The
FRAMING
and
RATIFICATION
of the
CONSTITUTION

The
FRAMING
and
RATIFICATION
of the
CONSTITUTION

LEONARD W. LEVY and DENNIS J. MAHONEY
editors

MACMILLAN PUBLISHING COMPANY
NEW YORK

Collier Macmillan Publishers
LONDON

Copyright © 1987 by Macmillan Publishing Company
A Division of Macmillan, Inc.

Macmillan Publishing Company
866 Third Avenue, New York, NY 10022

Collier Macmillan Canada, Inc.

Library of Congress Catalog Card Number: 87-1562

Printed in the United States of America

printing number
1   2   3   4   5   6   7   8   9   10

Library of Congress Cataloging in Publication Data

The Framing and ratification of the Constitution.

Includes index.
1. United States—Constitutional history.
2. United States. Constitutional Convention (1787)
I. Levy, Leonard Williams, 1923–   . II. Mahoney,
Dennis J.
KF4541.F7   1987   342.73′029   87-1562
ISBN 0-02-918790-7   347.30229

The Introduction by Leonard W. Levy appeared originally in
the *Encyclopedia of the American Constitution.* An abridged
version of the chapter on Constitutionalism and the American
Founding by Herman J. Belz also appeared in the *Encyclopedia.*
Copyright © 1986 Macmillan Publishing Company.

To
Our Teachers
Henry Steele Commager
and
Harry V. Jaffa

CONTENTS

LIST OF CONTRIBUTORS

Lance G. Banning, Professor of History, University of Kentucky

Herman J. Belz, Professor of History, University of Maryland

Judith A. Best, Professor of Political Science, State University of New York at Cortland

Jacob E. Cooke, MacCracken Professor of History, Lafayette College

Murray P. Dry, Professor of Political Science, Middlebury College

David F. Epstein, Analyst, Office of Net Assessment, Department of Defense

Edward J. Erler, Professor of Political Science, California State University, San Bernardino

Jack P. Greene, Andrew W. Mellon Professor of History, The Johns Hopkins University

James H. Hutson, Chief, Manuscript Division, Library of Congress

Leonard W. Levy, Andrew W. Mellon All-Claremont Professor of the Humanities and Chairman, Graduate Faculty of History, The Claremont Graduate School

Charles A. Lofgren, Roy P. Crocker Professor of American History, Claremont Mckenna College

Donald S. Lutz, Associate Professor of Political Science, University of Houston

Dennis J. Mahoney, Assistant Professor of Political Science, California State University, San Bernardino

Michael J. Malbin, Visiting Professor of Government and Politics, University of Maryland

John M. Murrin, Professor of History, Princeton University

Peter S. Onuf, Associate Professor of History, Worcester Polytechnic Institute

Jack N. Rakove, Associate Professor of History, Stanford University

Ralph A. Rossum, Alice Tweed Tuohy Professor of Government and Ethics, Claremont McKenna College

Robert A. Rutland, Professor of History, University of Virginia, and Editor-in-Chief, The Papers of James Madison

William M. Wiecek, Congdon Professor of Public Law and Legislation, Syracuse University

Michael P. Zuckert, Professor of Political Science, Carlton College

PREFACE

This volume comprises twenty-one essays on the framing and ratification of the Constitution of the United States. The essays treat the subject both chronologically and topically, and so, although this is not a single, continuous narrative, it is a comprehensive historical account of the creation of our frame of government and the emergence of a distinctively American theory of constitutionalism. The chapters in this volume were written by historians and political scientists representing a wide range of ages, interests, and political persuasions. In its scope and comprehensiveness, this volume is unique among the several volumes that have been or will be published commemorating the two-hundredth anniversary of the Constitutional Convention.

This volume was intended to make available to the general reader accounts of the issues and events surrounding the framing and ratification of the Constitution. We believed that such a work would be interesting and valuable to students as well as to the public generally. In order that the book should serve the needs of people who are not specialized scholars, we asked that the authors keep footnotes to a minimum. Not everyone was able to do so, consequently the documentation of the chapters may appear uneven. In general, footnotes to the records of the Convention and to *The Federalist* have been eliminated; in their place, references to the date of a particular debate or the number of a particular essay have been included in the text.

Many of the authors who wrote chapters for this volume also wrote for the *Encyclopedia of the American Constitution.* Generally, the chapters included here are different from what is found in the *Encyclopedia*. Where an article for the *Encyclopedia* may have compressed the whole history of a particular issue into 1,000 or 1,500 words, the chapters in this volume run between 5,000 and 7,500 words and focus on the period of the framing and ratification of the Constitution, not on its subsequent history. The editors commissioned twenty original essays, which their authors wrote expressly for first publication in this volume. There are two exceptions to this rule: Professor Levy's introductory chapter appears in substantially the same form in the *Encyclopedia,* for which it was originally written; Professor Belz's concluding chapter was originally written for this volume, but a significantly abridged version was included in the *Encyclopedia.*

We gratefully acknowledge the generous financial support of the Earhart Foundation of Ann Arbor, Michigan.

LEONARD W. LEVY
DENNIS J. MAHONEY

The
FRAMING
and
RATIFICATION
of the
CONSTITUTION

INTRODUCTION: AMERICAN CONSTITUTIONAL HISTORY, 1776–1789

LEONARD W. LEVY

On July 4, 1776, King George III wrote in his diary, "Nothing of importance this day." When the news of the Declaration of Independence reached him, he still could not know how wrong he had been. The political philosophy of social compact, natural rights, and limited government that generated the Declaration of Independence also spurred the most important, creative, and dynamic constitutional achievements in history; the Declaration itself was merely the beginning. Within a mere thirteen years Americans invented or first institutionalized a bill of rights against all branches of government, the written constitution, the constitutional convention, federalism, judicial review, and a solution to the colonial problem (admitting territories to the Union as states fully equal to the original thirteen). Religious liberty, the separation of church and state, political parties, separation of powers, an acceptance of the principle of equality, and the conscious creation of a new nation were also among American institutional "firsts," although not all these initially appeared between 1776 and 1789. In that brief span of time, Americans created what are today the oldest major republic, political democracy, state constitution, and national constitution. These unparalleled American achievements derived not from originality in speculative theory but from the constructive application of old ideas, which Americans took so seriously that they constitutionally based their institutions of government on them.

From thirteen separate colonies the Second Continental Congress "brought forth a new nation," as Abraham Lincoln said. In May 1776, Congress urged all the colonies to suppress royal authority and adopt permanent governments. On that advice and in the midst of a war the colonies began to frame the world's first written constitutions. When Congress triggered the drafting of those constitutions, Virginia instructed its delegates to Congress to propose that Congress should declare "the United Colonies free and independent states." Neither Virginia nor Congress advocated state

1

sovereignty. Congress's advice implied the erection of state governments with sovereign powers over domestic matters or "internal police."

On June 7, 1776, Congressman Richard Henry Lee of Virginia introduced the resolution as instructed, and Congress appointed two committees, one to frame the document that became the Declaration of Independence and the other to frame a plan of confederation — a constitution for a continental government. When Lincoln declared, "The Union is older than the States, and in fact created them as States," he meant that the Union (Congress) antedated the states. The Declaration of Independence, which stated that the colonies had become states, asserted the authority of the "United States of America, in General Congress, Assembled."

The "spirit of '76" tended to be strongly nationalistic. The members of Congress represented the states, of course, and acted on their instructions, but they acted for the new nation, and the form of government they thought proper in 1776 was a centralized one. In fact, Benjamin Franklin had proposed such a government on July 21, 1775, when he presented to Congress "Articles of Confederation and perpetual Union." Franklin urged a congressional government with an executive committee that would manage "general continental Business and Interests," conduct diplomacy, and administer finances. His plan empowered Congress to determine war and peace, exchange ambassadors, make foreign alliances, settle all disputes between the colonies, plant new colonies, and, in a sweeping omnibus clause, make laws for "the General Welfare" concerning matters on which individual colonies "cannot be competent," such as "our general Commerce," "general Currency," the establishment of a post office, and governance of "our Common Forces." Costs were to be paid from a common treasury supplied by each colony in proportion to its male inhabitants, but each colony would raise its share by taxing its inhabitants. Franklin provided for an easy amendment process: Congress recommended amendments that would become part of the Articles when approved by a majority of colonial assemblies. Franklin's plan of union seemed much too radical in July 1775, when independence was a year away and reconciliation with Britain on American terms was the object of the war. Congress simply tabled the Franklin plan.

As the war continued into 1776, nationalist sentiment strengthened. Thomas Paine's *Common Sense* called for American independence and "a Continental form of Government." Nationalism and centralism were twin causes. John Langdon of New Hampshire favored independence and "an American Consitution" that provided for appeals from every colony to a national congress "in everything of moment relative to governmental matters." Proposals for a centralized union became common by the spring of 1776, and these proposals, as the following representative samples suggest, tended to show democratic impulses. Nationalism and mitigated democracy, not nationalism and conservatism, were related. A New York newspaper urged the popular election of a national congress with a "superintending power" over the individual colonies as to "all commercial and Continental affairs," leaving to each colony control over its "internal policy." A populistic plan in a Connecticut newspaper recommended that the congress be empowered to govern "all matters of general concernment" and "every other thing proper and necessary" for the benefit of the whole, allowing the individual colonies only that which fell "within the territorial jurisdiction of a particular assembly." The "Spartacus" essays, which newspapers in New York, Philadelphia, and Portsmouth printed, left the state "cantons" their own legislatures but united all in a national congress with powers similar to those enumerated by Franklin, including a paramount power to "interfere" with a colony's "provincial affairs" whenever required by "the good of the continent." "Essex" reminded his readers that "the strength and happiness of America must be Continental, not Provincial, and that whatever appears to be for the good of the whole, must be submitted to by every Part." He advocated dividing the colonies into many smaller equal parts that would have equal representation in a powerful national congress chosen directly by the people, including taxpaying widows. Carter Braxton, a conservative Virginian, favored aristocratic controls over a congress that could not "interfere with the internal police or domestic concerns of any Colony. . . ."

Given the prevalence of such views in the first half of 1776, a representative committee of the Continental Congress probably mirrored public opinion when it framed a nationalist plan for confederation. On July 12, one month after the appointment of a thirteen-member committee (one from each state) to write a draft, John Dickinson of Pennsylvania, the committee chairman, presented to Congress a plan that borrowed heavily from Franklin's. The Committee of the Whole of Congress debated the Dickinson draft and adopted it on August 20 with few changes. Only one was significant. Dickinson had proposed that Congress be empowered to fix the western boundaries of states claiming territory to the Pacific coast and to form new states in the west. The Committee of the Whole, bending to the wishes of eight states with extensive western claims, omitted that provision from its revision of the Dickinson draft. That omission became a stumbling block.

On August 20 the Committee of the Whole reported the revised plan of union to Congress. The plan was similar to Franklin's, except that Congress had no power over "general commerce." But Congress, acting for the United States, was clearly paramount to the individual states. They were not even referred to as "states." Collectively they were "the United States of America"; otherwise they were styled "colonies" or "colony," terms not compatible with sovereignty, to which no reference was made. Indeed, the draft merely reserved to each colony "sole and exclusive Regulation and Government of its internal police, in all matters that shall not interfere with the Articles of this Confederation." That crucial provision, Article III, making even "internal police" subordinate to congressional powers, highlighted the nationalist character of the proposed confederation.

The array of congressional powers included exclusive authority over war and peace, land and naval forces, treaties and alliances, prize cases, crimes on the high seas and navigable rivers, all disputes between states, coining money, borrowing on national credit, Indian affairs, post offices, weights and measures, and "the Defence and Welfare" of the United States. Congress also had power to appoint a Council of State and civil officers "necessary for managing the general Affairs of the United States." The Council of State, consisting of one member from each of the thirteen, was empowered to administer the United States government and execute its measures. Notwithstanding this embryonic executive branch, the government of the United States was congressional in character, consisting of a single house whose members were to be elected annually by the legislatures of the colonies. Each colony cast one vote, making each politically equal in Congress. On all important matters, the approval of nine colonies was required to pass legislation. Amendments to the Articles needed the unanimous approval of the legislatures of the various colonies, a provision that later proved to be crippling.

The Articles reported by the Committee of the Whole provoked dissension. States without western land claims opposed the omission of the provision in the Dickinson draft that gave Congress control over western lands. Large states opposed the principle of one vote for each state, preferring instead proportionate representation with each delegate voting. Sharp differences also emerged concerning the rule by which each state was to pay its quota to defray common expenses. Finally some congressmen feared the centralizing nature of the new government. Edward Rutledge of South Carolina did not like "the Idea of destroying all Provincial Distinctions and making every thing of the most minute kind bend to what they call the good of the whole. . . ." Rutledge resolved "to vest the Congress with no more Power than what is absolutely necessary." James Wilson of Pennsylvania could declare that Congress represented "all the individuals of the states" rather than the states, but Roger Sherman of Connecticut answered, "We are representatives of states, not individuals." That attitude would undo the nationalist "spirit of '76."

Because of disagreements and the urgency of prosecuting the war, Congress was unable to settle on a plan of union in 1776. By the spring of 1777 the nationalist momentum was spent. By then most of the states had adopted constitutions and had legitimate governments. Previously, provisional governments of local "congresses," "conventions," and committees had controlled the states and looked to the Continental Congress for leadership and approval. But the creation of legitimate state governments reinvigorated old provincial loyalties. Local politicians, whose careers were provincially oriented, feared a strong central government as a rival institution. Loyalists no longer participated in politics, local or national, depleting support for central control. By late April of 1777, when state sovereignty triumphed, only seventeen of the forty-eight congressmen who had been members of the Committee of the Whole that adopted the Dickinson draft remained in Congress. Most of the new congressmen opposed centralized government.

James Wilson, who was a congressman in 1776 and 1777, recalled what happened when he addressed the Constitutional Convention on June 8, 1787:

> Among the first sentiments expressed in the first Congs. one was that Virga. is no more. That Massts. is no more, that Pa. is no more & c. We are now one nation of brethren. We must bury all local interests and distinctions. This language continued for some time. The tables at length began to turn. No sooner were the State Govts. formed than their jealousy & ambition began to display themselves. Each endeavored to cut a slice from the common loaf, to add to its own morsel, till at length the confederation became frittered down to the impotent condition in which it now stands. Review the progress of the articles of Confederation thro' Congress & compare the first and last draught of it.
> [Farrand, ed., *Records,* I, 166–67]

The turning point occurred in late April 1777 when Thomas Burke of North Carolina turned his formidable localist opinions against the report of the Committee of the Whole. Its Article III, in his words, "expressed only a reservation [to the states] of the power of regulating the internal police, and consequently resigned every other power [to Congress]." Congress, he declared, sought even to interfere with the states' internal police and make its own powers "unlimited." Burke accordingly moved the following substitute for Article III, which became Article II of the Articles as finally adopted: "Each State retains its sovereignty, freedom and independence, and every power, jurisdiction and right, which is not by this confederation expressly delegated to the United States in Congress assembled." Burke's motion carried by the votes of eleven states, vitiating the powers of the national government recommended by the Committee of the Whole.

In the autumn of 1777 a Congress dominated by state-sovereignty advocates completed the plan of confederation. Those who favored proportionate representation in Congress with every member entitled to vote lost badly to those who favored voting by states with each state having one vote. Thereafter the populous wealthy states had no stake in supporting a strong national government that could be controlled by the votes of lesser states. The power of Congress to negotiate commercial treaties effectively died when Congress agreed that under the Articles no treaty should violate the power of the states to impose tariff duties or prohibit imports and exports. The power of Congress to settle all disputes between states became merely a power to make recommendations. The permanent executive branch became a temporary committee with no powers except as delegated by the votes of nine states, the number required to adopt any major measure. Congress also agreed that it should not have power to fix the western boundaries of states claiming lands to the Pacific.

After the nationalist spurt of 1776 proved insufficient to produce the Articles, the states made the Confederation feckless. Even as colonies the states had been particularistic, jealous, and uncooperative. Centrifugal forces originating in diversity — of economics, geography, religion, class structure, and race — produced sectional, provincial, and local loyalties that could not be overcome during a war against the centralized powers claimed by Parliament. The controversy with Britain had produced passions and principles that made the Franklin and Dickinson drafts unviable. Not even these nationalist drafts empowered Congress to tax, although the principle of no taxation without representation had become irrelevant as to Congress. Similarly, Congress as late as 1774 had "cheerfully" acknowledged Parliament's legitimate "regulation of our external commerce," but in 1776 Congress denied that Parliament had any authority over America, and by 1777 Americans were unwilling to grant their own central legislature powers they preferred their provincial assemblies to wield. Above all, most states refused to repose their trust in any central authority that a few large states might dominate, absent a constitutionally based principle of state equality.

Unanimous consent for amendments to the Articles proved to be too high a price to pay for acknowledging the "sovereignty" of each state, although that acknowledgment made Maryland capable of winning for the United States the creation of a national domain held in common for the benefit of all. Maryland also won the promise that new states would be admitted to the Union on a principle of state equality. That prevented the development of a colonial problem from Atlantic to Pacific, and the Northwest Ordinance of 1787 was the Confederation's finest and most enduring achievement.

The Constitution of 1787 was unthinkable in 1776, impossible in 1781 or at any time before it was framed. The Articles were an indispensable transitional stage in the development of the Constitution. Not even the Constitution would have been ratified if its Framers had submitted it for approval to the state legislatures that kept Congress paralyzed in the 1780s. Congress, representing the United States, authorized the creation of the states and ended up, as it had begun, as their creature. It possessed expressly delegated powers with no means of enforcing them. That Congress lacked commerce and tax powers was a serious deficiency, but not nearly so crippling as its lack of sanctions and the failure of the states to abide by the Articles. Congress simply could not make anyone, except soldiers, do anything. It acted on the states, not on people. Only a national government that could execute its laws independently of the states could have survived.

The states flouted their constitutional obligations. The Articles obliged the states to "abide by the determinations of the United States, in Congress assembled," but there was no way to force the states to comply. The states were not sovereign, except as to their internal police and tax powers; rather, they behaved unconstitutionally. No foreign nation recognized the states as sovereign, because Congress possessed the external attributes of sovereignty especially as to foreign affairs and war powers.

One of the extraordinary achievements of the Articles was the creation of a rudimentary federal system. It failed because its central government did not operate directly on individuals within its sphere of authority. The Confederation had no independent executive and judicial branches, because the need for them scarcely existed when Congress addressed its acts mainly to the states. The framers of the Articles distributed the powers of government with remarkable acumen, committing to Congress about all that belonged to a central government except, of course, taxation and commercial regulation, the two powers that Americans of the Revolutionary War believed to be part of state sovereignty. Even Alexander Hamilton, who in 1780 advocated that Congress should have "complete sovereignty," excepted "raising money by internal taxes."

Congress could requisition money from the states, but they did not pay their quotas. In 1781 Congress requisitioned $8,000,000 for the next year, but the states paid less than half a million. While the Articles lasted, the cumulative amount paid by all the states hardly exceeded what was required to pay the interest on the public debt for just one year.

Nationalists vainly sought to make the Articles more effective by both interpretation and amendment. Madison devised a theory of implied powers by which he squeezed out of the Articles congressional authority to use force if necessary against states that failed to fulfill their obligations. Congress refused to attempt coercion just as it refused to recommend an amendment authorizing its use. Congress did, however, charter a bank to control currency, but the opposition to the exercise of a power not expressly delegated remained so intense that the bank had to be rechartered by a state. Congress vainly sought unanimous state consent for various amendments that would empower it to raise money from customs duties and to regulate commerce, foreign and domestic. In 1781 every state but Rhode Island approved an amendment empowering Congress to impose a 5 percent duty on all foreign imports; never again did an amendment to the Articles come so close to adoption. Only four states ratified an amendment authorizing a congressional embargo against the vessels of any nation with whom the United States had no treaty of commerce. Congress simply had no power to negotiate commercial treaties with nations such as Britain that discriminated against American shipping. Nor had Congress the power to prevent states from violating treaties with foreign nations. In 1786 John Jay, Congress's secretary of foreign affairs, declared that not a day had passed since ratification of the 1783 treaty of peace without its violation by at least one state. Some states also discriminated against the trade of others. Madison likened New Jersey, caught between the ports of Philadelphia and New York, "to a cask tapped at both ends." More important, Congress failed even to recommend needed amendments. As early as 1784 Congress was so divided it defeated an amendment that would enable it to regulate commerce, foreign and domestic, and to levy duties on imports and exports. Often Congress could not function for lack of a quorum. The requisite number of states was present for only three days between October 1785 and April 1786. In 1786 Congress was unable to agree on any amendments for submission to the states.

The political condition of the United States during the 1780s stagnated partly because of the constitutional impotence of Congress and the unconstitutional conduct of the states. The controversy with Britain had taught that liberty and localism were congruent. The 1780s taught that excessive localism was incompatible with nationhood. The Confederation was a necessary point of mid-passage. It bequeathed to the United States the fundamentals of a federal system, a national domain, and a solution to the colonial problem. Moreover, the Articles contained several provisions that were antecedents of their counterparts in the Constitution of 1787: a free speech clause for congressmen and legislative immunity, a privileges and immunities clause, a clause on the extradition of fugitives from justice, a full faith and credit clause, and a clause validating United States debts. The Confederation also started an effective government bureaucracy when the Congress in 1781 created secretaries for foreign affairs, war, marine, and finance — precursors of an executive branch. When the new departments of that branch began to function in 1789, a corps of experienced administrators, trained under the Articles, staffed them. The courts established by Congress to decide prize and admiralty cases as well as boundary disputes foreshadowed a national judiciary. Except for enactment of the great Northwest Ordinance, however, the Congress of the Confederation was moribund by 1787. It had successfully prosecuted the war, made foreign alliances, established the national credit, framed the first constitution of the United States, negotiated a favorable treaty of peace, and created a national domain. Congress's accomplishments were monumental, especially during wartime, yet in the end it failed.

By contrast, state government flourished. Excepting Rhode Island and Connecticut, all the states adopted written constitutions during the war, eight in 1776. Madison exultantly wrote, "Nothing has excited more admiration in the world than the manner in which free governments have been established in America, for it was the first instance, from the creation of the world that free inhabitants have been seen deliberating on a form of government, and selection of such of their citizens as possessed their confidence to determine upon and give effect to it."

The Virginia Constitution of 1776, the first permanent state constitution, began with a Declaration of Rights adopted three weeks before the Declaration of Independence. No previous bill of rights had restrained all branches of government. Virginia's reflected the widespread belief that Americans has been thrown back into a state of nature from which they emerged by framing a social compact for their governance, reserving to themselves certain inherent or natural rights, including life, liberty, the enjoyment of property, and the pursuit of happiness. Virginia's declaration explicitly declared that as all power derived from the people, for whose benefit government existed, the people could reform or abolish government when it failed them. On the basis of this philosophy Virginia framed a constitution providing for a bicameral legislature, a governor, and a judicial system. The legislature elected a governor, who held office for one year, had no veto power, and was encumbered by an executive council. The legislature chose many important officials, including judges.

Some states followed the more democratic model of the Pennsylvania Constitution of 1776, others the ultraconservative one of Maryland, but all state constitutions prior to the Massachusetts Constitution of 1780 were framed by legislatures, which in some states called themselves "conventions" or assemblies. Massachusetts deserves credit for having originated a new institution of government, a specially elected constitutional convention whose sole function was to frame the constitution and submit it for popular ratification. That procedure became the standard. Massachusetts's constitution, which is still operative, became the model American state constitution. The democratic procedure for making it fit the emerging theory that the sovereign people should be the source of the constitution and authorize its framing by a constitutional convention, rather than the legislature to which the constitution is paramount. Massachusetts was also the first state to give more than lip service to the principle of separation of powers. Everywhere else, excepting perhaps New York, unbalanced government and legislative supremacy prevailed. Massachusetts established the precedent for a strong, popularly elected executive with a veto power; elsewhere the governor tended to be a ceremonial head who depended for his existence on the legislature.

The first state constitutions and related legislation introduced significant reforms. Most states expanded voting rights by reducing property qualifications, and a few, including Vermont (an independent state from 1777 to 1791), experimented with universal manhood suffrage. Many state constitutions provided for fairer apportionment of representation in the legislature. Every southern state either abolished its establishment of religion or took major steps to achieve separation of church and state. Northern states either abolished slavery or provided for its gradual ending. Criminal codes were made more humane. The confiscation of Loyalist estates and of crown lands, such as the opening of a national domain westward to the Mississippi, led to a democratization of landholding, as did the abolition of feudal relics such as the law of primogeniture and entail. The pace of democratic change varied from state to state, and in some states it was nearly imperceptible, but the Revolution without doubt occasioned constitutional and political developments that had long been dammed up under the colonial system.

The theory that a constitution is supreme law encouraged the development of judicial review. Written constitutions with bills of rights and the emerging principle of separation of powers contributed to the same end. Before the Revolution appellate judges tended to be dependents of the executive branch; the Revolution promoted judicial independence. Most state constitutions provided for judicial tenure during good behavior rather than for a fixed term or the pleasure of the appointing power. Inevitably when Americans believed that a legislature had exceeded its authority they argued that it had acted unconstitutionally, and they turned to courts to enforce the supreme law as law. The dominant view, however, was that a court holding a statute unconstitutional insulted the sovereignty of the legislature, as the reactions to *Holmes v. Walton* (1780) and *Trevett v. Weeden* (1786) showed. *Commonwealth v. Caton* (1782) was probably the first case in which a state judge declared that a court had power to hold a statute unconstitutional, though the court in that case sustained the act before it. In *Rutgers v. Waddington* (1784) Alexander Hamilton as counsel argued that a state act violating a treaty was unconstitutional, but the court declared that the judicial power advocated by counsel was "subversive of all government." Counsel in *Trevett* also contended that the court should void a state act. Arguments of counsel do not create precedents but can reveal the emergence of a new idea. Any American would have agreed that an act against a constitution was void; although few would have agreed that courts have the final power to decide matters of constitutionality, that idea was spreading. The *Ten Pound Act Cases* (1786) were the first in which an American court held a state enactment void, and that New Hampshire precedent was succeeded by a similar decision in the North Carolina case of *Bayard v. Singleton* (1787). The principle of *Marbury v. Madison* (1803) thus originated at a state level before the framing of the federal Constitution.

The Constitution originated in the drive for a strong national government that preceded the framing of the Articles of Confederation. The "critical period" of 1781–1787 intensified that drive, but it began well before the defects of the Articles expanded the ranks of the nationalists. The weaknesses of the United States in international affairs, its inability to enforce the peace treaty, its financial crisis, its helplessness during Shays' Rebellion, and its general incapacity to govern resulted in many proposals—in Congress, in the press, and even in some states—for national powers to negotiate commercial treaties, regulate the nation's commerce, and check state policies that adversely affected creditor interests and impeded economic growth. Five states met at the Annapolis Convention in 1786, ostensibly to discuss a "uniform system" of regulating commerce, but those who masterminded the meeting had a much larger agenda in mind — as Madison put it, a "plenipotentiary Convention for amending the Confederation."

Hamilton had called for a "convention of all the states" as early as 1780, before the Articles were ratified, to form a government worthy of the nation. Even men who defended state sovereignty conceded the necessity of a convention by 1787. William Grayson admitted that "the present Confederation is utterly inefficient and that if it remains much longer in its present State of imbecility we shall be one of the most contemptible Nations on the face of the earth. . . ." Luther Martin admitted that Congress was "weak, contemptibly weak," and Richard Henry Lee believed that no government "short of force, will answer." "Do you not think," he asked George Mason, "that it ought to be declared . . . that any State act of legislation that shall contravene, or oppose, the authorized acts of Congress, or interfere with the expressed rights of that body, shall be *ipso facto* void, and of no force whatsoever?" Many leaders, like Thomas Jefferson, advocated executive and judicial branches for the national government with "an appeal from state judicatures to a federal court in all cases where the act of Confederation controlled the question. . . ." Rufus King, who also promoted a "vigorous Executive," thought that the needed power of Congress to regulate all commerce "can never be well exerciseu ..... ·- Federal Judicial." A consensus was developing.

The Annapolis Convention exploited and nurtured that consensus by adopting a resolution addressed to all the states and to Congress, calling for a constitutional convention to "meet at Philadelphia on the second Monday in May next (1787), to take into consideration the situation of the United States, to devise such further provisions as shall appear to them necessary to render the constitution of the federal government adequate to the exigencies of the Union. . . ." Several states, including powerful Virginia and Pennsylvania, chose delegates for the Philadelphia Convention, forcing Congress to save face on February 21, 1787, by adopting a motion in accord with the Annapolis recommendation, although Congress declared that the "sole and express purpose" of the convention was "revising the articles of confederation."

The Constitutional Convention of 1787, which formally organized itself on May 25, lasted almost four months, yet reached its most crucial decision almost at the outset. The first order of business was the nationalistic Virginia Plan (May 29), and the first vote of the convention, acting as a Committee of the Whole, was the adoption of a resolution "that a *national* Government ought to be established consisting of a *supreme* legislative, Executive and Judiciary" (May 30). Thus the convention immediately agreed on abandoning, rather than amending, the Articles; on writing a new Constitution; on creating a national government that would be supreme; and on having it consist of three branches.

The radical character of this early decision may be best understood by comparing it with the Articles. The Articles failed mainly because there was no way to force the states to fulfill their obligations or to obey the exercise of such powers as Congress did possess. "The great and radical vice in the construction of the existing Confederation," said Alexander Hamilton, "is the principle of legislation for states or governments, in their corporate capacities, and as contradistinguished from the individuals of which they consist." The convention remedied that vital defect in the Articles, as George Mason pointed out (May 30), by agreeing on a government that "could directly operate on individuals." Thus the Framers solved the critical problem of sanctions by establishing a national government that was independent of the states.

On the next day, May 31, the Committee of the Whole made other crucial decisions with little or no debate. One, reflecting the nationalist bias of the convention, was the decision to establish a bicameral system whose larger house was to be elected directly by the people rather than by the state legislatures. Mason, no less, explained, "Under the existing confederacy, Congress represent the States not the people of the States; their acts operate on the States, not on the individuals. The case will be changed in the new plan of Government. The people will be represented; they ought therefore to choose the Representatives." Another decision of May 31 was to vest in the Congress the sweeping and undefined power, recommended by the Virginia Plan, "to legislate in all cases to which the separate States are incompetent; or in which the harmony of the U.S. may be interrupted by the exercise of individual [state] legislation; to negative all laws passed by the several States contravening in the opinion of the National Legislature the articles of Union, or any treaties subsisting under the authority of the Union." Not a state voted "nay" to this exceptionally nationalistic proposition. Nor did any state oppose the decision of the next day to create a national executive with similarly broad, undefined powers.

After deliberating for two weeks, the Committee of the Whole presented the convention with its recommendations, essentially the adoption of the Virginia Plan. Not surprisingly, several of the delegates had second thoughts about the hasty decisions that had been made. Elbridge Gerry reiterated "that it was necessary to consider what the people would approve." Scrapping the Articles contrary to instructions and failing to provide for state equality in the system of representation provoked a reconsideration along lines described by William Paterson of New Jersey as "federal" in contradistinction to "national." Yet injured state pride was a greater cause of dissension than were the powers proposed for the national government. Some delegates were alarmed, not because of an excessive centralization of powers in the national government but because of the excessive advantages given to the largest states at the expense of the others. Three states — Virginia, Massachusetts, and Pennsylvania — had 45 percent of the white population in the country. Under the proposed scheme of proportionate representation, the small states feared that the large ones would dominate the others by controlling the national government.

On June 15, therefore, William Paterson of New Jersey submitted for the convention's consideration a substitute plan. It was a small-state plan rather than a states' rights one, for it too had a strong nationalist orientation. Contemplating a revision, rather than a scrapping, of the Articles, it retained the unicameral Congress with its equality of state representation, thus appeasing the small states. But the plan vested in Congress one of the two critical powers previously lacking: "to pass Acts for the regulation of trade and commerce," foreign and interstate. The other, the power of taxation, appeared only in a stunted form; Congress was to be authorized to levy duties on imports and to pass stamp tax acts. Except for its failure to grant full tax powers, the Paterson Plan proposed the same powers for the national legislature as the finished Constitution. The Plan also contained the germ of the national supremacy clause of the Constitution, Article Six, by providing that acts of Congress and United States treaties "shall be the supreme law of the respective States . . . and that the judiciary of the several States shall be bound thereby in their decisions, any thing in the respective laws of the Individual States to the contrary notwithstanding." The clause also provided for a federal judiciary with extensive jurisdiction and for an executive who could muster the military of the states to compel state obedience to the supreme law. Compulsion of states was unrealistic and unnecessary. Paterson himself declared that the creation of a distinct executive and judiciary meant that the government of the Union could "be exerted on individuals."

Despite its nationalist features, the Paterson Plan retained a unicameral legislature, in which the states remained equal, and the requisition system of raising a revenue, which had failed. "You see the consequence of pushing things too far," said John Dickinson of Delaware to Madison. "Some of the members from the small States wish for two branches in the General Legislature and are friends to a good National Government; but we would sooner submit to a foreign power than submit to be deprived of an equality of suffrage in both branches of the Legislature, and thereby be thrown under the domination of the large states." Only a very few dissidents were irreconcilably opposed to "a good National Government." Most of the dissidents were men like Dickinson and Paterson, "friends to a good National Government" if it preserved a wider scope for small-state authority and influence.

When Paterson submitted his plan on June 15, the convention agreed that to give it "a fair deliberation," it should be referred to the Committee of the Whole and that "in order to place the two plans in due comparison, the other should be recommitted." After debating the two plans, the Committee of the Whole voted in favor of reaffirming the original recommendations based on the Virginia Plan "as preferable to those of Mr. Paterson." Only three weeks after their deliberations, had begun the framers decisively agreed, for the second time, on a strong, independent national government that would operate directly on individuals without the involvement of states.

But the objections of the small states had not yet been satisfied. On the next day, Connecticut, which had voted against the Paterson Plan, proposed the famous Great Compromise: proportionate representation in one house, "provided each State had an equal voice in the other." On that latter point the convention nearly broke up, so intense was the conflict and so deep the division. The irreconcilables in this instance were the leaders of the large-state nationalist faction, otherwise the most constructive and influential members of the convention: Madison and James Wilson. After several weeks of debate and deadlock, the convention on July 16 narrowly voted for the compromise. With ten states present, five supported the compromise, four opposed (including Virginia and Pennsylvania), and Massachusetts was divided. The compromise saved small-state prestige and saved the convention from failure.

Thereafter consensus on fundamentals was restored, with Connecticut, New Jersey, and Delaware becoming fervent supporters of Madison and Wilson. A week later, for example, there was a motion that each state should be represented by two senators who would "vote per capita," that is, as individuals. Luther Martin of Maryland protested that per capita voting conflicted with the very idea of "the States being represented," yet the motion carried, with no further debate, 9-1.

On many matters of structure, mechanics, and detail there were angry disagreements, but agreement prevailed on the essentials. The office of the presidency is a good illustration. That there should be a powerful chief executive provoked no great debate, but the convention almost broke up, for the second time, on the method of electing him. Some matters of detail occasioned practically no disagreement and revealed the nationalist consensus. Mason, of all people, made the motion that one qualification of congressmen should be "citizenship of the United States,"and no one disagreed. Under the Articles of Confederation, there was only state citizenship; that there should be a concept of national citizenship seemed natural to men framing a constitution for a nation. Even more a revelation of the nationalist consensus was the fact that three of the most crucial provisions of the Constitution—the taxing power, the necessary and proper clause, and the supremacy clause—were casually and unanimously accepted without debate.

Until midway during its sessions, the convention did not take the trouble to define with care the distribution of power between the national government and the states, although the very nature of the "federal" system depended on that distribution. Consensus on fundamentals once again provides the explanation. There would be no difficulty in making that distribution; and, the Framers had taken out insurance, because at the very outset, they had endorsed the provision of the Virginia Plan vesting broad, undefined powers in a national legislature that would act on individuals. Some byplay of July 17 is illuminating. Roger Sherman of Connecticut thought that the line drawn between the powers of Congress and those left to the states was so vague that national legislation might "interfere . . . in any matters of internal police which respect the Government of such States only, and wherein the general welfare of the United States is not concerned." His motion to protect the "internal police" of the states brought no debaters to his side and was summarily defeated; only Maryland supported Connecticut. Immediately after, another small-state delegate, Gunning Bedford of Delaware, shocked even Edmund Randolph of Virginia, who had presented the Virginia Plan, by a motion to extend the powers of Congress by vesting authority "to legislate in all cases for the general interest of the Union." Randolph observed, "This is a formidable idea indeed. It involves the power of violating all the laws and constitution of the States, of intermeddling with their police." Yet the motion passed.

On July 26 the convention adjourned until August 6 to allow a Committee of Detail to frame a "constitution conformable to the Resolutions passed by the Convention." Generously construing its charge, the committee acted as a miniature convention and introduced a number of significant changes. One was the explicit enumeration of the powers of Congress to replace the vague, omnibus provisions adopted previously by the convention. Although enumerated, these powers were liberally expressed and formidable in their array. The committee made specific the spirit and intent of the convention. Significantly, the first enumerated power was that of taxation and the second that of regulating commerce among the states and with foreign nations: the two principal powers that had been withheld from Congress by the Articles. When the convention voted on the provision that Congress "shall have the power to lay and collect taxes, duties, imposts and excises," the states were unanimous and only one delegate, Elbridge Gerry, was opposed. When the convention next turned to the commerce power, there was no discussion and even Gerry voted affirmatively.

Notwithstanding its enumeration of the legislative powers, all of which the convention accepted, the Committee of Detail added an omnibus clause that has served as an ever-expanding source of national authority: "And to make all laws that shall be necessary and proper for carrying into execution the foregoing powers." The convention agreed to that clause without a single dissenting vote by any state or delegate. The history of the great supremacy clause, Article VI, shows a similar consensus. Without debate the convention adopted the supremacy clause, and not a single state or delegate voted nay. Finally, Article I, section 10, imposing restrictions on the economic powers of the states with respect to paper money, ex post facto laws, bills of credit, and contracts also reflected a consensus in the convention. In sum, consensus, rather than compromise, was the most significant feature of the convention, outweighing in importance the various compromises that occupied most of the time of the delegates.

But why was there such a consensus? The obvious answer (apart from the fact that opponents either stayed away or walked out) is the best: experience had proved that the nationalist constitutional position was right. If the United States was to survive and flourish, a strong national government had to be established. The Framers of the Constitution were accountable to public opinion; the convention was a representative body. That its members were prosperous, well-educated political leaders made them no less representative than Congress. The state legislatures, which elected the members of the convention, were the most unlikely instruments for thwarting the popular will. The Framers, far from being able to do as they pleased, were not free to promulgate the Constitution. Although they adroitly arranged for its ratification by nine state ratifying conventions rather than by all state legislatures, they could not present a plan that the people of the states would not tolerate. They could not control the membership of those state ratifying conventions. They could not even be sure that the existing Congress would submit the Constitution to the states for ratification, let alone for ratification by state conventions that had to be specially elected. If the Framers had strayed too far from public opinion, their work would have been wasted. The consensus in the convention coincided with an emerging consensus in the country that recaptured the nationalist spirit of '76. That the Union had to be strengthened was an almost universal American belief.

For its time the Constitution was a remarkably democratic document framed by democratic methods. Some historians have contended that the convention's scrapping of the Articles and the ratification process were revolutionary acts which if performed by a Napoleon would be pronounced a coup d'état. But the procedure of the Articles for constitutional amendment was not democratic, because it allowed Rhode Island, with one-sixtieth of the nation's population, to exercise a veto power. The convention sent its Constitution to the lawfully existing government, the Congress of the Confederation, for submission to the states, and Congress, which could have censured the convention for exceeding its authority, freely complied — and thereby exceeded its own authority under the Articles! A coup d'état ordinarily lacks the deliberation and consent that marked the making of the Constitution and is characterized by a military element that was wholly lacking in 1787. A convention elected by the state legislatures and consisting of many of the foremost leaders of their time deliberated for almost four months. Its members included many opponents of the finished scheme. The nation knew the convention was considering changes in the government. The proposed Constitution was made public, and voters in every state were asked to choose delegates to vote for or against it after open debate. The use of state ratifying conventions fit the theory that a new fundamental law was being adopted and, therefore, conventions were proper for the task.

The Constitution guaranteed to each state a republican or representative form of government and fixed no property or religious qualifications on the right to vote or hold office, at a time when such qualifications were common in the states. By leaving voting qualifications to the states the Constitution implicitly accepted such qualifications but imposed none. The convention, like the Albany Congress of 1754, the Stamp Act Congress, the Continental Congresses, and the Congresses of the Confederation, had been chosen by state (or colonial) legislatures, but the Constitution created a Congress whose lower house was popularly elected. When only three states directly elected their chief executive officer, the Constitution provided for the indirect election of the President by an Electoral College that originated in the people and is still operative. The Constitution's system of separation of powers and elaborate checks and balances was not intended to refine out popular influence on government but to protect liberty; the Framers divided, distributed, and limited powers to prevent one branch, faction, interest, or section from becoming too powerful. Checks and balances were not undemocratic, and the Federalists were hard pressed not to apologize for checks and balances but to convince the Anti-Federalists, who wanted far more checks and balances, that the Constitution had enough. Although the Framers were not democrats in a modern sense, their opponents were even less democratic. Those opponents sought to capitalize on the lack of a bill of rights, and ratification of the Constitution became possible only because leading Federalists committed themselves to amendments as soon as the new government went into operation. At that time, however, Anti-Federalists opposed a bill of rights because it would allay popular fears of the new government, lending the chance for state sovereignty amendments.

Although the Framers self-consciously refrained from referring to slavery in the Constitution, it recognized slavery, the most undemocratic of all institutions. That recognition was a grudging but necessary price of union. The three-fifths clause of Article I provided for counting three-fifths of the total number of slaves as part of the population of a state in the apportionment of representation and direct taxation. Article IV, section 2, provided for rendition of fugitive slaves to the slaveholder upon his claim. On the other hand, Article I, section 9, permitted Congress to abolish the slave trade in twenty years. Most delegates, including many from slaveholding states, would have preferred a Constitution untainted by slavery; but southern votes for ratification required recognition of slavery. By choosing a union with slavery, the Convention deferred the day of reckoning.

The Constitution is basically a political document. Modern scholarship has completely discredited the once popular view, associated with Charles Beard, that the Constitution was undemocratically made to advance the economic interests of personalty groups, chiefly creditors. The largest public creditor at the convention was Elbridge Gerry, who refused to sign the Constitution and opposed its ratification, and the largest private creditor was George Mason, who did likewise. Indeed, seven men who either quit the convention in disgust or refused to sign the Constitution held public securities that were worth over twice the holdings of the thirty-nine men who signed the Constitution. The most influential Framers, among them Madison, Wilson, Paterson, Dickinson, and Gouverneur Morris, owned no securities. Others, like Washington, who acted out of patriotism, not profit, held trifling amounts. Eighteen members of the convention were either debtors or held property that depreciated after the new government became operative. On crucial issues at the convention, as in the state ratifying conventions, the dividing line between groups for and against the Constitution was not economic, not between realty and personalty, or debtors and creditors, or town and frontier. The restrictions of Article I, section 10, on the economic powers of the states were calculated to protect creditor interests and promote business stability, but those restrictions were not undemocratic; if impairing the obligations of contracts or emitting bills of credit and paper money were democratic hallmarks, the Constitution left Congress free to be democratic. The interest groups for and against the Constitution were substantially similar. Economic interests did influence the voting on ratification, but no simple explanation that ignores differences between states and even within states will suffice, and many noneconomic influences were also at work. In the end the Constitution was framed and ratified because most voters came to share the vision held by Franklin in 1775 and Dickinson in 1776; those two, although antagonists in Pennsylvania politics, understood for quite different reasons that a strong central government was indispensable for nationhood.

THE BRITISH AND COLONIAL BACKGROUND OF AMERICAN CONSTITUTIONALISM

JOHN M. MURRIN

THE ENGLISH BACKGROUND

England changed dramatically during the century that elapsed between the founding of Virginia (1607) and the death of Queen Anne (1714). The government of James I (1603–1625) had been a monarchy that, until 1621, was assisted only on rare occasions by a Parliament. James ruled his subjects according to common law. He did not imprison them without trial, tax them without consent, or promulgate new laws by prerogative alone. In other words, the English monarchy was authoritarian but not very powerful.

The historical vision of England as an oasis of liberty triumphed after the Glorious Revolution of 1688–1689. Not only did the Glorious Revolution produce the Bill of Rights (1689) and the Toleration Act (1690) but it also led to other measures that defined the British state and its politics well into the nineteenth century. The British state that emerged from this process was far more stable and far more powerful, but much less authoritarian, than the Stuart monarchy had ever been. English liberty had become inextricably linked to Britain's ability to project power abroad. The defense of that liberty against the ever-present threat of corruption provided the central dialogue of British public life in the eighteenth century.

CONSTITUTIONAL EXPERIMENTATION IN THE COLONIES

The changing English heritage had a dramatic impact on North America. The time at which a settler crossed the Atlantic obviously conditioned the constitutional expectations he brought with him. Those who went to Jamestown before 1618 had very different ideas from those who in the 1680s rushed into Pennsylvania, a colony founded by a self-conscious neo-Harringtonian, William Penn. The early colonies reflected not a single line of obvious development but a series of experiments that put into practice most of the constitutional permutations available to seventeenth-century Englishmen. They differed strikingly in fundamentals — how much religious liberty they encouraged, the prerogatives exercised by ther governors, the powers claimed by their assemblies, the structure of local government, the authority wielded by magistrates, and the use of juries. Some colonies were highly authoritarian, some both authoritarian and consensual, others profoundly anti-authoritarian.

Several common points stand out, however. American settlers had to define over time what they meant by liberty and limited government. The absence of traditional institutions made these principles more vulnerable and uncertain in the wilderness than in England. The dispersed pattern of settlement and wide access to land also left authority weaker in the colonies than in England. The Mayflower Compact of 1620, for instance, was less a bid for broad political participation than an effort to commit all adult males to obey whatever laws the community should adopt. Armed force was seldom available to a governor, and he had few compelling awards to bestow on his followers other than land grants, which in the long run increased the recipient's autonomy, not his dependence. Standards of legitimacy also remained precarious and usually had to balance the expectations of the local community with trans-Atlantic demands from the crown or a lord proprietor.

Colonial constitutions emerged within this environment of weakened traditions and enfeebled authority. All of them drew heavily on English models and English ideas, but none ever replicated England. Despite serious efforts, no hereditary aristocracy took root in North America. No colonial council ever became a House of Lords. No colony ever adopted England's evolving formula for responsible government, largely because all were too small to have departments of state and ministries. Impeachments occurred very rarely in America and never played the central role that they had in English developments.

Although the commercial corporation had an extraordinary failure record as a colonizing device, it had one major constitutional function to perform after the collapse of the Virginia Company. The organizers of the Massachusetts Bay Company in 1629–30 decided to bring their charter with them to New England, where they converted it into a constitutional framework for the colony itself. Neighboring settlements, even without royal sanction, copied most of its features and embodied them in the early governments of Rhode Island, Connecticut, and New Haven. Rhode Island and Connecticut eventually won crown approval for their creations by securing formal charters from Charles II in 1662 and 1663.

The Massachusetts charter created a corporation or joint-stock company in which the "freemen," or shareholders, met four times a year in a

"Great and General Court." They also elected annually a board of eighteen "assistants" and a governor and lieutenant-governor, all of whom together were expected to manage the company's day-to-day affairs and to rule the settlers in a manner "not . . . repugnant to the laws and statutes" of England. The settlers, for their part, were to "have and enjoy all liberties and immunities of free and natural subjects within any of the dominions of" the crown.

By the end of 1630 only about a dozen investors in the project had accompanied the many hundreds of settlers arriving in New England. Legally this handful of men could have elected themselves assistants and governed the colonists almost without restraint, but they did not. At the first meeting of the General Court in October 1630, the leaders proposed that "the Freemen should have the power of chuseing Assistants when there are to be chosen, and the Assistants from amongst themselves to chuse a Governor and Deputy Governor, whoe with the Assistants should have the power of makeing lawes and chuseing officers to execute the same." This suggestion "was fully assented unto by the generall vote of the people, and ereccion of hands." At its next meeting, the General Court admitted 116 settlers as freemen, probably a large majority of the colony's adult males.

Over the next four years most of the remaining features of the Massachusetts system took shape. Freemanship was limited to church members in 1631. In 1632 freemen were allowed to elect the governor and deputy governor. More controversial because it had no charter sanction was their successful demand of 1634 that the freemen of each town be allowed to choose "deputies" to join with the governor, deputy governor, and assistants in the four annual meetings of the General Court. Only in the early 1640s did the deputies and assistants become distinct houses, sitting apart except when acting as the colony's highest court of law, usually to hear appeals or decide cases of equity.

At the local level, meetings of the first church congregations became distinct town meetings as the members gathered to discuss purely secular matters. The General Court gave them wide latitude, especially over the distribution of land. Judicial meetings of magistrates from neighboring towns evolved into county courts in the 1640s. In civil disputes they sought community consensus through an extraordinary reliance upon juries even to decide appeals. Against criminal offenders the magistrates enforced a rigorous puritan morality in noncapital cases for which they almost never resorted to juries before the 1660s and only infrequently for the next generation. Capital trials were held before the Court of Assistants in Boston with juries or, more rarely, before the full General Court, which heard notorious political cases. The General Court also assumed jurisdiction over offenses inadequately defined by colony law but declared capital by the Bible, such as being a stubborn and disobedient son.

This system was both authoritarian and participatory. To puritans the two characteristics were closely linked. As in their religious covenants, the settlers believed that men must consent to be bound, but then bound they are by the laws of God and man, and the state must hold them to their responsibilities. The orthodox lodged all power in the General Court and made no concessions to any embryonic notions of the separation of powers. Even though the government lacked conspicuous instruments of enforcement other than elective constables armed only with their staffs of office, magistrates relied heavily and successfully on internalized puritan values. In New Haven Colony, for instance, well over 90 percent of those accused of an offense were convicted and punished. Yet before trial few of them were jailed or even asked to post bail. Offenders received a simple summons, appeared in court nearly always on time, and accepted punishment, usually after pleading guilty. Only one offender out of about two hundred successfully fled from justice, and few others even tried.

The various New England colonies adopted interesting variations upon the Bay Colony system. Only Massachusetts and New Haven confined freemanship to church members, and even Massachusetts after 1647 permitted nonmembers to vote in town meetings on local issues. Only Massachusetts was truly bicameral before the 1690s. New Haven abolished all juries, civil and criminal, and developed a system of justice that was overtly inquisitorial, not adversarial. The magistrates accused, interrogated, tried, convicted, and sentenced offenders. In criminal justice, Massachusetts, Connecticut, and Plymouth resembled New Haven more than England. Even when juries did hear noncapital cases, they convicted the vast majority of the accused. All of these colonies, even New Haven, adopted formal legal codes between the 1630s and the 1650s.

Rhode Island went in a different direction, mostly because its founders had all tasted the rigors of magisterial justice in Massachusetts or Plymouth during the 1630s and 1640s. The colony welcomed religious dissent. In 1647 it actually proclaimed its government "Democraticall; that is to say, a Government held by ye free and voluntary consent of all, or the greater part of the free Inhabitants." Whatever else this passage meant, Rhode Island tried to create neutral magistrates. The legislature established the office of public prosecutor to deprive the bench of that role, routinely made defense attorneys available, and encouraged criminal juries that acquitted more people than they convicted. The colony also sought and obtained a charter from Parliament in the 1640s, mostly to ward off encroachments from its more orthodox neighbors, and the settlers boasted of their reliance on English rather than biblical law.

New England's innovations produced the most stable English colonies of the seventeenth century, but other provinces also experimented dramatically. Outside Virginia and New England, each of their governments began as a proprietorship, a legal device by which the crown bestowed upon one or more proprietors the maximum amount of power that lawyers could find a way to convey.

Maryland provided the most important early example. George and Cecilius Calvert, the first and second Barons Baltimore in the Irish peerage, received every power, liberty, or privilege that any bishop of Durham "ever heretofore hath had, used, or organized, or of right could, or ought to have, hold, use, or enjoy." The lord proprietor had full control over the colony's land and could even subinfeudate; that is, create his own privileged nobility. But he could make laws only "with the advice, assent, and approbation of the freemen" of Maryland, "or the greater part of them, or of their delegates or deputies. . . ." As in other colonies, these laws could not be "repugnant or contrary" but had to be "as conveniently may be" agreeable to the laws of England.

As Roman Catholics who envisioned a New World haven for persecuted coreligionists, the proprietors tried to build a tolerant society organized around the kind of feudal relationships all but dormant in seventeenth-century England. They created, for instance, more than a dozen lords of manors, each of whom received the right to hold his own feudal courts and also his own individual summons to early meetings of the General Assembly, a practice that imitated the English House of Lords whose members were similarly convened. Other free settlers could either attend in person or give their proxies to someone who would, presumably one of the manor lords.

This hierarchical system of government, resting at base upon highly personalized relations between lord and man, broke down in the 1640s when the passions of the English civil war swept across Maryland and bitterly divided its settlers. Most of the lords were Roman Catholics, while most ordinary colonists were Protestants. After this struggle very nearly destroyed the colony, Lord Baltimore reorganized the political system in 1649–50. His concessions included a Toleration Act applicable to all Christians and a bicameral legislature in which, he expected, Roman Catholics would normally dominate the upper house, and Protestants the lower. Representation also replaced proxies in the lower house. This arrangement failed to prevent another decade of acute civil strife, but it did define Maryland government until the Glorious Revolution.

As in Virginia, tobacco planters, servants, and slaves defined the society. The county court, not the manor, characterized local government. The proprietor insisted more stridently on his prerogatives than did most Virginia governors before the 1680s. Baltimore, for example, waited until 1684 to veto all laws passed in 1678. He arbitrarily confined each county to two representatives when several had been accustomed to choosing more. The last proprietary governor before 1689 even articulated an explicit divine-right defense of the Calvert regime. These claims inspired assemblymen to cite specific English precedents in defense of their privileges and probably encouraged Maryland's Protestant magistrates to look more favorably on trial by jury than did contemporary justices in Virginia. Surprisingly, the Maryland system was more stable than Virginia's despite the built-in tension between proprietor and assembly, Catholic and Protestant.

Other proprietorships also embarked upon major experiments. Carolina (chartered 1663), New York (1664), New Jersey (1665), and Pennsylvania (1681) all promoted religious toleration but in other respects stood for incompatible extremes. The Carolina proprietors (a board of eight) hoped to create not a nostalgic feudal order but a fully modern aristocratic society that would put into practice maxims about the relation between land and power. Because ordinary settlers had no reason to share these ambitions, embodied in several versions of the Fundamental Constitutions of Carolina after 1669, this plan never came close to full implementation. Particularly in what became South Carolina, assemblymen grew adept at resisting the prerogative claims of governors and the privileged demands of aspiring local peers. The Carolina nobility planned by the proprietors never took hold, and the Fundamental Constitutions were dead by 1700.

New York was organized by James, duke of York, the brother of King Charles. The colony probably represented his vision of how England ought to be governed, as a tolerant and efficient autocracy presided over by trained soldiers. The New York charter did not require James to obtain the settlers' consent to provincial laws, nor did he think such a process desirable even when it was urged upon him by one of his soldier-governors. Assemblies "would be of dangerous consequence," James affirmed, "nothing being more knowne then the aptness of such bodyes to assume to themselves many priviledges which prove destructive to, or very oft disturbe, the peace of the government wherein they are allowed."

The Dutch majority of New York had no experience with representative government and resented not the lack of such institutions but the English intrusion itself in nearly every form it took, whether in altering laws, imposing juries on people unused to them, permitting soldiers to batter civilians, degrading the status of the Dutch Reformed Church, or restricting trade with Amsterdam. New Englanders on Lord Island preferred their own law to that of the Dutch but expected to be consulted about taxes or changes in the law. Newcomers from England resented the economic power of the Dutch elite, distrusted the New Englanders, and — unless they were closely attached to the duke — also disliked the emerging autocratic regime. New York's first governor compiled a law code mostly from New England sources, summoned an assembly from the English towns on Long Island to meet at Hempstead in 1665, and insisted that the delegates accept the "Duke's Laws" without amendment. At first the code applied only to the English sections of the province and New York City, but it was gradually extended to some Dutch areas as well. After 1665 the governor and council ruled with no assembly but with assistance from the Court of Assizes, which contained all of the justices of the peace in the province.

New York's first legislative assembly met in 1683, nearly twenty years after the English conquest. It passed a Charter of Liberties that guaranteed an assembly at least every three years along with other rights. It also imposed an English county system and English law on the entire province. When the duke became King James II in 1685, he approved the Revenue Act but negatived the Charter of Liberties. Once more New York became autocratic.

Settlers still swarmed across the Atlantic in the early 1680s, but those heading for northern climates overwhelmingly chose the Delaware Valley over the Hudson. In that environment Quakers had been trying to erect an ideal society since the mid-1670s, first in West Jersey (after 1674) and then in Pennsylvania (after 1681). Both were proprietary colonies whose Quaker organizers showed an intense interest in constitutionalism. Indeed, West Jersey's "Concessions and Agreements" of 1677 became the most radical political document that Englishmen anywhere used to organize a society before the American Revolution.

Although a small colony, West Jersey was to have been governed by a large assembly of a hundred men, chosen by ballot and subject to popular instruction. A council of ten commissioners would have acted as a plural executive of sharply limited powers, while within the court system juries, not magistrates, would have decided both fact and law. Opposition from some of the proprietors (the Quakers split a single proprietorship into one hundred shares and then subdivided some of them) and from New York prevented the system from ever being implemented in full, but in Burlington County in the 1680s it came close to achieving the founders' ideal of a participatory regime of brotherly love.

Because William Penn (1644–1718) was an educated gentleman as well as a Quaker, his experiment was less radical but still bracing. More reflection and planning went into the drafting of his First Frame of Government than into the constitutional organization of any other colony. In the First Frame, Penn proposed an assembly of two hundred growing to an eventual size of five hundred. For the colony's first decade or so, he probably meant it to include virtually all free adult males. Although it could only accept or reject bills proposed by the council, this idea looks almost democratic within the context of the settlement process. The council was to contain seventy-two men elected to staggered three-year terms. Penn or his deputy would possess no veto, only a triple vote in council. Bills were to be printed for public distribution before annual meetings of the assembly. In short, Penn proposed what looks almost like a unicameral council whose decisions would have to be ratified by a virtual plebiscite, but as the colony matured, he did expect the system to evolve into a very large, bicameral structure.

These arrangements were far too ambitious for an infant colony to implement, and in 1683 the settlers persuaded Penn to set aside the Frame at least temporarily for a Second Frame, or Charter of Liberties, which reduced the assembly to thirty-six men and the council to eighteen. This system guaranteed tension between the two houses, and the assembly won the right to initiate legislation in the early 1690s when, following the Glorious Revolution, Penn briefly lost control of his colony. He reluctantly accepted this result in a Third Frame, which was replaced in 1701 by the Fourth, or Charter of Privileges, which endured until independence. It gave full legislative power to the assembly, subject only to the governor's veto and the crown's review. The council became an appointive body, but it could only advise the governor. It had no formal legislative role although, provided the governor requested its opinion, it could function informally as an upper house by advising the governor to sign or veto a bill or recommend amendments.

Between 1675 and 1685, Englishmen in America enjoyed an astonishing range of constitutional options. Although royal charters played a role in launching the mainland colonies or in legitimating most other regimes that the settlers created for themselves, the colonists placed a higher value on documents they had drafted and approved among themselves — the Fundamental Orders of Connecticut (1639) which the charter of 1662 mostly ratified, the various New England law codes, the Massachusetts Body of Liberties (1641), the West Jersey Concessions and Agreements (1677), and the Pennsylvania and New York Charters of Liberties (1683). The participatory but authoritarian regimes of Massachusetts and Connecticut contrasted sharply with the anti-authoritarian and participatory governments of Rhode Island, West Jersey, and to a lesser degree Pennsylvania. Proprietary forms characterized societies that varied from formal autocracy through feudal Harringtonian aristocracy to Quaker egalitarianism. Least conspicuous was an active royal presence: until 1679, Virginia was the only royal colony on the mainland.

IMPERIAL REORGANIZATION

During the generation after 1660, the institutional features of royal government became well established. Legally the government of each colony derived its legitimacy from the crown's commission to its governor. This document defined his powers and made provision for a council and assembly. Accompanying the commission was a set of instructions ordering the governor (and sometimes the settlers) to use these powers in specific ways. Both documents quickly became standardized, a process that also made the system exportable from one province to another. The crown appointed both governor and council, while landowning colonists elected the assembly.

The governor could veto bills, and even those approved by him could still be disallowed by the Privy Council in England, which also heard appeals from the highest court in each colony. Governor and council controlled most appointments to office and land grants.

Titanic struggles occurred over how much initiative an assembly should possess. At times the Lords of Trade (the permanent committee of the Privy Council that oversaw the colonies from 1675 to 1696) threatened to impose on a particular colony a statute that restricted its assembly to considering only bills approved in advance by the Privy Council. But the ministers of the crown were usually more interested in revenue, above all in making sure that each colony met its own internal expenses. After a prolonged battle with Jamaica, the crown compromised in 1681. In exchange for a perpetual revenue act, the assembly retained the power to initiate legislation.

As soon as the duke of York became King James II in 1685, this model acquired a rival in royal circles, in the form of the Dominion of New England. Since the Restoration, crown officials had pressured Massachusetts to accept royal appointment of a governor, toleration of all Protestants, and secularization of suffrage requirements. Bay Colony agents delayed in every way they could imagine until the crown had the Massachusetts Charter vacated in chancery in 1684. Some months later Massachusetts became the core of a much larger province, the Dominion of New England. By 1688 it incorporated every English colony east and north of the Delaware River.

Every major policy of the Dominion had been tried earlier in ducal New York—autocratic government, reliance on a military garrison, restrictions on the power of town meetings, reorganization of the land system to secure quitrents to the government, and broad religious toleration. Edmund Andros, governor of New York from 1674–1680, took charge of the Dominion in late 1686 and implemented the king's program. Despite abolition of the assembly, Andros had considerable merchant and gentry support at first, but his policies alienated nearly all New Englanders by 1689. News that William of Orange had landed in England brought this disaffection to a head, and in April 1689 the Boston militia rose, overpowered the small royal garrison, and captured Andros. Confirmation of William's success in England encouraged the rebels to restore the charter government but with a much broader suffrage to ensure popular support. The other New England colonies quietly resumed their pre-Dominion governments.

In New York City, the Dutch militia took possession of Fort James, drove Lieutenant-Governor Francis Nicholson from the colony, and established a temporary government under Captain Jacob Leisler. Maryland also faced revolution two months later. Led by longstanding opponents of the proprietary system, hundreds of settlers formed a Protestant Association, armed, took over the colony, and petitioned England for a royal government.

The Glorious Revolution utterly discredited autocracy and divine-right justifications in English North America. The Jamaica-Virginia model of royal government thus became the overwhelming preference among crown officials, and its only competition came from charter forms already in existence. Connecticut and Rhode Island managed to retain their charters, which had never been overturned by legal process.

Massachusetts, after more than two years of protracted negotiations, obtained a new charter in 1691. In it the crown reserved the power to name a governor and lieutenant-governor with broad patronage and a veto. Property, not church membership, determined suffrage, and the charter extended toleration to all Protestants. Legislation and lawsuits would both be subject to review by the Privy Council. For his part, William III also made significant concessions to the colony. Contrary to the practice in other royal colonies, the legislature rather than the governor and council controlled land grants. The most unusual feature of the 1691 charter involved the council, which became a body elected every year by the General Court, subject to the governor's veto. A blizzard of legislation in the decade after 1692 standardized town governments, ensured tax support for Congregationalist ministers, and created a court system that drew as much on Dominion and common-law precedents as upon the colony's earlier experience. Jury trials for misdemeanors became commonplace.

Outside New England, the crown accepted the Maryland revolution, imposed royal government on the colony in 1692, encouraged the establishment of the Church of England, and barred Roman Catholics from office. But when a Calvert heir converted to the Church of England, his proprietary was restored in 1716. William Penn, suspect because of his cordial relations with James II, lost his governing powers from 1693 to 1695, but, despite frequent complaints from imperial officials, his proprietary interest remained intact. Both East and West Jersey resumed their charter governments by 1692, but their politics became so tempestuous over the next decade that the proprietors willingly surrendered their powers of government to the crown, which created the united royal colony of New Jersey in 1702.

Only in New York did William and Mary repudiate and punish the revolutionaries of 1689. The duke's former men, the English agitators behind the Charter of Liberties of 1683, and Long Island Yankees all resisted Leisler, won London's sympathy, and took over the colony in 1691. New York politics, well into the decade 1700–1710, became and remained a series of vicious struggles between Anti-Leislerians and Leislerians; but the latter, through these contests, began to grasp the practical advantages of English judicial procedures and representative government even as they slipped from majority to minority status. But the biggest winner in these contests was the royal governor, who could often get his way by playing one

faction against the other and in the process made his office the most lucrative patronage post in British North America.

The French war of the 1690s also compelled the home government to
reform its administration of imperial affairs. Parliament passed its most
comprehensive Navigation Act in 1696, in consequence of which a series of
vice-admiralty courts became established in major colonial ports. These
Roman law tribunals used no juries and offered rapid and efficient justice to
maritime communities that could ill afford the frequent delays of common-
law litigation. When disposing of prize cases in time of war or resolving
disputes between a master and his crew, vice-admiralty courts were effective and even popular. They aroused controversy, however, when they tried
to replace colonial common law courts in enforcing the Navigation Acts and
other trade laws. Because the statutory basis for this jurisdiction was ambiguous, provincial supreme courts felt little compunction about issuing writs
of prohibition to remove such cases to their own purview.

Prodded by a threat of direct parliamentary participation in imperial
administration, William III reformed crown oversight of the colonies in
1696. He abolished the Lords of Trade and replaced that body with the
Board of Trade (or Lords Commissioners of Trade and Plantations), the
agency that would supervise the provinces until the Revolution. The board
was an advisory rather than a governing body. In its early early, it assumed a
dynamic, reforming stance. It tried to stamp out land speculation in Virginia
and to encourage small planters rather than large. It attacked the charters of
Pennsylvania, Connecticut, Rhode Island, and Massachusetts and urged
Parliament to annul them. When these initiatives failed, the board settled
into a more comfortable routine of preparing and processing royal commis-
sions and instructions, corresponding with officials overseas, and permitting merchants, colonial agents, and other interested or well-informed parties to present their cases and points of view to the government.

For most of the seventeenth century, political change had made the
colonies less like each other and quite different from England. The transformation that followed the Glorious Revolution reversed this momentum.
The settlers began to see in their provincial governments a plausible facsim-
ile of the metropolitan model. Assemblies directly copied the procedures of
the House of Commons, the smaller councils looks somewhat like both a
local House of Lords and a provincial Privy Council, and except in Rhode
Island and Connecticut, an appointive executive represented the crown or,
as in Pennsylvania and Maryland, the lord proprietor with royal approval.

Royal government, a mainland oddity as late as 1680, became the norm
by 1719 when a Carolina revolt overthrew the proprietary governor and
pleaded for royal protection. In the next decade, South and North Carolina
both became standard royal colonies, along with the Bahamas a few years
later. The only holdouts remained proprietary Maryland and Pennsylvania

(including Delaware, organized separately under the Penns after 1704), and corporate Connecticut and Rhode Island. Proprietors retained their land rights often to the detriment of political harmony. Pennsylvanians valued their statutory Charter of Privileges of 1701 over Charles II's proprietary charter to Penn, but the settlers of Connecticut and Rhode Island so cherished their royal charters that, in slightly modified form, they kept them as state constitutions after 1776. At first the people of Massachusetts were inclined to regard the 1691 charter as a badge of defeat, a measure of the province's inability to regain its pre-1686 autonomy. But by the 1730s at the latest, the new charter was widely venerated as a magnificent example of British constitutionalism in practice. Indeed, the Revolutionary War would begin in 1775 when London ordered redcoats to Concord to enforce Parliament's Massachusetts Government Act, a measure of 1774 that abrogated the second charter and tried to make Massachusetts into a conventional royal province.

The imperial system fit together as an informal federal system that never acquired a sustaining federal ideology. No one could quite explain why powers ought to be divided as they were. Royal apologists insisted that all legitimate authority derived from the crown and that colonial assemblies could not even exist without the sanction of a royal commission. This argument persuaded few settlers, if only because the colonists knew that in every mainland province other than New York, the assembly was older than royal government and confronted the first royal governor with a formidable body of privileges already in place. Rigid adherence to standardized instructions generated turmoil almost everywhere during the period of transition, until royal officials came to terms with the previous history of each society. The most intense conflicts occurred not when assemblies tried to expand their privileges but when governors attempted to exercise prerogatives no predecessor had actually used. Much like the British monarchy at home, governors gained in strength when they concentrated on political management rather than prerogative demands. In terms of practical effectiveness, the eighteenth century marked not the decline but the rise of the crown in North America.

Nevertheless, fairly consistent lines of authority did demarcate an imperial from a provincial sphere of government. Parliamentary legislation was overwhelmingly commercial and therefore oceanic in its objects. By the eighteenth century, the major goals of the basic Navigation Acts had been achieved. Colonial trade traveled exclusively in British ships after the Union with Scotland. Tobacco and sugar were marketed according to law, but some cheating probably occurred with lesser staples. Most colonial imports came from or through Britain, although violations of their requirement did occur and probably increased with the expansion of direct trade to southern Europe after 1730. Parliament's biggest oceanic failure was the Molasses Act of 1733, which tried to ban French and Spanish molasses from the

North American colonies even though the British sugar islands could not produce enough to sustain the New England rum trade. Massive evasion followed.

On balance, Parliament's oceanic policies were a great success. The imperial legislature made good its claim to power over the sea. But when it tried to intervene directly in the internal affairs of the colonies, it nearly always failed. It did establish an imperial postal service, a system that threatened no one's interests and could be sustained by user fees. But when it tried to prevent lumberjacks from destroying tall white pines, or regulate the number of apprentices a New York hatter could employ, or prevent the erection of new iron mills, it failed. Enforcement required the voluntary cooperation of unpaid local officials who had no interest in punishing neighbors who improved the prosperity of the area by pursuing such activities. Instead, internal colonial affairs belonged, under the crown, to the realm of politics. London was far more likely to get its way by consulting provincial interests and requesting local support through normal political channels. Government by consent was a social fact as well as a political ideal, and its ramifications affected far more than relations between governor and assembly.

The ministry did not conceptualize the empire in terms of these limitations. Parliament had no standing committee for America, no built-in dynamic for intervention. It legislated for the colonies only when the ministry asked it to do so, and what happened either through pressure from the merchant community or when royal policy in separate colonies had created conflicting precedents about important matters, and only Parliament seemed able to break the logjam. Examples include the uniform Piracy Act in 1700 and an act regulating the value of foreign coins in 1708. To the degree that such measures required active local cooperation, they did not work well. The colonists, on the other hand, seemed quite happy to let Parliament define the common rights of Englishmen everywhere. Virginia, though settled in 1607, claimed such benefits as habeas corpus (1679) and toleration (1690) even though these statutes never mentioned the colonies.

When Parliament passed laws affecting the colonies, it thought of itself as a sovereign imperial legislature. The empire ought to be as centralized as Parliament wished. Decentralization stemmed from concession, not right. If Parliament never taxed the colonies for revenue before 1764, that fact did not prove that it could not do so. Real power within the empire followed an external-internal (or oceanic-continental) axis, but no body of English law or theory explained why it should. The colonists, for their part, believed that these boundaries were substantive, but they could point to no single text to sustain this judgment. They relied instead upon a century of customary behavior which, they insisted, had actually defined the nature of the empire and could not be changed in fundamentals without the consent of all of the affected societies. In 1765, North Americans would insist almost unanimously that Parliament had no right to tax the colonies, externally or internally. A few argued that the "internal polity" of each colony was also beyond parliamentary reach, although this issue would not become urgent until 1774.

LATE COLONIAL CONSTITUTIONALISM

During the half-century before American independence, colonial spokesmen increasingly shared the widespread English adulation for the British constitution, absorbed most of the language of public debate in Britain, and learned to defend even unique colonial privileges in these terms. Because royal prerogative remained an active issue in North America much longer than in Britain, public life reflected both the older seventeenth-century dualism between prerogative and privilege and the newer civic humanist antagonism between corruption and liberty. When governors quarreled with an assembly majority, the debate was likely to be traditional, legalistic, and highly conscious of both local and English precedents. When an opposition lacked the strength to control the assembly, its members might appeal to the broader public through pamphlets, newspapers, and popular demonstrations that increasingly turned to country ideology, the language of Britain's permanent opposition. In the southern provinces, country ideology became a common denominator of politics, acceptable to governors and assemblymen and no particular threat to political stability. In northern colonies, on the other hand, country ideology before the 1760s continued to appeal most strongly to weak opposition groups.

This trend accompanied a growing elitism in colonial society. The number of public offices never kept pace after 1690 with the growth of population, and almost everywhere turnover in these positions slowed dramatically. The emulation of polite British society became part of the legitimation process in provincial politics, a way that a man justified his pretension to high office. A colonial judge of 1760 was far more likely than his predecessor of 1700 to have strong claims to gentility. American officeholders who became loyalists ultimately preferred this form of legitimacy to public approbation.

Appeals to the public were, however, central to the political process, especially as newspapers and pamphlets became available in nearly every colonial capital by the 1720s and 1730s. In most provinces, elections occurred more frequently than in Britain. New York's governors twice kept an assembly in being for more than seven years (1716–1726 and 1728–1737), but the colony secured its own Septennial Act in the 1740s. By law, elections were annual in Massachusetts, Rhode Island, Connecticut, Pennsylvania, and Delaware. By law or custom, they occurred triennially in New Hampshire, Maryland, and South Carolina. New Jersey and Virginia evolved toward a customary septennial system by mid-century, and North Carolina also moved toward longer assemblies after a biennial measure was disallowed.

What happened during elections varied widely across time and from one colony to another. At mid-century, South Carolina elections were seldom contested and attracted few voters. Virginia contests were vigorous but seldom after 1720 injected any serious factionalism into the House of Burgesses. In the two decades before 1765, electoral battles in Philadelphia, New York City, and Boston sometimes mobilized thousands of voters, aroused sharp class antagonisms, and had a dramatic effect on public life. Most of the time from 1740 to 1765, voters in New Hampshire, Massachusetts, Virginia, and South Carolina supported candidates friendly to the administration, while voters from New York through Maryland usually backed opposition men. Nevertheless, a strong potential existed everywhere to appeal to the public at large against unpopular imperial policies.

Important differences remained. Virginia, South Carolina, and Georgia successfully implemented the constitutional principles of country ideology. The use of royal patronage to manipulate an assembly proved counterproductive and on several occasions produced massive repudiation at the polls. Strong, financially independent governors had to persuade strong, independent assemblies to cooperate voluntarily with royal policies, and increasingly the two learned to work together in a "politics of harmony." In New Hampshire, Massachusetts, and New York, by contrast, royal governors relied heavily on patronage to gain control of their assemblies. Yet in both regions from about 1720 into the 1760s, royal governors achieved a level of practical success seldom approached by their predecessors.

Provincial politics strengthened the empire, but that is not the trend that many detected in London. Real gains in practical power might even appear as disastrous losses of vital prerogatives. The Massachusetts salary controversy illustrates this process. Beginning in 1702, royal governors demanded a fixed salary from the General Court, as their instructions required them to do. The legislature, which antedated royal government by two generations, always refused, citing its invariable custom of never granting a salary for more than a year. This struggle reached a peak between 1720 and 1734. The House of Representatives virtually drove Governor Samuel Shute from the province in 1723, and the British ministry threatened to revoke the 1691 charter unless the General Court complied on salaries. Governor Jonathan Belcher arranged a compromise in the mid-1730s. He ceased to demand a fixed salary, and in return the assembly agreed to vote the governor the equivalent of £1,000 as the first item of business in each legislative year. Beyond question the crown gained from this exchange. Belcher gave up only a prerogative that no one had ever exercised in Massachusetts. He acquired an assured salary that no predecessor had ever received and, by paying formal respect to an assembly privilege, took the issue out of politics until the eve of independence and thus deprived opposition groups of a favorite weapon. Yet many in the ministry and Parliament saw only the loss of prerogative. Measured against the expectations embedded in standard instructions, royal government appeared to be declining just when in fact it was on the verge of its most spectacular achievements in Massachusetts.

These perceptions had consequences. Toward mid-century, such reformers as the Earl of Halifax at the Board of Trade and his young assistant, Charles Townshend, demanded a rejuvenation of imperial authority. Frustrated by the depreciation of paper money in New England, reformers seriously considered such inflammatory proposals as a parliamentary declaration giving royal instructions the force of law, at least in the charter colonies, perhaps in all colonies. "The King in Council is the LEGISLATOR of the Colonies," Earl Granville told Benjamin Franklin in 1759; "and when his Majesty's Instructions come there, they are the Law of the Land . . . and as such, *ought to be* OBEYED."

During the first half of the Seven Years' War (1754–1763 in America), as the French won victory after victory, panicky royal officials called for coercive measures to make the colonists fight: direct taxation by Parliament, the prohibition of paper money, a draconian crackdown on smugglers, the compulsory quartering of soldiers on civilians, the imposition of harsh military justice on provincial volunteers, and the treatment even of colonial major generals as the equivalent of British junior officers. But after 1757, William Pitt's war ministry secured its heady triumphs through cooperative measures. Pump-priming parliamentary subsidies raised more revenue and men from America than direct taxes could have and, by providing a steady flow of specie, helped stabilize the value of paper money, which continued to be issued in huge amounts. The provinces built public barracks for redcoats and voted them ordinary supplies as they passed through. Military justice did stiffen, but provincial officers won from Pitt a rank immediately beneath that of their British counterparts, an arrangement that produced unprecedented cooperation. The tide of British conquest steadily reduced opportunities for smuggling.

Yet after the war the British government rejected the precedents of victory. The Sugar and Currency Acts of 1764 and the Stamp and Quartering Acts of 1765 drew quite directly on the panicky demands for coercive measures from 1754 to 1757, not on Pitt's voluntaristic policies that had won the conflict. The informal imperial constitution disintegrated under this strain.

Nevertheless, provincials entered the 1760s warmly committed to British political culture and the constitutional system that had shaped it. They exuberantly celebrated the victory over New France and hailed the accession of George III (1760–1820) as a new era of a patriot king, dedicated to British liberty and public virtue. North Americans shared Sir William Blackstone's admiration for a mixed and balanced constitution in which "all parts of it form a mutual check upon each other. In the legislature, the people are a check upon the nobility, and the nobility a check upon the people; . . . while the king is a check upon both, which preserves the executive power from encroachment. And this very executive power is again checked, and kept within due bounds by the two houses. . . ." This theory assumed that government must embody society, that for a system of balance to work, the government must contain within itself the major components of the social order—the monarchy, including the law courts, the armed forces, and all other officeholders; the titled aristocracy, including its numerous retainers and clients; and commoners who owned sufficient land to be independent of the will of another. Because it embodied society, government could be sovereign and, through the system of mutual checks, also just. Only by surrendering the potential self-interest of each could king, lords, and commons agree to enact a law.

While the empire came apart, American constitutionalism emerged as much by repudiating as by fulfilling this British and colonial heritage. A substratum of continuity remained in representative government, bicameralism, an independent judiciary, and trial by jury. But the denial of parliamentary sovereignty and the repudiation of the crown meant the abandonment of the mixed and balanced constitution and left Americans with no source of legitimacy beyond themselves.

To keep government limited—that is, to remain a constitutional society—Americans took sovereignty away from government and lodged it with the whole "people," a vital concept that replaced the idea of social orders. This process meant replacing the mixed and balanced constitution with the separation of powers, a theory with much weaker roots in the colonial period, that looked for checks and balances within government itself rather than in the broader society. The Revolution also permitted Americans to resolve the federal dilemma that had destroyed the empire. Because the people, rather than government at any level, must be sovereign, they can delegate some powers to their state governments and others to a national government. In 1787 they finally took the step that the empire could not take.

ORIGINS OF THE AMERICAN REVOLUTION: A CONSTITUTIONAL INTERPRETATION

JACK P. GREENE

Fundamentally, the American Revolution was the unforeseen consequence of the inability of the disputants to agree upon the nature of the constitution of the British Empire. As the controversy over this question became more intense during the thirteen years between 1763 and 1776, many other issues came to the surface. But the constitutional question always remained at the core of the controversy. So significant was it that, if it could have been resolved, no revolution would have occurred in the mid-1770s. The debate over this question proceeded in three sequential phases in association with three distinct crises: the Stamp Act crisis in 1764–1766, the long controversy initiated by the Townshend measures in 1767–1772, and the final crisis of imperial authority and independence in 1773–1776. The unfolding of this debate and the divergent conceptions of the imperial constitution it produced are the primary subjects of this chapter.[1]

When the Seven Years War ended in 1763, the only certainty about constitutional arrangements within the large extended polity that was the early modern British Empire was their ambiguity. There simply was no explicit definition of the balance of authority between the metropolis at the center and the colonies on the peripheries of the empire. Recurrent disputes over the extent of the *Crown's* colonial authority throughout the previous century and a half had left that issue unresolved, while the nature of *Parliament's* relation to the colonies had never been explicitly examined. Parliament's efforts to impose revenue taxes on the colonies in the mid-1760s precipitated the first intensive and systematic exploration of this problem on either side of the Atlantic.

Ostensibly, the issue raised by these efforts, especially by the Stamp Act of 1765, was no more than whether, in the succinct words of Massachusetts Governor Francis Bernard, "America shall or shall not be Subject to the

Legislature of Great Britain." But the controversy rapidly moved on to a more general level. In the process, it provoked a broad-ranging considera- tion of fundamental issues involving the nature of the constitutional rela- tionship between Britain and the colonies and the distribution of power within the empire. Far from producing either a theoretical or a practical resolution of these issues, however, the Stamp Act crisis revealed a deep rift in understanding between metropolis and colonies, a rift that would never be bridged within the structure of the empire.

Some metropolitan supporters later admitted that the Stamp Act was an innovation. For at least three decades, however, metropolitan officials had causally assumed that Parliament's colonial authority was unlimited. For over a century, moreover, Parliament had routinely laid duties upon colonial exports and imports for the purposes of regulating trade. But parlia- mentary legislation for the colonies had been confined almost entirely to commercial and other economic regulations of general scope. The only precedent for any other sort of tax was the Post Office Act of 1710, and revenue was not its primary objective. If, prior to the Stamp Act, there were no precedents for Parliament's taxing the colonies for revenue, neither had anyone ever explicitly articulated a theoretical justification for the exertion of parliamentary authority in that area.

The traditional link between taxation and representation in British constitutional thought and practice made this problem potentially trouble- some — for metropolitans *and* colonials. Indeed, metropolitan disquiet over this problem was clearly revealed during the Stamp Act crisis by proposals from several writers for colonial representation in Parliament. More impor- tant, the administration of Prime Minister George Grenville itself implicitly acknowledged its importance in the months just before final passage of the Stamp Act, when, to justify taxing the colonists, it invented the doctrine that, like the many residents of Britain who had no voice in elections, they were *virtually* represented in Parliament.

As soon as it was raised, the specter of parliamentary taxation produced enormous unease in the colonies. Arguing that it was both new and unprec- edented, colonial spokesmen insisted that no community of Englishmen and their descendants could be taxed without their consent, an exemption they claimed "as their Right" and not "as a *Privilege*." They dismissed the idea of virtual representation out of hand and argued that no legislature had any right to legislate for any people with whom it did not have a common interest and a direct connection. For people on the peripheries of an ex- tended polity like that of the early modern British Empire, this emphasis upon the local foundations of legislative authority made sense. Whatever Parliament might declare, few colonists had any doubt that their rights as Englishmen demanded both that they be exempt from taxes levied in a distant metropolis without their consent and that their own local assemblies have an exclusive power to tax them.

In analyzing the colonial response to the Stamp Act crisis, most scholars have tended to treat the colonists' claims as demands for their individual rights as Englishmen, as indeed they were. But this emphasis has tended to obscure the very important extent to which, especially during the Stamp Act crisis, the colonists seem to have believed that security of individual rights depended upon security of corporate rights, which they thought of as virtually synonymous with the rights of the provincial assemblies. Throughout the colonial period, the status and authority of the assemblies had been a prime subject of dispute between metropolitans and colonials. Whereas earlier the conflict had been between the assemblies and the Crown, after 1765 it was between the assemblies and Parliament.

During the Stamp Act crisis, colonial spokesmen put enormous stress upon the traditional conception of their assemblies as the primary guardians of both the individual liberties of their constituents and the corporate rights of the colonies. Noting that it was precisely because their great distance from the metropolis had prevented them from being either fully incorporated into the British nation or represented in the metropolitan Parliament that their assemblies had been initially established, they insisted that each of their own local legislatures enjoyed full legislative authority and exclusive power to tax within its respective jurisdiction. This identification of individual rights with the corporate rights of the assemblies ran right through the entire colonial argument.

The colonists based their claims for exclusive taxing authority and exemption from parliamentary taxation on their rights as Englishmen, their royal charters, and, especially, long-standing custom. For over a century, they argued, they had "uniformly exercised and enjoyed the privileges of imposing and raising their own taxes, in their provincial assemblies," and such "constant and uninterrupted usage and custom," it seemed to them, was, in the best traditions of English constitutional development, "sufficient of itself to make a constitution." With these arguments, colonial spokesmen merely turned against Parliament defenses they and their ancestors had developed over the previous century to protect colonial rights against abuses of prerogative.

Whatever the sources of the legislative authority of the assemblies, the most significant questions posed by the new intrusion of Parliament into the domestic affairs of the colonies, the most vital issues raised by the Stamp Act crisis vis-à-vis the constitutional organization of the early modern British Empire, were how extensive that authority was and how it related to the authority of the British Parliament. Linking authority to consent, few colonists could accept the metropolitan position that there were no limits to Parliament's colonial authority.

Although some argued that Parliament's authority was purely local and did not extend beyond the bounds of Britain, most colonists in 1764–1766 took a far more cautious approach, admitting, as the Virginia lawyer

Richard Bland put it, that the colonies were "subordinate to the Authority of Parliament" but denying that they were "absolutely so." But what was the nature of that subordination? Where should the line be drawn between the authority of Parliament at the center and that of the colonial legislatures on the peripheries?

The traditional view has been that during the Stamp Act crisis the colonists drew that line between taxation and legislation, that they denied Parliament's authority to tax the colonies for revenue but not its authority to legislate for the colonies. This argument is based on the fact that neither the Stamp Act Congress nor many of the assemblies explicitly commented on Parliament's authority outside the realm of taxation. But the failure of most of these bodies to challenge Parliament's legislative authority outside the area of taxation by no means constituted an admission of that authority, especially in view of the fact that there were several official bodies that explicitly denied that authority.

Indeed, considerable evidence suggests that the colonists' strong initial impulse was to exclude Parliament from all jurisdiction over the domestic affairs of the colonies. Denying Parliament's right to pass laws respecting either taxation or their internal polities, early protests from the Connecticut and Virginia legislatures and later declarations from the Virginia, Rhode Island, Maryland, Connecticut, and Massachusetts assemblies claimed for their constitutents a right not merely to no taxation without representation but even to no legislation without representation, and several writers, including Bland, Governor Stephen Hopkins of Rhode Island, and Samuel Adams wrote elaborate statements in defense of this position. An analysis of the works of these writers suggests that, as Bernard Bailyn has emphasized, the supposed colonial distinction between taxation and legislation was less important to the colonial attempt to demarcate the jurisdictional boundaries between Parliament and the colonial assemblies than a distinction between " 'internal' and 'external' spheres of government."

Richard Bland provided the most extensive and systematic exploration of this distinction. Claiming for the colonists the authority "of directing their *internal* Government by Laws made with their Consent," he argued that each colony was "a distinct State, independent, as to their *internal* Government, of the original Kingdom, but united with her, as to their *external* Polity, in the closest and most intimate LEAGUE AND AMITY, under the same Allegiance, and enjoying the Benefits of a reciprocal Intercourse." Though Bland did not specify precisely what matters were subsumed under the respective categories *internal* and *external*, he implied that Parliament's authority — to legislate as well as to tax — stopped short of the Atlantic coast of the colonies and did not extend over any affairs relating exclusively to the domestic life of the colonies. Such matters, according to Bland's formulation, were the exclusive preserve of the several colonial assemblies.

This distinction between external and internal spheres effectively described the pragmatic and customary distribution of authority within the empire as it had developed over the past century and a half. Notwithstanding metropolitan efforts to limit the extent of local self-government on the peripheries of the empire, the colonists had continued to enjoy considerable local authority. In the exercise of metropolitan authority, Crown and Parliament had, in fact, as Bailyn has noted, usually "touched only the outer fringes of colonial life" and dealt only "with matters obviously beyond the competence of any lesser authority" and with "the final review of actions initiated and sustained by colonial authorities." All other powers — the vast area of "residual authority" that both constituted "the 'internal police' of the community" and "included most of the substance of everyday life" — "were enjoyed . . . by local . . . organs of government." In view of this situation, it was only natural for the colonists to conclude that, insofar as their respective internal affairs were concerned, no part of the empire could be constitutionally subordinated to any other part.[2]

If, at the beginning of the Stamp Act crisis, the questions, in Franklin's words, of "how far, and in what particulars" the colonies were "*subordinate and subject* to the British parliament" were "points newly agitated [and] never yet . . . thoroughly considered," that was no longer the case by the time of the repeal of the Stamp Act in the late winter of 1766. Over the preceding two years, the colonists had slowly begun to construct what John Adams called "a formal, logical, and technical definition" of the imperial constitution under which they lived. As a result of this "great inquiry," they had learned that, as Richard Bland put it, it was "in vain to search into the civil Constitution of *England* for Directions in fixing the proper Connexion between the Colonies and the Mother Kingdom." The main underlying principles of that constitution were certainly relevant to their inquiry, but the British constitution was not, in and of itself, suitable as the constitution for an "extended and diversified" empire.

Instead, in their efforts to understand the nature of the relationship between Britain and the colonies, the colonists turned for guidance to the traditional rights of Englishmen and to their own experience with the actual pattern of customary relations within the empire as they had developed over the previous century and a half. One of the central conclusions of their inquiry — and one of the arguments they pressed most vigorously in their claims against the intrusion of parliamentary authority in the colonies — was that, like Britain itself, both the individual colonies and the empire as a whole had long-standing constitutional traditions that, at least from the point of view of the colonies, seemed to supply legitimacy to their determined efforts to resist what Bland referred to as this "new System of Placing *Great Britain* as the Centre of Attraction to the Colonies."

In 1764 – 1766, only the most advanced thinkers among the colonists were willing to argue that Parliament had *no* role in either the imperial or the several colonial constitutions, to suggest that there was "no *dependence* or relation" between Britain and the colonies except "only that we are all the common subjects of the same King." What all colonial protests did have in common, however, was a clear concern to fix the boundaries between the authority of the metropolis and that of the colonies, between the power of Parliament and that of the colonial assemblies. If Parliament had a constitutional role in the empire, they were persuaded, that role had to be a *limited* one. They were virtually unanimous in agreeing that that role did not include authority to tax the colonies for revenue, and a substantial body of sentiment also held that it did not include authority to legislate for the internal affairs of the colonies.

The colonial case against the Stamp Act got a generally hostile reception in Britain. Few seemed to understand that the colonists' challenge to parliamentary authority went beyond the realm of taxation, and even with regard to this more restricted conception of the colonial position, only a few men in Parliament agreed with the colonists that there were limits upon Parliament's colonial authority. Most both rejected the colonists' contention that they were not represented in Parliament and dismissed the argument that inheritance, charters, and custom exempted the colonies from parliamentary taxation. Lord Mansfield sounded the predominant argument when he flatly declared that, "as to the power of making laws," Parliament represented "the whole British empire" and had "authority to bind every part and every subject without the least distinction."

From this point of view, colonial claims for exemption from parliamentary taxation seemed, as Grenville had defined them when he first proposed to levy stamp duties on the colonies, to be nothing less than a challenge to British sovereignty. As it had gradually developed over the previous century and a half, the conventional conception of sovereignty was that in all polities, including "an Empire, extended and diversified, like that of *Great-Britain*," there had to be, as Blackstone wrote, "a supreme, irresistible, absolute uncontrolled authority, in which the *jura summi imperii,* or the rights of sovereignty reside[d]." Because, most contemporaries seem to have believed, the King-in-Parliament was sovereign in the British polity, it could accept no restrictions upon its authority without relinquishing the sovereignty of the nation over the colonies. By definition, there could be no limitation upon a supreme authority. It was either complete or nonexistent. For that reason, it seemed obvious that the King-in-Parliament had full authority over all matters relating to all Britons everywhere. For the same reason, it also seemed evident that no clear line could be drawn between Parliament's power to legislate for the colonies and its power to tax them.

In the metropolitan view, there was thus no distribution but a concentration of authority within the empire: "As the sovereign of the whole," the King-in-Parliament had "control over the whole British empire." To most metropolitans, in fact, the colonial position appeared incomprehensible because it seemed to imply the existence of more than one sovereign authority within a single state, and sovereignty, according to conventional theory, could not be divided. An "Imperium in imperio"—a sovereign authority within a sovereign authority—was a contradiction in terms. As Lord Lyttelton put it, the colonies were either "part of the dominions of the Crown of Great Britain," and therefore "proper objects of our legislature," or they were "small independent communities," each operating under its own sovereign authority. There was, according to metropolitan theory, no middle ground between these two extremes.

The intensity of colonial opposition to the Stamp Act forced Parliament to repeal that measure, but it accompanied repeal with passage of the Declaratory Act, modeled on the Irish Declaratory Act of 1720 and asserting Parliament's authority "to bind the colonies and people of America . . . in all cases whatsoever." But this fiat from the center by no means resolved the question of the distribution of authority within the empire. As Colonel Isaac Barre announced in the House of Commons early in 1766, the Stamp Act crisis had provoked "the people of America to reason . . . closely upon the relative rights of this country and that," and the undefined and "loose texture" of Britain's "extended and diversified" empire had fostered the development of two widely divergent interpretations of how authority was distributed between metropolis and colonies. Whereas most people in the former thought the empire a unitary state, most people in the latter thought of it as a federal polity in which the authority of the center was limited by the authority exercised by the peripheries.

If the Stamp Act crisis "first led the colonists into [systematic] Enquiries concerning the nature of their political situation," its resolution in early 1766 by no means put an end to those inquiries. Indeed, Parliament's renewed efforts early in 1767 to tax the colonies through the Townshend Acts quickly reopened the question. For the next six years, people on both sides of the Atlantic further explored the difficult problem of the constitutional organization of the empire.

The vast majority of people in the metropolitan establishment, in both Britain and the colonies, adhered strictly to the position articulated by Grenville and his supporters during the Stamp Act crisis. Interpreting all suggestions for any limitations upon Parliament's colonial authority as a challenge to the British constitution of parliamentary supremacy and to metropolitan sovereignty over the colonies, they continued to insist, as they had throughout the Stamp Act crisis, that sovereignty was indivisible and to view the maintenance of "the supremacy and legislative authority of Parliament" in its fullest extent over the colonies as "essential to the existence of the empire."

Notwithstanding the tenacity with which they held to this point of view, metropolitan authorities resisted the impulse to take sweeping coercive measures against the colonies during the late 1760s. Sensing the expediency of Thomas Pownall's declaration that *"You may exert power over, but you can never govern an unwilling people,"* they instead wound up in 1770 taking what they regarded as a conciliatory approach. At the same time that they indicated that they would seek no new parliamentary taxes and guided through Parliament a repeal of most of the Townshend duties, they retained taxes on tea and sugar products to stand as symbols of Parliament's colonial authority.

If anything, the urge toward conciliation during the crisis over the Townshend Acts was even more powerful in the colonies. This urge was evident in the grudging willingness of colonial merchants throughout the crisis to pay an unrepealed parliamentary tax on molasses. On both sides of the Atlantic, John Dickinson's *Letters from a Farmer in Pennsylvania,* published in 1767, was certainly the most widely circulated expression of colonial opinion. Obviously intending to confine the controversy within the narrowest possible bounds, Dickinson addressed his pamphlet exclusively to the issue of the moment—Parliament's right to tax the colonies for revenue—and did not consider the wider problems of the relationship between metropolis and colonies, the extent and nature of metropolitan sovereignty over the colonies, or the distribution of authority within the empire.

By focusing debate so closely upon the narrow question of taxation, Dickinson helped to deescalate the controversy. The widespread acceptance of his definition of the situation seems both to have inhibited the sort of wide-ranging discussion of the nature of the metropolitan–colonial relationship that had occurred during the Stamp Act crisis and to have been in no small part responsible for the fact that all but a few official colonial challenges to parliamentary authority during the late 1760s and very early 1770s were confined to the single issue of taxation for revenue.

If, during the crisis over the Townshend Acts, most colonial assemblies, as the Massachusetts legislator Thomas Cushing later observed, "acquiesced in the distinction between Taxation and Legislation and were disposed to Confine the dispute to that of Taxation only and entirely to wave the other as a subject of too delicate a Nature," a number of thinkers in both the colonies and Britain took a much deeper look at the controversy. As Benjamin Franklin wrote his son in March 1768, they concluded that, while "Something might be made of either of the extremes; that Parliament has a power to make *all laws* for us, or that it has a power to make *no laws* for us," "no middle doctrine" of the kind proposed by Dickinson could successfully be maintained. Although these thinkers regarded their conclusions as no more than an articulation and rationalization of long-standing constitutional practice within the empire, they in fact represented a radical challenge to the metropolitan belief in Parliament's supremacy over the whole empire.

This radical interpretation proceeded from three underlying assumptions. The first was that Parliament's claims to colonial jurisdiction had to be proved and could "not [simply be] take[n] . . . for granted" or permitted to rest on "the monstrous idea of a *Virtual Representation.*" The second was that the "civil constitution" of Britain "by no means" determined "the connection which ought to be established between the parent country and her colonies, nor the duties reciprocally incumbent on each other." The third was that the history of the colonies and of their relationship to the metropolis was the most authoritative guide to the exact nature of that connection.

Adherents of this interpretation put particular emphasis upon the history of the colonies, which seemed to them to make clear that the colonies had never been "incorporated with Great Britain in a legislative capacity." This being the case, it seemed equally obvious that Great Britain and the British Empire were distinct political entities. As the Georgia minister Johan Joachim Zubly explained, the British Empire was a far "more extensive word, and should not be confounded with the kingdom of Great Britain." Rather, it was a "confederal" polity that consisted of both the home islands and a number of "extrinsic Dominions," including "several islands and other distant countries, asunder in different parts of the globe." As the "head of this great body," England was "called the mother country" and "all the settled inhabitants of this vast empire" were "called Englishmen." But those phrases by no means implied that the empire was "a single state." On the contrary, each of its many separate entities had a "legislative power . . . within itself," and "the several legislative bodies of Great-Britain, Ireland and the British Colonies" were "perfectly distinct, and entirely independent upon each other."

In the view of its proponents, the real virtue of this emerging conception lay not in its foundations in past practice but in its appropriateness for the governance of an extended polity. The "Excellency of the Invention of Colony Government, by separate independent Legislatures," Franklin wrote in 1769, was that it permitted "the remotest Parts of a great Empire" to be "as well governed as the Center." By guaranteeing maximum autonomy to peripheral states and thereby helping to prevent wholesale "Misrule, Oppressions of Proconsuls, and Discontents and Rebellions" in those areas, the authority of the British monarch seemed to be infinitely expandable, capable, in Franklin's words, of being "extended without Inconvenience over Territories of any Dimensions how great soever."

This conception of the British Empire as consisting, in Benjamin Prescott's words, "of a great and glorious King, with a Number of distinct Governments, alike subjected to his royal Scepter, and each governed by its own Laws," also seemed to its proponents to offer a solution to the problem of the indivisibility of sovereignty. Posed by metropolitan protagonists during the earliest days of the Stamp Act controversy, the logical dilemma of "an *imperium in imperio*" had remained at the heart of metropolitan resistance to colonial claims for exemption from parliamentary authority. According to the emerging conception of empire among the most advanced defenders of the colonies, however, sovereignty within the extended polity of the British Empire resided not in Britain and not in the King-in-Parliament but in the institution of the monarchy alone. In the imperial realm, according to these writers, the theory of coordination, of the legal sovereignty of the King-in-Parliament, did not apply.

To its proponents, this view of the empire as "many states under one Sovereign" seemed thoroughly defensible on the basis both of the terms of the colonial charters and the customary constitutional arrangements that had grown up since the establishment of the colonies. For over a century and a half the colonists, without interruption, had "been trusted in a good measure with the entire management of their affairs." Of course, as they recognized, the doctrine of usage on which their developing conception of the empire rested so heavily cut two ways. If Parliament had no role whatever in their early history and if, subsequently, Parliament had not customarily interfered in their internal affairs, they could not deny that, from the mid-seventeenth century on, Parliament had "exercised its Authority in the Colonies, for regulating their Trade, and afterwards for directing their exterior Policy." Furthermore, they had to admit that, even though Parliament's authority had "in some Instances been executed with great Partiality to Britain and Prejudice to the Colonies," they had "nevertheless always submitted to it" and thereby "consented to consider themselves as united to Great Britain in a commercial capacity, and to have their trade governed by its parliament."

Deriving from a century and a half of experience, custom thus seemed to prescribe a clear allocation of authority within the broad extended polity of the early modern British Empire, an allocation precisely along the lines identified by Bland and other colonial writers during the Stamp Act crisis. The many provincial governments — Ireland on the near-periphery and the several colonies in the distant American periphery — had full jurisdiction over their own particular local and internal affairs, while the metropolitan government at the center had authority over all general matters, including the external relations of the several provincial governments.

In the absence of any impartial tribunal to settle constitutional disputes between the center and the peripheries, there was, as Pownall lamented in 1768, "no means of deciding the controversy" by law. Unwilling to give in, metropolitan leaders were, as yet, also unwilling to resort to force. They still understood that, in the words of Edmund Burke, there was "no such thing as governing the whole body of the people contrary to their inclinations," and such considerations were behind Parliament's decision in the spring of 1770 to repeal all of the Townshend duties except the tax on tea. This essentially political resolution of the crisis in effect went back to the settlement adopted in 1766. That is, it left the issue of the extent of Parliament's colonial authority to rest on the Declaratory Act and token taxes on sugar products and tea, with an implicit understanding that, as in the case of Ireland, Parliament would not thenceforth levy any further taxes on the colonies.

Like the Stamp Act crisis, the controversy over the Townshend Acts had helped to illuminate still further the ancient question of how, within the extended polity of the British Empire, authority was distributed between metropolis and colonies. To be sure, it produced little change in the metropolitan position as it had been articulated in 1764–1766, while the conciliatory thrust of both Dickinson's *Letters from a Pennsylvania Farmer* and most of the official colonial protests helped to obscure the radical drift of sentiment among spokesmen in both America and Britain who supported the colonial side. For, pursuing the logic of the customary constitutional arrangements that had obtained in the empire over the previous century, a great many writers between 1767 and 1770 had worked out detailed arguments to prove what a few colonial thinkers had already implied in 1764–1766: that the British Empire was a loose association of distinct political entities under a common king, each of which had its own legislature with exclusive jurisdiction over its own internal affairs. As in 1764–1766, a major constitutional crisis had thus functioned to intensify, rather than to resolve, differences in interpretations of the constitutional organization of the empire.

Nevertheless, repeal of the Townshend Acts brought a temporary respite from the turmoil that had beset metropolitan–colonial relations over the previous six years. For the next three and a half years, debate over the respective jurisdictions of Parliament and the several peripheral legislatures in Ireland and the American colonies fell into temporary abeyance. Yet, throughout the early 1770s, constitutional relations within the empire remained troubled. Coincident with the repeal of most of the Townshend duties there were a new series of quarrels over the scope of the Crown's colonial authority, quarrels in several colonies that punctuated the so-called period of quiet during the early 1770s and revealed that the debate over the extent of the Crown's prerogative in the colonies was still hotly contested.

From the perspective of the crises over the Stamp and Townshend Acts and the debate over Parliament's new pretensions to authority over the internal affairs of the colonies however, these old questions about the Crown's relationship acquired a new and heightened urgency in the colonies. If, as an impressive number of colonial spokesmen had begun to argue during the late 1760s, sovereignty within the empire rested not in the Crown-in-Parliament but in the Crown alone, then it became especially important for the colonists to establish the boundaries not just of parliamentary but also of royal authority in the colonies. For that reason, colonial defenders in all of the battles of the early 1770s revealed a pronounced tendency to build upon their own particular local constitutional heritages to argue, as their predecessors in earlier generations had often done, that, no less than in Britain itself, the Crown's authority — the freedom of its "will" — in the colonies had been effectively limited over the previous century by specific idiosyncratic constitutional developments in each of the colonies. Again just as in Britain, these developments had led irreversibly, colonial leaders believed, in the direction of increasing authority in the hands of the local legislatures and greater restrictions on the prerogatives of the Crown. By this process, they argued, the rights of the inhabitants in the peripheries had gradually been secured against the power of the center.

As refined and elaborated during the contests of the early 1770s, this view of colonial constitutional history powerfully helped to reinforce traditional views of the colonial legislatures both as the primary guardians of the local rights of the corporate entities over which they presided and, like Parliament itself in Britain, as the dynamic forces in shaping the colonial constitutions. Insofar as the constitution of the empire was concerned, this emphasis upon the peculiarity and integrity of the several colonial constitutions certainly constituted, as Peter S. Onuf has noted, a vigorous "defense of constitutional multiplicity" that had profound implications for the ongoing debate over the nature of sovereignty within the empire. For, together with the emerging conviction that Parliament had no authority over the colonies, the renewed contention that the Crown's authority in the peripheries was also limited by local constitutions as they had emerged out of not just the colonists' inherited rights as Englishmen and their charters but also local usage and custom pushed the colonists still further in the direction of a wholly new conception of sovereignty in an extended polity like the early modern British Empire. That conception implied that ultimate constitutional authority — sovereignty — lay not in any institution or collection of institutions at the center of the empire but in the separate constitutions of each of the many separate political entities of which the empire was composed.[3]

When Parliament's passage of the Tea Act in May 1773 revived the dispute over its colonial authority, colonial resistance to that measure provoked the crisis that would, in a mere two and a half years, led to the dismemberment of the early modern British Empire. At no time during this crisis did either side show much disposition to compromise. As each quickly took a determined stand upon the position marked out by its most extreme proponents during the previous crises, the spirit of conciliation that had marked the crisis over the Townshend Acts rapidly gave way to complete intransigence.

In both Britain and the colonies, supporters of Parliament's right to legislate for the colonies insisted, as they had ever since the beginning of the controversy during the Stamp Act crisis, that the British Empire, consisting of Great Britain *and* all its territories, was a single state composed of "ONE people, ruled by ONE constitution, and governed by ONE King." Reiterating the same central contentions that had underlain their argument from the beginning, they continued to interpret the controversy as a dispute over sovereignty. They dismissed the doctrine of no legislation without representation as "an obsolete maxim" that had no applicability to the distant parts of an extended polity like the British Empire, and persisted in asserting that "no maxim of policy" was "more universally admitted, than that a supreme and uncontroulable power must exist somewhere in every state." In the British Empire, they insisted, that power was vested "in King, Lords, and Commons, under the collective appellation of the Legislature," which as James Macpherson phrased it, was merely "another name for the Constitution of State," was, "in fact, the State itself."

Thus, if the colonists refused obedience to Parliament, they were "no longer Subjects, but rebels" who, by arrogating "to themselves all the functions of Sovereignty," were obviously endeavoring to put themselves "on the footing of a Sovereign State." "The question between them and Great Britain," then, as Macpherson gravely noted in summarizing the dominant position within the metropolitan political nation, was nothing less than "dependence or independence, connection or no connection." With "no common Principle to rest upon, no common Medium to appeal to," wrote Josiah Tucker, the dispute seemed to have no middle ground. To admit any qualification in "the controuling right of the British legislature over the colonies," its proponents devoutly believed, would mean nothing less than the abandonment of "the whole of our authority over the Americans."

While the metropolitan political nation refused to back down from its insistence that the King-in-Parliament was the supreme sovereign of the empire, the colonial assemblies and the First and Second Continental Congresses, composed of delegates from the thirteen colonies from New Hampshire to Georgia, gave official sanction to radical views that had previously been held only by private individuals, views that had been developed by Franklin and others during the late 1760s and early 1770s and called for complete colonial autonomy over the internal affairs of the colonies.

The colonial position, as it was enunciated in mid-1774 and elaborated over the next two years, was founded on a complete rejection of the prevailing metropolitan theory of an omnipotent Parliament. By ignoring the vital and traditional British constitutional principle of consent, of no legislation without representation, this "dreadful novelty," supporters of the colonial position declared, was at total variance with both "the ancient rights of the people" and "the settled, notorious, invariable practice of" imperial governance within the empire over the previous century and a half.

No less important, when applied to distant and unrepresented colonies, this "modern doctrine," it seemed to the colonists, obviously also represented "a total contradiction to every principle laid down at the time of the [Glorious] Revolution, as the rules by which the rights and privileges of every branch of our legislature were to be governed for ever." Indeed, by its insistence upon exerting a *"supreme* jurisdiction" over the colonies, Parliament seemed not merely to be violating the most essential principles of the Revolution but actually to have assumed and to be acting upon precisely the same "high prerogative doctrine[s]" against which that Revolution had been undertaken. Thus, the colonists believed, if, by resisting Parliament, they had become rebels, they were "rebels in the same way, and for the same reasons that the people of Britain were rebels, for supporting the Revolution."

By 1774, few colonial leaders any longer had any doubt that, over the previous decade, it had "been clearly and fully proved that the Assemblies or Parliaments of the *British* Colonies in *America*" had "an exclusive right, not only of taxation, but of legislation also; and that the *British* Parliament, so far from having a right to make laws binding upon those Colonies in all cases whatsoever," had "really no just right to make any laws at all binding upon the Colonies." Far from being subject to the "supreme" authority of Parliament, most American leaders now believed, the colonies had "always enjoyed a supreme Legislature of their own, and . . . always claimed an exemption from the jurisdiction of a *British* Parliament." Not the King-in-Parliament, wrote the Virginian Thomson Mason, but the "King, at the head of his respective *American* Assemblies," constituted "the Supreme Legislature of the Colonies."

Whether Parliament had any authority even over the external affairs of the colonies now became a point of contention. Already during the Townshend Act crisis, some colonial supporters were beginning to suggest that Parliament had no authority whatever over the colonies. By 1774, many of the most influential tracts, including those written by James Wilson of Pennsylvania and Thomas Jefferson of Virginia, unequivocally took this position. The legislative authority of each of the many independent legislatures within the empire, including Parliament, wrote Wilson, was necessarily "confined within . . . local bounds" and could not be imposed upon any of the other areas of the empire without their consent.

During the early stages of the crisis of independence, however, most American leaders seemed still to believe that Parliament did have authority over external affairs. As both Alexander Hamilton and John Adams pointed out, they thought that that authority derived from the "long usage and uninterrupted acquiesence" by which the colonists, since the middle of the seventeenth century, had given their "implied consent" to the navigation acts and other trade regulations.

But, if few of their protagonists yet claimed for the colonists "external as well as internal sovereign jurisdiction" as "independent nations," virtually everyone now agreed with those people who had begun to argue during the late 1760s that "all the different members of the British Empire" were "distinct states, independent of each other, but connected together under the same sovereign." Upon close examination, they had discovered that, as an entity "composed of extensive and dispersed Dominions," the empire was "in some degree a new case" in political history that had to "be governed . . . more by its own circumstances, and by the genius of our peculiar Constitution, than by abstract notions of government." Separated by vast distances, "inhabited by different people, [living] under distinct constitutions of government, with different customs, laws and interests," its several constituent elements could not possibly comprise a single civil state. Rather, each part had to be "considered as a [distinct] people, not a set of individuals." Presided over by its own legislature, each of these corporate entities was a separate realm that was entirely independent of all the others. According to this line of thought, no part of the empire was subordinate to any other part. As Franklin had remarked in 1770, there was no dependence among the several parts of the empire, "only a *Connection*, of which the King is the common Link."

In view of the economic success of the empire, both Americans and their supporters in Britain regarded it as absurd for the metropolis to risk so many palpable advantages in pursuit of what increasingly appeared to them to be nothing more than an academic and irrelevant political abstraction. Sovereignty might appear to be the grand question in dispute to the vast majority of the metropolitan political nation. Throughout the prerevolutionary debates, however, most colonial leaders had resisted such reductionism and had endeavored, unsuccessfully, to focus debate upon the seemingly more tractable and certainly less abstract problem of how power was or should be allocated in a polity composed of several related but nonetheless distinct corporate entities. For the colonists, resolution of their dispute with the metropolis had never seemed to require much more than the rationalization of existing political arrangements within the empire.

For them, the "great solecism of an *imperium in imperio*" seemed, as James Iredell declared, to be little more than "a narrow and pedantic . . . point of speculation," a "scholastic and trifling refinement," that had no relevance to the situation at hand. "Custom and continual usage" seemed to be "of a much more unequivocal nature than speculation and refined principles." Notwithstanding the fact that it had been "so vainly and confidently relied on" by their antagonists, that "beautiful theory in political discourses — the necessity of an absolute power residing somewhere in every state" — seemed, as Iredell wrote, to be wholly inapplicable to a situation involving "several distinct and independent legislatures, each engaged in a separate scale, and employed about different objects."

Colonial protagonists thus called upon the metropolitan government to abandon its pursuit of the "vain phantom of unlimited sovereignty, which was not made for man," and content itself with "the solid advantages of a moderate, useful and intelligible authority." As long as all members of the empire adhered to the customary arrangements that had developed over the previous century and a half, as long as the king was the "supreme head of every legislature in the British dominions," he would always have it in his power to "guide the vast and complicated machine of government, to the reciprocal advantage of all his dominions" and, by his authority to veto laws, would on any occasion be able to "prevent the actual injury to the whole of any positive law in any part of the empire."

In their efforts to explain — and to rationalize — existing constitutional relationships within the empire, colonial protagonists, between 1764 and 1776, had discovered that the locus of authority necessarily had to reside in each of the separate corporate entities that composed the empire. Contrary to metropolitan theory as it had developed following the Glorious Revolution and, more especially after 1740, Authority, they now clearly understood, had never been concentrated in a sovereign institution at the center. Rather, it had always been dispersed among the several parliaments that routinely had been established to preside over — and express the collective will of — each new polity within the empire. Indeed, this proliferation of legislatures was the only way that those traditional English rights that had been confirmed to the inhabitants of the metropolis by the Revolutionary settlement — especially that most fundamental right of no legislation without representation — could be extended to people in the peripheries of a large extended polity like the early modern British Empire. For the inhabitants of those, by then, quite ancient corporate entities, English liberty and their specific local corporate rights were identical. Just as it had been throughout the colonial era, the integrity of those rights and of the constitutions and assemblies that embodied and protected them was thus, not surprisingly, the central theme of colonial constitutional protest during the 1760s and 1770s.

Although this insistence upon the "autonomy and integrity" of the several colonial constitutions was certainly a "defense of constitutional multiplicity" within the empire, the ancient and continuing association of its several separate polities clearly implied the existence of a larger imperial constitution, a constitution of the empire. Though this constitution was obviously based upon and expressed the same fundamental constitutional principles, it was emphatically not identical to the British constitution. By the 1760s the British constitution had become a constitution of parliamentary supremacy. But the emerging imperial constitution, like the separate constitutions of Britain's many overseas dominions, remained a customary constitution in which, according to the colonial point of view, sovereignty resided not in an all-powerful Parliament but in the Crown, the power of which had been considerably reduced over the previous century by the specific "gains made over the years in the direction of self-determination" by each representative body within the empire.[4]

Regarding any diminution of parliamentary sovereignty as a prelude to the eventual loss of control of the colonies that seemed to be so intimately associated with Britain's rise to world power, the vast majority of the metro-politan political nation found it impossible to accept such arguments. Be-sides, from the perspective of Britain's own internal constitutional develop-ment during the previous century, colonial theories about the organization of the empire seemed dangerously retrograde. By placing the resources of Ireland and the colonies directly in the hands of the Crown and beyond the reach of Parliament, those theories appeared to strike directly at the root of the legislative supremacy that, for them, was the primary legacy of the Glorious Revolution.

By 1776, what had begun as yet another crisis over Parliament's right to tax the colonies had become a crisis over whether the colonies would be-come independent. The empire foundered over the inability of the center and the peripheries to agree on a formula for governance that would give the peripheries of that extended polity the same rights and control over their domestic affairs that was enjoyed by the center. Whether independence would be the first step toward the establishment of a viable union that would enable them to resolve the problem that had. brought the British Empire to grief, the problem of how in an extended polity authority should be distributed between center and peripheries was still an open question when the colonies declared independence in July 1776.

Driven by the specter of parliamentary taxation to investigate the con-stitutional organization of the empire, American colonials quickly decided in the 1760s that they were governed by a customary imperial constitution based upon the ideas of principled limitation and government by consent. As several legal historians have recently emphasized, the fact that metro-politan officials would not take the colonial case seriously does not mean that they were "right about the law." Constitutional arrangements within the British Empire were far from precise, and in the debates of the 1760s and 1770s each side could marshal effective legal arguments in behalf of its position. In this unsettled situation, constitutional questions were by no means so clear as they were said to be in London and as has been assumed by so many later historians.[5]

The early modern British Empire was by no means yet a modern unitary state. Imperial institutions in the colonies had little coercive power and depended for their effectiveness upon the consent of local populations. Authority within the empire had long been dispersed into the hands of authoritative, powerful, and "largely autonomous local institutions." Not dependent for their effectiveness "on the support or the acquiesence of a central authority" and highly "resistant to centralized control," these insti-tutions were regarded, both by those who composed them and those whom they served, as largely "independent recipients of constitutional power and authority." In this "diffuse and decentralized" political entity local institutions invariably determined the nature of the constitution as much as did authorities at the center.[6]

The argument of this essay has been that with regard to extended polities in the era before the development of the modern consolidated state in the wake of the French Revolution, one should not automatically assume that the perspective of the center is the correct or even the dominant one. In any polity like the early modern British Empire in which the authority and ideology of the center have been weak in the peripheries while local power and traditions have been strong, local institutions and customs have been at least as important in determining existing constitutional arrangements as those of the center. In such an entity, a *center* perspective will almost automatically be a *partisan* perspective. In the particular case of the British Empire at the time of the American Revolution, the antiquity of the notion of a customary imperial constitution of principled limitation and the strength of local institutions combined with the comparative recentness of the doctrine of parliamentary supremacy and weakness of metropolitan authority in the colonies to make the perspective of the center a "tory perspective." Perhaps even more important, the failure of the center to establish the legitimacy of its perspective in the peripheries rendered it an *anachronistic* perspective when applied to legal and constitutional arrangements within the empire as a whole.

THE DECLARATION OF INDEPENDENCE AS A CONSTITUTIONAL DOCUMENT

DENNIS J. MAHONEY

The important Consequences resulting to the American States from this Declaration of Independence, considered as the Ground & Foundation of a future Government, will naturally suggest the Propriety of proclaiming it in such a Mode, as that the People may be universally informed of it.
John Hancock to the New Jersey Convention, July 5, 1776

By the Declaration of Independence the inhabitants of the United States constituted themselves as a people. This is the great constituent act; the constitution of a government is merely secondary. A people may be more or less successful in constituting a government for themselves; they may have to have more than one try at it. But the constitution of a people is accomplished once for all. In this sense, the Declaration of Independence must be regarded as America's most fundamental constitutional document.

The constitution of the American people is different from the constitution of any people previously existing. The American people was constituted not by ties of common blood, or of a common language, or of a common historical experience. The American people was constituted by the recognition of the natural human rights of equality and liberty. From recognition of those rights, conclusions followed about what form the constitution of government must take. The Declaration is the definitive statement for the American polity of the ends of government, of the necessary conditions for the legitimate exercise of political power, and of the sovereignty of the people who establish the government and, when circumstances warrant, may alter or abolish it. No mere tract in support of a bygone event, the Declaration was and remains the basic statement of the meaning of the United States as a political entity.

The Founding Fathers were emphatic about the constitutional status of the Declaration of Independence. John Hancock, president of the Continental Congress, transmitting the Declaration to the several states, described it as "the Ground & Foundation of a future Government." Thomas Jefferson, with the concurrence of James Madison, called it "the fundamental Act of Union of these States." Adoption of the Declaration of Independence was the first step in the process of "establishing good government from reflection and choice" rather than from accident and force.

The Declaration of Independence was, strictly speaking, neither necessary nor sufficient to effect a dissolution of the bonds between America and Britain. A simple resolution was all that was necessary; and without a successful Revolution nothing would have been sufficient. But the delegates to the Second Continental Congress self-consciously chose the occasion of asserting independence for the promulgation of a constitutional document. Richard Henry Lee, on instructions from the Virginia convention, introduced three resolutions on June 7, 1776: to declare the colonies independent, to establish a confederation, and to seek foreign alliances. Each of the resolutions was referred to a select committee, one of which was charged with preparing "a declaration to the effect of the first resolution."

To draft the Declaration, Congress appointed a distinguished committee, including John Adams of Massachusetts, Benjamin Franklin of Pennsylvania, Roger Sherman of Connecticut, Robert Livingston of New York, and Thomas Jefferson of Virginia. The committee, in turn, delegated the task to a subcommittee comprising Adams, Franklin, and Jefferson; but it was the Virginian who actually penned the Declaration. So well did Jefferson express the sentiments of the Congress that his committee colleagues made only a few changes in his draft.

Jefferson, by his own account, turned to neither book nor pamphlet for ideas. Nor did he seek to expound a novel political theory. His aim was to set forth the common sense of the American people on the subject of political legitimacy. To be sure, there are ideas, and even phrases, that recall John Locke: the Declaration follows Locke in stressing the natural rights of man as the foundation of the political order. But the concept of man's natural autonomy, modifiable only by his consent to the rule of others in a social compact, was long acknowledged in the American colonies; it inhered in congregational church polity, and it was transmitted through such theoretical and legal writers as Emerich de Vattel, Jean-Jacques Burlamaqui, and Samuel Pufendorf, as well as by the authors of Cato's Letters and other popular works.

Considered as a tract for the times, as a manifesto for the Revolutionary cause, the Declaration marks an important step in American constitutional development. The resistance to British misrule in America had, at least since the French and Indian Wars, been based on an appeal to the British constitution. The Americans had charged that the imposition of taxes by a body in which they were not represented and the extension to them of domestic legislation by a Parliament to whose authority they had not consented violated the ancient traditions of British government. The constitution, that is, the arrangement of offices and powers within the government and the privileges of the subjects, had been overridden or altered by the British Parliament. Although the differences between the American provinces and the mother country were great, they were differences about, and capable of resolution within, the British constitutional framework. The liberties that the colonists had claimed were based on prescription.

There had been other revolutions in British history, but this one was different. From the barons at Runnymede to the Whigs who drove James II from the throne, British insurgents had appealed to the historic rights of Englishmen. The declarations they extracted—from Magna Carta to the Bill of Rights—were the assurances of their kings that the ancient laws obtaining in their island would be respected. The preamble of the Declaration of Independence makes clear that this is not the case with the American Revolution. The case of Britain's misrule in America was to be held up to a universal standard and exposed as tyrannical before a "candid world." Against the selfsame standard all government everywhere could be measured. Everyone who reads the Declaration with his eyes open must be struck by this fact: the Declaration justifies the independence of the American nation by appeal not to an English or an Anglo-American standard but to the universal standard of human rights.

When independence was declared, the British constitution became irrelevant. The liberties claimed in the Declaration are grounded in natural law; they are justified by reason, not by historical use. The American Revolution was, therefore, the first and most revolutionary of modern revolutions. In the Declaration was recognized a higher law to which every human law—constitution or statute—is answerable. The British constitution, as it then existed, was tried by the standards of that higher law and found guilty of tyranny. As the British constitution, so every constitution, including the American Constitution, may be tried; and on conviction the sentence is that the bonds of allegiance are dissolved.

STRUCTURE

The structure of the Declaration emphasizes its various purposes. There are five parts: the heading, the preamble, the declaration of the natural law of civil government, the indictment of the British king for his violation of that law (comprising both a general charge and twenty-five specifications), and a conclusion. At least one scholar has pointed out the similarity of this structure to the structure of a formal common law document, no longer in use in American pleading, called a "declaration," a methodical statement of a plaintiff's cause of action or assertion of right.[1] Jefferson, himself a lawyer and something of a scholar of legal history, was probably familiar with that type of document. Even if that were not the case, however, and even if the structure had been devised ad hoc by Jefferson, the point would be obvious to the reader.

THE HEADING

The heading of the Declaration of Independence exists in two distinct forms. The "authenticated copy," printed on the authority of Congress for distribution, was headed:

IN CONGRESS, July 4, 1776.

A DECLARATION

By the REPRESENTATIVES of the

UNITED STATES OF AMERICA,

In GENERAL CONGRESS assembled.

But the engrossed copy, the original parchment that was signed by the members of Congress and is now preserved in the National Archives, was headed:

IN CONGRESS, JULY 4, 1776.

The unanimous Declaration of the thirteen united States of America.

Both versions are significant.

The heading of the authenticated copy emphasizes the representative character of the Declaration. Although the Declaration expressed the common sense of the American people, it was not the product of a plebiscite or of a mass movement. Rather, it was the product of deliberation. *The Federalist* was to point out that deliberation was the characteristic introduced into popular (we would now say "democratic") government by the principle of representation.

The heading of the engrossed copy emphasizes the unanimity of the states in making the Declaration. The formula used in the heading of he engrossed copy foreshadowed the formula used by the Constitutional Convention in transmitting the new constitution to the people for ratification: "Done in Convention by the Unanimous Consent of the States present. . . ."

PREAMBLE

The Preamble sets forth certain facts pertaining to the situation that existed in North America in 1776. It had become necessary for "one people" (the Americans) to dissolve the political bands that had connected them to another (the British). But that supposes that the Americans had become, or by the adoption of the Declaration were becoming, "one people." It further supposes that the British had become, or were becoming, "another" people. Neither of these suppositions was indisputably necessary to be made — indeed, the American enemies of the Declaration in later generations were to deny the validity of both of them.

Was there really an American people? Were there not rather thirteen peoples, New Yorkers and Pennsylvanians, Virginians and Georgians, and so forth? Institutions of government were being established in the provinces, now become states; no institutions of government were established, or even proposed, for the Union of those states. And were there not three separate peoples, black, white, and red? Did these not have different rights and different aspirations and different claims to being peoples? Did the white people not hold the black people in bondage? And did the red people (the "merciless Indian savages" of the Declaration) not hold both the black and white peoples in terror? How could Jefferson, how could Congress, speak of the Americans as "one people"?

On the other hand, how could the British be regarded as "another people"? Ethnically, the British North Americans may have had a somewhat greater admixture of Scandinavian and continental European blood than their cousins in the home islands, but the difference was not very significant. The things that Englishmen had in common, whether they resided in Britain or in North America, far outweighed the things in which they differed. Foremost, of course, was the English language and its literature. But, in addition, they shared their religion (Protestant Christianity), their law (the common law of England), and a variety of institutions, social and political. With what justification, then, could the Declaration speak of the Americans as one people and the British as another people?

It turns out that the recognition of the natural equality of human beings is the defining characteristic of the American nation. By the Declaration of Independence a "new nation" was created, dedicated to the proposition that all men are created equal. The British nation, by contrast, recognized itself in its ethnic purity and historical continuity; and, far from being dedicated to the proposition of human equality, was organized on the principle that persons are born to various ranks and stations in society.

But the defining proposition of the American people was not that all men are treated equally, it was that all men are created equal. Justice dictates that equals be treated equally as regards those things in which they are equal. But the Declaration does not assert, nor did the American people then believe, that justice was everywhere established. (Thirteen years later, one of the purposes of ordaining a new constitution was said to be "to establish justice.") Nor did they believe or assert that every member of the new nation either acted or was treated justly. They did assert a common belief concerning what justice required.

The next supposition of the Preamble of the Declaration was that, by natural and divine law, a "people" is "entitled" to a "station" separate from and equal to the "station" of each other people. Given the suppositions that the Americans were one people and the British another people, why does it necessarily follow that the two peoples should not be connected? Why should they not share a common government (or at least a common sovereign)? The English and the Scots had been two people with a common sovereign from 1603 until 1707. And, separate or not, why should the two people be equal in stature? History afforded numerous examples of one people being the dependency or protectorate of another. A few generations later, the British would establish a worldwide "commonwealth of nations" on just that principle.

The answer seems to be that self-government requires and implies both separateness and equality. Those are the two conditions for the existence of what is known in international law as "sovereignty," which is to be distinguished from the domestic "sovereignty" of a king (or, now, of the people). The equality existing among nations, like that among people as individuals, is equality of right, not equality of size, or strength, or wealth, or wisdom, or beauty.

Finally, the Preamble speaks of a "decent respect for the opinion of mankind." The respect is a product of decency: a decent people respects the opinion of mankind. But what is the "opinion of mankind"? Mankind is made up of many peoples, to say nothing of many people. Individual people may have opinions; the separate peoples of the world may have opinions common to their members, but can mankind as a whole have an opinion?

Ultimately, the appeal of the Declaration is to be based upon truths that although "self-evident" were yet foreign to the opinions of most of the people and peoples in the world (just as they are foreign to most of the people and peoples of the world today). The Declaration appeals to the right opinion of mankind, that is, it appeals to the reason of mankind. The argument of the Declaration is directed to the faculty of reason that can reform opinion and cause opinion to become right opinion (if not actual knowledge). The respect that a decent people owes to the opinion of mankind is served by instructing that opinion in reason, and thus in enabling opinion to become right opinion.

But even in this, Jefferson and the Congress displayed a lawyerly prudence. For, although a decent respect for the opinion of mankind moves the American people to declare the causes of its actions, it is not the whole case that is left for the judgment of mankind. The Declaration submits the facts in its case against the British king "to a candid world"; that is, the world (or mankind) is to be the jury in the case. But the argument of law, that is, of the rectitude of the Americans' intentions, is submitted to "the Supreme Judge of the world." The issue of law cannot be decided by the opinion of mankind; instruction in the natural and divine law must be given by the Supreme Judge.

THE RIGHTS OF MAN

There follows next a statement of the ends of government and of the conditions under which obedience to government is proper. "All men are created equal . . . endowed by their Creator with certain unalienable rights . . . among [which] are life, liberty, and the pursuit of happiness." Equality is the condition of men prior to government — logically prior, not chronologically. But that equality is not equality of condition, or even equality of opportunity; certainly it is not equality of intelligence, strength, or skill. The equality that men possess by nature is equality of *right*. There is, among human beings, none with a right to rule the others; God may claim to rule human beings by right, human rights may rule the brutes by right, but no human being has a claim to rule another by right.

The rights with which men are endowed are said to be "unalienable." That is, human rights may be neither usurped nor surrendered, neither taken away nor given up. The Declaration rejects the false doctrine of Thomas Hobbes (more gently echoed by William Blackstone) that men on entering society and submitting to government yield their natural rights and retain only "civil" rights, dispensed and revoked at the pleasure of the sovereign.

"To secure these rights, governments are instituted among men." The purpose of government is to protect the natural rights which men possess, but which, in the absence of government, they are not secure enough to enjoy. Government in society is not optional, it is a necessary condition for the enjoyment of natural rights. But the institution of government does not create an independent motive or will in society. All just powers of government derive "from the consent of the governed."

The Declaration asserts that the people retain the right of revolution, the right to substitute new constitutions for old. But it also assets that the exercise of that right is properly governed by prudence — a prudence that the Americans had shown in the face of great provocation.

THE INDICTMENT OF THE KING

The next section of the Declaration is a bill of indictment against George III on the charge of attempted tyranny. The specifications are divided almost evenly between procedural and substantive offenses. The fact that the king — by his representatives in America — assembled the provincial legislatures at places far from their capitals or required persons accused of certain crimes to be transported to England for trial, evinced a tyrannical design by disregard of procedural safeguards. But even when the established procedures were followed, as in giving or withholding assent to legislation, the result could be tyrannical; for example, the suppression of trade, the discouragement of population growth, and the keeping of standing armies in peacetime were acts according to the forms of due process that unjustly deprived the Americans of their liberty. Still other acts, such as making the royal assent conditional on surrender of the right of representation and withholding assent from bills to create provincial courts, were tyrannical both in form and in substance.

The most critical charge, the thirteenth, was that the king had conspired with others—the British Parliament—to subject the Americans to a jurisdiction foreign to their constitution. The Americans had come to see that a relationship existed between the British king and each of his American provinces according to which the king exercised executive power in each even as he did in the home island, and that the common executive was the sole governmental connection between America and Britain. The imperial constitution, as the Americans had come to understand it, no more permitted the British legislature to regulate the internal affairs of Massachusetts or Virginia than it did the provincial legislatures to regulate the internal affairs of England or Scotland. But the British legislature could not breach the compact between the king and the provinces because Parliament was not a party to that compact. The king, however, by conniving at that usurpation, did breach the compact.

The final five accusations deal with the fact that Britain and America were at war. One charge that Jefferson included, but Congress struck out, accused the king of waging "cruel war against human nature itself" by tolerating the introduction of slavery into the colonies and sanctioning the slave trade. Only two states, Georgia and South Carolina, objected to the passage, but the others acquiesced to preserve unanimity. In any case, the condemnation of slavery was implicit in the opening paragraphs of the Declaration.

THE CONCLUSION

The conclusion of the Declaration of Independence comprises three paragraphs. The first of these, which marks the transition from the indictment of the king to a more general discussion of constitutional principle, emphasizes the self-restraint that had marked the American side of the controversy. The second paragraph returns to the theme of the preamble; it speaks of the dissolution of the bands connecting the peoples of America and Britain. The third paragraph contains the formal proclamation of American independence as well as the statement of what that independence entailed.

The first paragraph of the conclusion asserts that the Americans had tried peaceably to resolve their differences with the king. Prudence dictates that constitutional upheaval not be risked for light or transient causes; experience shows that people are disposed to suffer while evils are sufferable rather than to abolish the forms of government to which they are accustomed. The prudence of the American people is evinced by their repeated petitions for redress and by their humility in petitioning. The tyrannical character of the monarch is demonstrated by the fact that repeated petition brought only repeated injury.

The paragraph ends with one of the most enigmatic passages in the whole document: a tyrannical prince "is unfit to be the ruler of a free people." This seems to imply that there are "princes" who are fit to be the rulers of free peoples.

The next paragraph alleges that the Americans have dealt justly with the British people. The British are described, at the beginning of the paragraph as "brethren," but by its end they can be, in the best case, only "friends." The British people, by their Parliament, had usurped authority over the Americans, and the Americans had advanced two lines of persuasion to induce the British to desist. The British, however, proved deaf both to the appeal of justice and to the conjuration of consanguinity. Presumably, the American people would not have been impelled to dissolve the political bands connecting them to the British people if the latter had treated the former either justly or fraternally. Because just power is exercised only by the consent of the governed, justice would have permitted the Americans to separate from the British when British usurpation occurred. But "conjuring" the British by the "ties of common kindred" was dictated by prudence. Only when the claims of justice and prudence coincided did the "necessity of separation" arise.

In the final paragraph is the "solemn" publication and declaration that the American states are free and independent. The publication and declaration are made by the members of Congress in their representative capacity. And the rectitude of their intentions is to be judged, not indeed by "a candid world" or by "the opinion of Mankind" but by the Supreme Judge of the world, by nature's God, according to whose laws the American people are entitled to separate and equal status among the nations of the world.

The Declaration states that the erstwhile colonies are "free and independent states," and that "they" have the powers to make war and peace, and to do "all other acts and things" befitting independent states. Whether the colonies became independent collectively or individually was a matter of debate for at least a hundred years. At the Constitutional Convention of 1787, James Wilson and Alexander Hamilton advanced the former position, while Luther Martin maintained the latter. At least until the Civil War, different theories of the Union arose based on differing interpretations of the act of declaring independence.

THE CONSTITUTIONAL THEORY
OF THE DECLARATION

The central section of the Declaration of Independence is the quintessential statement of the meaning of constitutional (that is, limited) government. Constitutional government is founded upon the recognition that human beings are naturally and self-evidently equal in right. If this were not so, government would belong in the hands of those with the superior claim of right. But the right to rule is, in the first instance, the right to rule oneself only. All human beings have an equal right to rule themselves. Political life is made possible when that right is transformed into the ruling of others and being ruled in turn by them. Because the claim to rule onself is a claim of right, once cannot justly be ruled by another unless he first waives the right to rule himself. Such a waiver is not lightly or freely to be made. In fact, the only consideration sufficient to justify the waiver of one's own right to self-rule is the mutual waiver by one's fellows of their own respective rights to rule themselves.

In the earliest versions of the theory of constitutionalism, the consideration offered in exchange for a person's waiver of his right to self-rule was physical safety. Thomas Hobbes, as is well known, described the apolitical or prepolitical state as offering a life that is "solitary, poor, nasty, brutish, and short." That is, when everyone asserts his right to rule himself, then each is a law unto himself and each of his fellows is a potential danger to him. In Hobbes's view, what each person receives, upon entering civil society, in exchange for waiving his right to self-rule, is the assurance that he will be defended from that danger. Hobbes, therefore, conceived of every person as contracting with a "sovereign" that that sovereign should rule all.

The Declaration of Independence offers an alternative view. In the Declaration, each person is conceived to have agreed with his fellows that each consents to be ruled by all in exchange for having a share in ruling all. What is more, the agreement does not extend to arbitrary or total rule but only to rule that has as its aim the security of the rights that each person has to life, liberty, and the pursuit of happiness. The Declaration describes these rights as "unalienable," that is, as being properties that may neither be taken away nor given away. They are the essential properties of a human being, so that any creature without them is debased to a subhuman condition. Hence, no human being can consent to being enslaved, that is, to being subjected to total or arbitrary rule.

The power to rule, according to the Declaration, is justly exercised only when it is derived from the consent of those who are ruled. That consent is identical with the waiver of the right to rule onself. And the consent, that is, the waiver, cannot extend to the alienation of the essential properties of humanity.

The institution of government is to "secure," that is, to make safe, not the mere physical existence of the subjects, but those rights that are the essential properties of human beings: the right to life, the right to liberty, and the right to pursue happiness. Each of these rights has an end, a purpose or goal. The right to life has as its end existence (one might almost say, mere existence); the right to liberty has the end of autonomous existence; the right to pursue happiness has as its end the attainment of happiness.

The right of the people to alter or abolish their goverment does not arise until the government becomes destructive of these ends. The government must become destructive of the life of the people, or of their liberty, or of their happiness. (Happiness, and not the pursuit of happiness, is an end; the pursuit is instrumental to the end.)

What is to be made of the fact that the Declaration speaks of "forms of government" rather than of "governments"? Did the Congress, indeed, did Jefferson, mean to suggest that the Framers of a national constitution were free to institute any of the types of government classically referred to as "forms"?[2] That is, would monarchy be a permissible choice? Would aristocracy be an open option? Clearly monarchy and aristocracy (not to speak of tyranny and oligarchy) are incompatible with the doctrine of equality as taught by the Declaration. What, then, did the authors of the Declaration mean by "forms of government"?

They seem to have meant the constitutional arrangements of the regime themselves. That is, "forms of government" meant the formal structures and institutions of government. The teaching of the Declaration permits the substitution of one form of government for another, and thereby authorizes the replacement of one constitution by another. This is exactly what happened in 1787–1789. In the classical typology of political philosophy, the form of government had not changed. There was a democratic republic both before and after the replacement of the Articles of Confederation by the new Constitution. However, the *formalities* of the government, the terms of the distribution of power and of offices within the country, were altered.

THE DECLARATION AND THE CONSTITUTION

Congress did not proceed from the promulgation of the Declaration of Independence to the formulation of a constitution of national government. To be sure, the process of preparing a draft of the first national constitution (the Articles of Confederation) was begun in a committee of Congress at the same time that another committee began drafting the Declaration. But the Articles were a long time in production. It is a proposition that needs more than merely to be asserted that the Articles were the product of the same American mind that produced the Declaration.

Most of the state constituent assemblies, before proceeding to the business of outlining the form of government of the state, first made a declaration of rights. Following the pattern established by the Convention Parliament in 1688, they declared the authority for their constituent activities, the purpose of the government they were establishing, and the rights retained by the people. Such a declaration was the ground and foundation of any constitution subsequently erected by the state.

The convention that drafted the Constitution did not see the need for any new declaration of rights. The purpose of government, the limits of government, and the authority of the people to consent to a form of government and, subsequently, to alter or abolish their form of government, had already been declared, once and for all. The Constitutional Convention did not claim for itself, or for the people in the ratifying conventions (from whom, and not from the convention, the force and effect of the Constitution must derive), any new constituent authority. The Framers did not substitute any new conception of the legitimacy of governmental power. They assembled in the name of the people to alter the forms of government in accordance with the aims already declared and established. Even the Preamble was an afterthought, and it echoed the content and tone of the Declaration of Independence.

So at the national level the Declaration of Independence is the declaration of rights that is the ground and foundation of any government subsequently constituted. The Declaration of Independence is the Declaration of Rights of the American people. One may even say that it is the real preamble to the Constitution of the United States.

Certainly this is how the Framers themselves regarded the relationship between the American Revolution (and the Declaration of Independence, which set forth the principles of the Revolution) and the establishment of a constitution of government. Writing in the *National Gazette* less than four years after the Constitutional Convention, James Madison asserted that the significance of the Revolution was that while "[i]n Europe, charters of liberty have been granted by power," in America "charters of power [are] granted by liberty." The federal and state constitutions were thus "instruments, every word of which decides a question between power and liberty," and their framing was by solemn "acts, proclaiming the will and authenticated by the seal of the people."

It was not the Constitution of 1787 that deviated from the principles of the Revolution but rather the state constitutions adopted during and immediately after the war. As Benjamin Rush said, in an oration delivered at Philadelphia to members of the convention and others on July 4, 1787, the authors of those constitutions "understood perfectly the principles of liberty" but "were ignorant to the forms and combinations of power in republics." And Thomas Jefferson, author of the Declaration of Independence, wrote in his *Notes on the State of Virginia*, "an elective despotism was not the government we fought for."

Even in its treatment of the most sensitive and difficult issue of the Founding Era, the Constitution did not stray so far as it might appear from the predecessor document. Although the Continental Congress struck from the Declaration of Independence Jefferson's condemnation of slavery as "cruel war upon human nature itself," the Founders clearly understood that slavery was incompatible with the principles of liberty and equality that they espoused. Indeed, in the Declaration of the Causes and Necessities of Taking Up Arms, which they had adopted in 1775, the members of that same body had framed their accusation against the British parliament in terms of the latter's attempt to "hold an absolute property in, and an unbounded power over" the American colonists.

The Framers of the Constitution faced the circumstance that the institution of human slavery, acknowledgedly incompatible with the "principles of liberty" that were the foundation of their Revolution, was long established in a part of the country. Nevertheless, Northerners and Southerners, slaveholders and antislavery men, contrived together to keep the shameful word out of the Constitution. Although certain guarantees were written into the document for those who then depended upon the institution, Congress was given the power (after the lapse of but one generation) to proscribe the traffic in human beings, as well as the power to govern the territories, which power the Congress then sitting under the Articles of Confederation had used to provide that "there shall be neither slavery nor involuntary servitude" in the Northwest Territory.

It is indeed unfortunate that twentieth-century Americans are accustomed to reading our two great constitutional documents through the eyes of nineteenth-century slaveholders. Legal historians side either with Roger B. Taney, who sought, as a matter of constitutional law, to justify the existence of slavery by reading the black man out of the Declaration of Independence, or with John C. Calhoun, who, knowing that the Declaration included black people equally with whites, would have had the Declaration superseded by a Constitution that he chose to read as proslavery. But the common hostility of the slave power to the Declaration of Independence and the Constitution was pointed out by Abraham Lincoln, on July 4, 1861, when, referring to the secessionists of the South, he said:

> Our adversaries have adopted some Declarations of Independence; in which, unlike the good old one, penned by Jefferson, they omit the words "all men are created equal." Why? They have adopted a temporary national constitution, in the preamble of which, unlike our good old one, signed by Washington, they omit "We the People," . . . Why this deliberate pressing out of view, the rights of men and the authority of the people?

Lincoln, like Jefferson and Washington, saw and proclaimed the essential connection between the Declaration of Independence and the Constitution, between the rights of men and the authority of the people.

Nevertheless, the putative antagonism between America's two basic documents, invented by the slave power in the nineteenth century, has formed a recurring theme for historians and ideologues in the twentieth century. The Progressive Era writers Charles A. Beard and J. Allen Smith made war against the Constitution in the name of a Declaration of Independence that supposedly liberated the unfettered will of the people as a governing force. Smith and Beard alleged that the Constitution was the work of wealthy conservative counterrevolutionaries: a "Thermidorian reaction" against the infant American democracy.

After about 1937, when Franklin D. Roosevelt had appointed a majority of justices to the Supreme Court, the Constitution was no longer anathema to intellectuals. Indeed, the Constitution, severed from the Declaration of Independence, became the embodiment of the American ideal. Understood as a "living" document, that is, as a document almost infinitely malleable in the hands of enlightened judges, the Constitution represented positive law, and thus it was a refutation of the allegedly outdated natural rights philosophy of the Declaration of Independence. History (understood as progress) thus became the authority for constitutional interpretation, rather than "the laws of nature and of nature's God."

In a certain sense, it would be easy to read the Constitution as the sole constituent act of the American people. But the Constitution does not contain within itself any account of the ends for which it was adopted, other than the Preamble. But the Preamble was very nearly the last part of the Constitution to be written, a virtual afterthought of the delegates. Although all of the delegates to the convention were familiar with the theory that dictated that the first act of a constituent assembly should be the framing of a declaration of the rights of man and of the ends of government, none seems to have thought it necessary as the first step in erecting the new national government.

To be sure, at the end of the convention there were delegates such as George Mason, the author of the Virginia Declaration of Rights, who insisted that the Constitution should contain a bill of rights. During the ratifying process, there were those who felt so strongly that this should be the case that they opposed the ratification of the Constitution. (On the other hand, many of those who raised the issue of a bill of rights were, in fact, opposed to the creation of a national government with real governing power.)

It cannot be that the prudent and cautious men who participated in the Constitutional Convention were indifferent to the ends of government. Nor can it be supposed that they sought to establish a system of government that was indifferent to ends. Why, then, was there no discussion of the ends of government at the Constitutional Convention? No doubt because the delegates believed that the question had already been settled. No doubt they believed that the American people had already definitively spoken on the subject. The Framers of the Constitution could concern themselves with means, because the ends were already understood. They could concern themselves with procedures, because the substance was already agreed upon.

It is scarcely too much to say that the Declaration of Independence was both the Bill of Rights and the Preamble to the Constitution. In the Declaration of Independence, the American people set forth what it was that they wanted of their government and what the limits of the government's authority were to be.

CONCLUSION

The Constitution of the United States is sometimes pronounced, by scholars or politicians, to be neutral with respect to political principles. But the Constitution was not framed in a vacuum. It was devised as the Constitution of the nation founded by the Declaration of Independence. The Declaration prescribes the ends and limits of government, and proclaims the illegitimacy of any government that fails to serve those ends or observe those limits. The Constitution is thus ruled by the Declaration. The Constitution provides for the government of the regime created by the Declaration: the regime of equality and liberty.

THE FIRST AMERICAN CONSTITUTIONS

DONALD S. LUTZ

The modern written constitution was invented by English-speaking people on North American shores. The process of invention was lengthy and complex, and we can point to no one event or year as decisive. Certainly the writing of the United States Constitution in the summer of 1787 was a dramatic high point in the process, as well as the most important historical moment in American constitutionalism, but by then the modern written constitution had already been developed and was well represented in a number of earlier documents.

Furthermore, despite the Constitution's roots in European intellectual traditions derived from the Bible, classical Greek philosophy, Protestant theology, English common law, English Whig political theory, and the Enlightenment, no European precedent or model for our national constitution existed by 1787. The form and content of the United States Constitution derived largely from experience with the early state constitutions, by both borrowing from them and by reacting to them. These often overlooked state documents occupy a critical position in the development of American constitutionalism. They are at the same time the culmination of a long process, and the foundation upon which the United States Constitution rests.

One way to illustrate this is to consider a prominent, yet often unremarked feature of the Constitution written in that warm summer in Philadelphia. In this, our second national constitution, the states are explicitly or by clear implication mentioned more than fifty times in forty-two different sections. If the proverbial Martian traveler were to show up and attempt to understand the document, he would discover a fact that most Americans have never come fully to appreciate themselves — the United States Constitution is an incomplete document until and unless the state constitutions are also read.

If we want to know who can vote for members of the House of Representatives, we must look, says section 2 of Article I, at who can vote for members of the lower house in each state, and this requires reading the state constitutions. Senators are elected by the state legislatures, and in order to understand the character and composition of these legislatures we must read the state constitutions. The President is elected by electors "appointed" by the states in a manner determined by the respective state legislatures. Section 2 of Article IV creates a dual citizenship whereby all Americans are simultaneously citizens of the United States and of the states wherein they reside. One result of dual citizenship is the existence of a state court system as well as a national court system, and in order to understand the design and operation of the American judiciary we are once again driven to read the state constitutions.

The obvious point that should require no further belaboring is that the United States Constitution assumes, in fact requires, the existence of state constitutions if it is to make any sense. Put another way, the state constitutions are part of the United States Constitution and are needed to complete the legal text. The Framers of our national document, regardless of their attitude toward the already existing state governments, had no choice but to recognize their existence. The state constitutions are woven into the national constitution because they already existed and could not be ignored and because the interweaving allowed the national document to control the negative effects of the state documents and allowed the Founders to take advantage of the benefits of federalism.

The state constitutions are embedded in the United States Constitution in another, less obvious fashion. The design and theoretical underpinnings for the national document result to a significant degree not only from European theoretical ideas but also from the experience, both positive and negative, of living under the state constitutions. Complete foundation documents in their own right, the state constitutions each produced political systems more or less successful at solving the collective problems of their respective peoples. Viewed to a certain extent as experiments in self-government, the state constitutions were tinkered with and sometimes replaced in an effort to meet the twin goals of effective government and popular liberty. By the summer of 1787, the framers of our national constitution, many of whom had helped write state constitutions, could draw upon a rich experience in the design of institutions and the practical effects of those institutions. It is doubtful that they could have been as successful in their efforts, or been inclined to produce the kind of document they did, without their prior experience with state constitutions and the Articles of Confederation.

Although the early state constitutions were an integral part of the United States Constitution and the base upon which the national document was written, they were not the beginning of American constitutionalism. Instead they were themselves the culmination of a process begun much earlier. In 1776 Rhode Island and Connecticut readopted colonial charters written in the early 1660s as their respective state constitutions. After removing references to the king from the charters, the citizens of these two states simply continued to conduct business as usual. Massachusetts did not even bother to readopt its colonial charter, but continued until 1780 under its charter of 1691 as if it had constitutional status. These states could act in such a fashion because they already had institutions largely of their own design, based upon popular consent, under which they had successfully reached collective decisions both effective and widely accepted. The Connecticut Charter in turn essentially ratified a form of government adopted by the colonists in 1639, and Rhode Island's charter ratified a form of government designed by the colonists in the 1640s. Massachusetts could trace its basic institutions to documents written by the colonists stretching back to the 1620s.

Although the other states wrote new constitutions, they also built directly upon colonial documents, documents that provided extensive experience with elected legislatures, elected local government, and institutional design. Georgia's experience was the shortest, going back only a half-century in 1787. Pennsylvania and New York had experience stretching back a full century, New Jersey to the 1670s, the Carolinas to the 1660s, Maryland to the 1640s, and New Hampshire to the 1630s. Virginia's experience went back to its first legislative assembly in 1619. Without exception, the colonial charters provided for local self-government as long as legislation did not run contrary to the laws of England. The colonists took advantage of this provision and wrote a long string of documents designing and regulating their local and colony-wide governments.[1]

The early state constitutions thus stand as the fulcrum in American constitutional history. On the one hand, they were the culmination of colonial experience, and they embodied and summarized that rich experience. On the other hand, they formed the ground upon which first the Articles of Confederation and then the United States Constitution were erected. The design of our national constitution in 1787 deeply benefited from the experience of state constitutional design. There are few institutions in the national document, including federalism, that had not been tried our earlier in state or colonial documents. Even more, the state constitutions interpenetrated the national constitution to the point of virtually becoming part of it.

This is not to imply that the state constitutions were the inevitable product of what came before anymore than that the United States Constitution was simply a composite of state documents. The last three decades of the eighteenth century constituted a time of extraordinary political experimentation and innovation. Between 1776 and 1798 the first sixteen states wrote a total of twenty-nine constitutions, two of which were rejected. The two national constitutions bring the total for the era to thirty-one. The willingness to experiment with new institutions in the service of old, well-established political goals and principles was impressive. Surrounding the writing of constitutions there was an outpouring of pamphlets and newspaper articles commenting upon them that numbered in the thousands.

If we accept estimates that in the 1780s about 60 percent of white, adult males in America participated in politics at least to the extent of voting, then

we had about 300,000 persons, on average, generating about three constitutions every two years for twenty-two years, and during the same period
writing at least 1,300 pamphlets and newspaper articles a year on political
and constitutional matters. When we add the consideration that all but one
state had annual elections, and elections were used to fill at least 8,000
political positions from president to town surveyor, the numbers suggest a
virtual maelstrom of activity for several decades. At the center of all this
activity, and engaging the attention of some 30,000 men in the most active
political class, was the design, operation, and alteration of constitutions,
especially at the state level.

How successful were these extensive efforts? Despite seven of the first
states replacing their initial constitutions within a decade or less, the average
state constitution written during the era lasted for more than sixty years.
One of them, the Massachusetts Constitution of 1780, is currently the
world's oldest constitution. Also, despite the tremendous changes that have
occurred in America, the state constitutions we write today are deeply
indebted to, and, with only a handful of exceptions, are essentially based
upon the models developed between 1776 and 1787. The United States
Constitution, erected upon and derived from these state documents, has
survived for two centuries with only twenty-six amendments. Finally, the
symbols, principles, and values found in the early state constitutions continue to inform our political thinking in late-twentieth-century America.

THE EARLY STATE CONSTITUTIONS—
A GENERAL OVERVIEW

It is useful to divide eighteenth-century state constitutions into three
"waves" of adoption. The first wave followed quickly after the Continental
Congress in May of 1776 recommended that the states erect new govern-

FIRST WAVE	SECOND WAVE	THIRD WAVE
1776 New Hampshire	1777 New York	1789 Georgia
1776 South Carolina	1777 Vermont	1790 South Carolina
1776 Virginia	1778 South Carolina	1790 Pennsylvania
1776 New Jersey	1780 Massachusetts	1792 Delaware
1776 Maryland	1784 New Hampshire	1792 Kentucky
1776 Delaware	1786 Vermont	1792 New Hampshire
1776 Rhode Island		1793 Vermont
1776 Connecticut		1796 Tennessee
1776 Pennsylvania		1798 Georgia
1776 North Carolina		
1777 Georgia		

ments. The second wave included three constitutions that were the result of longer deliberations than those of the first wave plus three constitutions in which states reconsidered and replaced earlier documents. The third wave will not concern us in this study. It includes constitutions by three new states plus a reconsideration by seven states of their earlier constitutions in light of federalist political principles.[2]

Each of these constitutions defines a political system — a set of institutions for reaching collective decisions. Each constitution also defines a political culture — the values that inform and animate a political system. What is striking about the early constitutions as a group is that, despite considerable inventiveness, there are strong institutional similarities and a basic political culture underlying all of them.

Looking at the first eighteen state constitutions (including, here, Massachusetts's 1691 charter), we find the following inventory of basic institutions.

1. Except for Pennsylvania (1776) and Georgia (1777), the states used a bicameral legislature (Georgia adopted bicameralism in 1789 and Pennsylvania in 1790).

2. In all seventeen constitutions the lower house was elected directly by the people.

3. Although the percentage of white, adult males enfranchised varied from state to state, on average the percentage was eight to ten times what it was in England.

4. If the sixteen constitutions using bicameralism, all but one had the Senate elected directly by the people, usually by the same electorate for both houses. Maryland voters elected an electoral college, which in turn elected the Senate.

5. With only one exception (South Carolina, 1776), all constitutions provided that the lower house be elected annually.

6. Of the sixteen bicameral constitutions, ten had annual elections for the Senate, and three had staggered, multi-year terms.

7. Nine of the constitutions had the executive elected by the legislature, and six more used a popular election essentially to identify the major candidates from among whom the legislature picked the governor.

8. Fourteen constitutions provided for annual elections of the governor, two for biennial elections, and two for triennial elections.

9. Twelve of the constitutions required voters to own property, usually between twenty and fifty acres or the equivalent, four required them to be taxpayers, and two had no property requirement.

10. Of the sixteen bicameral legislatures, thirteen had the same property requirement to vote for the upper house as for the lower house.

11. Of the nine states that involved the people in selecting the governor, eight required the same amount of property to vote for the executive as to vote for the lower house.

12. All but two of the constitutions required ownership of property to run for the legislature, with few exceptions requiring more property to run for office than to vote.

13. Ten of the sixteen bicameral legislatures required more property to run for the upper house than for the lower house, and usually even more property was required to run for governor.

14. Except for Massachusetts, Connecticut, and Rhode Island, which initially operated as states under colonial charters, and two states that wrote constitutions before the Declaration of Independence (New Hampshire, 1776; South Carolina, 1776), most early state constitutions included bills of rights.

15. With only two consistent exceptions, the rights listed in the bills of rights, including the right to property, were alienable by the legislature (the exceptions were the right to free exercise of religion and the right to trial by jury).

16. Thirteen of the seventeen constitutions were written by the respective state legislatures, usually after an election in which it was made clear that the new legislature would also write a new constitution. Only two constitutions, Massachusetts in 1780 and New Hampshire in 1784, were written by a convention elected solely for that purpose and submitted to the people for ratification.

17. Only four constitutions in the first wave mention an amendment process, and in two of those instances the legislature is the amending agent. During the second wave, an amendment process is mentioned more frequently, but except for Massachusetts and New Hampshire — which give the amendment power to the people — the power is invariably given to the legislature.

One should not conclude that the differences among the state constitutions were insignificant. It was a time of experimentation, and the willingness to try out new ideas and institutions was impressive. Nevertheless, the most significant fact about the early state constitutions is that despite the many differences there was a common set of commitments, assumptions, and institutions defining the continuing American constitutional tradition. The commonalities produced not only shared strengths but also widely shared weaknesses that required addressing.

THE EARLY STATE CONSTITUTIONS AS A COHERENT YET INCOMPLETE SYSTEM

This list of similarities is not exhaustive, but it is sufficient to permit us to outline the essential form of government produced by the early state constitutions. Perhaps most obvious is the manner in which the early state constitutions produced political systems where a bicameral legislature was supreme. The executive was invariably quite weak and a creature of the legislature. Courts were placed directly under the legislature, whereas in colonial times they had been under the executive.

That the framers of early state constitutions were strongly inclined toward legislative supremacy is not surprising. The locus of colonial politics was the perennial struggle between a governor appointed by the crown and the legislature elected by the colonists. Using a suffrage much broader than that found in England, the colonists kept very close control of legislatures, which gradually gained the upper hand in most colonies. The relationship between the colonists and their legislatures was so close that when they spoke of "the government" they usually referred only to the executive and not the legislature. The legislature was their protector for governmental tyranny, and was viewed as much more effective than bills of rights and courts in this regard.

With the coming of independence, Americans naturally retained their preference for the legislature. The executive branch, although recognized as performing necessary functions, was stripped of power and made dependent upon the legislature. Typical provisions in state constitutions, in addition to having the legislature elect the executive, required legislative approval for executive appointments, and refused the executive any veto power. Often they created a small body drawn from the legislature to assist the governor in giving executive approval to legislation and granting pardons, or just generally to tell him what to do, and, of course, the courts were moved from the executive to the legislative branch. One characteristic that distinguished first-wave documents from second-wave ones was that in the latter the executive recovered somewhat from his position of virtual political servitude. The first tentative steps were taken in the 1777 New York constitution, and the 1780 Massachusetts document describes a resurrected executive. Still, by 1787 only four states had executives worthy of the name, and all states had, if not legislative supremacy, then legislative predominance.

Legislative supremacy, direct election of both houses, annual elections for all offices including governor, property requirements for voting, the same property requirements to vote for all offices, and above all a broadly defined electorate were among the many manifestations of a general commitment to government resting upon popular consent. If legislative supremacy be excluded, the list also represents most of the devices whereby the powerful legislatures were kept close to the people and made highly responsive to popular majorities.

Linking voting rights with the ownership of property does not seem to belong on any list of instruments for resting government on popular consent or keeping the legislature close to the people; yet it does belong there. The framers of the state constitutions made four arguments for property qualifications: owning property gives a person an independent will; property gives a person a stake in the community and thus ties the owner to the well-being of the community; anyone who levies taxes must also be subject to them; and the use of property should be subject to the majority decisions of property owners only.[3]

The ownership of property had long been linked with liberty in the English-speaking world. Owning one's land meant that one did not depend upon another for livelihood. Such a secure economic base gave one freedom to speak and vote without danger of the kind of economic reprisal to which tenant farmers were subject. It also implied a relative immunity to bribery so that votes were not so likely to be bought. In America, with plenty of cheap land available, the link between property and liberty meant that there would be a much higher percentage of independent wills than in England.

The framers of the state constitutions also believed that owning land in a community would change the manner in which an individual viewed that community. Based upon a shrewd assessment of human psychology, they assumed that involvement in community affairs would be higher among property owners, and that involvement would be based upon a realistic assessment of the relationship between public policy and its consequences. There is plenty of room for questioning whether this justifies making property a test of one's being permitted to vote, but modern social science provides ample proof that political behavior is affected in precisely the manner predicted.

The slogan "No taxation without representation" has two sides to it. Anyone who is taxed should be represented, and anyone levying taxes should be subject to them as well. English common lawyers had held since Magna Carta that no one should be taxed without his consent. In England that restricted suffrage almost exclusively to the landed gentry. In America it opened suffrage to exercise by most males. As there were too many whose consent was needed to bring them together in one place, the alternative was to choose from among them representatives who would stand for the majority of landowners. With these assumptions, and under the conditions to be found in America, it made good sense to many that both voters and representatives should be property owners.

Despite property requirements, these constitutions produced the broadest suffrage in the history of the world up to that time. The electorate thus enfranchised varied from about 80 percent of white adult males in some northern states to a low of about 35 percent in Georgia. In the 1780s there was a rough gradient, with the New England states generally having the highest suffrage rates and the percentage falling off as one moved south. The most conservative of the careful studies in recent years finds that nationwide about 50 percent of white adult males were enfranchised by the property requirements. The property requirement established the minimum electorate. On average about 60–65 percent of white adult males were able to vote in the 1780s, which meant that other tests were also available for enfranchising. Ironically, this is a higher average turnout than has been the case in the last half of the twentieth century in an America with no property requirements.[4]

The major problem with state constitutions was not an electorate limited by property requirements. Instead it was that a broad electorate closely tied to a supreme legislature was an unbalanced constitutional system. Put another way, Americans brought with them to independence only a portion of the successful constitutional system to which they had belonged as colonists. Independence brought with it a new political situation to which their constitutional system had to adjust. There was an inevitable period of adjustment during which political institutions lagged behind political needs. It is worth contrasting the operation of the colonial system with that in effect shortly after independence.

To recapitulate, colonial experience had led not only to a preference for the legislature but also to the strong expectation that the legislature would be very close to the voters and highly responsive to majority will. The eighteenth-century view of majority rule was not as legalistic as ours, and rather than straining toward one-half plus one as the basis of decision making, the colonists usually strained toward consensual decisions. Given the highly homogeneous populations found in most colonies, this is not surprising. On the most important issue about which they were not consensual, Christian sectarianism, they responded by removing sectarian considerations from politics, although they continued to inject broadly Christian values into constitutions.

The straining toward consensus was aided by what historians sometimes call "the politics of deference." There was a tendency to defer to the "better sort" as possessing more of the virtues needed to be good legislators. Although there was no true aristocracy in America, colonial legislatures were nonetheless dominated by the wealthier, more educated members of the community. The higher standards of civility and more pronounced preference of this sort of men for stability and order, in addition to the people's straining toward communitarianism over factionalism, created a situation in which highly democratic legislatures operated largely free of what are usually viewed as the natural excesses of democracy. Nor did it hurt that a governor, usually appointed by the crown, stood as a barrier to unbridled majoritarianism.

Independence rapidly altered circumstances. With only a few exceptions, most notably in Connecticut and Rhode Island, the governors who had functioned as barriers disappeared and were replaced by anemic executives. The politics of deference seemed to disappear almost overnight. In part this resulted from the rhetorical and theoretical stance necessitated by the opposition to Britain. It was not a time of calm argument. Also, about a third of the "better sort" were abruptly expelled from American politics for being Tories. In many cases the legislatures left over from the colonial governments contained so many of these British sympathizers that alternate legislatures were elected in a successful attempt to bypass Tory efforts at moderation. In the operating state legislatures, and in those created by the new constitutions, the "better sort" declined sharply as a percentage of the body. On the whole, the wealthy and well-to-do declined from being clear majorities in the legislatures, sometimes running as high as 80–85 percent of the body, to being distinct minorities. They were replaced by moderately well-off citizens, often similar to the yeoman farmer that Jefferson seemed to prefer so strongly.[5] Along with this change went a drastic decline in the number of lawyers sitting in legislatures. Finally, there was a broadening of the electorate as suffrage requirements were relaxed somewhat, or simply not enforced as rigorously. In this regard there was not much room for change in most states. Probably, on average, the electorate expanded by about 10–15 percent. However, because the Tories were usually disenfranchised, and because they represented about 10–15 percent of those who voted regularly, the net change was not so much an expansion in the electorate as a redistribution in the economic classes now voting.

In effect, the situation was not really much more democratic than it had been before independence. However, the circumstances were significantly altered. The governors were now missing. Not only had they been a source of restraint on legislative excess, they had also served the function of providing a common enemy for the many colonial factions who papered over their differences to do political battle together. With the common enemy gone, factionalism seemed suddenly to worsen. The electorate included many more voters from the lower end of the socioeconomic scale in replacement of many at the higher end, who were now excluded. This altered electorate used the highly democratic means available to them under the institutions inherited from their colonial past to press demands upon legislatures that now lacked most of the experienced, legally trained members of previous years. The balances induced by the system of deference were gone with the changes in legislative membership and the revolutionary rhetorical style. An artificial yet useful communitarian consensus on monetary matters had existed among legislators before independence, but that was swept away by the changes in legislators and replaced by economic and social factionalism as the legislatures more accurately reflected in their personnel the divisions within society. In sum, it was a classic case of lagging political culture in the face of rapid change. The constitutional system was out of balance—part of the old system had been kept but another part was lost. A new constitutional system was needed.

A NEW CONSTITUTIONAL SYSTEM

The response was conservative in a positive sense, not in a reactionary one. Efforts were made to keep the old system intact as much as possible while replacing the lost or obsolescent portions of that old system with new institutions that made sense in terms of the permanently altered circumstances. The process began not with the Federalists but with those framing state constitutions. The second wave of constitutions reflects experimentation in this regard. By 1787 four states had revised their initial documents in ways that kept the strong legislatures closely tied to the population but introduced new institutions of retraint. A somewhat stronger executive, stronger bills of rights, and attempts to distinguish between normal legislation and the writing and amending of constitutions are examples of this trend at the state level. Two states, Connecticut and Rhode Island, functioned quite well without constitutional revision. Their governors had been subject to popular election for many years, and the balances in their constitutional systems had already been worked out and could be retained intact.

In this context the national constitution written by the Federalists can be called conservative. Although it is true that the Federalists worked hard to replace some of the more radical state constitutions, especially the most radical one (the 1776 Pennsylvania document), the net effect of their efforts was to introduce a new constitutional system that preserved, perhaps we should say conserved, what remained of the prewar system that was still of value. For example, the Federalists' concern over majority tyranny is sensible only if they intended to retain ultimate majority rule. They were not so much antimajoritarian as seeking ways to restore balance to a system of majority rule. Another example is the 1790 Pennsylvania constitution that the local Federalists wrote to replace the radical 1776 document. In it we can see no real retreat from ultimate majority rule. A senate was added with four-year staggered terms. The governor was given a three-year term instead of one year, and he was also given some significant power. But both branches of the legislature and the governor were to be elected directly by the people, there was no property requirement to run for any office, and there was no property requirement for voting—producing the broadest electorate of any state, virtually universal manhood suffrage. The Federalists did this knowing full well that the same broad electorate would be used to elect the members of the House of Representatives from Pennsylvania, as well as to elect a state legislature that in turn would elect the two Pennsylvania senators.

The United States Constitution is usually viewed as conservative or reactionary because the President and Senate are not elected directly by the people, devices for filtering and slowing down the majority, but not for replacing majority rule with something else. The Electoral College is elected by the broad state electorates, and meet in their respective states. Those engaged in an antimajority cabal would more likely have used the Senate to elect the executive, or at least brought the electors together in one place where their deliberations could be better controlled. Under the Articles of Confederation the Congress was elected by the state legislatures, but in the Constitution the lower house of Congress is elected directly by the people. If the Federalists were bent only on removing government from the people, this hardly seems the way to do it.

Nor is this all window dressing to cover a power grab by nonmajoritarians. The three most important powers of government — the power to tax, the power to appropriate money, and the power to declare war — are all given to Congress, and one house of Congress represents a direct majority of the people while the other represents the state legislatures closely tied to state majorities. The President has a veto power and powers of appointment and treaty making, but the first is subject to congressional override and the other two are subject to Senate approval. Certainly this is a resuscitated executive, but the national Constitution retains legislative predominance, although not legislative dominance. A close examination of constitutional checks shows that they are mainly for use by the legislature to check the operation of the executive and judicial branches. The President can veto, but Congress can override, set the salaries of the other two branches, create or destroy offices in the executive branch beyond those mentioned in the Constitution, set the size of the Supreme Court, determine the Court's appellate jurisdiction, impeach members of the other two branches (while controlling its own membership), withhold appropriations, and have a role in amending the Constitution. The check usually mentioned most prominently as limiting Congress — judicial review — is not in the Constitution.

In many respects the closest model to our national constitution, after taking out the parts that result from federalism, is the Massachusetts constitution of 1780. There is no mention of religion in the United States Constitution, as there is in the Massachusetts document, but the federal Constitution originally left religious matters to the states anyway. The Bill of Rights was added primarily at the insistence of the friends of state government, and has the effect of making the Constitution look even more like a state constitution.

One lesson learned from the earlier state documents was to take the judiciary away from the legislature. Putting the national courts under the executive would have been a conservative response, but instead the judiciary is made a separate branch. This salutary innovation, one of America's major contributions to constitutional history, was copied later at the state level and by many nations around the world. A separate judiciary helps to make the federal legislature weaker than those found at the state level, and is one of the clear instances in which the United States Constitution incorporates features devised in reaction to negative aspects of the state constitutions.

The United States Constitution is forward looking. It successfully created a new constitutional system appropriate to new political circumstances, conserved that which was best and most central to the earlier American constitutional tradition, and built upon and in many important respects derived from earlier state constitutions. It is not useful to imply that the Constitution is primarily a reaction to the evils perpetrated by fundamentally flawed state constitutions. Most state constitutions were retained intact for many years after 1787. When they were finally revised significantly or replaced, it was done to make them even more democratic than they had been — hardly evidence that excessive democracy had been their primary flaw. And from 1787 onward the state constitutions were made an integral part of the national Constitution.

The deep commitment to popular control of government continued at both state and national levels, and has been extended at the national level through perhaps the most revolutionary idea to come out of the founding era — the amending process institutionalized in the Constitution itself. Any attempt to characterize the United States Constitution as simply conservative is likely to be misleading, unless one asks what it was supposed to conserve. It conserved the American constitutional tradition, which stretches back deep into the colonial experience and of which the Constitution is the ultimate expression. It conserved the basic commitments, values, and institutions of the early state constitutions, both in its own institutions and in its inclusion of the state constitutions in a new, federal constitutional system. The United States Constitution is best described as creating a federal republic, and both federalism and republicanism are legacies to us from the early state constitutions.

THE FIRST FEDERAL CONSTITUTION: THE ARTICLES OF CONFEDERATION

PETER S. ONUF

The Articles of Confederation were the first federal constitution. But they never gained widespread acceptance across the new nation. Congress adopted the Articles in November 1777 and sent them out to the thirteen states for the unanimous approval necessary to put them into operation. Complaints and suggested revisions flowed in from all quarters. By the summer of 1778 only ten states had ratified; after Congress made an urgent appeal to their "patriotism and good sense," Delaware (November 1778) and New Jersey (January 1779) joined the fold. But Maryland, unhappy about the failure of the Articles to limit the western claims of the large, "landed" states, held out until March 1781. The unpopularity of the Articles raises an important question: why was it so difficult to establish a constitutional structure for the union at a time when patriotic Americans were willing to suspend their mutual suspicions and conflicts of interest and make enormous sacrifices for each other in the war effort?

Through the entire history of their drafting and ratification, no one had much good to say about the Articles. In 1776 Edward Rutledge of South Carolina was convinced that "we have made such a devil of it already that the Colonies can never agree to it." Even congressmen who favored ratification could muster little enthusiasm. "It is the best Confederacy that Could be formed," concluded Cornelius Harnett of North Carolina in late 1777, "especially when we consider the Number of States, their different Interests, Customs &c &c." Yet no one pretended that the Articles fully secured all these conflicting interests. The states were deeply divided on the "landed" states' western claims (apparently guaranteed by the proviso in Article IX "that no State shall be deprived of territory for the benefit of the United States") and on the equality of state votes in Congress (Article IV). There was also considerable grumbling about the mode of apportioning quotas — Northerners felt that the formula laid down in Article VIII, keying quotas "to the value of all land within each State, granted . . . or surveyed," favored the southern states, where land values were relatively low.

82

Compromises on taxation, representation, and land claims gave everyone something to dislike in the Articles. While most congressmen agreed with Charles Carroll that they would have to rise above the "little and partial interests" of their own states, the drafting process also seemed to jeopardize larger, more general interests, if not fundamental principles. Some provisions clearly represented expedient, political concessions to groups with leverage in Congress: thus the small states, fearful of being "swallow'd up & annihilated," threatened not to confederate if they were not guaranteed equal voting power. Delegates from large states, like John Adams of Massachusetts, were bitterly opposed to such a guarantee, insisting that representation proportional to population was along "equitable." For Adams, the compromise of principle seemed all the more glaring—and dangerous—in a document that purported to found a "perpetual" union.

The government of the union carried on without constitutional authority until the war was nearly over. Because political compromises and concessions were so conspicuous in the completed Articles, ratification did not retard—and may even have hastened—the rapid deterioration of Congress as an effective governing body. From 1781 on, "nationalist" proponents of a stronger central government emphasized defects in the Articles as they campaigned for amendments to give Congress greater control over commerce and an independent revenue. In 1784, a disgusted commentator asserted that Congress, having lost much of the effective authority it had exercised during the war, was now a mere "burlesque on government, and a most severe satire on the wisdom and sagacity of the people." By early 1787, Henry Knox spoke for a growing number of Americans who were convinced that "the poor Federal government is sick almost unto death."

Yet it would be a mistake to conclude that the history of the Articles was one of unmitigated failure, relevant only as a negative model to the new Constitution that superseded them. The Philadelphia convention adapted the broad division between state and national powers under the Articles; in drafting the Articles, essential state and sectional interests that would have to be accounted for under any enduring constitutional order were sharply defined. The immediate result of political controversies in the drafting process was to secure state rights and weaken central authority: dissatisfaction with the resulting patchwork of compromises made the Confederation seem a provisional, temporary arrangement at best. But the definition of particular interests *in relation to each other* was a necessary first step toward the creation of a more perfect union.

INDEPENDENCE AND UNION

The states confederated under desperate pressure. "Nothing but Present danger will ever make us all Agree," wrote New Jersey delegate Abraham Clark in August 1776, "and I sometimes even fear that will be insufficient."

Clark's chief concern was to preserve the union of states against the British. "A Confederation of the Colonies" was also "absolutely necessary," added William Whipple of New Hampshire, "to enable Congress to Conclude foreign alliances." Diplomatic concerns were compounded by recognition of the potential danger unconfederated states presented to each other. Terms of union had to be secured now, warned John Witherspoon, or the Revolution might prove only "a prelude to a contest of a more dreadful nature," a true "civil war" pitting patriot against patriot.

If the "Present danger" worked toward union, it also promoted the expression of local interests. Taking advantages of the wartime crisis, state leaders claimed that the survival of the union hinged on concessions from other states. When provoked by Congress's apparent unwillingness to uphold their essential rights or interests, they hinted that their states might abandon the war effort. Given the importance of preserving the union and showing a common front to friends and foes, congressmen took such warnings to heart. As a result, successive drafts of the Articles, beginning with a plan submitted by Benjamin Franklin in 1775, diluted congressional authority and secured state rights. The character of the union thus was shaped by growing awareness of the need to guarantee particular interests as far as possible.

Franklin's draft was inspired by his own Albany Plan of Union (1754), a precocious proposal for continental union under the British Empire. The Albany Plan, drawn up in response to the French and Indian threat, would have established a strong central authority. Franklin argued that the colonies, in their present disjointed condition, could not coordinate effective defensive measures. Because they were so "extremely jealous of each other," union was "absolutely necessary for their preservation." Franklin called on Parliament to create an American constitution consisting of a crown-appointed "President General" and a "Grand Council" comprised of delegates chosen by the assemblies of each colony. Representation would be proportional to population, a principle Franklin later incorporated in his draft of the Articles.

The Albany Plan met a chilly reception in England and in the colonies. "The Crown disapprov'd it," Franklin later explained, "as having plac'd too much Weight in the democratic Part of the Constitution; and every Assembly as having allow'd too much to Prerogative." His 1775 proposals fared little better. Congress was already operating on the basis of state equality, and a new system of representation was politically impossible. Franklin's proposal to allow a majority of the colony assemblies to amend the Articles also raised the specter of a bloc of states imposing its will on all the others. But the main problem with the Franklin draft was its timing. At this point, few delegates were willing to forfeit the possibility of reconciliation by such an irrevocable move toward independence.

The following year severely tested the patience of Franklin and other patriots who knew it was hopeless to expect the British government to repeal the long list of obnoxious laws that had precipitated the revolutionary crisis. Because sentiment for a complete, formal break with Britain was most advanced in the New England colonies, Franklin thought they should "enter into" a regional confederation of their own "& invite the other Colonies to accede to it." But prudent Yankees were well aware that their radical reputation was a liability to the resistance movement. Though they shared Franklin's frustration, New Englanders kept a low profile in these critical months, encouraging men from other colonies to assume leading roles in Congress and the army. In the interests of union, they waited for the other colonies to see the need for confederation—and to set its terms.

The movement toward independence and union guaranteed the centrality of state claims under the Articles. During the first few confusing months of 1776, congressmen faced three distinct tasks: to formalize the break with Britain and declare the colonies independent; to establish a confederation, in order to secure what John Adams called "our internal Concord"; and to negotiate an alliance with France in the interests of "external Defence." The crucial question was one of timing and sequence. Conservatives like Carter Braxton of Virginia and John Dickinson of Pennsylvania thought confederation should come first. In April Braxton wrote, "Previous to Independence all disputes must be healed & Harmony prevail. A grand Continental League must be formed & a superintending Power also." Braxton and other conservatives were acutely aware of the many intercolonial controversies—notably over boundaries—that might easily subvert the American union. They were afraid that Josiah Tucker, a sympathetic British commentator, was right in predicting that "intestine quarrels will begin" in America "the moment a separation takes effect." To conservatives the prospect of civil war was even more horrifying than the ongoing conflict with Britain. It was therefore imperative for the colonies to resolve their differences, thus removing the occasion for domestic conflict, and institute an effective "superintending Power" to take Britain's place.

As independence approached, conservatives focused their energies on securing a "Continental Constitution." Dickinson prepared a new draft of the Articles, thus setting the framework for subsequent discussion and revision. According to Jefferson's notes, congressmen from the middle colonies threatened that "their colonies might secede from the Union" if their impetuous colleagues pushed them too fast. Just as confederation had to precede independence, union would be jeopardized by precipitous action. By withholding his signature from the Declaration of Independence, Dickinson registered his misgivings about the sequence as well as the rapidity of congressional moves.

The association of confederation with the obstructionist tactics of congressional moderates and conservatives drove radicals to discount the importance of drafting an elaborate "Continental Constitution." At first, John

Adams even hesitated to use the term "constitution" to refer to arrangements for governing the colonies collectively. Adams would be satisfied, he wrote in March, with a central government much like the present Congress, empowered to coordinate the war effort and keep the peace among the states. His chief interest at this time, apparent in his *Thoughts on Government*, was with the reconstitution of colony governments, not with intercolonial organization. It was easy for patriots like Adams to conclude, often unfairly, that concern with establishing a strong confederation cloaked loyalist leanings or, at least, a determination to minimize the impact of the transfer of authority in the states.

The conservatism of many delegates, particularly from the middle colonies, combined with the need to preserve consensus to keep Congress on a frustratingly moderate course. The link between national politics and a conservative agenda was reinforced as congressional conservatives preempted the argument for a strong central government. Consequently, radical patriots were forced to look to the separate states to take the final crucial steps toward independence. In May 1776 Congress called on colonies to establish popular, revolutionary governments where existing arrangements proved inadequate to the "exigencies of their affairs." With royal authority overthrown at the colony level, a Declaration of Independence would simply formalize a political — as well as military — *fait accompli*. Thus, Adams wrote his wife Abigail, "Confederation among ourselves, or Alliances with foreign Nations are not necessary, to a perfect Separation from Britain. That is effected by extinguishing all Authority, under the Crown, Parliament and Nation as the Resolution for instituting Governments, has done, to all Intents and Purposes."

The sequences determined by political "exigencies" in Congress and the colonies — Independence, followed by alliance and confederation — exacerbated centrifugal tendencies in revolutionary politics. The states, functioning as proxies for radicals with generally cosmopolitan perspectives and commitments, became the leading actors in the revolutionary drama. Certainly there are other explanations for the suddenly inflated importance of the states at this time: the end of royal rule together with emerging notions of popular sovereignty and republican government made the states logical claimants to legitimate authority. As colonies, their corporate identities stretched back as far as a century and a half. But in the moment of revolutionary transformation, loyalties were fluid and contingent, and the precise balance between local and national authority remained to be fixed. The move toward independence in the separate colonies — whether prompted or simply ratified by Congress — and the subsequent development of state constitutions gave the states a preeminent place in the new order. The states' plausible claims to *priority* strengthened their claims to constitutional *primacy*.

Within weeks of Congress's May resolves, Adams betrayed second thoughts about the sequence which he and fellow radicals had inaugurated. In early June he wrote Patrick Henry, describing what he considered the "natural Course and order of Things." First, each colony would "institute a Government"; next, "all the Colonies" would "confederate, and define the Limits of the Continental Constitution"; this confederation would then "declare the Colonies a sovereign State, or a Number of confederated Sovereign States" and, "last of all . . . form Treaties with foreign Powers." By making the confederated states the source of American sovereignty and reducing the original state governments to a provisional status, Adams's sequence would have secured for the central government a coordinate, if not preeminent, role in the new system. If the United States did not constitute a single "sovereign State," at least the separate states would be coincidentally "confederated" and "Sovereign." But alas, Adams confessed, "We cannot proceed Systematically." Logic notwithstanding, "We shall be obliged to declare ourselves independent [that is, separately sovereign] States *before* we confederate" (emphasis added).

With independence finally declared, the drafting of a continental constitution was no longer tainted with obstructionism or crypto-loyalism. ("It is obvious," Arthur Lee wrote in July 1777, "that those generally, who were marked foes to the declaration of independence are the men that now thwart and delay Confederation.") Most patriotic Americans agreed that confederation was crucial to the quest for foreign aid. "What Contract will a foreign State make with Us," asked Samuel Chase of Maryland, "when We cannot agree among Ourselves?" Yet if the diplomatic situation made confederation seem imperative, it also defined the goals of union narrowly and instrumentally. The wartime emergency forced Americans to seek an alliance with each other as well as with foreign powers. Thus the confederation began to take on the form of the international agreements it was designed to make possible.

Writing home to North Carolina in May 1777, when differences over the terms of union seemed most intractable, delegate Thomas Burke dejectedly concluded that it was "far from improbable that the only Confederation will be a defensive alliance." Like most other congressmen, Burke was ambivalent about the prospects for a more perfect union. The challenge of "preserving the independence of the States [separately], and at the same time giving each its proper weight" seemed beyond Congress's collective wisdom and ingenuity. Burke's solution, incorporated in what was to become Article II, was to guarantee "Each State . . . its sovereignty, freedom and independence, and every power, jurisdiction and right, which is not by this confederation expressly delegated to the United States, in Congress assembled." While Article II cleared the way for state delegations to endorse the draft, it did so by resolving any questions about the allocation of authority in favor of the states. Through such revisions, the confederation became little more than the "defensive alliance" Burke had hoped to avoid.

The diplomatic and military situation encouraged delegates to see union as the product of a series of hard bargains in which each state sought to protect its interests. The point of confederation was not only to promote the American war effort at home and abroad but also to keep the states from making war on each other. The threat of civil war led some congressmen to conceive of the United States as a collective security organization, thus reinforcing the legitimacy of each state's claims. Charles Carroll emphasized the extent to which union would serve state interests: "a Confederacy formed in a rational Plan will certainly add much weight & consequence to the United States, [and] collectively give great security to each individually."

American independence apparently presented an unprecedented opportunity to put into practice an international "peace plan." John Witherspoon made the most enthusiastic case for union in these terms, arguing in late July 1776 that confederation would represent an epochal development in the "progress" of international relations. "It is but little above two hundred years since that enlarged system called the balance of power, took place," Witherspoon told his congressional colleagues, maintaining "that it is a greater step from the former disunited and hostile situation of kingdoms and states, to their present condition, than it would be from their present condition to a state of more perfect and lasting union." In Witherspoon's scheme of world history — and in his vision of the American confederation — states were constants. "Progress" was measured by their ability to perfect arrangements among themselves for perpetuating collective "security and peace." Witherspoon's conception of union thus reflected and rationalized the preeminence of distinct sovereign states established by the original movement toward, and definition of, American independence. The failure of the states to confederate when they declared their independence assured that the goal of the Revolution for most Americans would be to preserve their states' rights: union — confederation — would only be a means to secure "independence" — state sovereignty.

CONFEDERATION POLITICS

The drafting process dragged on for more than a year after a committee headed by John Dickinson submitted its version of the Articles to Congress in July 1776. The basic outlines of Dickinson's plan survived intact, despite important concessions to state and sectional interests. Key provisions concerning voting were identical in the 1776 report and in the Articles sent out to the states in late 1777: each state would have one vote; nine state delegations would have to agree on important issues; and amendments depended on unanimous consent of the state legislatures. Prohibitions on state action interfering with the exercise of congressional authority over war and diplomacy (Article VI of the completed confederation) were drawn from several articles (IV, V, VIII, IX) in the Dickinson draft. The guarantee that "free inhabitants" of each state would enjoy "all privileges and immunities of free citizens," including "privileges of trade and commerce," throughout the union (Article IV) was also taken from the earlier draft (Articles VI and VII).

Most Americans agreed on the scope of congressional power, particularly in managing the war effort. The structure of the British empire—as Americans understood it—provided a model. During the Imperial Crisis, Patriot agitators had insisted that Britain's "superintending" authority could be distinguished from the "internal police" of the colonies. General acceptance of this "external"–"internal" distinction helps explain why there was so little theoretical debate over the distribution of authority between Congress and the states after independence. Carter Braxton, a conservative Virginian, asserted that Congress should "have power to adjust disputes between Colonies, regulate the affairs of trade, war, peace, alliances, &c." The more radical John Adams formulated a similar list. He thought congressional powers should be "confined to . . . war, trade, disputes between Colony and Colony, the Post-Office, and [jurisdiction over] the unappropriated lands of the Crown."

But applying the principle of congressional superintendence to particular cases proved nearly impossible. The biggest practical problem was to guarantee Congress's disinterestedness when that body was comprised of representatives of the very states whose interests it was supposed to adjudicate and guarantee. George III and his Privy Council had enjoyed a distinct advantage over Congress in this respect, precisely because they were *not* directly responsible to the colonies but exercised an unquestioned authority over them in cases where their respective claims conflicted. But if the confederation Congress enjoyed only modest success in resolving interstate conflicts, it helped set in motion a broad readjustment of interests. The great achievement of American politics during these troubled years was to define the range and character of interests that would have to be secured under a continental constitutional order: only then would it be possible to agree on an impartial, disinterested role for a superintending authority.

The immediate impact of efforts to protect particular interests—whether of the landed states in the western lands controversy or of small states or slaveholders in debates over representation and taxation—was, of course, *disintegrative*. The problem, Edward Rutledge and other critics recognized, was that the protracted drafting process became hopelessly entangled with the ongoing crush of congressional business. This meant that the Articles would be considered piecemeal, not as a coherent document, thus offering numerous opportunities to affected interests to press for concessions. Rutledge's solution, to have the "States . . . appoint a special Congress"—or convention—to draft a continental constitution, anticipated the direction of state and national constitution writing. Though few would concur with Rutledge's bold suggestion in 1776, Congress's subsequent travails provided a powerful negative model for the Philadelphia convention.

But other congressmen realized that there were long-run advantages to the mixture of constitutional and political questions in the drafting process. First, it is very likely that the confederation would have failed altogether, with potentially disastrous results for the war effort, if the states had been forced to act definitively on any document that could have been produced in 1776. By leaving the outcomes of specific, controversial provisions in suspense, Congress helped reinforce the states' commitments to the union — even if each state defined the union differently. The drafting process may have exposed the full range of "little and partial interests" that divided Americans, but those interests were at the same time being defined *in relation* to each other. In dialectical fashion, then, conceptions of union emerged out of the articulation of state interests. Recognizing that this process was necessarily "political" and would involve long-drawn-out negotiations on apparently trivial as well as momentous issues, Congress invited the states to raise objections to the Articles when they were transmitted for their approval. New Hampshire delegate Nathaniel Folsom explained that Congress meant "if Possible to give satisfaction and ease to each and every of the States."

The protracted drafting process also helped contain intersectional animosities. Attempts to secure states' rights through limits on congressional power and the equal representation of states reflected fears that the central government would be exploited by *groups* of states with distinctive interests. Rutledge of South Carolina was unusually candid in denouncing New Englanders as men of "low Cunning . . . and . . . levelling Principles." For Rutledge, a strong union could only be a Yankee plot: "The Idea of destroying all Provincial distinctions and making every thing of the most minute kind bend to what they call the good of the whole, is in other Terms to say that these Colonies must be subject to the Government of the Eastern Provinces." Rutledge was also wary of entering into a "Union" or alliance with potential allies, thus "placing ourselves in [their] Power." From his perspective, "union" at home or abroad jeopardized states' rights and sectional interests.

Rutledge's suspicions were widely shared in the South: Jefferson, for instance, was notoriously hostile toward New Englanders. For their part, Yankees like John Adams wondered whether the hardy yeomanry of the North could ever form a lasting union with the great slaveholding "Barons of the South," or with "the Proprietary Interests in the Middle Colonies." Adams believed that the "popular Principles," which alone could support a durable "Continental Constitution," were unique to his own section. "Gentlemen in the other Colonies have large Plantations of slaves, and the common People among them are very ignorant and very poor. These Gentlemen are accustomed, habituated to higher Notions of themselves and the distinction between them and the common People, than We are." Sectional differences were nearly as deep and abiding, Adams feared, as those among "several distinct Nations."

If intersectional suspicions were pronounced in 1776, the framework for collective action established by the continental congresses helped control and deflect them. After all, the challenge was to create a union of *states:* sections as such had no political standing. The interests of states often cut across vaguely defined sectional lines (it was unclear, for example, whether Pennsylvania was naturally aligned with the northern or the southern states). Because large and small states and landed and landless states were scattered across the continent, congressmen had to cooperate with representatives from other parts of the country. In the same way, proponents of radical measures, like the Lees of Virginia and the Adamses of Massachusetts, developed close ties despite differences in economic interest and social structure in their home states.

By muting sectionalist politics, the emphasis on states' rights enhanced the prospects for a durable union — if not for an effective central government. This does not mean that delegates lost sight of sectional interests. Indeed, the emerging structure of the Confederation protected vital sectional interests by allowing a small group of states to block action on questions concerning war, peace, and finance (Article IX in the final draft) and a single state to veto fundamental, constitutional changes (Article XIII). The price of union, or of an intersectional modus vivendi, was an exaggerated solicitude for states' rights. As a result, the national government was doomed to powerlessness: even before the Articles were ratified it became clear that state "sovereignty" had to be curbed before an effective government could be established for the union. But union itself would have been impossible without guarantees to the states.

WESTERN LANDS

Political and constitutional issues were most conspicuously confused in deliberations over the status of the "unappropriated lands of the Crown." Dickinson, representing Pennsylvania, a "landless" state, inserted a provision in his draft guaranteeing the territorial integrity of the states, but only when their limits had been established (Article XV). A later article (XVIII) explained how the western boundaries of the "landed" states would be fixed: Congress would simply have the power of "limiting the Bounds of those Colonies, which by Charter or Proclamation, or under any Pretence, are said to extend to the South Sea, and ascertaining those Bounds of any other Colony that appear to be indeterminate." Not surprisingly, the "landed" states would have nothing to do with such provisions: for them, congressional disinterestedness was hopelessly compromised by measures plainly favoring their "landless" rivals. Spokesmen for the landed states further charged that Congress's interest in acquiring a national domain precluded impartial judgments on their territorial rights.

Concern that particular states or interest groups would be able to advance their interests by controlling Congress encouraged moves to curb congressional power and secure states' rights. The impetus for these moves was not so much principled opposition to a strong central government but rather the justifiable fear that coalitions of narrow, local interests, and not "the real Interests of America," would determine the course of national policy. Implicit in the elusive standard of disinterestedness was the idea that Congress should function as a kind of court. Only as impartial arbiter of the numerous, inevitable disputes between states could Congress preserve the union in peace. Yet in sorting out boundary claims, just where its judicial mandate was most compelling, Congress's political character became most apparent. Thus there was a disjunction between judicial ends — the generally accepted scope of congressional authority — and political means. Congress was unable to perform its expected role effectively because it was so obviously the creature of the states, and therefore too responsive to their narrow interests. As a result, opposition to congressional power reflected not only a parochial and defensive loyalty to the states but also legitimate misgivings about Congress's standing as a disinterested, limited, constitutional government for the union.

The most important revisions of the Articles in 1776–1777 focused specifically on the role of the central government in resolving jurisdictional controversies. The landed states would not allow Congress to set their western limits by fiat. In the August 1776 debates on the Articles, Benjamin Harrison of Virginia warned that "Gentlemen shall not pare away the Colony of Virginia." Samuel Huntington of Connecticut spoke for all the landed states, united "against mutilating [colonial] Charters." Landless state delegates were equally obdurate, refusing to confederate on terms they thought would reduce them to a permanently inferior position in the union.

The immediate result was stalemate. But it was clear there would be no agreement on Dickinson's western lands article (XVIII), and when discussions resumed a year later, Congress replaced the offending provisions with a new article (IX in the final draft) satisfactory to the landed states. Not only were state claims protected from congressional interference ("no State shall be deprived of territory for the benefit of the United States"), but an elaborate procedure was established for setting up special courts to settle jurisdictional disputes. The effect of these provisions was to remove controversial issues from Congress: even when its authority was exercised, it would be delegated to impartial tribunals insulated from political pressures.

Landless Maryland argued that the new Article IX would guarantee the primacy of Virginia and the other landed states and withheld its approval of the confederation until 1781. These fears proved unfounded. The landed states were willing to give up their western claims, provided they could do so under conditions securing their own interests. Cession offers poured in from the landed states, resulting in agreements with New York (1782), Virginia (1784), Massachusetts (1785), and Connecticut (1786). By receiving cessions instead of asserting its own title or its right to set boundaries, Congress could act impartially on behalf of all the states: it would no longer be an interested party, incapable of acting disinterestedly.

The new provisions on jurisdiction also marked a crucial, if awkward, step toward a more perfect union. The adjudication of *Connecticut v. Pennsylvania* by an Article IX court in 1782 showed that Congress could rise to the disinterested impartiality of a constitutional government. One enthusiastic commentator thought the court's decision, upholding Pennsylvania's jurisdiction in the Wyoming Valley, presented "a new and extraordinary spectacle" to the world. "Two powerful and populous States, sovereign and independent" had accepted "the arbitration of judges mutually chosen from indifferent states." In other words, the drafters of the Articles had, in this extraordinary instance, discovered a way for states to submit to a higher authority without sacrificing their "sovereignty." By contrast, Congress in its ordinary deliberations was too responsive to the states to command such deference.

STATE EQUALITY

The preeminent issue for small, and usually landless, states was to maintain their corporate identities by preserving equal representation in the national legislature. In predicting, as did William Williams of Connecticut, that "the smaller Colonies will be in effect swallow'd up and annihilated" under a scheme of proportional representation, small state delegates agreed with their landed state adversaries that congressional power inevitably would be exploited to advance state interests. Stephen Hopkins of Rhode Island pointed out "that the 4 largest [states] would contain more than half the inhabitants of the Confederating states, & therefore would govern the others as they should please." Large state delegates responded with reciprocal concerns. According to John Adams, "an equal vote [for the small states] will endanger the larger."

Opposition to a "consolidated" national government grew out of the small states' concerns about being overwhelmed and absorbed by their larger neighbors. For them, a confederation not premised on state equality would invite the larger states to extend their power. Witherspoon's vision of the United States as an enlightened international system, or "federal union," reflected his determination to guarantee the survival of New Jersey and other small states. Considered as corporate entities, the small states had as much to lose as the large: "in questions of war" they were "as much interested" and "therefore should vote equally." Though Witherspoon conceded that "equality of representation was an excellent principle," he insisted that "nothing relating to individuals could ever come before Congress; nothing but what would respect colonies."

Representatives of small states at the Philadelphia convention echoed their predecessors' arguments. The primary concern at both times was with the dangerous implications of state inequality in a federal union, not with extending state power at the expense of the central government. On the contrary, relatively small, weak, and vulnerable states had a strong interest in preventing disunion and strengthening national power. Their advocacy of states' rights was a preemptive, defensive response to the threat of being dominated by larger, more populous states. When the Articles were being drafted, the apparent determination of the large, landed states to hold on to their extensive western claims reinforced the small states' insistence on state equality in Congress. Virginia, for instance, already held an enormous advantage in land and population over Maryland; the disproportion would increase, Marylanders complained, once the Old Dominion began to develop the West, causing the "depopulation, and consequently the impoverishment" of the small, circumscribed eastern states.

For Maryland, particularly, an equal vote in Congress was an invaluable resource in its ongoing campaign to create a national domain and so equalize state size and power. The success of the small states in preserving equal state votes balanced that of the large states in revising the Articles to prevent encroachments on their claims. The principles of state equality and of territorial integrity thus were both incorporated in the confederation. Yet, as long as the sizes of the states remained so disproportionate, these principles in practice tended to immobilize congressional authority. "So unequal as the States are," bemoaned Burke of North Carolina in May 1777, "it will be nearly impossible" to confederate; even when the Articles were ratified, the problem of state inequality continued to drive a wedge through Congress.

The guarantees of state and sectional interests in the Articles all worked negatively, to *prevent* Congress from acting in sensitive areas. The state equality provision, guaranteeing the small states majorities in Congress, was offset by the requirement that no less than nine states agree on any "question relative to peace & war or other important matters." In this way, the principle of proportional representation was at least roughly upheld: by combining their votes, the most populous states could be assured that no measure could be adopted by delegates representing a minority of the American people as a whole. The characteristic paradox here was that the interests of the majority could be secured only by giving a minority of the states (five, if every state were voting) the right to override the will of the majority.

Yet if the Articles, in reflecting the conflicting interests of large and small states, seemed to guarantee the "imbecility" of the union, they also anticipated and shaped the development of a new and more complex constitutional order in which differing principles of representation were deployed to give the union a limited—rather than imbecilic—national government. Under the federal Constitution, the principle of state equality would be preserved in the Senate (which Madison said was "only another edition" of the old Congress), while claims of larger states that were expressed negatively and indirectly in the Articles were now given positive form through proportional representation in the House.

TAXATION AND REPRESENTATION

The precondition for a durable union, John Adams wrote in May 1777, was that "the great and small States must be brought as near together as possible." Even at that time, congressmen recognized the desirability of a more complex, possibly bicameral system representing both people (and property) as well as states. Chase of Maryland suggested that Congress switch back and forth between equal and proportional schemes, depending on the issue: "the smaller states should be secured in all questions concerning life or liberty & the greater ones in all respecting property." He therefore proposed that in votes relating to money, the voice of each colony should be proportioned to the number of its inhabitants. Jefferson thought that "the Representatives of a Majority of the People, or of a Majority of the States," presumably sitting in distinct houses, should be able to "negative" any offensive proposition.

These promising lines were not pursued, primarily, historian Jack N. Rakove writes, because "the overriding need for wartime efficiency" made a more elaborate and cumbersome national legislature "an impracticable option" at this time. In any case, the small states were unlikely to relinquish their established advantage. And even though the large states insisted that some proportional scheme would be much more "equitable," it was not yet clear who (or what) would be represented proportionally.

Confusion over how to determine the "proper weight" the respective states should exert "in the public councils" first became apparent in bitter debates over tax quotas in July 1776. Delegates from states with large numbers of slaves parried efforts to set quotas according to total (white and black) population. Again, Marylanders threatened not to confederate on such terms, arguing, in Chase's words, "that Negroes in fact should not be considered as members of the state more than cattle & that they have no more interest in it." For their part, Northerners were unwilling to link taxation *and* representation to total population, agreeing with their southern colleagues that slaves could not be represented. Instead, Adams asserted, "the numbers of people [slave and free] were taken . . . as an index of the wealth of the state." Chase and fellow Southerners agreed that "taxation should be always in proportion to property," but argued that the white population was the most reliable indicator of state wealth (including slaves).

When debates over quotas resumed in 1777 Congress sought to break the stalemate by omitting population — of whatever description — from its tax provision. Because both sides in the earlier exchange linked taxation (and implicitly representation) with property, the solution was to discover a less controversial "index" to wealth. The formula incorporated in Article VIII, basing quotas on the value of surveyed lands, though unpopular in New England, constituted an important step toward intersectional accommodation. When, in 1783, the scarcity of reliable data on land values pushed Congress back toward a population standard, delegates negotiated a compromise between the New Englanders' whites only and the Southerners' total population formulas. Modifying a suggestion made by Benjamin Harrison of Virginia in the first round of debates in 1776 that "two slaves should be counted as one freeman," Congress for the first time endorsed the infamous "three-fifths compromise" (five slaves would count as three freemen in determining quotas), subsequently employed in the federal Constitution.

CONCLUSION

The drafting of the Articles exposed radically divergent positions on taxation, representation, and jurisdiction. These differences were deeply rooted in the political and economic heterogeneity of the early United States. The timing of the confederation, lagging far behind the independence of its constituent states, and the confusion of constitutional and political issues during the drafting process guaranteed that state and sectional interests would get a full airing. Though the resulting controversies seemed to call into doubt the very survival of the union, the articulation of distinct interests was an essential step toward discovering and defining enduring common interests.

The process of reconciling interests began, haltingly, as congressmen struggled toward consensus on the draft of the Articles sent out to the states in late 1777. That the process was still far from complete was apparent in the unwillingness of the landless states to ratify, in continuing grumbling in the large states about small state "equality," and in New Englanders' complaints about the inequities of tax quotas based on land values. At the same time, however, critical interests had gained important victories that helped secure their commitment to the union: as a result, they would prove increasingly responsive to the interests of their erstwhile adversaries. Thus the landed states, guaranteed against jurisdictional challenges, began to cede their western claims to Congress. The result was that the large and small states were, in John Adams's words, "brought as near together as possible." With the old states made more equal, and with the prospect of new states further reducing the danger of a few large states exercising despotic power, the practical difference between proportional and equal state representation diminished. It was then less unthinkable for the two schemes to coexist in a more complex constitutional scheme. So, too, the initial stand-off on how or if to count slaves in assessing tax quotas set the stage for intersectional accommodation.

Few contemporaries believed that the Articles could be a successful constitution for continental government. The very fact that the drafting process lasted so many years—and that reformers began campaigning for amendments immediately thereafter—made the Articles seem provisional at best. In the meantime, the states (beginning with Massachusetts in 1780) set new standards for drafting and ratifying constitutions establishing more elaborate governments, generally with bicameral legislatures. The state constitutions exposed the constitutional defects of the Confederation Congress and provided models for national reformers.

The failures of the Articles, often exaggerated for rhetorical effect, helped shape the new constitutional order that superseded them. But the contributions of the Articles were not only negative. The distribution of authority between the states and central government was not radically different under the federal Constitution, and several key principles of the new system were worked out in and under the Articles. Most important, the Articles established a necessary framework for working toward a continental constitutional order.

THE ROAD TO PHILADELPHIA, 1781 – 1787

JACK N. RAKOVE

The framing and adoption of the federal Constitution was the culminating event in the American revolutionary generation's experiment in republicanism. The work had begun a decade earlier, with the drafting of the first state constitutions and the Articles of Confederation; but it was only in the great debates of 1787 and 1788 that American ideas of politics and government achieved mature form. Because the Constitution rightly commands this central place in the history of the Revolution, scholars have often been tempted to view earlier debates and disputes about the structure of the Confederation from the perspective of 1787. In the works of the leading Progressive historians, for example, the decisions of the late 1780s marked the final round of a continuing struggle that began with independence, when conservative and elitist groups first sought to establish a strong national government in order to check the dangers from more radical and democratic forces within the states. Seen in this way, the Constitution appears as a conservative repudiation of the liberal and egalitarian impulses of 1776.

Continuities there certainly were between early discussions of the problem of federalism and the chains of events that ultimately led to the Philadelphia Convention. Many of the most important Framers of the Constitution had indeed been long associated with proposals to create a vigorous and more powerful union, among them such prominent figures as John Dickinson, Benjamin Franklin, James Madison, Alexander Hamilton, James Wilson, Gouverneur Morris, Robert Morris, and George Washington himself. Moreover, some of the key initiatives that were taken to strengthen the Confederation during the 1780s clearly anticipated the strongly nationalist policies that Hamilton would pursue, with great success, as first secretary of the treasury under the Constitution. So, too, the recognition that managing the vast domain of western lands beyond the Appalachian chain would become one of the foremost responsibilities of the union was a continuous motif of national politics throughout the decade after independence.

Yet for all this, the history of the movement that led to the great assembly in Philadelphia is not one of steady progress toward some long foreseen end. It is, rather, a story of years of partial and modest efforts at reform abruptly yielding to a new situation in which radical changes could suddenly be proposed and adopted within almost a matter of months. Though a few visionaries like Hamilton and Franklin may have glimpsed the prospect of national government at an early point, it was only during the months and even weeks preceding the gathering of the Constitutional Convention that serious discussions of the issue began to move beyond the rather limited range of amendments to the existing articles of union that had preoccupied debate on this issue throughout the 1780s. Perhaps the most striking development that took place during the months that followed the adjournment of the Annapolis Convention in September 1786 was that it at last became possible to fashion a new agenda of reform far more expansive than anything that had been considered previously. Instead of vesting modest additional powers in the existing Congress, reformers like James Madison and James Wilson could now seriously envision a radical transfer of authority from the states to a national government that would be reconstructed along more familiar lines, with an independent executive and judiciary enforcing the laws framed by a bicameral legislature.

Why had this transition taken so long? To a large extent, the problem of conceiving of a truly national government required a major leap of intellect and imagination. It was no easy task to imagine just what a national government would do, or how a legislature composed of representatives from so extensive a country could possibly prove competent to draft laws dealing fairly and intelligently with so many complex and diverse interests as the new nation embraced. The idea of a national republic was itself something of a novelty, and before any major reform of the Confederation could be attempted, certain stock assumptions about the nature of government would have to be challenged. Foremost among these was the received wisdom which held that republican governments could exist only in small, relatively homogeneous societies.

But this intellectual task was made all the more difficult by the political obstacles against which all supporters of a stronger federal union had to struggle. The first and most important of these was the requirement (in Article XIII) that amendments to the Articles of Confederation secure the unanimous approval of the state legislatures. In practical terms, this barrier was set so high that there was little point even in contemplating proposing anything more than the most carefully drawn amendments, proposals that needed to command virtual consensus within Congress if they were to enjoy a plausible hope of adoption by the states.

Prudence indeed dictated that the reform of the Confederation could occur only as the piecemeal benefits derived from particular amendments gradually taught both the state legislatures and their constituents that a more vigorous federal government would not ride roughshod over their rights as states and citizens. For in the 1780s Americans still harbored many of the radical fears of government that had carried them from resistance to revolution in the decade after the Stamp Act. Many of them believed that it was wrong "to unite the purse with the sword" — to endow a national government with both the power to declare war and the means to wage it. Many of them doubted whether the basic purposes of representation could be honored at the national level — where an elected representative would no longer feel any sense of obligation to his electors or even possess an informed awareness of their wishes and interests. And many of them had further reason to wonder whether their own particular interests would be well secured within a government in which they might find themselves members of a permanent minority. The dominant planting class of the southern states feared that their economic interests would be sacrificed to the commercial concerns of northern merchants — and a few of them may even have begun to recognize that the security of their property in other men might be threatened if antislavery opinion continued to grow in the North. New Englanders believed that the movement of population away from the intensely farmed lands of their states to new territories in the West would continually erode their influence within the union. Residents of small states like Delaware and Rhode Island, which enjoyed an equal vote in Congress, similarly suspected that any major changes in the structure of the Confederation would lead to calls for proportional voting within the national legislature, and thus reduce their weight to miniscule proportions.

One additional factor made the task of allaying these objections even more difficult. Since Congress itself could only recommend measures to the state legislatures, the revision of the Articles required an ability to bring political influence and pressure to bear upon the individual legislatures. But in the absence of the national political parties that would themselves begin to develop only after the Constitution took effect, there were no ready available mechanisms for mobilizing popular opinion or coordinating political activity within the thirteen states. Occasionally, men like Robert Morris or Madison might realistically identify particular interest groups who could be counted upon to rally to support a specific proposal. Yet again, the task of conducting an effective *national* campaign virtually outran both the imagination and the experience of even the most seasoned revolutionary leaders. The only precedents for mass mobilization that they could readily draw upon came from the early episodes of the Revolution — from the remarkable upsurge of popular resistance that had greeted the parliamentary Stamp Act of 1765 and the Coercive Acts of 1774. Perhaps for this reason, many of the supporters of a stronger federal union concluded that the general population would become convinced of the need for federal reform only after continued instances of British malevolence toward its former colonies would conclusively demonstrate the "imbecility" of the Confederation.

In practice, then, the events of 1787 were the outgrowth not of a sustained and self-conscious movement leading inexorably toward the Constitution, but rather of the failure of a series of efforts to deal with specific problems that arose once the Articles of Confederation took effect on March 1, 1781. The Constitutional Convention was made possible only by the collapse of all previous attempts to amend the Articles of Confederation. Had any of these proposals ever been adopted, it would have been far more difficult to circumvent the formal requirements of Article XIII. Only after the futility of this procedure became evident could would-be reformers of the Confederation begin to think seriously about what the establishment of a national government would entail.

The various campaigns to strengthen the Confederation that were launched during the six years that separated the formal inauguration of the Articles from the gathering of the Philadelphia Convention in late May 1787 can be divided into three major phases. The first of these was primarily a response to the shortage of money and supplies that threatened to cripple the American war effort after 1779. This phase of activity can be said to have come to an end in April 1783, when the coming of peace coincided with the submission to the states of a comprehensive plan for establishing national finances on a secure and permanent basis. A second set of concerns gradually became apparent during the months that followed, as Americans sought both to restore prewar patterns of commerce and to secure access to new markets. The lack of federal revenue remained, as before, an obsessive worry throughout this period, but now proponents of reform were also convinced that the national interest required vesting Congress with substantial power over the regulation of commerce. Revenue and commerce continued to dominate the agenda until September 1786, when the adjournment of the Annapolis Convention marked the failure of the last effort to find a way of amending the Articles of Confederation on a piecemeal basis. Only during the months that followed did the possibility of using a general convention to propose major changes in the union become a viable alternative, and with it the recognition that the work of reform would now involve not only saving Congress from the states but also the states from themselves.

The Articles of Confederation, as finally drafted in November 1777, reflected the patriotic assumptions that had carried the colonists through the critical early stages of independence. As Madison would later observe, the framers of the Articles had assumed that the state governments would simply bear whatever duly authorized requisitions — for men, money, and supplies — Congress imposed on them. But the three and a half years that separated the submission of the Articles to the states from their final ratification in early 1781 had revealed just how naive that assumption had been. When runaway inflation forced Congress to stop printing paper currency in the fall of 1779, it adopted a cumbersome system of asking the states to collect "specific supplies" of everything from beef to blankets and cartridges to flour. Such a scheme was entirely consistent with the principles of the Confederation, which had envisioned that the states would act in effect as the administrative auxiliaries of Congress. But the states, which were already overburdened and underfinanced themselves, found compliance with these requests beyond their means.

Since the mere ratification of the Articles would allow Congress to exercise no more authority than it already possessed, delegates began contemplating amendments to the Confederation even before the long-delayed accession of Maryland was at last secured. Congressional thinking about amendments ran along two lines. One was directed toward asking whether Congress should be vested with some sort of coercive authority over the states, so that a state that failed to meet its obligations could conceivably find itself subjected to pressure either from the Continental Army or from a naval blockade. Such a scheme was so obviously unworkable that it testifies more to the desperation of Congress than anything else.

The second and more likely line of thought revolved around the idea of giving Congress independent sources of revenue. Such precedent for this could already be found in the cessions of claims to western lands that the states of New York, Virginia, and Connecticut were now beginning to offer Congress. But while the creation of a national domain would give the union a resource of enormous permanent value, it did not provide an answer to immediate problems, since these lands could only be developed gradually in time of peace. To collect the revenue it needed now, however — as well as to provide a fund to secure the loans it hoped to attract overseas — most delegates came to support the idea of asking the states to allow Congress to levy a 5 percent impost (or duty) on foreign imports. This proposal was submitted to the states in early February 1781, a few weeks before the Articles of Confederation took effect.

Events on the battlefield outpaced the desultory progress of the impost proposal through the states. In the summer of 1781, Lord Cornwallis made his fatal encampment at Yorktown, George Washington marched a substantial detachment of his army southward to lay siege, and the timely arrival of a French fleet in the Chesapeake led, in October, to the surrender of Cornwallis and the end of major combat on the North American mainland. But the prospect of independence could not redeem unpaid debts to public creditors and the army; nor could it enable Congress to meet its ongoing responsibilities, however they were defined. From the late summer of 1782 until the next spring, questions of finance dominated the daily congressional calendar.

Hope that the impost proposal of 1781 might provide a partial foundation on which to rebuild a federal treasury were quashed in the fall of 1782, when Rhode Island definitely rejected the measure and Congress learned that Virginia had repealed its earlier endorsement. By then, however, Congress was already beginning to consider more comprehensive measures. In the spring of 1781, at the start of its effort to establish permanent executive departments, Congress had appointed Robert Morris, the great merchant prince of Philadelphia, to be the first superintendent of finance. The pressures of the military campaign of 1781 had originally prevented Morris from addressing long-term problems. But in July 1782 he presented Congress with a major message on public finance, and in the months to come he launched a protracted campaign to induce the delegates to accept his program. This called, in brief, for balancing accounts between the states and Congress; settling a certain segment of the public debt on the states while consolidating other obligations into a national debt to be serviced by the union; and using this latter responsibility in turn to justify asking the states to vest Congress not only with the impost already proposed but also with additional authority to levy poll, land, and excise taxes.

The character and fate of these measures are deeply indicative of both the scope of early proposals to strengthen the Confederation and the formidable difficulties that would inhibit reform before 1787. Like other measures that Congress considered during the early 1780s, the Morris program was far more a response to the lessons of war than a plan for the radical expansion of federal authority. While Morris certainly hoped to free Congress from its dependence on the states, his proposals would not have reallocated the basic tasks of government between the union and the states. They were meant instead simply to enable Congress to discharge the responsibilities it either enjoyed already under the Articles or would acquire when the states completed their cessions of western lands. Arguably the establishment of fiscal stability, coupled with the creation of a national bank (which Morris also supported), would aid the postwar development of the domestic economy; but his program nonetheless stopped well short of asking the states to authorize Congress to regulate trade or other forms of economic activity.

Morris was well aware of the political difficulties his program would have to surmount before it could be approved by both Congress and the states. He could rely on Hamilton, James Wilson, and Thomas FitzSimons to support his measures vigorously within Congress, but rather than rely on the force of argument alone, he also sought to enlist both public creditors and the Continental Army to bring pressure to bear on the delegates and the state assemblies. Congress had to conduct its debates amid rumors that the regular troops now posted at Newburgh, New York, would mutiny if it did not provide for the payment of back wages and the pensions that had been promised to the officer corps. When these pressures seemed inadequate, Morris threatened to resign if his proposals were not enacted.

In the end, these heavy-handed tactics backfired. Aware as most delegates were of the just demands of soldiers and civilian creditors alike, they could not ignore the objections that any plan of national taxation would encounter from their constituents in the state legislatures. Led by Madison, a critical nucleus of delegates broke with Morris and began to fashion a compromise plan which all the states might be persuaded to accept if it could be presented as a reasonable program supported by a strong consensus within Congress. After prolonged debate, Congress adopted a comprehensive set of resolutions on April 18, 1783. In brief, its three major elements called upon the states to levy specific taxes dedicated to servicing the national debt, and to amend the Confederation by granting Congress a revised version of the impost and by approving a change in Article VIII, so that the expenses of the union would be allocated among the states not according to the existing impractical formula based on land values but simply by population (with five slaves being counted as equivalent to three free men). To preserve the various bargains upon which these proposals rested, Congress further insisted that they had to be approved in their entirety to take effect.

Four of the five delegates who voted against these resolutions did so because they opposed any federal taxes in general—but the fifth dissenter was Alexander Hamilton, who, like Robert Morris, felt that the proposed measures did not go nearly far enough. Hamilton was also one of a circle of delegates and other nationally oriented leaders who had privately discussed the idea of calling a general convention to consider the entire state of the union. He had broached this notion as early as 1780, and now, in the first weeks of peace, he even went so far as to draft an appropriate resolution. Yet even Hamilton had to concede that neither his colleagues in Congress nor their counterparts in the state legislatures were likely to endorse so radical a measure—especially since the coming of peace was rapidly defusing the sense of urgency that had accompanied earlier discussions of amendments to the Confederation. Hamilton filed his resolution among his personal papers, and retired to the practice of law.

He was hardly alone in preferring to substitute private pursuits for public obligations: all Americans welcomed the chance to resume activities and enterprises too long disrupted by eight years of war. Congress itself suffered from this pervasive transition. After a group of mutinous soldiers provoked Congress to abandon Philadelphia and take up residence elsewhere (first in Princeton, then Annapolis and Trenton, and finally New York), the national assembly was continually pressed just to maintain a quorum.

Then again, it was not entirely clear what functions the national government would continue to serve in peacetime. True, once Virginia tendered its final offer of cession in the fall of 1783, the long-delayed establishment of a national domain was close to completion. But without the revenues required to sustain adequate military forces on the frontier, Congress was in a poor position to restrain either the settlers who were already spilling across the Ohio River or the Indians whose lands they coveted. The other tasks that would now fall to the union, however, remained to be discovered.

The most important challenges arose, as it turned out, within the realm of foreign affairs, the one area in which the need for effective federal authority would seemingly be least disputed. But in practice, even here postwar developments revealed that Congress lacked the ability to enforce its legitimate powers or to act in behalf of the national interest. One set of problems involved American compliance with the treaty of peace of 1783. At the behest of the British government, the treaty contained two articles protecting the rights and interests of British creditors and American loyalist refugees. When various states refused to honor these provisions, Britain cited these violations of the treaty as a pretext for retaining its frontier forts in the Northwest, an action that seemed likely to stiff Indian resistance to American expansion. These state actions, in turn, led some American leaders to begin to consider how international treaties properly ratified under the terms of the Confederation could be made binding upon the states.

While few Americans were affected by events on the frontier, another dimension of Britain's policy toward its former colonies soon appeared far more consequential. At war's end, American merchants were anxious to restore commercial connections severed after 1774, and American consumers were similarly eager to purchase goods they had gone without or obtained only at great expense during the years of scarcity. Britain was willing to satisfy the second of these demands but not the first. A stream of British ships began to cross the Atlantic, bringing all those items of European manufacture that Americans desired while often seeking to cut American importers out of their marketing. At the same time, the British government acted to prevent American merchants from reestablishing prewar patterns of commerce. By order of the Privy Council, American ships were prohibited from carrying exports to the British West Indies, which before the Revolution had provided them with their most valuable markets, as well as from carrying imports from the home islands.

The logical American response to these discriminatory measures was retaliatory: the United States should curtail the access of British ships to American ports until imperial harbors were opened to American merchants. Such a strategy was urged with characteristic zeal by John Adams, whose major task as the first American minister to Great Britain was to negotiate a treaty of commerce with the former mother country. But under the Articles of Confederation, Congress lacked authority to regulate either foreign or interstate commerce. Individual states could impose whatever restrictions they pleased—and many states did attempt to protect the interests of American merchants and artisans—but without a uniform set of regulations these efforts proved pointless. Goods legally imported in one state could easily find their way overland to interior markets.

With the revenue plan of April 1783 still making the rounds of the state legislatures, Congress was reluctant to request further powers. But in April 1784 it did ask the states to consider two further amendments to the Confederation. The first would have authorized Congress to bar from American harbors ships owned or navigated by citizens of nations that had not concluded commercial treaties with the United States. The second would have empowered Congress to prohibit foreign merchants from importing goods manufactured in any country but their own.

By 1785, these measures seemed inadequate to the depression that was reputedly engulfing the merchants and artisans of the northern cities. At the particular behest of James Monroe, who had replaced James Madison in the Virginia delegation, Congress appointed a committee to consider whether it should solicit comprehensive powers over commerce. But when the committee did draft an amendment to grant Congress the power to regulate both foreign and interstate commerce, Congress failed to muster a consensus in its favor, and the proposal was effectively tabled.

Why did Congress fail to act? First, a number of southern delegates (other than Monroe) feared that federal power over commerce would be effectively controlled by the northern states. Much as they resented the British merchants who were even now demanding the repayment of prewar debts — with interest! — southern planters seemed almost as fearful of their own countrymen. Second, a group of New England delegates, led by Elbridge Gerry of Massachusetts, saw the committee's recommendation as the insidious first step of a scheme to subvert the Articles of Confederation. Associating this proposal with the controversial plans of Robert Morris, whom they had bitterly opposed, they defied the apparent interests and even the instructions of their constituents, and refused to endorse the committee's report.

Without consensus in Congress, no amendment could possibly be approved by the states. But there was a third reason why Congress failed to act, and which pointed the way to the thinking that would lead Madison and Monroe, among others, to accept the conclusion that Alexander Hamilton had reached years earlier: that effectual reform required going beyond Congress and using the still novel device of a specially called convention to frame appropriate measures.

For by 1785 Congress had fallen into such disrepute that any amendment it issued would itself be tainted. Opponents of the revenue measures of 1781 and 1783 had repeatedly predicted that a Congress possessed of independent funds would destroy the entire fabric of republican liberty protected by both the Articles of Confederation and the state constitutions. Supporters of Congress answered these charges as reasonably as they could, but repetition had its effect. Congress had been so effectively discredited that further efforts to follow the amendment procedures of Article XIII seemed doomed to failure.

A slim hope still existed that state ratification of the revenue plan of 1783 or the commercial amendments of 1784 would demonstrate that this procedure was workable. None of these proposals ever received unanimous state support, however. When New York definitively rejected the revenue scheme early in 1786, the inadequacy of the Confederation's formal amendment procedures seemed evident.

It was against this background that Madison and other national leaders began to think seriously about using the route of a convention to discuss changes in the Articles. Previously they had been reluctant even to consider such an idea on the grounds that it would sap even further not only the prestige of Congress but also the authority of the Confederation. Yet at some point a decision had to be made as to how much longer the formal requirements of Article XIII were to be honored. The turning point came during the fall 1785 meeting of the Virginia legislature. At the start of the session, Madison and a group of assemblymen introduced a bill to vest Congress with the power to regulate foreign trade. So severely was this measure attacked, however, that its supporters decided it would be better to table the bill than risk approving the eviscerated version that seemed likely to pass the assembly.

But on January 21, 1786, the very last day of the session — in one of those closing rushes for which state legislatures were famous even then — a substitute proposal prepared by John Tyler was adopted. On its face, it was a simple measure. The resolution named seven commissioners — among them Madison, Edmund Randolph, and the crusty old whig George Mason — who were authorized, in the name of Virginia, to invite deputies from other states to attend a meeting "to consider and recommend a federal plan for regulating commerce." In early March, the commissioners set a time and place: the first Monday in September, at Annapolis — a city that would be free from the kinds of suspicions that would arise should a more obvious locale, such as Philadelphia or New York, have been proposed.

Madison at first doubted whether this experiment would succeed, and Monroe, who was still in Congress, was even more skeptical. If the defects of the Confederation were to be remedied by a convention, Monroe argued, the proposed conference at Annapolis was too narrowly conceived to do much good. But Madison had reached a different conclusion, and in his letters to Monroe he linked the need to act beyond the rule of the Articles with his continuing conviction that reform still had to be gradual. "The efforts of bringing about a correction thro' the medium of Congress have miscarried," he wrote in March 1786. "Let a Convention then be tried. If it succeeds in the first instance, it can be repeated as other defects force themselves on the public attention, and as the public mind becomes prepared for further remedies." [1] Monroe found this reasoning persuasive, and his conversion to Madison's views gained added urgency because Congress was itself again considering whether it should propose additional amendments to the Articles of Confederation or even issue a call for a general convention. Deploying the arguments that Madison had provided in his private letters, Monroe led the successful opposition to both ideas.

Almost by default, then, the Annapolis conference was left as the one remaining alternative worth pursuing. Whether it would prove any less futile than earlier efforts was another matter. A poorly attended conference might do more harm than good, and by mid-August only eight states had accepted Virginia's invitation. Two states—including the host, Maryland—balked at appointing delegates precisely because they feared the conference would detract even further from Congress's stature. Key New England leaders still suspected that Virginia had ulterior motives in calling for the meeting; while William Grayson, a Virginia congressman, thought that the nation's "affairs are not arrived at such a crisis as to ensure success to a reformation on proper principles." On the other hand, the fact that a convention of any kind was finally being held encouraged speculation about the possibility of proposing more adventurous changes. Thus in mid-August, Madison could inform Thomas Jefferson that "Many Gentlemen both within & without Congress wish to make the meeting subservient to a Plenipotentiary Convention for amending the Confederation. Tho' my own wishes are in favor of such an event," he continued, "yet I despair so much of its accomplishment at the present crisis that I do not extend my views beyond a Commercial Reform. To speak the truth *I almost despair even of this.*" [2]

Madison's ambivalence illustrates why the Annapolis Convention marked the transition from the tactics of gradual reform that had prevailed since 1781 toward the more ambitious and potentially open-ended political activities that preceded the actual gathering at Philadelphia in May 1787. Had the conference actually been well attended, the original scenario of confining discussion to the sole subject of commerce might still have been followed. As it happened, however, only twelve commissioners from five states appeared at Mann's Tavern by September 12, and although a few days might have brought the arrival of stragglers from Massachusetts and Rhode Island, the predicament facing the convention would have been no different. Any substantive proposal concerning trade framed by such a body would carry little weight. Far from advancing the cause of reform, such a recommendation would only demonstrate anew how difficult it was to get the American states to unite.

Yet what purpose would be served if the convention simply adjourned without taking any action? Among those present, Madison, Hamilton, and John Dickinson were all deeply committed to the cause of federal reform, and rather than confess failure, they and their colleagues preferred to risk one further gamble. In their report, which is customarily attributed to Hamilton, the commissioners invited the state legislatures to appoint delegates to attend a second convention, to be held in Philadelphia the following May, which would be called "to take into consideration the situation of the United States, [and] to devise such further provisions as shall appear to them necessary to render the constitution of the Federal Government adequate to the exigencies of the Union."

Since the road from Annapolis did lead to the Constitutional Convention, it is easy to see the commissioners' report as the act of a group of seasoned politicians who knew exactly what they wanted. But it would be more faithful to the circumstances in which they acted to recognize that their call was as much a desperate final maneuver as a bold stratagem for constitutional revolution. Having exhausted every likely method of proposing modest amendments to the Confederation, nothing was any longer to be lost by taking a greater risk; but neither were the commissioners confident that the states would accept the invitation, or that a convention, once assembled, would be able to reach agreement.

Beyond the realization that the strategy of gradual reform had proved bankrupt, the commissioners were probably spurred by one further consideration. At the close of the Revolutionary War, the supporters of a stronger federal union had believed that time was on their side, and that, indeed, radical political measures could not be expected immediately from a people exhausted by eight years of war. By late 1786, such patience was far less easy to justify. In part this reflected the failure of the states to approve even one of the prudent amendments Congress had already proposed. But fears that the time for reform was limited were now reinforced by the possibility that the union itself might dissolve before constitutional change could be effected. The early debates over vesting Congress with power over commerce had revealed the potential for sectional divisions between northern and southern states.

Even more alarming, however, was the course of the dispute that preoccupied Congress while the preparations for Annapolis were well under way. During the summer and fall of 1786, Congress was deeply divided over whether the United States should attempt to force Spain to open the Mississippi River at New Orleans to American navigation, or whether it should temporarily abandon such claims in order to obtain a commercial treaty with Spain. Southern congressmen, protecting the interests of the rapidly growing populations of what would become Kentucky and Tennessee, insisted that American navigation rights not be yielded; but northern delegates, anxious to alleviate the commercial difficulties of their constituents, argued that a treaty was currently more valuable. Prolonged debate over this issue split Congress into two sectional blocs, with the five southernmost states arrayed against their eight northern counterparts. While the American public as yet knew little about this dispute, the Annapolis commissioners did. What they now had to consider was whether the existing union might dissolve into two or three separate confederacies if an adequate federal government was not reconstituted fairly soon. This, too, justified a political risk-taking that would have been unacceptable only months earlier.

From the early fall of 1786 on, then, the prospect of a general constitutional convention served, as one Virginia congressman put it, "as a Beacon" upon which the thoughts and activities of American politics began to fasten.[3] By February 1787, after eight states had appointed delegations to attend the meeting at Philadelphia, Congress overcame its nervousness about circumventing the formal rules of the Confederation to add its own imprimatur. By the early spring, every state but Rhode Island had responded favorably to the call. James Madison, recalling the disappointment of Annapolis, still wondered whether George Washington should withhold his attendance until a respectable quorum was actually mustered, but in the meantime his own preparations for the convention went forward.

These preparations were primarily intellectual in nature, and were devoted to establishing the agenda that Madison hoped to convince the convention to follow. To place too great an emphasis on the ideas and plans of one man may seem unwarranted (especially since Madison himself was originally disappointed in the results of the convention). Yet in one critical respect, his efforts to think through the entire problem of republican government vividly illuminate what was distinctive about the final phase of political activity that preceded the gathering of delegates in late May.

Well into 1786, the problem of amending the Articles of Confederation had not been regarded as a means of correcting the failings of republican governments within the states. The central task of return was to free Congress from its dependence on the states, not to undo the damage done to sound principles of governance by the republican enthusiasm of 1776. Efforts to revise the Articles and to improve the functioning of the state governments thus proceeded on separate tracks, and it was difficult to see how these could be made to intersect. But as Madison examined what he called "the vices of the political system of the United States" in the spring of 1787, he found it impossible to disentangle the two. In part this was because the refusal of the states to accede to genuine considerations of national interest demonstrated just how "vicious" their individual governments were. But more to the point, he now believed that the states were incapable of legislating wisely for their own constituents. To the frustrations he had himself recently encountered as a member of the Virginia assembly, Madison added lessons drawn from observations of events in other states, especially from the growth of paper money factions in states like Rhode Island and North Carolina, and from the outbreak of actual rebellion in Massachusetts.

All of these reflections led toward a notion of constitutional change that would be radical rather than incremental. As Madison defined the issues, the work of the convention would extend to saving not only the union from the states but the states from themselves. Substantial powers would have to be transferred from the states to the union; new limitations would have to be placed on the residual authority of the states; and lessons drawn from the republican constitutions of the states would determine the form the national government itself would now take: three independent branches of government, including a bicameral legislature.

These ideas began to coalesce only in March and April 1787, but they led directly to the Virginia Plan which Madison's colleague, Edmund Randolph, presented to the convention on May 29. At this final stage of preparation, and well after, the range of political obstacles that would have to be surmounted before any new constitution could be adopted remained formidable. But the critical developments that had to occur for the Constitution to be written were as much intellectual as political, and it was in raising the understanding of what was at stake from the constrained views of earlier years to the broad perspectives so manifest at Philadelphia that Madison played so important a role.

THE CONSTITUTIONAL
CONVENTION

LANCE BANNING

Meeting at the Pennsylvania State House (Independence Hall), the Constitutional Convention found a quorum on May 25 and sat until September 17. Fifty-five delegates participated in its work, though there were seldom more than forty in the room for any single session. Representing every state except Rhode Island, the delegates comprised a good cross-section of the early national elite. Lawyers (34), merchants (7), farmers (27), public creditors (30), and public servants (10), nearly all were wealthy men, and most had taken generally conservative positions in their states. Yet members came from a variety of local factions and from all the major regions of the several states except the west. The nation might have organized an equally impressive meeting from the ranks of leaders who did not attend. John Adams and Thomas Jefferson were representing the United States abroad in 1787. John Jay and Samuel Adams were passed over. Patrick Henry "smelt a rat" and turned down his election. Still, most states attempted to select their most experienced and best, usually with slight regard to factional considerations, and they succeeded well enough that Jefferson described the roster as a gathering of "demigods." George Washington was present. Inevitably, he was quickly chosen to preside.

Among the delegates as well was young James Madison, Jefferson's close friend, an influential member of the Annapolis Convention, and long a leading advocate of national reforms. Madison had led Virginia, which had led the other states, in organizing the convention and selecting delegates whose talents and distinguished reputations signaled a profound commitment to its work. In the weeks before the meeting, he had taken careful notes on ancient and modern confederacies and prepared a formal memorandum on the "Vices of the Political System of the United States," thinking problems through to a degree that no one else had done and urging other members of his delegation to arrive in Philadelphia in time to frame some introductory proposals with which the meeting might begin. Virginia's seven delegates assembled daily while they waited for the full convention to obtain a quorum, agreeing on a set of resolutions that might serve as a preliminary basis for discussions. Speaking for the delegation as a whole, Governor Edmund Randolph introduced these resolutions on May 29, as soon as the convention had agreed upon its rules.

Reassembling in the character of a Committee of the Whole, the meeting turned immediately to a consideration of the Randolph (or Virginia) Plan. Along with the adoption of a rigid, carefully respected rule of secrecy, which freed the members from external pressures and encouraged them to feel that they could alter their positions if discussion changed their minds, the Virginia Plan was among the great convention's most important acts. For its provisions, which were based primarily on Madison's ideas, did not propose to make the Articles of Confederation "adequate to the exigencies of the union." Rather, they envisioned the complete replacement of the current central government by a republican regime of national extent. The present, single-chamber central government would be reorganized in imitation of the balanced constitutions of the states. Based directly on the people, it would have the right "to legislate in all cases to which the separate States are incompetent, or in which the harmony of the United States may be interrupted by the exercise of individual Legislation." To guarantee the central government's supremacy wherever common measures were required, the articles of union would be ratified by state conventions chosen by the people, and federal powers would include authority "to call forth the force of the Union against any member of the Union failing to fulfill its duty" or to veto state legislation inconsistent with the federal charter.

By starting with the resolutions of May 29, the Constitutional Convention set its course from the beginning toward a thorough-going reconstruction of the present system. Meeting at least once with Pennsylvania's delegation and doubtless talking privately with others as the members trickled into town, Madison and his Virginia colleagues had correctly sensed that early sentiment was overwhelmingly opposed to patchwork, piecemeal efforts. The members opened their deliberations deeply moved by the momentousness of the occasion, as was the country as a whole. Many recognized that the convention might afford the last alternative to fragmentation of the union. Many feared, as Madison had put it in his preconvention letters, that America's republican experiment could not indefinitely survive the loss of this protective shield. Madison himself believed that popular commitment to the Revolutionary order was already flagging as the ineffectuality of the Confederation Congress reinforced a tendency in all the states toward fluctuating, ill-considered legislation which reflected slight regard for either private rights or long-term public needs. He therefore warned the other delegates that they were not assembled merely to attend to the debility of Congress. Their ultimate objective, he insisted, must be nothing less than to "perpetuate the union and redeem the honor of the republican name."

A solemn sense of high responsibility and urgent, common purpose was indispensable to the Convention's great achievement, not least because most delegates were only partially prepared for the enormous changes sketched by the Virginia Plan. Seizing the initiative for radical reform, Madison's proposals demonstrated an instinctive grasp of several broad, though hazy, understandings that would limit and direct the course of the proceedings. Leaders of a democratic Revolution, including thirty veterans of the war, the delegates had not forgotten the complaints and hopes that had propelled them into independence. Nearly all of them had come to think that an effective central government would have to have, at minimum, an independent source of revenues, authority to regulate the country's trade, and power to compel obedience to its legitimate commands. Nearly all agreed, as well, that powers that the colonies had stubbornly denied to England would have to be accompanied by careful checks against the possibility of their abuse. Many, nonetheless, were far from willing to consent to the specific kinds of checks proposed by the initial resolutions. The Pennsylvanians and Virginians were prepared from the beginning to insist that powers of this sort could be entrusted only to a well-constructed, fully representative republic. Overawed by the Virginia Plan, accepting many of its goals, and unprepared to offer comprehensive counterresolutions, dissenters were uncertain how to counter its proponents in debate. They nevertheless objected from the start that the convention was empowered only to reform the present federal system, not to overturn it. The framing of the Constitution thus became a complicated story of a fundamental conflict that occurred within the context of a common quest.

One of the finest recent studies of the Constitutional Convention calls its early weeks a period of "nationalist assault." Certainly, the members from the smaller states felt thoroughly assaulted by a plan that offered to apportion legislative seats according to the populations of the several states. George Read immediately protested that the delegates from Delaware, who were specifically instructed to insist upon the equal vote that every state had always had in Congress (as in the convention), might have to leave the meeting if the larger states were bent upon this change. Neither Read nor any of his fellows really planned to quit before the business had begun. Yet it was clear from the beginning that the smaller states anticipated total domination, even loss of their identities, in a national republic grounded on proportional representation. Nor were theirs the only worries prompted by the resolutions of May 29. No sooner was the first one taken up than Elbridge Gerry of Massachusetts and Charles C. Pinckney of South Carolina, both representing larger states, questioned whether the convention could or should propose so radical a reconstruction. The Virginia Plan not only terrified the smaller states, it also seemed to many other members to depart too far from the essential spirit of a limited confederation and to call for more participation by the people than the people were equipped to make to national affairs. By offering what Madison described as a republican corrective for the defects of democracy, as well as an extreme solution to the problems of the union, the Virginia Resolutions complicated the convention's task and multiplied the sources of contention. They entangled the convention in so many overlapping arguments that it is easy to neglect the members' early sense of common purpose. But the "miracle" at Philadelphia resulted from a complex interplay of disputation and consensus, during which the delegates collectively developed a conception of a form of government so novel that it lacked a name. To understand this process, it is necessary both to simplify a set of disagreements so complex as to defy a brief description and to recognize that these disputes were only one dimension of the story.

Between May 30 and June 13, the Committee of the Whole conducted a complete consideration of the Randolph Plan. During these two weeks, with Madison and James Wilson of Pennsylvania at their head, a brilliant group of delegates from larger states developed a compelling case for radical reform. Distinguishing between a "national" government and one "merely federal," Wilson, Madison, Randolph, George Mason (Virginia), Gouverneur Morris (Pennsylvania), and others argued that the fatal weakness of the old confederation was its unavoidable dependence on the thirteen states for revenues and for a host of intermediary actions necessary to enforce its laws and treaties. Lacking independent means to carry its decisions into action, they explained, Congress had been baffled by the states even when its measures were supported by a huge majority and undeniably were within its proper province. Paper grants of new responsibilities would only add new sources of frustration if the states retained the power to ignore or counteract the central government's decisions; and yet a federal power to compel the states might introduce a constant threat of war between the union and its members. The inescapable necessity, the nationalists maintained, was to abandon the unworkable idea of a government over governments, a sovereignty over sovereignties, and give the central government the courts and other independent means to act directly on the individual members of society. Revolutionary principles required, however, that any government possessing the authority to reach the people's lives and purses would have to represent its citizens immediately and fairly. Given the necessity for larger federal powers, the traditional equality between the states would have to be abandoned in order to preserve equality among the people and majority control.

Intellectually outclassed by men like Madison and Wilson, most members from the smaller states squirmed silently through the convention's early days. A large majority of delegates had quickly fallen in with Madison's attempts to postpone action on the most divisive resolutions until the meeting could define some common ground. But as the skeleton of the Virginia Plan acquired some flesh and as it grew increasingly more difficult to settle lesser questions while the great ones went unanswered, the confrontation that had loomed from the beginning could no longer be contained. New Jersey's delegates demanded a decision on apportioning the

Congress, insisting on June 9 that proportional representation would destroy the smaller states and place the whole confederation at the mercy of a coalition of its largest members: Massachusetts, Pennsylvania, and Virginia. Ten of thirteen states, warned William Paterson, would certainly reject this scheme. If he could not defeat it in the hall, he would oppose it in his state. New Jersey would "never confederate on the plan before the committee."

Sunday intervened and tempers cooled, but not before James Wilson answered Paterson in kind. "If the small states will not confederate on this plan," he assured them, Pennsylvania and some others "would not confederate on any other." The division that would dominate proceedings for the next five weeks had burst into the open. It would prove the clearest, most dramatic, most persistent argument of the convention — the single conflict over which the gathering repeatedly approached collapse.

For all its threatening potential, nevertheless, the clash between the small states and the large cannot explain developments between May 30 and June 13. It was not the only conflict that emerged, nor can an exclusive emphasis on conflicts and divisions properly illuminate the course of the proceedings. The Constitutional Convention was successful, in the end, because its battles almost always raged in multiple dimensions, because the push-and-pull that marked its course was never *simply* a result of clashing interests, and because the men involved were more than merely clever brokers for their states. We do not need to resurrect old myths to recognize that the Constitutional Convention was, at once, a battleground for disagreeing politicians and a theater for one of the most brilliant exercises in creative statesmanship that history has ever witnessed. The famous compromises that reshaped the resolutions of May 29 into the document completed on September 17 were necessary consequences of contrasting state and sectional desires, capably advanced by representatives who were acutely conscious of competing interests. But each decision was a product, too, of a *cooperative* endeavor to achieve a better understanding of the nation's needs and to resolve its problems in accord with its ideals. Moreover, this was not the sort of meeting at which everyone arrived inflexibly committed to a set of clear objectives and compromised no more than he was forced to. It was the sort in which not even the Virginians knew exactly what they wanted at the outset, the sort from which the great majority departed rather awed by what they had achieved and with their thinking greatly changed by the collective effort.

The first two weeks of the convention seem most helpfully described as an initial exploration during which a complicated pattern of divisions rapidly emerged within a framework of evolving, general understandings. Like Madison, most delegates had come to Philadelphia as worried by conditions in the states as by the problems of the union. They readily agreed with the Virginian that the will of unrestrained majorities was often inconsistent with the rights of the minority or long-term public needs, and that the early

Revolutionary constitutions had neglected dangers of this sort by trusting too much power to the lower houses of assembly, which were not effectively restrained by governmental branches less immediately responsive to majority demands. Everywhere, as Elbridge Gerry phrased it, the country seemed to suffer from "an excess of democracy." Good government appeared to have been sacrificed to revolutionary fears of unresponsive rulers.

Few members of the Constitutional Convention carried their alarm about majority misrule so far as to suggest nostalgia for aristocrats or kings. Most genuinely shared the people's fierce commitment to a democratic system. Yet nearly all were powerfully determined not to replicate the errors they believed had been committed in the early Revolutionary constitutions. Here, again, the resolutions of May 29 successfully defined the boundaries of disagreement. Sound republics, they suggested, must be built upon two legislative houses: one elected by the people; the other chosen in a manner that would shield its members from the whims of the majority and thus assure continuing protection for the rights of the minority and continuing attention to the nation's long-term needs. The legislature should be counterbalanced by a forceful, separate executive, and the judiciary should be independent of them both. Through almost four months of often bitter quarrels, there was never any serious dispute about these fundamental principles of governmental structure. The Virginia Plan not only forced the meeting to consider a republican solution to the Revolutionary fear of concentrated central power, which had resulted in a general government unable to advance the nation's interests or even to fulfill its legal obligations. It also both elicited and guided a collective reconsideration of the nature of a sound republic. It did not specifically define which powers were beyond the competence of individual states. It offered only a preliminary sketch of an improved republic — not even indicating, for example, whether the executive should be a council or a single man. But it involved the delegates from the beginning in exchanges to which most contributed a determination not only to protect specific interests but also to advance a general search for principles and structural devices that could guarantee a place for governmental energy and wisdom as well as for responsiveness to popular demands.

The Virginia Plan survived its first examination fundamentally intact, its sketchy outline filling rapidly as the debates suggested and improved upon the broad agreements present from the start. As the Pennsylvanians helped elaborate the concept that the general government might act directly on the people, the Virginians dropped the resolution calling for a federal power to coerce the states, but found new reasons for their view that states should not participate directly in the choice of federal officials. Wilson, Madison, and their lieutenants made it clear that what they wanted was to build a wise and energetic central government upon a broadly popular foundation, blending a responsibility to the majority with multiple securities against an overbearing, popularly elected lower house. Impressed by their analysis of the debilities of the existing system, the convention speedily agreed to substitute a complex and authoritative central government for the present, feeble, unicameral regime. Sharing their dissatisfaction with the constitutions of the states, it worked from the beginning to establish genuinely independent, fully countervailing branches.

Through these early days, Madison and Wilson towered over the convention like a team of titans. On May 31, with only South Carolina and New Jersey voting no, and with Connecticut and Delaware divided, the Committee overwhelmingly approved the popular election of the lower house, a decision reaffirmed a few days later with the two divided delegations going opposite directions. With Madison successfully resisting a divisive argument about the scope of federal powers until some structural decisions could be made, the meeting easily decided on a three-year term for representatives, and seven years for the executive and members of the upper house. Insisting that the surest way to guarantee a safe, but firm, executive was to confer responsibility on one accountable individual, Wilson led a winning struggle for a single chief executive, though he could not prevent the fearful delegates from ruling that this magistrate could serve only a single term and was to be elected by the legislature, not the people. Both Madison and Wilson would have reinforced the veto power by involving the judiciary in the process, but Madison approved of the majority's decision that the veto was to be reversible instead of absolute. He and Wilson both were pleased, of course, by the decision on apportioning the Congress. On June 11 the Committee voted 7 states to 3, with Maryland divided and New Hampshire not yet present, for proportional representation in the lower house. Only tiny Delaware and antinational New York, where Alexander Hamilton was outvoted by Robert Yates and John Lansing, sided with New Jersey.

Still, the nationalist assault by no means carried everything before it. Although the smallest states seemed relatively isolated in the earliest debates and were severely beaten on the matter of the lower house, the fierce resistance vocalized by Paterson and Read became increasingly imposing as it coalesced with opposition based on different concerns. Three delegates — no more — were rigidly committed to a "merely federal" system, but Yates and Lansing could control New York while Luther Martin often managed to divide the Maryland contingent. For each obstructionist, moreover, there were several others for whom the pervasive fear of popular misrule, which made the resolutions of May 29 a universally attractive model for republican reform, could also reinforce a natural reluctance to surrender local powers to a national majority. Although the delegations from Connecticut and South Carolina were especially inclined to be distrustful of a scheme that would erect a stronger central government on greater popular involvement, almost every delegation was composed of men who differed widely in their judgments of the people's competence as well as in their willingness to shift additional responsibilities to federal hands. As the smaller states discovered partial allies, sometimes here and sometimes there, it seemed increasingly unlikely that a national republic could secure approval both from a majority of states and from the representatives of a majority of the people. Even optimistic nationalists resigned themselves to a campaign that promised to extend throughout the summer.

Confronted with so many overlapping fears, the democratic national-ists encountered rising opposition during the convention's first two weeks and suffered one decisive check. The Virginia Plan provided for election of the senate by the lower house from persons nominated by the states. On June 7, over loud objections from Madison and Wilson, majorities in every delegation disapproved this proposition in favor of election of the senate by the legislatures of the states. Nearly everyone agreed that the selection of the senate by the lower house might give the house of representatives an overweaning influence, while few were willing to entrust the choice directly to the people, as Wilson recommended. Doubting that the people were equipped to make a fit selection or insisting that a senate chosen in that way would prove unable to defend minorities against majority demands, many members saw election by the local legislatures simply as a lesser evil. Many others, though, including several delegates from larger states, were force-fully impressed by the insistence of John Dickinson (Delaware) and Roger Sherman (Connecticut) that selection by the local legislatures could collect the sense of states as states, assure a federal harmony, and offer firm securi-ties against potential federal usurpations.

Committed nationalists were deeply disappointed. Fearing that selec-tion of the senate by the states would build into the system exactly the flaw that was destroying the confederation, they also rightly sensed that an insistence on a federal role for states as states would reinforce demands for an equality between them. On June 11, just before the crucial votes, Sher-man urged that representation in the lower house might be appointed to free population, while every state might retain an equal vote in the senate. By moving to revive an old confederation formula, which counted a slave as three-fifths of a man, Wilson promptly headed off an argument that might have split the large-state coalition. But the overwhelming vote for propor-tional representation in the lower house was followed by a very close deci-sion on the senate, where Sherman's motion for equality was narrowly rejected, 6 to 5: Connecticut, New York, New Jersey, Delaware, and Mary-land, aye; Massachusetts, Pennsylvania, Virginia, North Carolina, South Carolina, and Georgia, no. A combination of concerns had joined to check the nationalist momentum. Two days later the Committee of the Whole reported its amended resolutions to the House, but the convention then immediately adjourned in order to permit opponents to prepare alternatives to the Virginia Plan.

William Paterson's New Jersey Resolutions, introduced on June 15, were thrown together quickly by the coalition that had voted for an equal senate days before. This coalition was united only by its opposition to the Randolph Plan, and its proposals did not represent the real desires of any of their framers. As Dickinson suggested in a private talk with Madison, many members from the smaller states were not opposed in principle to an effective, "national" system. In order to protect themselves from large-state domination, they were willing to ally themselves with the minority who were: "we would sooner submit to a foreign power than submit to be deprived of an equality of suffrage in both branches of the legislature." But if the large-state nationalists would bend a bit, the Delawarean was hinting, both his own state and New Jersey would support a vigorous, bicameral regime. To them, the contest with the larger states was not a controversy over which responsibilities should be entrusted to the central government, not even a debate about the merits of a complex system. On both these points, their fundamental preferences were closer to the nationalists' than to their temporary allies', and Paterson's proposals did not hide that fact. Under the New Jersey Plan, the general government would still have had the power to impose a stamp tax, postal duties, and an impost, to compel compliance with its requisitions, and to regulate the country's interstate and foreign commerce. Federal laws would still have overridden local legislation. A separate executive and federal courts would still have shared authority with Congress. For Luther Martin and the two New Yorkers, this was clearly rather much. For Dickinson and others, just as clearly, Paterson's proposal that the legislature should remain a single house, in which each state would keep its equal vote, was mainly an attempt to force concessions from the other side.

Switching back into the Committee of the Whole, the delegates debated the Virginia and New Jersey Plans on Saturday, June 16. Paterson and Lansing argued that the Randolph Resolutions would exceed the meeting's powers and could never win approval from the states. The nationalists refused to budge. Wilson argued that the gathering was free to *recommend* whatever changes it considered proper and should not consent to an enlargement of the powers of a single legislative chamber that would not derive directly from the people. Randolph pointed out again that the convention had to choose between a power to coerce the states, which would not work, and power to command the people, for which the present Congress was unfit. Alexander Hamilton monopolized the floor on Monday to suggest that even the Virginia Plan might leave excessive powers with the states, that full security against the instability inherent in a democratic system might require a closer imitation of the British constitution than anyone was willing to support. Madison concluded the discussion Tuesday morning with his longest speech to date, listing several ways in which a merely federal reform would fail to overcome specific problems and appealing to the smaller states to recognize that none had more to lose if the convention proved unable to preserve the union. The Committee of the Whole then voted 7 states to 3, with Maryland again divided, to adhere to the Virginia Plan. The delegates had needed less than three full days to reconfirm their general agreement that a purely federal reform, however thorough, could not meet the needs of union.

Little else, however, was decided by the vote of June 19, on which Connecticut had merely signaled its commitment to accommodation. As soon as the convention turned to the committee's resolutions, Lansing moved a substitute that would have vested legislative powers in a single house. Connecticut switched sides again to reproduce the characteristic 6-4-1 division: Massachusetts, Pennsylvania, and the four states south of the Potomac facing Connecticut, New York, New Jersey, and Delaware, with Maryland divided. Indeed, it soon became apparent that the conflict over representation overshadowed every lesser disagreement. The convention managed, with increasing difficulty, to confirm its preference for a bicameral regime. It voted once again for popular election of the lower house and state election of the upper. It reached agreement on a two-year term for representatives and six years for the senate. At every step, however, members fearful of a wholly national plan attempted to insert provisions that would give the states a larger role in paying or selecting federal officials. Small-state delegates attempted a variety of schemes that might disrupt the large-state coalition. Though Madison and Hamilton insisted that the small states need not fear a combination of the large, because the most important differences within the union were between the North and the South, William Samuel Johnson of Connecticut responded that a general government was being framed for states as well as people and that even Mason had admitted that the states should have some means to guarantee their rights and place within the system.

By the end of June, when the Convention voted 6-4-1 (as usual) for proportional representation in the lower house, the meeting was approaching dissolution. At this point Connecticut again proposed the compromise that Sherman had suggested weeks before, putting the proposal now in the language of an ultimatum. Remarking that the union might be "partly national," but should continue "partly federal" as well, Oliver Ellsworth said that he was not entirely disappointed that the meeting had approved proportional representation in the lower house, which would conform to national ideas and offer safety to the larger states. But he could see no ground for compromise and no alternative to the collapse of the convention and the union if the larger states would not concede an equal senate.

Madison and Wilson still refused to blink. "If the minority of the people of America refuse to coalesce with the majority on just and proper principles," the Pennsylvanian said, "a separation . . . could never happen on better grounds." Already, Madison complained, by voting that the upper house should be elected by the states, the meeting threatened to create a senate totally dependent on those bodies. If the states were also to be given equal votes, a small minority within the nation would retain the power to defeat every useful measure. Rufus King of Massachusetts also indicated his amazement that the smaller states were willing to renounce the prospect of a just and stable government "from an attachment to the ideal freedom and importance of *states*." "A government founded in a vicious principle of representation," King declared, "must be as short-lived as it would be unjust."

Gunning Bedford's sharp reply suggested that the next few days could settle the convention's fate. *"I do not, gentlemen, trust you,"* the Delaware attorney said. The coalition of the large states during the convention seemed to Bedford a sufficient warning of the consequences that could follow if the smaller states submitted to the "degradation" of the Virginia Plan, and he refused to be intimidated by the prospect that the large states would permit the union to collapse. "If they do," he warned, "the small ones will find some foreign ally . . . who will take them by the hand."

Bedford soon apologized for this remark, but his apology did not diminish its effects. Adjourning over Sunday, the convention moved without additional debate on Monday, July 2, to a decision on Connecticut's proposal. The motion for an equal senate failed on an even division: Connecticut, New York, New Jersey, Delaware, and Maryland, aye; Massachusetts, Pennsylvania, Virginia, North Carolina, and South Carolina, no; Georgia now divided. With the meeting at a deadlock and the large-state coalition showing obvious internal stress, Charles C. Pinckney recommended the appointment of a grand committee to devise a compromise. Only Madison and Wilson disapproved, fearing that the tide was turning irreversibly toward an accommodation — as, indeed, it was. Voting for a member from each state, the meeting chose a grand committee that included Ellsworth, Bedford, Paterson, Yates, and Martin, but not a single member from the larger states who had not hinted at a commitment to conciliation. The convention then adjourned till Thursday to celebrate the anniversary of Independence and permit the grand committee to prepare its plan.

To Madison and Wilson, the result was not a compromise at all, but a surrender to the smaller states — and one that seriously marred the symmetry of the evolving system. In exchange for equal representation in the upper house, the smaller states accepted proportional representation in the lower *and* agreed to give the lower house exclusive authority over money bills. This last provision, Madison and Wilson argued, might rob the senate of the power to restrain the lower house on matters where restraint was needed, but it would not prevent minorities from using their position in the senate to defeat the national will. Pleading with the smaller states to give up their demand for a concession plainly incompatible with democratic principles and larger federal powers, the leading nationalists continued to oppose the compromise throughout the next two weeks. They swam against a swelling current.

During these two weeks, the meeting saw a jumble of confusing motions and appointed two additional committees to distribute seats in the first house of representatives. Regional considerations, which had lurked beneath the early 6–4–1 divisions—in which all the southern states had voted with the large-state bloc—now bubbled to the surface. In arguments about a periodic census and admission of new states, as well as in maneuvers over seats in the lower house, members hostile to the three-fifths rule or fearful of the west confronted Southerners who realized that they would be outnumbered 8 to 5 in the projected senate and insisted on provisions that would guarantee their speedy reinforcement from the west, which was a southern section at that time. The smaller northern states proved willing to concede a little on these points in order to secure their more immediate objective. Meanwhile, it became increasingly apparent that several influential members from the larger states were less and less inclined toward a continued confrontation. Not only did they realize that the convention's work would surely be rejected if the smaller states walked out, but some of them conceded that a senate that would represent the states as states might help maintain a federal equilibrium while standing at a proper distance from the lower house. Genuine consolidationists were every bit as rare in the convention as were members who were totally opposed to the replacement of the Articles of Confederation. The moderates were moving to the front. George Mason said that he would "bury his bones in this city rather than expose his country to the consequences of a dissolution of the Convention without anything being done."

Sniffing the prevailing breeze, Yates and Lansing withdrew from the convention on July 11, depriving New York of its vote. (Hamilton had left some days before and would return, as a nonvoting member, only to be present at the finish.) Three days later, Wilson, Madison, and other foes of the committee's plan delivered last appeals for an alternative that would have minimized disparities between the states without conceding equal representation in the senate. Despite the absence of New York, this was defeated 6–4. On July 16, the convention voted 5–4–1 for the committee's compromise proposal: Connecticut, New Jersey, Delaware, Maryland, North Carolina, aye; Pennsylvania, Virginia, South Carolina, Georgia, no; Massachusetts divided.

The decision of July 16, as Randolph quickly noted, was not as narrow as the margin might suggest. New York, New Hampshire, and Rhode Island were unrepresented. All would probably have favored equal representation in at least one house. In addition, several moderates from Georgia, Pennsylvania, and Virginia sympathized with those in Massachusetts, Maryland, and North Carolina, who had voted for the Connecticut plan. The large states held a caucus in the aftermath of the decision. Wilson, Madison, and others still preferred to try to face the small states down. The caucus failed to reach agreement. All the members from the larger states returned to the convention, and the smaller states were satisfied from that point forward that opponents of the compromise would make no serious attempt to countermand the vote.

Randolph also said that the decision of July 16 "embarrassed the business extremely." Every previous decision, he explained, had been directly influenced by the supposition that proportional representation would prevail in both branches of the legislature; all would have to be thought through again in light of this new ruling. The implications, for that matter, were even more profound than the Virginian immediately perceived. With the adoption of the Great (or Connecticut) Compromise, every delegate was forced to make new calculations as to how the actions of the central government might touch his state or section. Assured an equal vote in one part of the Congress, the members from the smaller middle states, as Dickinson had predicted, immediately began to favor ample federal powers. Southerners, by contrast, suddenly became more wary, especially of the enormous powers that the gathering had earlier intended for the senate. Madison and Wilson, who had disapproved not merely state equality but any role for the state legislatures in selecting national officials or making national decisions, were compelled to come to terms with the convention's ruling that the new regime would not be wholly national in structure. As Madison would put it after the convention ended, the delegates were working now to frame a government that would be neither national nor federal, but a novelty compounded of elements of both. And none of them could fully understand what this unprecedented compound would be like.

Amazingly, on first appearances at least, the members needed only ten more days to reach agreement on the basic features of the Constitution. As Randolph failed to see, however, the decision that the general government would represent both individuals and states prepared the way for resolution of more than just the conflict over representation. Both the large states and the small, the North together with the South, could now anticipate control of one part of the legislature. With every state and section armed with a capacity to counter threats to its essential interests, every delegate felt freer to address the national ills that none of them denied. Almost all the delegates had made it clear by now that they intended to define a middle ground between the ineffectuality of the confederation and excessive concentration of authority in central hands. Nearly all agreed, as well, that what they wanted in a senate was a body that would stand at a sufficient distance from the people or the lower house to check majority oppression, yet one that would be wholly democratic in its derivation. With the ruling that the upper house would represent the states, whose legislatures would select its members, the delegates had satisfied demands for more protection for states' rights. They had also reconfirmed a mode of indirect election that promised to secure the senate's independence from the lower house without provoking popular suspicions. Cutting through a thicket of entangled problems, the compromise permitted the convention to resume a path along which arguments among its members could again be guided by their general agreements.

This is not to say that the completion of the work proved quick and easy. Several complicated passages remained, and more than one debate became quite heated. Yet none of the remaining difficulties blocked the members' progress as completely as the conflict over representation, and nearly everyone appears to have assumed that the convention would succeed.

Among remaining difficulties, the most perplexing centered on the powers and selection of the chief executive. From July 17 through July 25, the convention literally revolved around these questions, which were rendered formidable because most delegates were dedicated to a complex, balanced government, yet reasoned from a heritage in which the influence and ambitions of executives had always been identified as constant dangers to a balanced system. Under the Virginia Resolutions, as modified by the Committee of the Whole, the head of the executive would be elected by the national legislature for a single term of seven years. Seconded by Morris, Wilson powerfully opposed both the election by the legislature, which might end in the executive's dependence on that body, and the ineligibility for reelection, which could remove a strong incentive to good conduct and deprive the nation of the services of an experienced and able man. The Pennsylvanians argued that election by the people might remove these difficulties. Pennsylvania was the only state, however, to favor this proposal on July 17. A large majority in the convention doubted that the people had the information or ability to make a wise selection. Many delegates, moreover, led by Mason, were concerned that a reeligible executive would prove, in practice, an executive for life. The convention reaffirmed election by the legislature, struck the clause confining the executive to a single term, agreed that this would probably result in an improper link between the branches, moved to an election by electors chosen by the local legislatures, and then moved back again to an election by the Congress. By the 24th, as Gerry put it, the members seemed "entirely at a loss."

Madison reviewed the options on the 25th. Election by the legislature, he explained, might introduce intrigues and render the executive incapable of acting as a check on legislative usurpations — plainly so if the executive was eligible for reelection. Election by the local legislatures or the state executives, however, might introduce the influence of the very bodies whose "pernicious measures" the convention still intended to control. Two alternatives remained: election by electors chosen by the people, which had been suggested on July 19 by King and Paterson, but handily defeated; or direct election by the people, which he had come to favor but which seemed to put the smaller states, together with the South, at a considerable disadvantage. Hugh Williamson (North Carolina) suggested that the disadvantage to the smaller states could be corrected if the people were required to vote for more than a single candidate. Morris added that the citizens might cast two ballots, one of which would have to be for someone from another state. Yet, reinforced by Gerry, Mason still insisted that the people were *least* qualified to make a good selection. On the 26th the meeting came full circle to the proposition with which it had started: selection by the national legislature for a single term.

Few were really satisfied with this "solution." The Pennsylvanians, who had argued for a powerful, reeligible executive since the beginning of the meeting, had been winning influential converts, of whom Madison was probably the most important. The major architect of the Virginia Plan had entered the convention sharing much of the traditional suspicion of a strong executive. But as he listened to the Pennsylvanians and struggled to adjust to the decision on the senate, which he considered both undemocratic and a barrier to the pursuit of national interests, Madison supported an attempt to switch the power to appoint ambassadors and judges from the senate to the head of the executive, acting with concurrence of a portion of the upper house. Discontent with state equality, fear of legislative domination, and a wish to make it possible for an experienced executive to succeed himself, which seemed impossible to reconcile with legislative choice, were moving Madison and other large-state nationalists toward popular election and larger executive powers. Yet fear of an elective monarchy, distrust of popular election, and sheer impatience to complete the meeting's tasks still counterbalanced these considerations. On July 24, the House had chosen a Committee of Detail to put its resolutions into order. Now, the members eagerly agreed to an adjournment until Monday, August 6, in order to allow ten days for this committee to report.

While Washington went fishing and visited the old encampment at Valley Forge, John Rutledge (South Carolina), Edmund Randolph, Nathaniel Gorham (Massachusetts), Oliver Ellsworth, and James Wilson assumed responsibility for much more than a careful ordering of the decisions reached in the convention by July 26. In sessions from which only fragmentary records still survive, the Committee of Detail apparently assumed — without objection from their tiring colleagues — that they were free to make significant contributions of their own. Taking note of nearly everything that had transpired in the course of the deliberations, the committee added numerous details to the convention's resolutions and offered several significant additions. Besides providing more elaborate descriptions of executive and judicial powers, their report advanced a new procedure for resolving arguments among the states and recommended that agreement by two-thirds of Congress should be necessary for admission of new states or passage of commercial regulations. It inserted prohibitions of a tax on exports or on interference with the slave trade, which Pinckney had demanded as conditions for his state's agreement. Most significant of all, it offered an enumeration of the powers of the central government, a matter that the full convention had repeatedly postponed, and introduced a range of prohibitions on the sort of local legislation that Madison had planned to counter by a federal veto on state laws, a power that the full convention had decisively refused.

All of August was consumed in close consideration of the work of the Committee of Detail, most of it on two related issues which produced quite different divisions. Reluctant to resume the tedious debate on the executive, the delegates postponed this matter until all the other articles could be considered. Assisted by their broad agreement on the nation's needs and by their general alarm about majority abuses, they reached agreement relatively quickly on the prohibitions on the states and most of the enumerated powers of the Congress. But Morris, Madison, and Wilson had objected from the start to the provision in the Connecticut Compromise that gave the lower house exclusive power over revenues; and the Committee of Detail had given in completely to the South's demands for prohibition of a tax on exports, prohibition of congressional taxation of or interference with the international slave trade, and requirement of a two-thirds vote in Congress for commercial regulations. Opposition mounted day by day to all of these concessions.

On August 8 the smaller middle states joined nationalists in Pennsylvania and Virginia to strike the clause concerning money bills. Insisting that the clause had been a valuable concession from the smaller states, denouncing the involvement in taxation of a body that would not directly represent the people, Mason, Randolph, Williamson, and others bitterly objected, warning that it might compel them to retract their unenthusiastic willingness to go along with state equality in the upper house. Attempting to protect the compromise on which the hopes of the convention now depended, Caleb Strong of Massachusetts moved that money bills might be amended by the senate, but would have to be originated in the lower house. With many delegations thoroughly confused by the variety of questions that had come to be encompassed in this issue, the convention narrowly decided to postpone Strong's motion.

On August 8 all three of the New England delegations voted with the worried Southerners to keep the clause on money bills. From that day forward, compromisers in these Yankee delegations struggled to secure the vital interests of their section without provoking a significant secession by the South. Seconded by Morris, Rufus King condemned the plan of the Committee of Detail as so unreasonably biased in favor of the South that Northerners would justifiably reject it. For purposes of representation, King and Morris pointed out, the Southerners could count three-fifths of their slaves, and it was little consolation that the three-fifths rule would also be applied for purposes of direct taxation, which might never be employed. Hating slavery in any case, King and Morris were infuriated by the prohibitions on congressional interference with new importations and by the ban on export taxes. The Constitution, they protested, would commit the North to defend the South, which would be free not only to increase the evil but to shield the products of slave labor from taxation. Meanwhile, the requirement that two-thirds of Congress would be necessary to impose commercial regulations would impede the very national actions in the area of trade that were among the most important reasons why the shipping states, with their depressed economies, favored constitutional reform.

Complicated, often heated arguments concerning these provisions dominated the convention through the second half of August. Though Madison and Wilson joined with King and Morris to condemn the ban on export taxes, protesting that it would deny the government an easy source of revenues and an important weapon in its efforts to compel the Europeans to relax their navigation laws, the planting states were virtually unanimous in their insistence on this prohibition. Georgia and the Carolinas, though opposed by the Virginians as well as by the antislavery members from the North, were equally insistent on prohibiting congressional restrictions on the slave trade, making this an absolute condition of their states' approval of a plan. On August 21 the compromisers from Connecticut and Massachusetts voted with the Southerners to reaffirm the prohibition of a tax on exports, 7 states to 4 (New Hampshire, New Jersey, Pennsylvania, Delaware, no). Sherman, Gerry, Ellsworth, Gorham, and their colleagues indicated, though, that they expected their conciliatory efforts to be met in kind, that they had voted to accept the South's demands in expectation that the Southerners would now prove willing to protect New England's vital interests. On August 22 Morris moved referral of the slave trade, export taxes, and commercial regulation to another grand committee, where these subjects might provide materials for a "bargain" between the North and the South. Several Southerners approved.

The August compromise between the North and the South, Massachusetts and South Carolina, was second in importance only to the bargain of July 16 to the completion of the Constitution. On August 24 the grand committee chaired by William Livingston of New Jersey reported a proposal to prohibit legislative interference with the slave trade until the year 1800, to reaffirm the ban on export taxes, but to strike the clause requiring two-thirds of Congress for the passage of commercial regulations. On August 25, Pinckney moved extension of the prohibition until 1808, Gorham seconded the motion, and the prohibition carried 7 states to (New Jersey, Pennsylvania, Delaware, Virginia, no). Several Southerners continued to oppose control of trade by a majority in Congress, where they would be outvoted in both houses. This asked the South, said Mason, to "deliver themselves bound hand and foot to the Eastern states." It "would complete the deformity" of a system "so odious," objected Randolph, that he might be forced to disapprove it. Despite their fierce resistance, South Carolina abided by its bargain. A motion to reinstitute the two-thirds rule failed 4 to 7 with only Maryland, Virginia, North Carolina, and Georgia voting for it. Then, on August 31, on Sherman's motion, the convention voted to refer all postponed questions to still another grand committee. The procedure had become the members' standard strategy for handling issues too complex or too divisive for resolution by the whole.

Chaired by David Brearley of New Jersey, the Committee on Unfinished Business (or on Postponed Parts) untangled the convention's last remaining snarls, the knottiest of which was certainly the long-debated question of a sound executive. Having each secured supremacy in one house of the Congress, both the small and the large states had proved determined not to give the other a predominant advantage in selecting the chief magistrate. Fear of legislative dominance or of corrupting links between the branches, along with the desire to make it possible for the executive to succeed himself, had seriously discredited appointment by the Congress. To this expedient, however, the convention had reluctantly returned. Although the dominance of smaller states in the projected senate had encouraged several large-state nationalists to favor more executive authority — the Committee on Unfinished Business gave the president the leading role in making treaties as well as in appointment of ambassadors and judges — fear of an elective monarchy and strong objections to election either by the people or the states had brought the meeting to an impasse. Provisions that appeared to favor the selection of an able man seemed inconsistent with his reelection. The vigor and stability demanded by the Pennsylvanians seemed incompatible to some with popular election, to others with a due republican suspicion of this branch. Theoretical disputes were complicated by the lingering suspicions of the large and smaller states.

Reporting on September 4 and drawing on the meeting's previous debates, especially on the exchanges of July 25, the Brearley committee sought to cut this knot by recommending an election for a four-year term by electors chosen in such manner as the local legislatures should direct. Each state would be entitled to as many electors as the total of its seats in Congress, and each elector would cast two ballots, at least one of which would have to be for someone from another state. If a single candidate obtained an absolute majority of the electors' votes, he would be president. If not, the president would be elected by the senate from the five who had the highest totals. (In either case, the person placing second in the voting would become vice-president, an office first suggested and defined by this committee.) Both the cumbersome procedure and the introduction of an officer who was essentially superfluous were carefully contrived to balance the demands of the larger and smaller states. Reliance on electors, as committee member Sherman soon explained, would "get rid of the ineligibility" for reelection, which had seemed inseparable from an election by Congress. In addition, Sherman might have said, opponents of election by the people and opponents of election by the states could both find solace in a mode of indirect election that might start with either, yet secure a certain independence of them both.

Some of these details proved problematic. Assuming that the college of electors would seldom show an absolute majority for any single person, most members realized that the committee's plan was meant to give the larger states the largest role in making a preliminary nomination, from which the senate, dominated by the smaller states, would make the final choice. Since the smaller states would have a disproportionate advantage even in the number of electors, several members from the larger states objected that the senate should be forced to choose from fewer nominees. Others argued that selection by the senate, whose cooperation with the president would be required for treaties and appointments, would encourage these two branches to combine against the lower house. In an excellent example of the way in which the delegates had periodically applied collective wisdom to a common problem, these difficulties were resolved by shifting final choice of the executive from the senate to the house of representatives, which would vote by states on this occasion, and by narrowing to three the individuals from among whom the selection must be made.

Several delegates were still concerned about the way in which the president and senate would combine in making treaties and appointments. On September 7, Mason, Wilson, Madison, and Dickinson all favored the revival of a privy council to assist and check the head of the executive in matters where these functions had been trusted to the senate. This was easily defeated, though the members did attempt to reconcile opponents of a senate role in framing money bills by passing Caleb Strong's suggestion of a clause requiring lower-house origination, but permitting upper-house amendment. By September 8 the House was ready to confide a finished plan to a Committee of Style. There, with help from Johnson, Hamilton, Madison, and King, Gouverneur Morris imparted final polish to the phrasing.

September 10 saw final pleas for reconsideration of some features over which several members had become increasingly alarmed. Randolph said that he had introduced "a set of republican propositions" on May 29, but that these resolutions had been so disfigured in the course of the convention that he might "dissent" from the completed plan unless the meeting would provide that state conventions could propose amendments to a second general convention, whose alterations would be final. Sharing Randolph's dread of hazy wording and majority control of commerce, together with his fear that an objectionable senate might combine with a powerful executive to overbalance the people's representatives in the lower house, Mason argued on September 12 that the convention also ought to add a bill of rights. Gerry readily agreed.

Responding partly to these fears, the members did consent to substitute two-thirds of Congress for the three-fourths previously required to override a presidential veto. But with Sherman pointing out that nothing in the Constitution would repeal state declarations or infringe the liberties that they protected, the states unanimously declined to draft a bill of rights. As the convention speedily considered the report of the Committee of Style — obviously eager to adjourn, repeatedly refusing to consider major changes — the final drama was at hand. Mason failed to win insertion of a clause requiring two-thirds of the Congress for the passage of commercial regulations until 1808 (by which date, he may have hoped, the planting states would get their reinforcements from the west). Randolph moved again for a procedure under which the plan would not be ratified until a second general convention could consider changes recommended by the state conventions, warning that he could not sign without some such provision. Concluding that the finished plan "would end either in monarchy or a tyrannical aristocracy," Mason followed with a similar pronouncement, as did Gerry. Randolph's motion was unanimously defeated. Every delegation present voted to approve the finished Constitution and to order it engrossed.

On September 17, Benjamin Franklin, who was eighty-one and so enfeebled that James Wilson read his speeches for him, intervened once more, as he had done at several anxious moments, to plead with everyone who still retained objections to "doubt a little of his own infallibility" and join in signing. Hamilton appealed for unanimity as well, observing that "no man's ideas were more remote from the plan than his own were known to be," but that he could not hesitate "between anarchy and confusion on one side and the chance of good . . . on the other." No one, to be sure, had gotten everything he wanted in the course of the convention. No one, four months earlier, had entered the convention able to conceive the sort of Constitution that the members' compromises and collective wisdom had created. No one fully understood as yet — not even Hamilton or Madison — that the collective reasoning of the convention, together with the clashing interests of its delegations, had resulted in a system that would prove not only adequate to the exigencies of union but capable of serving as a new foundation for significant revision of the theory of constitutional democracy. Of the forty-two still present on September 17, however, all but three felt able to subscribe their names to the completed work. Whereupon, as Washington confided to his diary, "the members adjourned to the City Tavern, dined together, and took a cordial leave," nearly all of them agreeing with the venerated Franklin that the emblem on the chair in which the general had presided over their deliberations — testifying by his presence to the gravity of the occasion and the possibility that great executive authority might be entrusted to great virtue — was, indeed, a *rising* sun.

A SYSTEM WITHOUT PRECEDENT: FEDERALISM IN THE AMERICAN CONSTITUTION

MICHAEL P. ZUCKERT

When the Constitution was up for debate in 1787–1788 those who favored ratification called themselves "Federalists" and those who opposed it were called "Anti-Federalists."[1] Federalism thus appears to have been the issue around which the controversy over the Constitution turned. Many years later, James Madison underscored the centrality of federalism in an essay he prepared to stand as the preface to his notes on the Proceedings of the Constitutional Convention.

> It remains for the British colonies, now United States, of North America, to add to those examples [of ancient and modern confederacies], one of a more interesting character than any of them: which led to a system without a precedent ancient or modern, a system founded on popular rights, and so combining the federal form with the forms of individual Republics, as may enable each to supply the defects of the other and obtain the advantages of both.

The Americans, Madison implies, did not invent the federal form itself, but their creation of a federal system "without a precedent ancient or modern" was their most notable achievement. Their unprecedented system emerged from a number of innovations the Americans, under the tutelage of Madison, introduced into the federal models they inherited. In explaining those innovations I hope, at the same time, to clarify the connection of American federalism to the "precedents," the most important of which was, surprisingly, the British empire against which the colonists had rebelled a decade earlier.

Conventional wisdom explains Madison's claims to novelty in terms of the now well-worn distinction between federalism and confederalism. Both combine a central government with local governments that are not merely subordinate units of the central government, as they would be under a unitary or simply national government. In a confederal system, however, the government of the confederacy, or general government as we shall call it here, represents and acts solely on the member states in their corporate capacity. In a classical federal system, by contrast, the general government acts on individual human citizens and not on the subordinate levels of government; at the same time, its individual citizens and its member states are both represented in it. Like most conventional wisdom, this contains much truth; but, we must note at the outset, this usage of ours is not the usage of the founding generation nor of those who considered the issue of federalism before them. In Madison's "Preface," for example, he clearly uses "federal" and "confederal" as synonyms, a practice Martin Diamond has documented as universal at the time. We will never understand the Framers' achievement if we listen to their language with twentieth-century ears.[2]

The prevailing theoretical statement on federalism at the time of the founding was no doubt that contained in Book IX of Montesquieu's *Spirit of the Laws:* to that discussion both Federalists and Anti-Federalists adverted in order to find a touchstone by which to measure the proposed Constitution. Montesquieu had captured the dominant idea of federalism when he wrote of it as "an agreement by which several small states agree to become members of a larger one. . . . It is a kind of society of societies." The members or citizens of the federal societies are the smaller societies, and not the individuals who in turn compose the smaller societies. Beyond that fundamental point, however, Montesquieu himself treats federations very flexibly. For example, he commends the Lycian republic as the "model of an excellent confederate republic," even though that confederacy violated many of the principles later held to be fundamental to the federal form: the Lycian member cities did not have equal votes in the general government, and even more strikingly, the general government appointed the judges and city magistrates in the member cities. These features led even Madison to wonder about Lycia: "the name of a federal republic may be refused" to it.

Madison's doubts reflected more adequately the status of opinion in America than did Montesquieu's flexibility, for by 1776, the time of the drafting of the Articles of Confederation, Americans had adopted a rather rigid approach to federalism. In the context of Montesquieu's discussion and of the historical evidence of the variable character of historical confederacies (as unearthed by Madison in his researches, "On Ancient and Modern Confederacies," and displayed by Madison and Hamilton in *The Federalist* #18–20), the most striking characteristic of the confederacy the Americans first made was neither its strength relative to other confederacies (as some scholars maintain) nor its weakness (as the Federalists maintained), but rather its rigid adherence to a set of principles taken to embody the essential characteristics of confederacies. Those principles derived in large part from the lessons Americans believed they had learned in the intense struggle with Britain leading up to the Declaration of Independence.

Where Montesquieu had been content to leave the federal principle at "a society of societies," without specifying too closely any necessary mode of relations among the member societies, the Americans in the second Article of Confederation insisted on explicitly recognizing the "sovereignty, freedom, and independence" of the member states. By contrast, Montesquieu nowhere affirms the sovereignty of the members (although he does not deny it either). Indeed, he speaks of confederates as "deprived of the executive and legislative power," a description that seems to imply suspension or surrender of sovereignty.

The insistence on state sovereignty not only reflects the pride and self-assertion of the newly independent (or aspiring to be independent) states but it also recapitulates ten years of constitutional conflict with Britain. The doctrine of sovereignty holds that in any political community there must be a supreme, uncontrollable, undivided, absolute, and even arbitrary power. As the seventeenth-century French thinker D'Oyseau put it, the idea of supremacy necessarily implies that there can be "no degrees of superiority," a thought echoed during the British–American conflict by Samuel Johnson: "In sovereignty, there are no gradations." The power or right to give law, the characteristic of the state, implies or derives from "supremacy"; that power or right cannot be controlled or controllable, for then the controller would be "supreme" over the controlled; there can then be no enforcement of limits on the sovereign power. For all practical purposes the sovereign power is absolute and arbitrary. As Martin Howard, a Parliamentary sympathizer, said during the Stamp Act crisis in 1765: "It is of the essence of government, that there should be a supreme head, and it would be a solecism in politicks to talk of members independent of it."

The medieval struggle between sacred and secular authorities had led to the initial emergence of the doctrine of sovereignty, and the struggles between Crown and Parliament in seventeenth-century England ultimately committed Britain to a doctrine of parliamentary sovereignty. It was as though the very idea of sovereignty had a Midas-like power to transform whatever it touched, for the Parliamentary party, at first only attempting to redress or restore the constitutional order unbalanced by the Stuarts and to resist the claims to sovereignty raised by Stuart spokesmen, ended up claiming for itself the powers it denied the king.

That same Midas power was visible in the colonial contests preceding the American Revolution. The most common American position, up until around 1774, was to dodge the issue of sovereignty. "Tacitly acknowledging that by accepted definition sovereignty was both absolute and arbitrary, but convinced nevertheless that there were things that Parliament could not rightly do," says Bernard Bailyn, the Americans "set out, silent on the metaphysics of the problem, to locate pragmatically a line of separation between powers of Parliament that were valid when exercised in America and those that were not." [3] At first, then, American opinion was not dominated by the logical juggernaut of sovereignty. As the conflict wore on, however, they too fell under the sway of the idea of sovereignty. But they refused to concede the British position. If sovereignty there must be, then, agreed the Americans, Parliament cannot be the possessor of it. The Americans insisted that political power as such must be understood as subordinate to and for the sake of security of rights. Under the conditions of life in the British empire, recognition of parliamentary sovereignty did not promise to conduce to the ends of government, for the governed could act adequately without the governors in that large and distant empire. Sovereignty therefore must lie elsewhere — not in Parliament, but in agencies more politically responsible to the community. The legislative power must lie in the colonial legislatures. Not Parliament but the king was the head and unifying force of the empire.[4] This "mature" constitutional position was premised on an acceptance of the logic of sovereignty, as well as certain views of the necessity of republican control of government. It was not possible to recognize a general authority in Parliament, certainly not a general "supremacy" from which one could make exceptions or around which one could draw limits. Only that parliamentary legislation which the Americans voluntarily accepted had any validity.

By the time they came to make their new confederation, the Americans had thus come to interpret the empire as itself a confederacy of a certain sort — although in many ways an imperfect one. The empire was a unit composed of separate and independent political entities, sharing a common king, but possessing separate legislative authorities. The imperial federation possessed an agent, Parliament, with very limited, consent-based legislative power for the confederation as a whole. That authority at most extended to matters of genuine common concern to all the members, for example, regulations of the commerce of the whole.

Since the Americans, under the aegis of the idea of sovereignty, had reinterpreted the empire as a certain sort of confederacy, it is no wonder that when they had a freer hand they constructed, under the aegis of the same idea, a particularly pure or principled sort of "society of societies." They bannered the principle of sovereignty in Section II of the Articles of Confederation, preceded only by the article giving the name of the confederation. The concern with sovereignty went much deeper than mere declarations, however. The Articles created a system especially scrupulous in treating its member states as its citizens, treating them as sovereign entities in their own right. Each state was therefore equal in political rights in the confederacy. Changes in the terms of the agreement, that is, amendments to the Articles, required unanimity. Article III stated the purpose of the confederacy: the states created a "firm league of friendship," for the sake of "their common defense, the security of their [the states'] liberties, and their [again, the states'] mutual and general welfares." How the last two goals were understood is made clear in Article III's statement that the states bind themselves "to assist each other against all force . . . or attacks made upon them. . . ." The powers of the general government and limitations on the states correspond to this statement of purposes — powers of war and peace and treating with foreign nations belong more or less exclusively to the general government; internal matters, even many that are relevant to matters entrusted to the general government (for example, raising armies) belong to the states. In carving out these spheres of concern for each level of government, the Articles follow scrupulously Montesquieu's observations that confederations are the mode by which republics can generate "the external force of a monarchical government" while maintaining "all the internal advantages of a republican" government. So dominated by the idea of sovereignty was the constitution of the confederacy that its government even lacked powers, arguably for the "mutual and general welfare" of the member states, that had been frequently if not universally granted to Parliament under the reinterpreted imperial confederacy. The power to regulate commerce was such a power, the lack of which later contributed to the failure of the confederation.

The mode of operation and the system of construction of the confederal government faithfully reflected the commitment to the purist federalism animating the whole. If the system could be called a government at all, then, to paraphrase Lincoln, it was government of the states, by the states, and for the states. It was government of the states because the confederacy respected the federal idea in acting principally on or through the states "in their corporate capacity." The general government had responsibility for matters of peace and war, but had no control of the instrumentalities of peace and war, depending entirely on requisitions or requests to the states for men and money. Indeed, so sovereignty-obsessed was the Articles system that the very name of government could be denied to it in *The Federalist* #15:

> Government implies the power of making laws. It is essential to the idea of a law, that it be attended with a sanction; or, in other words, a penalty or punishment for disobedience. If there be no penalty annexed to disobedience, the resolutions or commands which pretend to be law will, in fact, amount to nothing more than advice or recommendation.

With no enforcement power, it is probably too much even to say that the Articles set up a central system with powers in certain areas; rather, it set up a structure with a certain range of concerns, or objects, the powers to effect which remained with the states, acting voluntarily under a certain moral obligation (cf. Article XIII) but with nothing legally or practically enforceable in that obligation.

The structure established embodied the same architectural principle. Lacking an enforcement function, it lacked any enforcement agencies, that is, it had no proper executive or judiciary institutions. Lacking a true legislative power, its sole constitutional agency, the Congress, had more the character of an assemblage of delegates from the individual states than of a true legislative body. The delegates were agents of, appointed by, sent to serve at the pleasure of, and paid by their states. Delegates even lacked seats of their own — each state was to have at least two and no more than seven members in its delegation, although each state was to have but one vote, no matter what size its delegation. Finally, the Articles "government" was made a creature of the states in the deepest way: the Articles had no higher legal status than any ordinary piece of legislation passed by a state legislature.

As an intellectual fabric the Articles of Confederation possessed an austere beauty, deriving from the consistency and purity of the logic of its construction. It became, in the minds of students of politics for all time after, the very model of the confederate principle, an honor it does not deserve if it is viewed in the light of previous experience and theory; but it too shows the power of that transformative idea of sovereignty, which made over the idea of federalism and gave to the world a beautiful model of pure federalism.

Unfortunately, it did not work. Not only the Federalists but even those who became Anti-Federalists conceded that the system required remodeling. The story both of the failures of the confederacy and of the efforts to reform it has been told so many times it need not be recounted here. But the source of the failure and the source of the beauty of the confederation surely were the same — the sovereignty-intoxicated political vision of the Revolutionary generation. A successful remodeling of the union would require, at the minimum, a taming of sovereignty.

We must guard against a facile assumption of the inevitability of reform — either that it would occur at all, or that the federalism "without precedent, ancient or modern" would emerge. The more natural idea for reform, an idea that was appearing around the continent, would have kept the essentially federal character of the confederacy but would have transformed it into a genuine government by arming the general government with enforcement powers and a few other substantive powers, in particular a power to regulate commerce. For the most part, this agenda of reform was later embodied in the New Jersey Plan presented to the Constitutional Convention as a less daring departure from the existing confederacy than the plan drafted by James Madison and presented by the Virginia delegation. Those reforms, however extreme the prospect of the general government's calling upon armed force against recalcitrant states may appear, remained firmly federal systems — governments of the states, by the states, and for the states. That America did not make the experiment of this alternate version of the new, pure federalism is due to James Madison.

In order to bring forth the newer federalism, the idea of sovereignty that lay beneath the Articles of Confederation needed to be tamed. James Madison, who made the decisive contribution to the new federalism, did not begin his rethinking of the issue with sovereignty, however, but only, in effect, ended up there after he had traversed his new path; and then he was able to deal with sovereignty almost as an afterthought.

Madison had spent most of the 1780s as a delegate to the Articles Congress and had experienced first-hand what *The Federalist* called its "imbecility." Already in 1783, the Articles barely in operation, Madison called for a reform of the union. He took it for granted that the revolution had produced "separate sovereignties of our respective states," that they were "different states." He likewise took it for granted that reform required not something drastically different from this, but rather an effective version of what America already had. The point of departure for Madison, then, was the federal idea of union of the sovereign states as states.

Convinced of the necessity of reform of the confederacy Madison undertook a systematic survey of the theory and practice of federations in history. In the course of his studies, he grasped the flexible Montesquieuan approach to federal systems. Montesquieu was liberating for Madison but seems to have provided little help beyond that. As we have seen, Madison seemed genuinely puzzled over whether Montesquieu had any firm criteria for the federal form.

More important, however, Madison came to have more radical doubts about historical confederacies than Montesquieu expressed. The French philosopher had not only praised the Lycian confederacy but also the Dutch and Swiss confederacies, both of which Madison found to be very defective. By the time he wrote *The Federalist,* Madison could forcefully assert that the past experience of confederacies "can furnish no other light than that of beacons, which give warning of the course to be shunned, without pointing out that which ought to be pursued." The first "beacon" Madison seems to have discovered was that confederations have an irresistible centrifugal force which fatally weakens them. They neither provide the defensive strength small republics require nor do they make for internal harmony among the member states, nor do they last very long. Their apparent successes are often due to accidental circumstances, like the geographic situation of the Swiss. But Madison also discovered political forces that tend to overcome these centrifugal pulls, for example, the role of the *stadhouder* (the executive) in the Dutch republic. Unfortunately, Madison saw, those forces exact their own price, in the Dutch case, for example, endangering republicanism through the development of an overswollen hereditary executive power.

Madison's retrospective statement in his "Preface" captures very well what the task must have appeared to him to be on the basis of his intensive consideration of the federal experience — to develop a new kind of federalism that succeeds where others had failed but that does so with "a system founded on popular rights," that is, a system itself republican and in which republicanism remains secure. Madison saw that this required new departures in three areas: (1) the development of a compound system in which the federal ends of union are achieved by an unprecedented kind of structure, operating in a wholly novel way; we might describe this as the realization of the need for novel national means to achieve traditional federal ends; (2) the development of explicit devices for umpiring the different elements of the new complex system, in particular the relations among the component states and between them and the general government: we might call this the need for new federal means to achieve newly realized federal ends; and (3) the development of altogether novel devices within the federal system to solve the internal problems of republicanism, which, Madison believed, had to his time resisted resolution in both theory and practice; we might call this the use of novel federal means to achieve novel national ends. The Constitution produced by the Constitutional Convention did not perfectly embody the new federalism he projected, but its features can best be understood as modifications of his plans.

A COMPOUND SYSTEM: NATIONAL MEANS TO FEDERAL ENDS

Madison, and many others in the 1780s, realized that government under the Articles of Confederation was not going well. The system depended on the voluntary compliance of the states, which all too often was not forthcoming. Madison traced that failing to the "want of sanction to the laws and of coercion in the government of the confederacy." So serious did Madison see this latter problem to be that he denied the very name of a "political constitution" to the Articles: "Under the form of such a constitution, it is in fact nothing more than a treaty of amity of commerce and of alliance, between independent and sovereign states." But unlike most, Madison did not limit himself to recommending the obvious remedy of arming the general government with coercive powers to enforce its determinations on the states. In his earliest thinking on the subject he did in fact recommend that expedient, but he also proposed, far more radically, that the general government be transformed into a full-scale government, with its own executive and judicial agencies, so that it could enforce its own laws, with its own institutions, directly on the citizens. The received wisdom that focuses on the last point correctly emphasizes the importance of that great innovation, but misses the point that it is but one part of a broader conception. The general government is to be, so far as possible, a self-contained system, drawing its powers and personnel directly from the people, and operating directly on them. The key is avoiding the intermediation of the states in any form, either in the composition of the general government or in its operation.

Madison made the great leap to this very different kind of federal structure because he came to a deeper-going diagnosis of the defects of the confederation (and of confederacies in general) than his contemporaries. As Hamilton states the point in *The Federalist* #15: "The great and radical vice in the construction of the existing Confederation is the principle of LEGISLA-

TION for STATES or GOVERNMENTS, in their CORPORATE or COLLECTIVE CAPACITIES, and as contradistinguished from the INDIVIDUALS of which they consist." The great and radical vice" was the federal principle itself, or the federal principle as it had come to be understood by 1776. Merely arming the general government with coercive powers to be employed "in the federal manner" would not remedy the root problem, and, indeed, might make matters worse. Governor Edmund Randolph of Virginia, at the Constitutional Convention one of the chief spokesmen for the Madisonian system, identified some of the problems with the use of coercion against the states: "Coercion he pronounced to be impracticable, expensive, cruel to individuals. It tended also to habituate the instruments of it to shed the blood and riot in the spoils of their fellow citizens, and consequently trained them up for the service of ambition." Every effort to enforce the laws must threaten civil war; every threat of civil war must be a temptation to leave the laws unenforced; the end result of coercive federalism is either widespread violence or widespread evasion of the law. Neither would be better than the situation prevailing under the Articles.

Not that the Framers believed recourse to coercion inappropriate or unnecessary. Neither individuals nor collective bodies like states can be expected to comply with law unless law is supported by coercion. To say nothing of other reasons, Madison and his fellows understood what is now called the "free-rider" problem: it may be the common interest of all to obey the law, or to make one's fair contribution to the whole, but it is even more to one's advantage to be a "free-rider," that is, to derive the benefits of the compliance or contributions of others without oneself complying or contributing. It is thus rational for all parties to avoid their obligations to the common good. Not a pretty conclusion about human nature, but, as Madison asked in *The Federalist* #51, "What is government itself but the greatest of all reflections on human nature? If men were angels, no government would be necessary."

Coercion there must be, therefore; coercion against the states as such is singularly ineffective, however. The great advantage of applying coercion against individuals rather than against states is the relative weakness of the former, which makes such coercion far more effective, for then the organized force of the community faces the puniness of the individual.

Not only must effective law be law operating on individuals but the agencies that make and enforce this law must also be constructed on the basis of independence from the states so far as possible. The states, as collective entities, possess common interests, it is true, in the goods of the union, but they have their separate and partial interests as well. Among these separate interests are the stakes the officeholders in the states have in the structures from which they derive power. That centrifugal tendency which one observes in all federal systems "has its origin in the love of power. Power controlled or abridged is almost always the rival and enemy of that power by which it is controlled or abridged." State agency in the operation or structure of the general government thus involves entrenching potential or even likely enemies in the midst of the system, which enemies would further the centrifugal tendencies in need of curbing.

The result of this line of thought was the development of a new theory of federalism, as pure in its way as the older doctrinaire theory on which the Articles had been constructed. The system as a whole remains federal, that is, a "state of states," in which the general government serves the common ends or purposes of the member states and not directly the ends of the individuals who compose the member states. The "subordinate" or local units are not legally derivative from or subject to overriding sovereign control by the general government. In these respects, the new federalism is as much a federal system as the old confederacy was; it is not a "national" or "unitary" or, in the language of the eighteenth century, a "consolidated system" in which the central government is simply supreme over the constituent parts.[5]

The federal character is to inhere in the system as a whole, however, and not in the constitution or operation of the general government itself. The general government is to be purely national, that is, operating on and through individuals, in its construction and operation. The states are to be by-passed entirely — neither acting upon nor acted on by the general government. In addition to its own institutions of government, then, the general government also requires a set of powers adequate to its responsibilities. The powers of the general government must be sufficient for it to carry out its tasks without recourse to the states. In particular, the general government must have access of its own to men and money; the single most important new power given to the general government in the Constitution is the general power to raise revenue entirely independently of the states.

Thus the compound system contains two sets of governments ruling over the same population and territory, dividing up the objects of concern between them with each set of governments possessing perfectly self-contained instrumentalities for effectuating its objectives without the involvement of the other set. The whole system is a federal compound, but each level of government is uncompounded. It employs new national means — action on and constitution by the human individuals — in order to achieve traditional federal ends.

Madison's uncompounded compound surely was a new departure in federalism, and a great shift from the system of the Articles. It is one of those great acts of creative insight for which no adequate explanation can be given, but we can to some degree retrace the steps that led to that great inspiration. Madison's study of Montesquieu and the history of confederacies revealed to him the doctrinaire character of the federalism embodied in the Articles, but in itself, that study failed to provide insight into the principles by which one ought to construct more effective federations. The key insight, it seems, was supplied by reflection on the British empire. In his 1783 "North America" essays Madison very boldly assessed the situation in America:

> A revolution then effected by joint efforts has destroyed the general government [the British empire], under which taxes were collected for the common benefit, and substituted in its place separate sovereignties, which are to exalt one part of the Empire to the utter depression and impoverishment of the others.

Surely by 1783 Madison had not worked out his new federalism, but this passage gives insight into how the germ of his new thought might have developed. He referred here to the British empire as the "general government," that is, he assimilated it to a federal system, and, at the same time, he spoke of America, as organized under the Articles of Confederation, as an "empire." He had thoroughly broken down the distinction between federation and empire so that he could think across the two categories and draw conclusions from the one relevant to the other. And that is precisely what he did here. The British imperial system was effective in acting for the common good (relatively); the Articles government was not. All Madison had to do was to reflect further on the reasons for British success and American failure: the British system did not (entirely) depend on the "federal principle" of acting on and through the states. The empire had its own agents — governors, executive establishments — and to the extent that it did not, it failed to carry through its policies also. The empire was at best an imperfect model for the new federalism, but in its idea of separate spheres (at least as interpreted by the Americans), and of self-contained government, acting on and through individuals rather than states, it provided a pointer toward the way along which one could move in order to build an effective federal system. Madison needed to abstract that principle and systematize it to produce his model; he also needed to make the general government properly republican, which the British empire surely was not: it acted directly on individuals with its own instrumentalities, but its government did not in turn derive from the individuals on whom it was to act.

THE PROBLEM OF ENCROACHMENTS: FEDERAL MEANS AND FEDERAL ENDS

Self-sufficiency and separateness are the watchwords of the new federalism. They are not, however, sufficient, and American federalism contains a number of features reflecting that insufficiency. The central difficulty here is the problem of encroachments — it is not enough to establish on paper or in principle the separate spheres; it is also necessary to find a way to make effective the separation. The failure to deal with the problems of encroachment was seen by Madison as among the chief failings of the Articles as well as of confederacies in general. Moreover, the problem of encroachment is multifaceted: the member states may encroach on each other, the states may encroach on the general government, or the general government may encroach on the states. Up through 1787–88 Madison tended to take seriously only the first and the second of these threats. Others at the Constitutional Convention were more impressed with the third than he was, however, and insisted on building into the Constitution features responsive to that fear, features which Madison and his closest allies at the convention resisted with all their might. In the 1790s, however, Madison himself became more convinced of the dangers of the third sort of encroachment, and attempted to energize subconstitutional, political checks against it.

The various dangers of encroachment arise from two main sources. The "separateness" of the different levels and layers of government depends, in the first instance, on the adequacy with which the lines of separation can be conceived and then captured in the constitutional apportionment of powers. In the Constitution that apportionment is executed via the enumerated powers of Article I, section 8. The powers of Congress are specified; all other powers not elsewhere explicitly denied to the states belong to them, as the Tenth Amendment makes explicit but as the original constitution already clearly implies. But it is very "arduous" to "make the proper line of partition between the authority of the general and that of the state governments." The different objects to be distributed to the different governments do not themselves possess fully clear and distinct boundaries that make them easily perceptible; the human mind is, at best, an imperfect instrument for perceiving such boundaries, even where they are perfectly clear in nature; and finally, language, the medium in which legal recognition of such boundaries must be expressed, is very imperfect. As *The Federalist* #37 says, "No language is so copious as to supply words and phrases for every complex idea, or so correct as not to include many equivocally denoting different ideas." These various imperfections imply that, even in governments administered with the best will in the world, the possibility, nay, probability of conflicts of authority between different governments will emerge.

Men not being angels, one cannot expect governments to be administered with a will uncorrupted by power and its blandishments. This is particularly true of the states vis-à-vis the general government, for the pull of partial interests is always great compared to the relative weakness of common interest. Thus encroachments by the states on the general government are most to be feared. "All the examples of other confederacies prove the greater tendency in such systems to anarchy than to tyranny; to a disobedience of the members than to usurpations of the federal head." Besides, Madison and his allies believed, the internal structure of the general government would prevent encroachment on the states from the center, in that the attachment of the people to their states would make itself felt in the general government. The reverse would not apply, nor would that check be available to safeguard the states from each other. Constitutional modes of preventing encroachments by the states were therefore indispensable.

The problem of encroachments required a breach in the principles of the new federalism: for the sake of the separateness and independent operation of the different governments, the governments must occasionally operate on each other. The chief device responding to the encroachment problem in Madison's original plan is a proposal that the Congress of the general government be armed with a veto power over the laws of the states, to be used to prevent encroachments by the states on each other and on the general government itself. The convention found Madison's proposal unsatisfactory and unworkable. Other delegates worried that this power would not only allow the general government to interfere too much with the states and prove a drain on the time and resources of the Congress but also would run counter to the main principle of the new federalism. In place of this device then, the Constitution substitutes a constitutional delimitation of spheres together with a firm specification of various acts the states may not perform, all to be enforced by the courts. The Constitution declares itself, and laws made under it, "supreme law of the land," that is, as taking precedent over the laws and constitutions of the states; it obliges state judges to recognize that supremacy and provides for a right of appeal from state courts to courts of the general government where ultimate enforcement of the encroachment-resolving provisions occurs. This solution is indeed more in line with the principle of action of the new federalism, for under it courts resolve questions of political jurisdiction in ordinary law suits, often between individual private parties. Even in this form, however, the anti-encroachments device is a step away from the separateness and self-sufficiency characteristic of the system in general; on the one hand, an agency of the general government, the federal courts, operates on an agency of state government, the state courts, in taking appeals from them and requiring disposition of cases in them in specified ways. On the other hand, while private individuals are often the parties to such cases, the states also may be, and when that happens, there is a particularly direct form of action by one government on the other.[6]

The convention went beyond Madison on the problem of encroachments by the general government on the states. Where Madison would leave ordinary political forces to resolve this danger, the convention agreed that the Constitution itself should contain some specific institutional safeguards for the states. While many such safeguards were debated, only a few were accepted — the principle of equal state representation in the Senate, the selection of senators by the states, and the involvement of the states in the Electoral College. Madison resisted all these modes of safeguard, for he believed they introduced a false principle into his new federalism. The system as a whole was to be a compound, but the general government was itself to be uncompounded, that is, not to have state agency in its constitution or operation. Thus the concern about encroachments led to a compromise of the purity of the Madisonian system, but the system remains clearly Madisonian in its dominant inspiration.

In seeing so clearly that the problem of encroachments had to be provided for, Madison seems once again to have been inspired by the example of the British imperial constitution. In 1787 he wrote to Thomas Jefferson, explaining his thoughts on the encroachments problem:

> If the supremacy of the British Parliament is not necessary, as has been contended, for the harmony of that Empire; it is evident I think that without the royal negative or some equivalent control, the unity of the system would be destroyed. The want of some such provision seems to have been mortal to the ancient Confederacies, and to be the disease of the Modern.

The genesis of Madison's own proposal is evident here: he conceived the Congress of the general government playing the role in the American system that the king played in the British empire through his veto power over the laws of the individual legislatures of the empire. That royal veto could be and was in fact used to prevent encroachments of the sort Madison feared. The parallel with the royal veto power is instructive, for it indicates Madison's view that the power to deal with encroachments is not part of the ordinary legislative power but is indeed closer to an executive power. It was, after all, a negative power, a veto, a power to refuse assent to laws, and not a positive power to make law which Madison turned to here. There is no hint that Madison favored granting the legislature of the general government plenary or full legislative power. In any case, Madison's favored device was rejected, but his concern to provide against encroachments became a firm part of the constitutional system. And therewith, so did another transformed version of the old imperial constitution.

THE PROBLEM OF REPUBLICANISM: FEDERAL MEANS TO NATIONAL ENDS

Montesquieu had one further lesson for Madison: Not only do confederal republics serve external, defensive purposes for their member states, they apparently have internal functions as well: "Should a popular insurrection happen in one of the confederate states, the others are able to quell it. Should abuses creep into one part, they are reformed by those that remain sound." Madison took this suggestion of Montesquieu's and attempted to go very far with it. When he came to catalogue the "vices of the political system of the United States" in 1787 he included a set of political evils which, strictly speaking, did not inhere in the confederacy but in the member states.

In developing the evils which viciate the political system of the United States, it is proper to include those which are found within the states individually, as well as those which directly affect the states collectively, since the former class have an indirect influence on the general malady and must not be overlooked in forming a compleat remedy.

Among those vices Madison discussed three in particular: the multiplicity, the mutability, and the injustice of the laws of the states. These vices derive more or less directly from the character of republican government itself. In his most daring departure from federal theory, Madison propounded the view that federalism can supply the cure for the evils inherent in republican government.

This part of Madison's thought is, paradoxically, both the best and the least known of all his political views. It is best known because this is the set of concerns that was embodied in his famous essay on factions and the extended republic (*The Federalist* #10). It is least known because the bearing the argument had for Madison, in particular the connection to federalism, is hardly ever appreciated properly.[7]

Madison's contemporaries developed an approach to politics that suggested to them that the creation of properly controlled republican institutions was the necessary and sufficient condition for the solution of the political problem of securing just rule, that is, rule in the interests of the ruled. If the community rules itself, or the well-controlled representatives of the community rule, then the rulers will act to secure the interests of the community and not the partial and special interests that ruling groups separate from and not responsible to the community always seek.

Madison broke as radically with contemporary opinion on the promise of republicanism as he had with contemporary orthodoxy on federalism. The prevailing view of republicanism was based on an abstraction: The community did not exist as an undifferentiated whole with an immediately visible common interest. Rather, "all civilized societies" were "divided into different sects, factions, and interests, as they happened to consist of rich and poor, debtors and creditors, the landed, the manufacturing, the commercial interests, the inhabitants of this district, or that district, the followers of this religious sect or that religious sect." To make the government answerable to, or controlled by, the community meant in practice to make it answerable to the majority; that, in turn, meant it was controlled by whatever interest might happen to be in the majority. Republicanism did not therefore guarantee just rule, that is, rule in the common interest, but might instead arm the majority interests in the community against all other interests.

The dominant theory of republicanism saw the requirements of just rule too simply, as if the one thing needful were control of the government by the majority of the community. In fact, said Madison, the requirements are more complex than that: "The great desideratum in government such a modification of the sovereignty as will render it sufficiently neutral between the different interests and factions, to control one part of the society from invading the rights of another, and at the same time sufficiently controlled itself, from setting up an interest adverse to the whole society." Madison's identification of the political task was not only more complex than the prevailing theory holds; it was also extremely difficult to achieve, for the two elements of his "great desideratum" seem to point in opposite directions. On the one hand, government must be neutral vis-à-vis the interests in society, so that it can act "disinterestedly," and control them rather than be controlled by some of them. This seems to require a certain distance or independence of the political authorities from the forces in society. On the other hand, the government must remain dependent on and controlled by society so that it does not impose a separate interest of its own on society as a whole.

Each requirement can be met tolerably well in a form of government well known in history. The kind of republic his compatriots favored could respond to the second problem. Keeping government on a very "short leash" could prevent it from developing or pursuing an interest separate from that of the community. Hereditary monarchy, on the other hand, can supply the other requirement. The prince, not dependent on the forces in society for his position or for the exercise of his powers, is free to be neutral or disinterested vis-à-vis those interests. But, as he is free to disregard the particular claims of any faction, so he is free to disregard the interests of the whole as well. Neither pure form — republic or principality — satisfies both requirements.

Madison saw the possibility of a solution in a combination of the two regimes: "a limited monarchy tempers the evils of an absolute one." A limited monarchy, like Britain's, combines the two pure forms — a hereditary prince and an elected republican legislature. The one supplies neutrality, the other controls. As was the case in other aspects of the new federalism, Madison saw that the British constitution could be the model for a new departure on the problem of republicanism in America: "As a limited monarchy tempers the evils of an absolute one; so an extensive Republic meliorates the administration of a small Republic." Madison saw the solution to the problem of republicanism not in the replacement of the small republic by the large, as many contemporary scholars believe, but rather in the combination of the two, in the new kind of federal system he invented. It was a "system without precedent" which "so combines the federal form with the form of individual republics, as may enable each to supply the defects of the other and obtain the advantages of both."

In the new kind of combination he projected, the "large republic" was to supply the disinterest, neutrality, and distance from society characteristic of the monarchic element in the British limited monarchy. Madison counted on two mechanisms to achieve this goal. In a large republic, majorities will have less likelihood of existing naturally, and, if they exist, greater difficulty in acting together. Instead of natural majorities, with their spontaneously formed interests contrary to the interests of others in society, governance will be enabled or required to proceed in the large republic via constructed majorities, that is, majorities which have been put together on the basis of a search for common interests less immediate and less obvious than the interests that spontaneously appear in society. That process pushes toward common interests, toward more neutral and disinterested rules of decision.

In the limited monarchy the monarchic element exercises its role through the possession of a negative power on legislation. The king is not given a positive legislative power, but makes his contribution of neutrality through a veto power. The republican legislature, Parliament, possesses the positive legislative power. The balance between the institutions and the powers they possess secure that combination of the two requirements which seemed so difficult to achieve.

In the American federal system, Madison envisaged the same combination of structures and powers, in this case with the government of the extended republic in place of the prince possessing a negative power, and the small republics of the states possessing positive legislative powers. Just as the limited monarchy does not arm the prince with positive legislative powers so the large-small republic combination of the new federalism does not arm the large republic with positive legislative power. Madison wanted to grant the Congress of the general government a power analogous to the king's — the power to negate all laws made by the states. Through the exercise of this veto power, the large republic, in concert with the small republics of the states, could achieve the two desiderata as the limited monarchy did. But the American solution would be, as Madison put it, "wholly republican."

The Constitutional Convention, of course, did not follow Madison's advice on this matter, and from his point of view produced a constitution that was a mere shadow of his hopes; at the close of the convention, when we might expect him to have rejoiced at the degree of success he had enjoyed, he wrote instead to Jefferson despairing of the convention's product because it had failed to endorse his plan for the solution of the republican problem. The convention rejected this part of Madison's plan for the same reasons that it rejected his way of dealing with the encroachments problem (the same negative power). The power went farther into the states than most were willing to countenance, the practical details seemed unworkable, and the mode of operation went too far astray from Madison's own insight into the problematic character of "federal operation" of one government on another. This part of Madison's schema sought to achieve national goals, the sort of goals a simply unitary system seeks — the protection of citizens in their rights, the securing of the public interest — by using in a radical way the federal means of a universal negative in the general government over the states.

Madison could not win the convention to his proposal, but he did not fail altogether. Some of the more obvious evils in the states — paper money, impairments of contract, bills of attainder — were directly forbidden in the Constitution. These were then to be enforced by the courts as were the provisions aimed at the encroachments problem. Madison considered this an unsatisfactory and pale version of his negative, but it went at least part way toward serving the ends peculiar to his vision of union, and stands as a key part of American federalism. Immediately following the adoption of the Constitution, Madison tried again to move the federal system closer to his original plan; he proposed an amendment analogous to those that became part of the Bill of Rights that would apply to the states. That effort also failed. But Madison's idea proved too powerful to die and his efforts to use federal union as a way of securing good rule in the member states became the germ for the far more successful effort to do the same following the Civil War in the Fourteenth Amendment. As originally understood, the Fourteenth Amendment would have achieved something very similar to Madison's universal negative.[8]

REPRISE: THE PROBLEM OF SOVEREIGNTY

The Articles of Confederation may have been sovereignty-obsessed, but when the new federalism posed the question once again, the founders slid past it with remarkable ease. The Constitutional Convention had few discussions that centered on the issue, and none of the rancor that characterized it in the era just before the Civil War. And during the debate over ratification of the Constitution the matter of sovereignty hardly arose. As John W. Burgess long ago described it, the Americans solved the riddle of sovereignty by drawing an altogether novel distinction between the sovereign and the government.[9] They insisted that the people were and remain sovereign, delegating only so much political authority as they chose to their government, or, as in the new federalism, dividing it between different governments. Neither government is sovereign; both, as James Wilson said, were "derived from the people — both meant for the people." Both governments are subordinate to the sovereign authority, the people, but, deriving equally from the sovereign, are equal to each other. No constitutional right of nullification or secession remains in the states, but no claim to general supremacy inheres in the nation.

We can conclude then that the new federalism is "without a precedent ancient or modern" not only because it contains novel approaches to old problems but also because it so complexly represents a response to a combination of problems. The federal system is a genuine composite, not only of its elements — states, individuals, and the general government — but also of problems addressed and modes of solutions proposed. American federalism combines features responsive to three somewhat separate problems: effective federalism, encroachment, and republicanism. It responds to these problems in a variety of different ways, some national in character, others federal. But the character of the whole composite is destined to appear confused and a hodge-podge, a "bundle of compromises" unless one sorts out the various elements of problem and solution it embodies. When one does that, it appears as a wonderfully wrought if not quite perfect structure, truly deserving of the pride Madison expressed in his late preface, and of the praise of imitation it has received ever since it was invented.

THE CONSTITUTION AND THE SEPARATION OF POWERS

EDWARD J. ERLER

"If it be a fundamental principle of free Govt. that the Legislative, Executive & Judiciary powers should be separately exercised; it is equally so that they be independently exercised."

James Madison[1]

During the framing and ratification of the Constitution, there was no political opinion more widely accepted than that which proclaimed the separation of powers to be an essential ingredient of constitutional government. James Madison reflected the universality of this opinion when he wrote in *The Federalist* that "[n]o political truth is certainly of greater intrinsic value, or is stamped with the authority of more enlightened patrons" than this "essential precaution in favor of liberty." The Framers of the Constitution were virtually unanimous in accepting Madison's statement in *The Federalist* #47 that "the accumulation of all powers, legislative, executive, and judiciary, in the same hands, whether of one, a few, or many, and whether hereditary, self-appointed, or elective, may justly be pronounced the very definition of tyranny." If, indeed, the proposed Constitution did evidence a design or a tendency to such an accumulation of powers — as some Anti-Federalists alleged — Madison conceded that "no further arguments would be necessary to inspire a universal reprobation of the system."

While there was general agreement that a separation of powers was essential for the rule of law, the precise form the separated powers should assume in the new Constitution provoked vigorous debate. In the view of the leading Federalists, it was not enough to provide a negative check upon the powers of government; it was also necessary to provide for energetic government. Theophilus Parsons, in his influential *Essex Result*, published in 1778, wrote that "the principles of a free republican form of government" require "modelling the three branches of the supreme power in such a manner, that the government might act with the greatest vigour and wisdom, and with the best intention." The three departments should also "retain a check upon the others, sufficient to preserve it's independence."

The whole object of such "modelling" was, of course, to serve the leading republican principle that "no member of the state should be controuled by any law, or be deprived of his property, against his consent."[2] In a word, the separation of powers held out the prospect that constitutional government could be nontyrannical government as well as good government.

Madison and most of the leading Federalists maintained that by itself the representative principle was insufficient. While a "dependence on the people is, no doubt, the primary control on government," Madison wrote, "experience has taught mankind the necessity of auxiliary precautions." Separation of powers — and its attendant checks and balances — was the central constitutional precept embodied in the new Constitution. Separation of powers, of course, is essentially a modern doctrine, one of those principles Hamilton listed as being either among "the wholly new discoveries" or those which "have made their principal progress towards perfection in modern times."[3] The Anti-Federalist "Centinel," although maintaining that "the highest responsibility is to be attained in a simple structure of government," nonetheless concurred with Hamilton, calling the separation of powers "the chief improvement in government in modern times." Although the idea of the separation of powers as a constituent element of constitutional government was not unknown either to the ancients or to the moderns, the version of that doctrine propounded in the American Constitution is unique in that it was intended to operate in an *unmixed* regime. As M. J. C. Vile correctly notes, "The division of functions between agencies of government who will exercise a mutual check upon each other *although both are elected, directly or indirectly, by the same people,* is a unique American contribution to modern constitutional theory."[4]

In *The Federalist* #47 Madison wrote that "the oracle who is always consulted and cited" on the subject of the separation of powers is "the celebrated Montesquieu. If he be not the author of this invaluable precept in the science of politics, he has the merit at least of displaying and recommending it most effectually to the attention of mankind." Indeed, Montesquieu's great work on politics, *The Spirit of the Laws*, published in 1748, was the source most cited by both proponents and opponents of the Constitution. Given the weight of Montesquieu's authority, therefore, it was necessary for Madison and the Federalists to understate their disagreements — and thereby overstate their agreements — with him. Like all oracular interpretations, Madison's discussion of Montesquieu concealed as much as it revealed. *The Federalist,* I believe, presents, if not the first full-scale account of the separation of powers, then certainly the first full-scale republican account. And, if it is true, as W. B. Gwyn remarks, that the doctrine of the separation of powers had republican origins, then certainly *The Federalist* must be credited with the first complete and definitive account of that doctrine.[5]

Montesquieu's famous discussion of the separation of powers in Book

XI, Chapter 6, of *The Spirit of the Laws* is brief and seems almost to be out of place in the economy of the work, since it occurs in the chapter on "The Constitution of England" but does not purport to be an accurate account of that system. At any rate, Montesquieu prefaced his remarks on the separation of powers with a definition of the "political liberty of the citizens." This is, he wrote, "a tranquility of mind arising from the opinion each person has of his safety." This "tranquility" is to be found "only where there is no abuse of power." And it is in the prevention of the abuse of power that the separation of powers becomes the central institution of "moderate government":

> When the legislative and executive powers are united in the same person, or in the same body of magistrates, there can be no liberty; because apprehensions may arise, lest the same monarch or senate should enact tyrannical laws, to execute them in a tyrannical manner.
>
> Again, there is no liberty, if the judiciary power be not separated from the legislative and executive. Were it joined with the legislative, the life and liberty of the subject would be exposed to arbitrary control; for the judge would be then the legislator. Were it joined to the executive power, the judge might behave with violence and oppression.

The Framers of the American Constitution were mindful of the fact that Montesquieu's major contribution to the separation of powers "doctrine" was the addition of an independent judiciary.

Prior to Montesquieu, the modern separation of powers theory — including that of John Locke — extended only to the legislative and executive departments; judicial power was seen as a part of executive power, the application of law in particular cases.[6] Montesquieu's attempt to distinguish judicial power is somewhat ambiguous in that it appears to be more of an attempt to "disguise" judicial power than to distinguish it. Even though Montesquieu remarks that the power of judging is "in some sense nothing," it

> ought not to be given to a standing senate; it should be exercised by persons taken from the body of the people at certain times of the year, and consistently with a form and manner prescribed by law, in order to erect a tribunal that should last only so long as necessity requires. By this method the power of judging, *so terrible to mankind,* not being annexed to any particular state or profession, becomes, as it were, *invisible and nothing.* People have not then the judges continually present to their view; they fear the office, but not the magistrate [L'Esprit des Lois XI, 6, emphasis added].

This power of judging was to be exercised by juries drawn periodically from the people, and in the exercise of the jury function the people were themselves to be judges. Juries would continually emerge from the people and then dissolve back into the mass of society. Since no magistrate exercised this "terrible power" directly, its influence would thereby be almost "invisible." It remained for the Framers of the American Constitution to complete the establishment of an independent judicial power by transforming Montesquieu's jury system into a judiciary and juries into judges.

The principal reason that Montesquieu's doctrine of the separation of powers was in need of modification, however, was that it rested on the mixed regime principle. As Thomas Pangle notes, "Montesquieu still believed that the competition which keeps powers limited requires a real class division among the citizenry." [7] Like Locke before him, Montesquieu sought to distribute the powers of government among different classes — monarchy, aristocracy, and democracy. The legislative function was to be divided between the democracy and a hereditary nobility with the executive branch held by the monarchy. The natural class antagonisms that pre-existed in society would thus be reflected on the level of government, preventing one class from dominating the government.

This balanced or mixed government would provide the stability or moderation necessary for the rule of law and prevent government from becoming too powerful. It was therefore a system that looked not primarily to the protection of the rights and liberties of individuals but to the protection of the rights and liberties of the various classes. Montesquieu may have alluded to this when he wrote that "the three powers can be well distributed with regard to the liberty of the constitution, although they are not so well distributed with regard to the liberty of the citizen" (L'Esprit des Lois XI, 18). As Martin Diamond cogently noted,

> the mixed regime was . . . defended, partly, as a barrier against oppression by one class of another — not, be it noted, as a protection of the liberties of individuals — and it was further defended, even more importantly, on the ground that by bringing together two partial conceptions of justice, statesmanship could hope to achieve a complete justice by harmonizing these opposing conceptions. Thus, in the mixed regime, rival claims regarding justice were in the very structure of the system.[8]

For Montesquieu, constitutional government — and hence the rule of law — was rooted in the class-based structure of society itself. Without this agency, it would be impossible to contrive an effective separation of powers because there would be no "rival claims regarding justice" among an undivided people which could serve as the source of the checking function that the separation of powers was designed to provide.

This class structure was, of course, lacking in America. There was no hereditary nobility and no prospect of creating one. Indeed, the Constitution's prohibition against the creation of titles of nobility was considered to be "the cornerstone of republican government," because, Alexander Hamilton wrote in *The Federalist* #84, as long as titles of nobility are "excluded there can never be serious danger that the government will be any other than that of the people." Almost everyone recognized that a class-based constitutional arrangement was contrary to the "genius of the American people." Several delegates to the Constitutional Convention noted the inappositeness of predicating a separation of powers upon class. Charles Pinckney, for example, remarked that, although he believed the "Constitution of G. Britain" to be the best in existence,

> it might easily be shown that the peculiar excellence, the distinguishing feature of that Governmt. can not possibly be introduced into our System — that its balance between the Crown & people can not be made a part of our Constitution.—that we neither have or can have the members to compose it, nor the rights, privileges & properties of so distinct a class of Citizens to guard.—that the materials for forming this balance or check do not exist. . . .

It was thus necessary to find a republican substitute for the mixed regime principle. This substitute was found in the constitutional system of checks and balances, and in the manner in which all the powers of government were derived "directly or indirectly from the great body of the people" (*The Federalist* #39). It was, of course, a task of particular delicacy to determine the precise configuration the constitutional system was to assume, and it was here that the bulk of the debate over the separation of powers took place during the founding period.

In *The Federalist* #47 Madison noted that one of the "principal objections" levied against the Constitution "by the more respectable adversaries" was that it had so blended and intermingled the powers of government as "to expose some of the essential parts of the edifice to the danger of being crushed by the disproportionate weight of other parts." An "Officer of the Late Continental Army" expressed a widely held Anti-Federalist opinion when he wrote that "The LEGISLATIVE and EXECUTIVE powers are not kept separate as every one of the American constitutions declares they ought to be; but they are mixed in a manner entirely novel and unknown, even to the constitution of Great Britain." "Cincinnatus" wrote in a similar vein, citing Montesquieu and Jean Louis DeLolme as his authority: "It would have been proper, not only to have previously laid down, in a declaration of rights, that these powers should be forever separate and incommunicable; but the frame of the proposed constitution, should have had that separation religiously in view, through all its parts. It is manifest this was not the object of its framers, but, that on the contrary there is a studied mixture of them." And "Federal Farmer," who conceded the necessity of some mixing and balancing of the powers of government, nevertheless contended that the particular admixture represented in the Constitution had a dangerous tendency toward the accumulation of executive power. Republican government, he maintained, did not need such a complicated system of checks and balances: "Where the members of the government, as the house, the senate, the executive, and judiciary, are strong and complete, each in itself, the balance is naturally produced, each party may take the powers congenial to it, and we have less need to be anxious about checks, and the subdivision of powers." The mixed system contemplated in the Constitution would, "Federal Farmer" alleged, establish a dangerous "new species of executive."

What Madison understood, and the Anti-Federalists did not, was that checks and balances, entailing the extensive sharing of constitutional power, was made necessary by the republican principle itself, a principle that did not give constitutional status or recognition to class. Checks and balances, of course, are superfluous in a mixed regime. It is not necessary to contrive defensive mechanisms for the different branches of government because those defenses will be supplied by the competing class interests. The Anti-Federalists interpreted Montesquieu's "pure theory" of the separation of powers as if it had been intended for a republic rather than a mixed regime. Madison thus had to modify Montesquieu to make his "doctrine" of the separation of powers compatible with the principles of an "unmixed" regime.

> [I]t may clearly be inferred that Montesquieu could not have meant that the legislative, executive, and judiciary ought to have no *partial agency* in, or no *control* over, the acts of each other. His meaning, as his own words import, . . . can amount to no more than this, that where the *whole* power of one department is exercised by the same hands which possess the *whole* power of another department, the fundamental principles of a free constitution are subverted.

The Anti-Federalists rigorously held to the traditional view that the principal purpose of the separation of powers was to augment legislative power against the prerogatives of executive power. They were never able to reconcile themselves to the idea of energetic government—energy and liberty were simply irreconcilable. For the Anti-Federalists, liberty could exist only within the interstices of the *exceptions* to sovereign power, never in its vigorous exercise, however well constructed government might be to control the abuse of power. Thus the Anti-Federalists tended to regard constitutions as little more than extended bills of rights. They still adhered to the older notion that the mass of sovereign power always resided in the government and that the people's liberties depended upon the extent to which they could carve out exceptions to that mass of sovereign prerogative. Thus Magna Carta and the English Bill of Rights were models for the Anti-Federalists. But these great documents were the source of the "historic" rights of Englishmen, whereas the American Constitution claimed to rest on natural rights—the necessary incidents of "the laws of Nature and Nature's God." The doctrine of natural rights derived legitimate government from the consent of the governed, not from history. The radical core of the American Revolution was precisely this change from historical rights to natural rights.

Hamilton argued in *The Federalist* #84 that those who supported the inclusion of a bill of rights in the Constitution mistook the nature of the government contemplated by that instrument. However impolitic Hamilton's argument may have been, he was correct in principle. The government established by the new Constitution, Hamilton argued, was a government whose sovereignty was limited to the accomplishment of certain specified objects. It did not have the prerogative of regulating "every species of personal and private concerns." Thus the people's liberties did not reside in the narrow sphere of excepted power; rather, the power of government depended upon positive delegations of power from the people. "Here," Hamilton noted, "in strictness, the people surrender nothing; and as they retain everything they have no need of particular reservations." Because the new form of government contemplated the sovereignty of the people, the Federalists maintained that the calculus of separated powers had changed. Executive power now had to be augmented to serve as a check against the prerogatives of legislative power.

The Anti-Federalist reliance on legislative power was connected to the small republic argument of Montesquieu. "Centinel" proclaimed "the form of government, which holds those entrusted with power, in the greatest responsibility to their constituents, the best calculated for freemen. A republican, or free government, can only exist where the body of the people are virtuous, and where property is pretty equally divided; in such a government the people are the sovereign and their sense or opinion is the criterion of every public measure; for when this ceases to be the case, the nature of the government is changed, and an aristocracy, monarchy or despotism will rise on its ruin." Citing Montesquieu as his authority, "Centinel" concluded that "it will not be controverted that the legislative is the highest delegated power in government, and that all others are subordinate to it." According to "Federal Farmer," a "fair representation" of the people was therefore the essential guarantee of republican principle. "A full and equal representation, is that which possesses the same interests, feelings, opinions, and views the people themselves would were they all assembled—a fair representation, therefore, should be so regulated, that every order of men in the community, according to the common course of elections, can have a share in it."

With a virtuous citizenry there is little need for complicated schemes of separated powers because the principle of representation itself will insure the enactment of just policies. But as *The Federalist* #35 countered, not only is this argument for proportional representation "altogether visionary" in the sense that the legislature could never be sufficiently numerous to represent the "interests and feelings of every part of the community," it also fails to account for the possibility that legislative power itself could be a source of danger to republican liberty. A virtuous citizenry may be necessary for republican government, but, as Hamilton argued in the New York ratifying convention, it is also necessary to rely on "auxiliary" institutions that connect "the virtue of . . . rulers with their interest." And once the principle of separation is conceded to be necessary to republican government, it is no longer possible to adhere to the proposition that republican government must be simple government. As Hamilton continued his description of the new Constitution, he remarked that "in the form of this government . . . you find all the checks which the greatest politicians and the best writers have ever conceived. . . . The organization is so complex, so skillfully contrived, that it is next to impossible that an impolitic or wicked measure should pass the scrutiny with success."

The Anti-Federalist view was represented in most of the state constitutions prior to 1787. Charles Thatch accurately described the situation when he wrote that "in actual operation, these first state constitutions produced what was tantamount to legislative omnipotence. . . . Separation of powers, whatever formal adherence was given the principle in bills of rights, meant the subordinate executive carrying out the legislative will." [9] The example of the state governments was a great concern to the members of the Constitutional Convention. James Wilson inquired: "Is there no danger of a Legislative despotism? Theory & practice both proclaim it. If the legislative authority be not restrained, there can be neither liberty nor stability."

The state constitutions contained strong commitments to separation of powers. The Massachusetts constitution of 1780 best illustrates:

> In the government of this Commonwealth, the legislative department shall never exercise the executive and judicial powers, or either of them: The executive shall never exercise the legislative and judicial powers, or either of them: The judicial shall never exercise the legislative and executive powers, or either of them: to the end it may be a government of laws and not of men.

But the framers of the state constitutions did not take adequate measures to establish in practice what they conceded to be necessary in theory. As Madison remarked in *The Federalist* #48, "in no instance has a competent provision been made for maintaining in practice the separation delineated on paper." The principal reason for this, according to Madison, was that the framers of the state constitutions were so preoccupied with curtailing "the overgrown and all-grasping prerogative of an hereditary magistrate, supported and fortified by an hereditary branch of the legislative authority," that they failed to foresee "the danger from legislative usurpations." These "legislative usurpations," Madison laconically notes, "must lead to the same tyranny as is threatened by executive usurpations."

In a republic there is no analogy between the power of a monarch and the power of an elected magistrate—a powerful executive was not, as many opponents of energetic government claimed, "the foetus of monarchy." In a monarchy, executive power is indeed the source of danger. But in a republic, where the executive is carefully limited and the legislature "is inspired by a supposed influence over the people" and possesses "an intrepid confidence in its own strength," the legislature possesses a natural advantage over the other branches. It is against the "enterprising ambition" of the legislative department, Madison concludes, "that the people ought to indulge all their jealousy and exhaust all their precautions." The particular danger of legislative supremacy to republicanism is that the legislature is the natural representative of majority faction, the disease "most incident to republican government." The principal defect of the state governments was not, of course, their lack of an effective separation of powers, but the smallness and lack of diversity that allowed their legislatures to be dominated by majority factions. Separation of powers is only an "auxiliary" consideration.

In *The Federalist* #48, Madison described the twofold character of an effective separation of powers: first, it is necessary to discriminate "in theory, the several classes of power, as they may in their nature be legislative, executive, or judiciary"; the second and "most difficult task" is to devise a means of providing "some practical security for each, against the invasion of the others." It is significant that Madison does not say here that the theoretical discrimination of the various powers according to their nature is an easy task, only that providing "practical security" is the "most difficult." The reason is that in *The Federalist* #37 he had already made the case for the difficulty of the classification of the various powers according to their nature.

> Experience has instructed us that no skill in the science of government has yet been able to discriminate and define, with sufficient certainty, its three great provinces—the legislative, executive, and judiciary; or even the privileges and powers of the different legislative branches. Questions daily occur in the course of practice which prove the obscurity which reigns in these subjects, and which puzzle the greatest adepts in political science.

We learn in *The Federalist* #51 that the task of providing "practical security" consists "in giving to those who administer each department the necessary constitutional means and personal motives to resist encroachments of the others." The "constitutional means" comprise the various modes of mixing and interblending the different powers of government that we have come to know as checks and balances. The argument for checks and balances, then, depends, in no small measure, on the fact that there is some indistinctness in the nature of the powers to be separated. The fact that by nature the powers are indistinct makes it appear that their combination can also be "natural."

The practice of the separation of powers depends upon the fact that the legislative, executive, and judicial powers can be blended and intermingled in a manner consistent with republican principles. As Madison remarked in

The Federalist #48, "unless these departments be so far connected and blended as to give to each a constitutional control over the others, the degree of separation which the maxim requires, as essential to a free government, can never in practice be duly maintained." The "great problem to be solved," then, is not a theoretical but a practical one; or at least it is a problem in which nature (the indistinct nature of the powers to be separated) lends itself fully to the support of practice. We would not add, however, that this is an instance where it is necessary for practice to inform theory.

Practice requires something more than mere "parchment barriers." Yet, this is the "security which appears to have been principally relied upon by the compilers of most of the American constitutions." Parchment barriers will be inadequate to resist "the encroaching spirit of power" by the "more powerful members of the government" against the "more feeble." And as Madison was fond of remarking, "the legislative department is everywhere extending the sphere of its activity and drawing all power into its impetuous vortex." The predominance of the legislative branch is natural in any popular form of government; it results from the fact that the legislature is the most immediate representative of sovereign power, the people. It derives advantages from other sources as well: besides the fact that the legislature will have exclusive "access to the pockets of the people," it has "constitutional powers . . . at once more extensive and less susceptible of precise limits." From this latter circumstance, "it can, with the greater facility, mask under complicated and indirect measures, the encroachments which it makes on the co-ordinate departments."

It is not possible, however, "to give to each department an equal power of self-defense." Since the "legislative authority necessarily predominates" in republican government, this "inconveniency" is met by dividing the legislature into rival branches. The "weakness of the executive may require, on the other hand, that it should be fortified." The "natural defense" appears "at first view" to be an absolute veto. The absolute veto, however, may be inconsistent with the principles of republican government; more important, an absolute negative might not be as frequently exercised as the qualified veto. The nature of republican government and the necessity of an energetic executive seem therefore to require the qualified veto. The other "constitutional means" possessed by the executive, such as the power to propose legislation, the appointment of judges, and the power of pardon, are designed to fortify the executive branch against the legislative. This scheme of checks and balances is designed to make the different branches independent, so that independence can serve as the means of defense for the weaker branches against the stronger. Throughout the construction of the executive branch the principle that guided the Framers of the Constitution was to combine, "as far as republican principles will admit, all the requisites to energy."

This principle is well illustrated by Hamilton's discussion of the treaty-making power. Acknowledging that objections had been made on the ground of "the trite topic of the intermixture of powers," Hamilton defended the Constitutional Convention's decision to place the treaty-making power in the executive "by and with the advice and consent of the Senate." Hamilton remarks that "the particular nature of the power of making treaties indicates a peculiar propriety in the union." The nature of this power, Hamilton maintained in *The Federalist* #75, is more legislative than executive, "though it does not seem strictly to fall within the definition of either of them." The "objects" of treaty making "are CONTRACTS with foreign nations which have the force of law, but derive it from the obligations of good faith. They are not rules prescribed by the sovereign to the subject, but agreements between sovereign and sovereign. The power in question seems therefore to form a distinct department."

Hamilton here alludes to Locke's distinction between "federative power" and "executive power." The federative power, according to Locke, is concerned with "all the Transactions, with all Persons and Communities without the Commonwealth" and is therefore "much less capable to be directed by antecedent, standing, positive Laws, than the Executive; and so must necessarily be left to the Prudence and Wisdom of those whose hands it is in, to be managed for the public good." Locke calls this "Federative" power "natural," because it corresponds "to the Power every Man naturally had before he entred into Society." Even though the executive and federative powers are by nature distinct, "yet they are always almost united" in the same person. But, as Hamilton admits, the republican principle demands that federative power—at least insofar as it involves treaty making—be divided between the executive and the Senate. To have entrusted the power of making treaties solely to the President would have been "utterly unsafe and improper."

> The history of human conduct does not warrant that exalted opinion of human virtue which would make it wise in a nation to commit interests of so delicate and momentous a kind, as those which concern its intercourse with the rest of the world, to the sole disposal of a magistrate created and circumstanced as would be a President of the United States.

Entrusting the treaty-making power solely to the Senate, on the other hand, "would have been to relinquish the benefits of the constitutional agency of the President in the conduct of foreign negotiations." The union of the treaty-making power in the executive and the Senate is thus made necessary by the nature of the powers involved and the nature of republican principles.

There were several proposals at the Constitutional Convention to have the President elected by the legislature. But, as James Wilson argued, such a mode of selecting the executive would render it "too dependent to stand as the mediator between the intrigues & sinister view of the Representatives and the general liberties & interests of the people." Wilson's view was seconded by Gouverneur Morris, who charged that "If the Executive be chosen by the Natl' Legislature, he will not be independent of it; and if not independent, usurpation & tyranny on the part of the Legislature will be the consequence." The leading architects of Article II were well aware of the fact that, in Hamilton's terms, "energy in the executive is the leading character in the very definition of good government," although Madison always referred to "energy in government" as being essential to "the very definition of good government."

In the Constitutional Convention Madison failed in his attempt to persuade the delegates to adopt another "auxiliary precaution" that he regarded as essential in translating the theory of separation into secure practice, a Council of Revision. This council would have been composed of the executive and a specified number of Supreme Court justices. Its function would have been to provide a "Revisionary check on the Legislature" through the prior review of legislative proposals. It would, Madison argued, provide a defensive mechanism against "Legislative encroachments" for both the executive and the judicial branch. Madison regarded the defeat of the revisory council and his failure to secure a national veto on state legislation as his two greatest defeats in the convention.

The Council of Revision was rejected because many delegates believed that this intermixture would violate the separation of powers, primarily because it would give the judiciary a double check on legislative power, once as part of the revisory power and again in the normal course of judicial review of legislation. James Wilson countered this argument, arguing that the council would give the Supreme Court a proper role in policy determination.

> It had been said that the Judges, as expositors of the Laws would have an opportunity of defending their constitutional rights. There was weight in this observation; but this power of the Judges did not go far enough. Laws may be unjust, may be unwise, may be dangerous, may be destructive; and yet not be so unconstitutional as to justify the Judges in refusing to give them effect. Let them have a share in the Revisionary power, and they will have an opportunity of taking notice of these characters of a law.

A majority of the convention reasoned that such a mixture would make "statesmen of the Judges," thus setting them up — instead of the legislature — as the guardians of the rights of the people. Most delegates seemed to believe that republicanism demanded that the judiciary not be involved in policymaking, because policymaking involves more than the exercise of judgment. There is, of course, some question as to whether the council would have genuinely contributed to executive independence, or whether it would have only served to strengthen judicial power at the expense of executive power. In the latter case, the council would have failed to provide an effective check on legislative omnipotence.

The natural superiority of the legislative branch also made it necessary for the Framers to construct an independent judiciary. A "complete independence of the courts of justice" was necessary to insure the legislature's —and the people's—adherence to the Constitution in those instances where it is inspired by an intrepid sense of its own strength to ignore the Supreme Law of the land. An independent judiciary is therefore necessary in order to place the courts in the role "as the bulwarks of a limited Constitution against legislative encroachments." This is the main reason that the independence of the judiciary depends upon the permanent tenure of judges, which "must soon destroy all sense of dependence on the authority conferring" the appointments. Richard Epstein recently remarked that "the judiciary is on a long leash at the edge of the strictly republican regime, reflecting the hope that good government can promise repose and tranquility to every individual man." [10] The only thing that saves the judiciary from being that un-republican "will independent of society" that Madison warns against in *The Federalist* #51 is the fact that the judiciary has no will—only judgment.

This independence does not, however, "suppose a superiority of the judicial to the legislative power. It only supposes that the power of the people is superior to both, and that where the will of the legislature, declared in its statutes, stands in opposition to that of the people, declared in the Constitution, the judges ought to be governed by fundamental laws rather than by those which are not fundamental" (*The Federalist* #78). This idea of an independent judiciary as the bulwark of a limited constitution received its greatest explication in Chief Justice Marshall's opinion in *Marbury v. Madison* (1803). There is some doubt, however, whether the Framers of the Constitution or Marshall would endorse the present-day version of judicial review. Today's version casts the Supreme Court in the role "as ultimate interpreter of the Constitution" in all matters involving the separation of powers (*Baker v. Carr*, 1962). This notion of judicial supremacy renders the Court too prone at times to confuse the Constitution with constitutional law. The Supreme Court has gone so far as to imply— supposedly relying on Marshall's argument in *Marbury*—that its *interpretations* of the Constitution are "the Supreme Law of the land" (*Cooper v. Aaron*, 1958). Marshall, however, had argued that "the framers of the constitution contemplated that instrument as a rule for the government of courts, as well as of the legislature."

In addition to providing the "constitutional means" for maintaining the independence of the branches of government, it is also necessary to provide the requisite "personal motives." For, without personal motives, there is the danger that government will not be energetic, that those who occupy the various constitutional offices will not employ the "constitutional means" of independence that are attached to their office. In a mixed regime, the motives for independence are provided by the rival claims and interests of the different classes in society. Republican government must replace class motives with personal ones. Madison remarks that "ambition must be made to counteract ambition. The interest of the man must be connected with the constitutional rights of the place." It is in this manner that interest and public spiritedness are combined so that "the private interest of every individual may be a sentinel over the public rights." These are in some sense, Madison laconically remarked in *The Federalist* #51, "inventions of prudence."

The great problem in arranging a separation of powers in a popular government is in devising a method of introducing different interests into the government. Discussing the Virginia Constitution in the *Notes on the State of Virginia,* Jefferson noted that "The senate is, by its constitution, too homogeneous with the house of delegates. Being chosen by the same electors, at the same time, and out of the same subjects, the choice falls of course on men of the same description. . . . We do not therefore derive from the separation of our legislature into two houses, those benefits which a proper complication of principles is capable of producing." The result is that "all the powers of government, legislative, executive and judiciary, result to the legislative body," thus forming an "elective despotism." The Constitution supplied "a proper complication of principles" by the use of differing modes of election. By deriving power from the people by means of different channels — directly or indirectly — different interests can be introduced into the level of government and serve as the basis for the ambitions and personal motives of those who occupy the various offices of government.

The Senate, for example, is ultimately responsible to the majority of society, but it is a different majority than the one that elects both the House of Representatives and the President; and the different branches are responsible not only to majorities derived in different ways but to majorities formed at different times. Presumably, in a large, diverse republic majorities formed at different intervals will express different views and interests. With these "transient" majorities being the most characteristic feature of modern republicanism, the government is free to represent the public good.[11]

The Federalist's explication of the separation of powers proceeds in terms of interest and ambition rather than virtue. As Hamilton wrote, the "best security for the fidelity of mankind is to make their interest coincide with their duty. Even the love of fame, the ruling passion of the noblest minds," would be insufficient for ensuring an energetic executive where there is no immediate prospect for enhancing one's reputation. The language of interest does not deny the possibility — or even the necessity — of virtue or public spiritedness. But *The Federalist* is "disposed to view human nature as it is, without either flattering its virtues or exaggerating its vices. . . ." There is no doubt that the Framers placed ultimate reliance on the "genius of the people of America" for the success of the experiment in republicanism. The honor of human nature—"the principles of the Revolution"—demanded such reliance. But the Framers were always mindful of the necessity of "auxiliary" precautions to account for the "ordinary depravity of human nature."

Republican government in which the separation of powers is to be the practical guarantee of liberty must be energetic government. But as some observers have pointed out, the term "energy"—only recently having made its way into political discourse from physics—is neutral with respect to forms of government. An energetic executive can be either a monarch or a republican executive. Energy is not identical with virtue, although the two are not necessarily incompatible. With a properly constructed government, however, energy can be the source of republican virtue. Without the proper constitutional forms the connection between energy and virtue will be less certain: "Had every Athenian citizen been a Socrates, every Athenian assembly would still have been a mob."

The great object of republican statesmanship is to insure not only that government will be energetic, but also that the objects of ambition are the objects worthy of "the noblest minds." The love of fame partakes of the same neutrality as "energy." As Abraham Lincoln pointed out in his Lyceum Speech in 1838, "Towering genius disdains a beaten path. . . . It thirsts and burns for distinction; and, if possible, it will have it, whether at the expense of emancipating slaves, or enslaving freemen." When such genius springs up in the midst of self-governing society, Lincoln noted, it will require a united people attached to the Constitution and the laws to be able to frustrate his designs.

Since energy and ambition are ambiguous springs to public spiritedness, the structure of government must be designed to insure that both will be directed to the public good. This is the reason that "ambition must be made to counteract ambition." The honor and ambition of those who occupy the constitutional offices will only be served when the nation prospers. Thus it is not so much the virtue of the rulers as the virtue of constitutional forms that insures the public good. The noblest minds will not be the product of a noble class. The various constitutional offices will be open to talent, but those who occupy the offices will not be the products of talented classes—their motives will be personal, not derived from class interests. The people will choose those who are most qualified for office, and their virtue—and perhaps their spiritedness—will be reflected in those whom they elect. Madison made this illuminating remark in the Virginia ratifying convention: "I go on this great republican principle, that the people will have virtue and intelligence to select men of virtue and wisdom. . . . If there be sufficient virtue and intelligence in the community, it will be exercised in the selection of these men; so that we do not depend on their virtue, or put confidence in our rulers, but in the people who are to choose them."

Republics can invite ambitious men to fill their constitutional offices because there are constitutional devices—most particularly the separation of powers which has now received its principal perfection in the American Constitution—to insure that however ambitious rulers might be, they will be confronted not only by the ambitions of other constitutional officers but ultimately by the ambition of the people. The people, in choosing their constitutional officers, are thus not merely deferring to the greater virtue of their representatives. As Madison remarked, "those ties which bind the representative to his constituents are strengthened by motives of a more selfish nature. His pride and vanity attach him to a form of government which favors his pretensions and gives him a share in its honors and distinctions." The people's ambitions are derived from the "manly spirit" of the revolution, a spirit "which actuates the people of America—a spirit which nourishes freedom, and in return is nourished by it." This is the ultimate ground of republican government, and all other considerations—however important they may be—are merely auxiliary.

THE WITCH AT THE CHRISTENING: SLAVERY AND THE CONSTITUTION'S ORIGINS

WILLIAM M. WIECEK

As America celebrates the constitutional bicentennial, we recognize that the Constitution of 1787 sanctioned evils as well as blessings. One of these evils was slavery. We perceive, uneasily, that slavery somehow was *there* at the constitutional beginning, like an unbidden, malevolent spirit at a festive celebration: the fairy-tale witch who was not invited to the christening but who came anyway and in an act of spite left a curse on the child. From our late-twentieth-century perspective, we find slavery's presence in the charter of our liberties hard to accept. How could the Framers, who embraced the noble principles of the Declaration of Independence, have compromised themselves by clinging to the squalid reality of enslavement? The cynic counsels us that they were hypocrites, too pusillanimous to give up slaveholding yet not candid enough to acknowledge what they were doing. The desperate idealist, repelled by such an ignoble attitude, instead invents a past that forces historical reality to conform to the ideals of our present. Down that path lie comforting myths that present a *fable convenue*—Napoleon's "agreed-upon fable"—and that reshape our view of our nation's beginnings and assuage our shame over slavery.

Reflecting a comparable embarrassment at the taint of slavery in the Constitution's origins, American historical writing has fluctuated since the Civil War. Abolitionists and the first generation of professional historians in America, writing at a time when memories of the Civil War were still fresh, naturally accorded slavery a prominent place in their accounts of the Constitution's beginnings. But in 1913 the eminent Yale historian Max Farrand overthrew this interpretive tradition and in its place established what was to reign for most of this century as the canonical interpretation. Farrand maintained that slavery had almost no influence at all on the Philadelphia Convention. Rather, the real conflicts there were between large and small states, and the focus of dispute was representation in Congress. But Farrand's own valuable edition of the *Records of the Federal Convention* (1911) belied this interpretation, demonstrating as it did how slavery recurrently surfaced to distract the delegates.

Farrand's vision was challenged first by Charles A. Beard and then by some of his intellectual descendants who shared his belief that what happened at Philadelphia was driven by a counterrevolution. For Beard, the counterrevolution was economic, with conservatives creating a national regime that could stifle democratic aspirations in the states in the interests of a centralized direction of the national economy. For neo-abolitionists who accepted a variant of the counterrevolution hypothesis, the convention embodied what John Hope Franklin calls "a conservative reaction" [1] that stifled social reform movements like antislavery in the interests of establishing a national government that would protect the rights of property, including the interests of slaveholders. Others, including Aileen Kraditor and Staughton Lynd, go further, accepting the contention of Garrisonian abolitionists that the Constitution was a proslavery document. In an elaboration of that approach, I have elsewhere contended that "in 1787 slavery was wholly compatible with the American constitutional order; indeed, it was an essential component of it." [2]

Unpersuaded by this neo-Garrisonian onslaught, eminent historians have sought a more balanced evaluation of the motivations and the accomplishments of the Framers. William Freehling has persuasively argued that the legacy of the Framers' attitudes concerning slavery eventually doomed it as an institution, thanks to gradual abolition in the North, the antislavery provisions of the Northwest Ordinance, the closure of the international slave trade in 1807, and the general notion they promoted that slavery was an evil. Don Fehrenbacher has offered a most subtle and convincing argument in this vein, suggesting that the Constitution was "bifocal": the Framers acknowledged the existence of slavery, but at the same time they hedged it about with restrictions that, they hoped, would eventually doom it. "It is as though the framers were half-consciously trying to frame two constitutions, one for their own time and the other for the ages, with slavery viewed bifocally—that is, plainly visible at their feet, but disappearing when they lifted their eyes." [3]

What are we to make of this scholarly disagreement? Did the Constitution establish slavery in America? Clearly not; slavery had been an established legal institution for over a century when the delegates met at Philadelphia. Did the Constitution support slavery? Certainly, in no less than ten clauses. Was slavery legitimate under the Constitution, or, as the ordinary person would phrase the question today, was slavery constitutional? Or was slavery inconsistent with the Constitution? When white people claimed to own a black man or woman, did that claim have the sanction of our highest law, or was it nothing more than the pretension of power backed by brute force? Surprisingly much has turned, and still turns, on how these questions are answered. Americans resorted to a bloody civil war to resolve them.

Even today, our way of thinking about this ghostly issue determines our attitudes toward such questions as affirmative action and enforcement of civil rights statutes. Judge Leon Higginbotham records the late Chief Justice of the United States Earl Warren as having expressed his anxiety about the meaning of slavery in the American experience: "not only what it meant in the past but the danger of what it will still mean to the future." [4]

Regrettably, Americans in the past have tended to answer that question by creating myths about our constitutional beginnings. The most pernicious of these myths at this two-hundredth anniversary of the Constitution is that slavery was somehow an exception to our otherwise libertarian political order, an anomaly slipped furtively into the Constitution. It follows from this premise that Americans were not responsible for enslavement here; it was foisted off on us. This was the position of Thomas Jefferson, in his widely misunderstood condemnation of the slave trade in the draft of the Declaration of Independence, as well as of succeeding generations of Southerners, who blamed first the British, then the New Englanders, for forcing slavery on them. With the burden of responsibility thus sloughed off, we are able to believe that slavery and the American constitutional order were incompatible. We *intended* to create a regime of liberty under the Constitution; we had no intent to establish slavery (it just happened somehow); therefore the liberating features of the Constitution overrode enslavement. One recent version of this myth holds that slavery was an "incredible aberration" from the Anglo-American tradition of liberty, making its appearance in America only through a "conspiracy of silence" on the part of American lawyers and judges. Slavery was an alien system; the "colonists borrowed the institution of slavery from . . . Spain," imposing it despite a supposed "common-law doctrine against slavery" in the English legal order. [5] It follows from this supposed conflict between social reality and legal ideal that "the fathers [of the Constitution] did include all men when they recognized that 'all men are created equal,' " and those men included black slaves. [6]

To escape the mind-fog that such myths engender, it might be useful to begin by framing our questions in a neutral fashion, asking: "What relationship did slavery have to the origins and drafting of the Constitution?" In answer, this chapter propounds the following theses:

1. Slavery was legally established in the British colonies by the eighteenth century.

2. It was therefore a legitimate institution in America at the beginning of the Revolution, and continued so through 1787.

3. The American Revolution nevertheless had a subtle and delayed effect: it created a cloud over slavery's legitimacy under the principles that it established as the foundation of the new nation's government.

4. The role of slavery at the Philadelphia Convention was central, not peripheral. The delegates wrote generous concessions to slavery into the Constitution. These enhanced the political power of the slave states and protected slavery's future.

Slavery existed in America long before the Constitution, but its legal origins in some of the colonies are frustratingly vague. Two addictive food-stuffs accounted for its appearance in the New World: sugar, grown in the West Indies, and tobacco, grown in the Chesapeake. The island colonies, among them Barbados, Kitts and others of the Leeward Islands, Jamaica, and the short-lived settlement on Providence Island, pioneered in importing blacks and imposing a lifetime condition of unfreedom on them. By the middle of the seventeenth century, slavery was solidly established in the islands.

Concurrently, it was also making its appearance on the mainland, but in quite different ways. In New England and Carolina, it was established abruptly and by statutory enactment; by way of contrast, in Virginia and Maryland, it evolved gradually, not emerging as a legal institution until around 1660. The New Englanders resorted to slavery as a solution to the future of Indian prisoners after the Pequot War (1637), shipping them off to Providence Island. In exchange, Providence shipped some black slaves to Massachusetts Bay. The Bay leaders promptly recognized the legal existence of slavery in the Massachusetts Body of Liberties (1641), permitting enslavement of "lawfull captives taken in just warres, and such strangers as . . . are sold to us [as well as those] who shall be Judged thereto by Authoritie." Slavery similarly came into being almost instantaneously in Carolina after the Restoration, the rights of the master being guaranteed in John Locke's Fundamental Constitutions of 1669. Within twenty years, the Carolinians were borrowing wholesale from the Barbados slave code to create their own body of slave statutes, as the black population quickly expanded to work the rice swamps and clear the back country.

In the Chesapeake, on the other hand, blacks were a part of the population for thirty years before the colony laws clearly identified negritude with lifetime unfreedom inherited by one's offspring. In the meantime, blacks lived in a legal status comparable to that of many unfree whites, as servants or poor freemen. But gradually white Virginians identified race with a condition of permanent unfree condition, assumed that the children of mothers in that status inherited the same condition, and embodied those social customs into occasional laws. In 1705, Virginia collected these scattered laws into a comprehensive slave code; Maryland followed suit in 1715.

Slavery's legal origins in New York were unique. When the English conquered New Netherlands in 1664, they found slavery already established there, but in a mild form that contrasted markedly with the uniquely harsh slavery of the English colonies. Blacks could intermarry with the Dutch, and served in the militia; manumissions were easy, and were often preceded by that particular condition known in Dutch law as "half-freedom," a sort of part-time slavery in which the slave worked to buy his own full freedom. The English settlers quickly replaced this relatively benign system with their much more severe regime.

By 1760, every mainland colony had laws governing slavery and race; nine of them had full slave codes. These laws legitimated slavery's presence in the mainland colonies. They also established its basic characteristics as a provincial domestic institution, which would carry over into the laws of the new states after Independence. The codes embodied all of the following five characteristics:

First, American slavery was racial: its subjects were defined by law in racial terms—"all Negroes, Mullattoes, Indians, and mustizoes," in the words of the 1740 South Carolina slave code. Only nonwhites could be slaves. This, in turn, produced a legal presumption of an identity between race and slavery: in the laws of the southern slave states, a person of African descent was presumed to be a slave unless he could affirmatively prove himself free.

Second, the colonial law of slavery legalized the brutality of discipline necessary to force unfree people to work, and to impose subordination of the black race to the white. The slave codes shared the presumptions of South Carolina's 1696 code that all blacks "are of barbarous, wild, savage natures, . . . such as renders them wholly unqualified to be governed by the laws, customs, and practices of this Province," who if unchecked by legitimated violence would indulge themselves in "the disorders, rapines and inhumanity, to which they are naturally prone and inclined." From this racist assumption, all the laws' brutality flowed. The scope of violence permitted to the master may be gauged from Virginia and North Carolina statutes that exonerated whites responsible for the death of "any Slave dying under moderate Correction." In the face of such a law, one must ask the obvious question: if slaves' deaths occurred routinely enough under "moderate Correction" to merit the notice of the law, what was *harsh* punishment like? Some answer to that is suggested in South Carolina's 1740 Code and Georgia's derivative code of 1755, which imposed only a trifling fine as punishment for any white who might "wilfully cut out the tongue, put out the eye, castrate, or cruelly scald, burn, or deprive any slave of any limb or member." A 1729 Maryland statute provided that a slave convicted of arson first have his right hand chopped off, then he himself was to be hanged, then the corpse's head was to be chopped off, the corpse quartered, and all these gruesome remains be "set up in the most public places of the county." The southern colonies sometimes offered bounties for the scalps or ears of runaway slaves. In New York, following the slave insurrection scare of 1712 and the 1741 "Negroe Plot," judges ordered convicted slaves to be put to death by being burned (in one recorded case the judge ordered that the fire be slow enough that the slave's death agony would be prolonged for at least eight hours), being broken on a wheel, being hung in chains (to die of starvation), and being impaled.

Such laws permanently seared the consciousness of people in slave societies. Chief Judge Thomas Ruffin of North Carolina, a humane man and one of the greatest judges of his era, wrote of such laws in *State v. Mann* (1829) with unflinching anguish: "The power of the master must be absolute, to render the submission of the slave perfect. I most freely confess my sense of the harshness of this proposition; I feel it as deeply as any man can. . . . But in the actual condition of things, it must be so. — There is no remedy. This discipline belongs to the state of slavery." [13]

Third, the slave was defined by law to be property. A human being was reduced to the condition of a thing, a vendible capital asset. Sometimes that worked, theoretically anyway, to the slave's benefit, as when southern laws prohibited wanton cruelty to slaves, in part to preserve the colony's laboring stock in good health. But often the indignity of being considered a thing in the eyes of the law was exacerbated by the side-effects of such status, as where a 1669 South Carolina statute created a presumption that a master who killed his slave in the course of punishment lacked criminal intent: "It cannot be presumed that prepensed malice (which alone makes murther ffelony) should induce any man to destroy his owne estate."

Fourth, the colonial laws made slavery a lifetime condition, thereby distinguishing it from servitude, which, however harsh, at least held out some hope that it would come to an end some day.

And fifth, this lifetime status was passed on to one's children, but only through the maternal line. That is, a child of a slave mother was born a slave; a child of a free mother was born free.

The cumulative impact of the colonial slave codes was profound. They transformed the colonies from settlements that happened to have slaves into authentic slave societies: polities whose legal order, as well as the ordering of ranks and races in its society, was predicated on slavery. In slave societies, the influence of slavery is diffused throughout the laws and consciousness of all people. It is not a matter of the tail wagging the dog (the tail being slavery and the dog being society as a whole); the tail *becomes* the dog.

The colonial statutory law of slavery was extensive, emphatic, and explicit. The law of the mother country was none of these things, and that produced legal and constitutional anomalies before American Independence that were to cast a long shadow over the legitimacy of American slavery. British law, to be sure, recognized the legitimacy of slavery in the plantations. But statutory law was wholly lacking on the subject of slavery at home, and the case law was confused, indistinct, and inconsistent. Baron Mansfield, Chief Justice of Kings Bench, attempted to introduce some specificity into the English law of slavery in the celebrated case of *Somerset v. Stewart* (1772), where he declared that

> The state of slavery is of such a nature, that it is incapable of being introduced on any reasons, moral or political; but only [by] positive law, which preserves its force long after the reasons, occasion, and time itself from whence it was created, is erased from memory: It's so odious, that nothing can be suffered to support it but positive law.

Because this opinion was handed down in 1772, when the American colonies still derived their common law from that of the mother country, the *Somerset* case passed into the body of American law, where it was to bedevil American jurists a half-century later in questions of conflicts of laws and comity, and where its plangent condemnation of slavery heartened blacks and white abolitionists.

The American Revolution had a curiously ambivalent impact on slavery. On the one hand, it soon became obvious that the ideals of the struggle for independence were incompatible with slavery. At the onset of the Revolution, Americans condemned "slavery" in purely rhetorical terms, as an absolute political condition that the mother country threatened to impose on them. But they could not long mouth such rhetoric without coming to see that they themselves imposed the real thing on blacks. Philadelphian Richard Wells asked how his fellow citizens could "reconcile the exercise of slavery with our professions of freedom," while the Rhode Island legislature, which bore as much guilt as any body in America for the iniquity of the slave trade, conceded that "those who are desirous of enjoying all the advantages of liberty themselves should be willing to extend personal liberty to others." [7]

These sentiments were not confined to an occasional New England jeremiad or to pamphlets published by political malcontents. They found expression in the work of the nation's first antislavery organizations, later collectively known as the Abolition Societies after they had been organized into a national federation in 1794. They were most effective in the crucial states of New York and Pennsylvania, where they memorialized effectively for state and federal action against the international slave trade. The societies promoted works of benevolence for free blacks, finding jobs for them and providing for their religious and secular education in Sunday schools. They vigilantly protected free blacks against kidnapping under the guise of fugitive-slave rendition, and propagandized about the evils of slavery.

Southerners sidestepped the problem posed by the ideology of the Revolution by adopting the expedient of declaring blacks outside the scope of those principles. Chief Justice Roger B. Taney reaffirmed this evasion in the *Dred Scott* Case (1857) when he wrote that black slaves could not have been included within the terms of the Declaration of Independence, "for if the language, as understood in that day, would embrace them, the conduct of the distinguished men who framed the declaration of independence would have been utterly and flagrantly inconsistent with the principles they asserted." We read this passage and condemn Taney for failing to grasp the liberating potential of the Declaration; yet we should recognize that he was doing no more than speaking the mind of southern statesmen, both in his time and in 1776. Taney and other southern spokesmen failed to perceive that two interpretations of the American revolutionary experience were possible. They assumed that blacks were not a part of anything that happened between 1760 and 1790, and consequently played no active role in the struggle for human freedom that gave the American Revolution its only lasting meaning. Blacks saw the matter differently. As Benjamin Quarles has recently noted, the Revolutionary War was in effect "a black Declaration of Independence in the sense [that] it spurred black Americans to seek freedom and equality. [They] viewed the war as an ongoing revolution in freedom's cause." [8]

In some ways the struggle for the political liberty of white people had the paradoxical effect of strengthening the enslavement of their black fellow Americans. Samuel Johnson, hostile to the cause of American Independence, sneeringly dismissed American pretensions to liberty as mere hypocrisy: "How is it that we hear the loudest yelps for liberty among the drivers of negroes?" But the American position was more complex than that. The Negro-drivers who were the objects of Johnson's Tory scorn were torn in their own minds about the conjunction of revolutionary principles and slavery. Abolition, wrote an anonymous Carolinian in 1774, would "complete the ruin of many American provinces, as well as the West India islands." Patrick Henry conceded that "the general inconvenience of living here [Virginia]" without slaves made abolition proposals unrealistic. Slaveholders could abandon neither revolutionary ideals nor slavery; therefore both had to be reconciled somehow. Southern Whigs had to advance libertarian principles from within a slave society. They accomplished this by devising an explicit racist justification for slavery, under which the principles of the Revolution and the Declaration of Independence did not embrace black slaves because blacks were so racially distinct that they could never be embodied in a free society composed of whites. Thomas Jefferson and his contemporaries elaborated a coherent, pseudo-scientific racist doctrine posited on black inferiority that underpinned a slave society whose basic premise was human liberty — for whites. Thus the paradox of the Revolution in the South: the creed of the Declaration of Independence actually strengthened the legal bonds of slavery and encouraged the elaboration of a racist ideology that had only been incipient before the Revolution.

A 1790 freedom suit in Pennsylvania (*Blackmore v. Pennsylvania*) provides a striking example of this ideological transformation working itself into the fabric of the law. The slave's counsel claimed that under the Constitution all people were free, with no implicit exceptions for race. Opposing counsel replied: "But we live under an express constitution; and on constitutional principles, there can be no slave, for the constitution declares all men born free; and the question is are these [slaves] of human species?" Having broached that dangerous question, the lawyer backed off to a more moderate, ambiguous position:

> These sections [of the Constitution] relate only to the parties to the contract. These negroes were not parties to it; they were none of the people. If [the Constitution] apply to all men, and a negroe be a man, there is an end of the question. [But] if negroes be property, this can only be taken away by consent of the owner.

This successful reconciliation of ideology and practice did not dispel all dangers to the slave societies of the South, however. For one thing, Southerners had to confront a spreading antislavery sentiment, not only in the states above the Chesapeake but also among their own people. Worst of all, the pre-Revolutionary near-perfect coincidence of slavery and race had been disturbed.

The War for American Independence resulted in an extensive growth of a free black class throughout America. Emancipation came about in several ways. Both sides in the war offered freedom to slaves who enlisted, the southern states doing so retroactively by liberating the slaves who had been volunteered by their masters as substitutes for a white man. Social disruption in the theaters of war made it possible for literally innumerable blacks to liberate themselves simply by running away, some to the maroon colonies of the swamps and the highlands, others to cities, most just to a new place where they were not known and could pass themselves off as free. Conscience-stricken whites who took revolutionary principles seriously manumitted their slaves. Whites found this emergent class of free blacks disturbing, and their fears were not soothed by contemporary slave insurrections in Martinique, Guadaloupe, and Saint-Domingue. Americans viewed these risings with fascinated horror, and drew two lessons from them. First, blacks could not become free *en masse* peaceably. Second, the violence of racial civil war was caused by a misguided antislavery sentiment that encouraged meddling with the stability produced by enslaving a racially distinct underclass.

The world refused to stand still for the slave societies of the South, however. Emancipation proceeded dramatically in the northern states. Some jurisdictions were free from their very beginnings: independent Vermont by its 1777 constitution, which abolished slavery outright in the Green Mountain republic, and the states carved out of the Northwest Territory by the Northwest Ordinance of 1787. In others — New Hampshire and the

Territory of Maine — slavery had never existed to any significant extent, and it simply vanished by economic desuetude. This process took a little longer in Maine's mother-state, Massachusetts, and was hastened by *Quock Walker's Case* (*Commonwealth v. Jennison*, 1783), in which Chief Justice William Cushing of the Massachusetts Supreme Judicial Court was supposed to have held that the all-men-are-born-free-and-equal provision of the Massachusetts Declaration of Rights "as effectively abolished [slavery] as it can be by the granting of rights and privileges wholly incompatible and repugnant to its existence." In Rhode Island, Connecticut, New York, New Jersey, and Pennsylvania, slavery was gradually abolished by statute, a long-drawn-out process that lasted into the 1840s in New Jersey. Pennsylvania's Gradual Abolition Act of 1780 was the model for the others; it provided that all children born to slave mothers after the Fourth of July 1781 would be born free, but would be held in servitude till majority (a means of allowing the master to recoup costs of raising the child to freedom). It also provided for registration of all persons claimed to be enslaved, and reversed the racial presumption of slave status by declaring that any person not so registered would be deemed free.

Slavery's incompatibility with the ideals of the Revolution would not have mattered as much as it did had the Americans not created a national Union. But because they did, slavery concentrated in one section of the nation became a concern to Americans everywhere. This extraterritorial impact of slavery made its presence felt at the Philadelphia Convention.

In seeking to understand the relationship of slavery to the Constitution, it is customary to begin with the Framers' intent. This is a misleading line of inquiry, however, when we begin with the assumptions that:

1. there even *was* such a thing as the "Framers' intent," identifiable and distinct concerning slavery;

2. it described the attitudes of all or a majority, or even a sizable minority, of the delegates;

3. it was *a priori* to the drafting of the Constitution, was reasoned and articulate, and was capable of statement uncontaminated with passion and irrationality;

4. it was expressed in the text of the Constitution or at least made explicit in Madison's *Notes* of the Philadelphia proceedings.

None of these assumptions is valid with respect to slavery. What we call the "Framers' intent" was no more than an incomplete lattice of expectations and moral convictions. This matrix of guess and judgment was too fragile and incomplete to provide us with black-letter rules that the Framers intended should guide our behavior into the future. When we seek the intentions of 1787, we find ambiguity, evasion, compromise, and ambivalence.

Instead of a fruitless search for an intent not to be found, let us take another approach, interpreting the slavery-related provisions of the Constitution as products of the immediate problems of the times. We might also usefully recognize that nearly all the fifty-five delegates arrived at Philadelphia sharing the common assumption that slavery as such had no place in the deliberations there because it was a "domestic institution" of the states, no different than such things as marriage or ecclesiastical governance, something of no concern to the national government, but rather exclusively within the responsibility of the states. Our skepticism about finding a clear intent need not blind us to the fact that each of the fifty-five had attitudes and assumptions about slavery. But at the outset they did not formulate those attitudes as an agenda item. They had more pressing and relevant matters to resolve. One of the most urgent of those was sectionalism.

Sectional divergences were a component of every problem that James Madison and other nationalists sought to remedy by drafting a new Constitution; in some ways, it was a key to all these other problems, something that had to be solved if the other issues were to be successfully resolved too. Sectional differences had plagued the Continental and Confederation Congresses for over a decade. As might be imagined, the questions were framed in the terms of economic interests and political power, and were most acutely perceived by the aggrieved minority. Richard Henry Lee, a Virginia delegate to the Confederation Congress, wrote Madison in the summer of 1785 that "giving Congress a power to Legislate over the Trade of the Union would be dangerous in the extreme to the 5 Southern or Staple States, whose want of ships and seamen would expose their freightage and their produce to a most pernicious and destructive Monopoly." This produced a dilemma for southern statesmen that received only a partial and fleeting solution in 1787. Staughton Lynd frames it thus: "Recognizing the need for stronger Federal powers, [Southerners] feared to create them until . . . assured that the South could control their use."[9]

Madison noted at Philadelphia on June 30 that

> the States were divided into different interests not by their difference of size, but by other circumstances; the most material of which resulted partly from climate, but principally from the effects of their having or not having slaves. These two causes concurred in forming the great division of interests in the U. States. It did not lie between the large & small States: it lay between the Northern & Southern.

Two weeks later, he reminded his colleagues that "it seemed now to be pretty well understood that the real difference of interests lay, not between the large & small but between the N. & Southn. States. The institution of slavery & its consequences formed the line of discrimination." Maryland delegate Luther Martin was equally attuned to the power of sectional division. "At the Eastward Slavery is not acknowledged," he observed, referring to the New England and Middle Atlantic states; "with us [the Chesapeake] it exists in a certain qualified manner, at the Southward [the Carolinas and Georgia] in its full extent." No interpretation, not even Farrand's and its half-century of distinguished progeny, that attempts to explain away this sectional clash by hypothecating a large-state–small-state division can be adequate to account for the dynamics of Philadelphia. Madison was explicit on this point:

> The great danger to our general government is the great southern and northern interests of the continent, being opposed to each other. Look to the votes in congress, and most of them stand divided by the geography of the country, not according to the size of the states.

With slavery-based sectionalism reestablished as one of the principal problems on the convention's agenda, we can examine how the constitution evolved in response to three sectionalism issues:

1. How would sectional differences be reflected in all the specific allocations of power, such as weighted representation in Congress?
2. How would the section most interested in slavery — South Carolina and Georgia — protect itself and its interests by constitutional arrangements?
3. How would the sections account for the projection of their interests in the future, as Americans streamed into the trans-Appalachian frontier?

These urgent interests overrode all assumptions that slavery was a domestic institution of the states and thus of no concern to the new national government. It was not necessary to address slavery questions directly; the words "slave" and "slavery" do not appear in the document (out of Deep South deference to "the religious and political prejudices of the Eastern and Middle States," as James Iredell put it in the North Carolina ratifying convention). But slavery and its manifestations in political sectionalism permeate the document.

This pervasive influence might seem odd, given the widespread and heart-felt opposition to slavery expressed by so many of the Framers. Freehling and others who have vindicated the reputation of the Framers from the imputation of hypocrisy are doubtless correct in ascribing some degree of antislavery sentiment to most of them; yet they produced a document that, in his words, "perpetually protected an institution the Fathers liked to call temporary." [10] This inconsistency between attitude and result is explained by the varying intensity of feeling about slavery, which corresponded to the rough three-way sectional division sketched by Martin much better than it did the more crude bipolar analysis favored by Madison. That is to say, there were not simply two binary forces at Philadelphia, an antislavery Ormazd and a proslavery Ahriman. Rather, there were gradations along a continuum, from the moderately antislavery views of Massachusetts' Rufus King and Pennsylvania's Gouverneur Morris, through the apologetic resignation of the Virginians, to the determined, defiant proslavery of the Carolinians, abetted by the Connecticut delegates' desire to salvage a compromise at any cost. Given this configuration of attitudes, weak and diffuse moderate antislavery attitudes were easily overawed by the determination of the Deep South to protect slavery.

Sectional self-interest made itself felt from the outset, using as its vehicle the debates over representation in Congress. Curiously, it was an antislavery Pennsylvanian, James Wilson, who originally suggested a representation scheme based on counting three-fifths of the slave states' slaves for purposes of representation in the House. (This was an adaptation of a formula originally devised in 1783 by the Confederation Congress to apportion taxes among the states.) The proposal immediately came under fire from Pennsylvania, New York, and Massachusetts delegates, with the Bay State's Elbridge Gerry demanding that if the Carolinians enumerate slaves, New Englanders should be allowed to count their cattle. (Benjamin Franklin had already given the answer to that rhetorical demand during the 1776 debates in the Continental Congress on slave representation: "Sheep will never make any Insurrections." Northern resistance provoked Carolinian intransigence, as it had been doing for over a decade in the Continental and Confederation Congresses. The Carolinians, together with all other delegates, entertained the erroneous expectation that the future increase of population would be predominantly southern and western, below the Ohio River. They confidently expected the slaveholding states to contain a majority of Americans in the nineteenth century, and they feared that the New Englanders, conscious of their dwindling population advantage, would try to impose some check on this growth of southern population or would concoct some economic stranglehold on southern growth through their position as the maritime carriers for the staple-exporting South. To bring political power into a correct alignment with this anticipated demographic future, the slave states sought to enhance their voting strength in the House of Representatives.

The northern delegates were aware of the distortions of political power that would flow from concessions to the southern demands. Consequently, the first six weeks of the convention were consumed by an intense debate over the allocation of political power. The realities of the struggle were obscured, however, by a peculiar shadow debate over the supposed large-versus-small-state struggle, in which delegates from states with small populations sought to preserve the one-state–one-vote apportionment of the Confederation Congresses, and delegates from some of the states with large populations and territories sought to have representation apportioned according to population. By mid-July, this sham issue, as well as the real struggles over sectional strength, were resolved by the expedient known as the Great Compromise, by which voting in the Senate was to be based on equal numbers for each state, and in the House by population. But the linchpin of the compromise was the three-fifths clause, under which the slave states were permitted to include 60 percent of their slaves in the enumeration that would determine the apportionment of representatives. This provided the first of four major concessions to slave interests, which were embodied in no less than ten clauses of the Constitution (rather than the three conventionally assumed to refer to slavery.) By 1820, this slave-holding premium for the southern states gave them eighteen more members in the House than they would have had if slaves were not counted at all in the enumeration.

In the ratifying conventions, southern delegates touted the three-fifths clause as "an immense concession in our favour," which, in reality, it was. Skeptical Northerners would have to be persuaded by altogether different arguments, though, and both Madison and Alexander Hamilton gamely put the best face they could on the matter, Madison in *The Federalist* #54 and Hamilton in the New York ratifying convention. They rejected the northern contention that slaves should be entirely eliminated from enumeration, in favor of "the compromising expedient of the Constitution . . . , which regards them as inhabitants, but as debased by servitude below the equal level of free inhabitants, which regards the slave as divested of two-fifths of the man." A peculiar way of putting it, perhaps, but as Massachusetts delegate Nathaniel Gorham said at Philadelphia, "pretty near the just proportion."

The dominant historiographic tradition of the twentieth century asserts that there was only one Great Compromise in the summer of 1787, and that agreement on its details assured the success of the convention. The older neo-abolitionist interpretation is nearer the truth, however, in seeing a second major crisis erupt in early August, as the convention took up a recommendation of the Committee of Detail that Congress be prohibited from abolishing or taxing the international slave trade. This provoked a second crisis, persisting through most of August, as northern and Chesapeake delegates, outraged by the Carolinians' overreaching and amorality, explicitly condemned the slave trade, and implicitly, the Carolinians' greed. Gouverneur Morris complained that the limitation on Congress's power, read together with the federal number clause,

> comes to this: that the inhabitant of Georgia and S.C. who goes to the Coast of Africa, and in defiance of the most sacred laws of humanity tears away his fellow creatures from their dearest connections & damns them to the most cruel bondages, shall have more votes in a Govt. instituted for protection of the rights of mankind, than the Citizen of Pa. or N. Jersey who views with a laudable horror, so nefarious a practice.

In response, the Carolinians and Abraham Baldwin of Georgia threatened to take their states out of the Union if they were prohibited from carrying on slave importations. The leverage of this threat was impressive. It alarmed Oliver Ellsworth and others responsible for the July compromise, who feared that the August debates had taken on "a threatening aspect. If we do not agree on this middle & moderate ground he was afraid we should lose two States [South Carolina and Georgia] with such others as may be disposed to stand aloof, should fly into a variety of shapes & directions, and most probably into several confederations and not without bloodshed." An ad hoc committee worked out a compromise that extended the ban on congressional power for twenty years and in the interim permitted Congress to levy a tax of up to $10 a head on imported slaves.

Eventually, the basic sectional compromises of the Constitution included the following elements: All direct taxes had to be apportioned among the states according to the federal number (that is, three-fifths) formula (this was redundantly required by two clauses in Article I, section 2, and Article I, section 9); the purpose of these redundant provisions was to prevent Congress from encouraging emancipation or enacting fiscal disincentives to slaveholding by laying a head tax on slaves. In addition, the latter clause was one of two made unamendable (by Article V), a superstatus conceded to only one other provision: the slave-trade clause. Two clauses in Article I, section 9, and Article I, section 10, prohibited the federal government and the states from taxing exports; one objective of these provisions was to prevent both governments from taxing slavery indirectly by taxing the products of slave labor. The southern delegates were acutely conscious that their slave economies depended on export staples, and they were not about to permit a discriminatory taxation that would disadvantage their dependence on black unfree labor. As a quid pro quo for these concessions, southern delegates abandoned their demand for requiring a congressional supermajority to enact laws affecting navigation, a sop to the carrying interests of the New England states.

Even after having twice brought the convention to stalemate and crisis, the Deep South's delegates had not sated their demand for the security of slavery. Near the close of the convention, the Carolinians proposed a fugitive slave clause. The Confederation Congress had recently incorporated such a clause into the Northwest Ordinance. Without it, the rendition of fugitive slaves would be left to considerations of comity between the states. Abolitionists long contended, with reason, that the fugitive slave clause did not modify that comity-based responsibility but only recognized it. Their insistence that the clause gave the federal government no independent powers was borne out by two considerations. First, the clause was drafted entirely in the passive voice, leaving the location of responsibility for its enforcement entirely unclear and ambiguous. Second, it is located in the Fourth Article, a bundle of provisions dealing with interstate relations, rather than Article I, which dealt with the powers of Congress and the federal government. Justice Joseph Story contended in *Prigg v. Pennsylvania* (1842) that

> the full recognition of this right and title was indispensable to the security of this species of property [slavery] in all the slaveholding states; and, indeed, was so vital to the preservation of their domestic interests and institutions, that it cannot be doubted that it constituted a fundamental article, without the adoption of which the Union could not have been formed.

Story was wrong about the fugitive slave clause. The federal number and slave trade clauses were both *sine qua non*, however. Alexander Hamilton, at the New York ratifying convention, said of the federal number clause that "without this indulgence, no union could possibly have been formed," and his remark was just as applicable to the slave trade clause.

One other matter vital to the well-being of the slave states was handled more diffusely: the problem of internal security against slave uprisings. Under the Confederation, the states were left to their own resources in dealing with slave insurrections. Congress's handling of Shays' Rebellion in the winter of 1786–1787 was such an exercise in futility that it prompted the convening of the Philadelphia Convention, to replace the Articles with a more effectual federal government. This lesson and opportunity were not lost on the slave-state delegates, and they welcomed a Constitution that provided in two places that the federal government had power to suppress insurrections and "domestic Violence." It needed little imagination, particularly for residents of slave societies, to read into those words the promise of national assistance against slave risings. Curiously, Madison suggested, in *The Federalist* #43, that the domestic violence clause of Article IV could be used to suppress not only black revolts but even black efforts to achieve political power nonviolently. He referred with exquisite circumlocution to "an unhappy species of population abounding in some of the States, who during the calm of regular government are sunk below the level of men; but who in the tempestuous scenes of civil violence may emerge into the human character, and give a superiority of strength to any party with which they may associate themselves." Such a breach of the racial barrier, he assured his readers, lay within the power of the federal government to quash.

In 1787, slavery was an integral part of the American constitutional and social order. Before that time, it had appeared in all human societies. As a form of labor discipline, it had proved itself remarkably adaptable, not only to plantation agriculture but to mining, the semi-skilled trades, and even the higher reaches of civil service and education. Enslavement was not some bizarre aberration from the norm of social organization, like binding feet or ritual suicide. Instead, coerced labor in one form or another appeared in all societies. Slavery in the United States added a racial overlay, however, in that only members of one race could be enslaved. Slavery and racism thus were fused in the American experience, and it remains impossible to disentangle them today.

Black people's struggle for freedom and equality consequently has not been an effort to realize some authentic promise or potentiality of the Constitution. For blacks, freedom was not an immanent promise of the Constitution, as it was for all other peoples (at least all other white peoples). Nor was eventual black freedom an authentic element of the constitutional system whose realization was frustrated by historic accident or sinister conspiracy. An egalitarian racial constitutional order has never been even an aspiration for white Americans until after World War II. Thus the black experience under the American Constitution has not consisted of an effort to claim something rightfully theirs. Rather, they have had to struggle for three hundred years to overthrow elements integral to the constitutional system: enslavement and racism.

The Constitution of 1787 was not a counterrevolution against the aspirations to freedom of the American Revolution. As far as slavery was concerned, it was instead the product of sober second thoughts about the meaning of revolutionary ideology for blacks. Matured by experience after 1776, white Americans concluded that enslavement of blacks not only had to be tolerated by the Constitution but protected and enhanced as well.

Yet, no matter how essential to the document of 1787, the provisions dealing with slavery were peculiar in several ways. From a certain perspective, they were somehow inconsistent with the document, and no amount of euphemism or ambiguity could conceal that inconsistency. Frederick Douglass wrote in 1850 that "Liberty and Slavery—opposite as Heaven and Hell—are both in the Constitution. . . . If we adopt the preamble, with Liberty and Justice, we must repudiate the enacting clauses, with Kidnapping and Slaveholding." Such inconsistency faithfully mirrored the anomalous status of blacks, slave and free, in white America. The slavery provisions were also ambiguous, both in their euphemistic approach to their subject and in their substantive content. This quality derived from the compromise nature of the provisions. The Framers gladly put off to some indefinite future troubling problems that they recognized they could not solve in Philadelphia and still produce a Constitution that would be ratified by enough states to be viable. Both sections assumed that time and demography were with them, and could gladly infuse the ambiguities and evasions of the Constitution with their own interpretations and expectations.

But the compromises of the Constitution, and the resolution of the slavery conflict that they accomplished, were both inherently unstable, and they recurrently came undone during the next seventy-five years. The Constitution and the Northwest Ordinance together provided what proved to be a short-term resolution of the great confrontation posed by slavery's expansion into the western empire. That proved insufficient by 1820, and a new fundamental settlement, the Missouri Compromise, became necessary. But that too proved only a short-run expedient, and it had to be revised again in 1846, and 1850, and again in 1854, and then again in 1857. This inability of the American constitutional order to remain coherent over a long period of time reflected not only territorial expansion and technological change but more fundamentally the forced marriage of incompatibles that Douglass identified. This incompatibility persists, and will last until the Constitution fully realizes the Revolution's promise of freedom and equality for all people.

CONGRESS DURING THE CONVENTION AND RATIFICATION

MICHAEL J. MALBIN

"The first and fundamental positive law of all Commonwealths," wrote John Locke, "is the establishing of the Legislative Power." [1] The delegates to the Constitutional Convention recognized this point during the summer of 1787. That is why Article I, the congressional portion of the Constitution, was placed first. It is also why more than half of the recorded debates at the convention were about how to organize Congress and what powers to give it.

The delegates were not making precisely the same point as Locke's of course. Anyone who reads the convention debates looking for theoretical completeness is bound to be disappointed. The Constitution may rest on important theoretical assumptions, but the document itself is a practical one, and so were the debates that produced it. If anything, the delegates with the deepest theoretical understanding of the proposed constitution also had an interest in not unnecessarily raising the broader issues their own proposals implied.

The Convention began its substantive work on May 29. For two weeks, until June 13, the Virginia Plan dominated the agenda as delegates considered and amended its proposals twice. The plan provided for a two-chamber legislature. The first branch was to be elected directly by the people and the second chamber was to be elected by the first. In both chambers, representation among the states was to be allocated on the basis of a population or taxation formula not fully spelled out in the original Virginia resolutions. The Virginia Plan, in other words, created a legislature that was to be chosen by, and therefore represent, the people.

The New Jersey Plan introduced by William Paterson on June 15, in contrast, would have maintained Congress as a unicameral legislature. Members of Congress would continue to be appointed by the states and not

NOTE: The research for this essay was supported in part by a grant from the American Political Science and American Historical Association's Project '87. Portions have been published as "Framing a Congress to Channel Ambition," in Project '87's periodical, *This Constitution*, Winter 1984, pp. 4–12, and are used here with permission. My thanks also go to Thomas W. Skladony, who helped do the initial research for this project as a research associate at the American Enterprise Institute.

be elected by the people. Each state would continue to have an equal vote. In short, the Congress would have remained a collection of people whose members represented the states in their sovereign capacities, as they had under the Articles of Confederation.

There was a consensus at the convention (and even, as Herbert Storing has shown, among Anti-Federalists during the subsequent ratification debates[2]) that the Confederation Congress was too weak to raise revenues, provide for defense, or adequately regulate commerce among the states. This common understanding meant there was at least one basic point of agreement among delegates who ended up on opposite sides of many convention votes. This agreement explains why advocates of a powerful, popularly elected Congress were able ultimately to carry the day.

Despite the underlying agreement, it took more than six weeks to settle the issue. On the surface, the convention's decisions leading up to and including the Great Compromise, adopted on July 16, make it look as if delegates split the difference, letting the House represent people and the Senate represent states. I shall argue later that the Senate was not meant simply to represent states, but even if it were, the convention moved the United States definitively away from a league or confederation when it let the people elect even one branch of Congress and then let the government operate directly on the people.

Whether the government should represent states or people — whether the United States should be a nation or confederation — was seen by most delegates as being the most important issue before the convention. As a result, the convention's records pose some problems for understanding other aspects of the Framers' views about Congress. Questions of power, purpose, and institutional form became thoroughly entangled in the debates. Different views about how Congress should be organized rested on different views about how Congress should work. These in turn rested, in part, on different premises about what Congress should do or about how the people would best be able to protect their liberty. In sorting out some of these tangled strands we shall be able not only to learn about Congress, but also about the importance of institutions more generally for the Constitution's Framers.

HUMAN NATURE AND FACTION: THE
BACKGROUND TO INSTITUTIONAL DESIGN

The Federalist and Anti-Federalist views of representation both began with a common understanding of the purpose of government. Government exists, according to the Declaration of Independence, to secure the unalienable rights of life, liberty, and the pursuit of happiness. But the liberty to be secured within government is not the same as the untrammeled liberty people may exercise in a state of nature. Liberty within civil society means liberty subservient to law, because without law civil society could not exist. This subservience to law, or to the legal system, is considered to be just if it is based upon consent. If ever a government fails to serve its essential purpose, the people always retain their natural right to change the government's form and start fresh.

The Federalists saw three different ways in which a government founded upon consent might betray its basic purpose: (1) the people might consent to a government—be it a monarchy, aristocracy, or even a representative government—only to find that those in government may act upon interests of their own that are distinct from the interests and needs of the people themselves; (2) the people could retain the power of government themselves, but a majority of the people could ride roughshod over the minority's rights and make the government serve only the majority; (3) a government could avoid either majority or minority tyranny, and still fail to serve its essential purpose, if it simply ended up pandering to the people's most immediate wishes. People form governments, according to the theory underlying the Declaration, because governments are necessary for people to enjoy the rights they possess, but cannot enjoy, in a state of nature. To survive and remain healthy, though, any government may occasionally have to act against the people's wishes for the people's own long-term good. A government, therefore, must find a way to say no to the people in the short term, while preserving the people's own right over the long term to say no to the government.

The first two of these dangers make up what *The Federalist* #10 defined as the problem of faction. The first corresponds to what James Madison described as the danger of a minority faction. The relief, Madison wrote, "is supplied by the republican principle, which enables the majority to defeat sinister views by a regular vote." Superficially, the republican principle ought to be enough by itself to guard against a minority faction. Freely elected legislators, however, may end up developing their own interests, contrary to those of the people. That is, the problem may not be a minority faction in the country at large: the legislators themselves may begin to act like a faction. Legislators can get away with behaving like a faction, though, only if they are able to persuade a majority to support them, at least temporarily.

In a republic, in other words, legislators are not likely to act as a separate minority faction unless they are first able to play upon the wishes of the majority. Majority factions therefore raise more fundamental issues in a republican government than minority factions. The Federalists believed that no amount of education or civic virtue could ever produce a body of citizens so united in their opinions and so motivated by a common passion for the public good that the problem of faction would simply disappear. "Liberty is to faction, what air is to fire," wrote Madison in *The Federalist* #10. Human beings by nature will have different passions, opinions, and interests. Even if all citizens could be made to care about the common good, they could not all be given the same opinions. Inevitably, their opinions will be colored by their self-love, no matter how virtuous their intentions. And opinions, once formed, will lead to faction, coalition, and political action.

The constitutional solution was an extended commercial republic in which factions would be encouraged to multiply. The more factions there are, the more difficult it will be to form any majority willing to use its position to oppress a minority. Those who want to be part of a governing majority in a large, diverse country are forced by the political arithmetic of coalition building to think about the needs of others if they want to achieve their own objectives. Legislative majorities will have to be made up of coalitions of minorities that come together only after a process of accommodation and compromise. Factions that help form today's legislative majority will have to moderate their demands, both because their coalition partners will demand it of them and because the politics of coalition may find them part of tomorrow's minority. For the same reason, today's minorities will not feel so frustrated as to think of rebellion, because they might be part of tomorrow's majority.

But the arithmetic of coalition building is not the only reason offered for large republics in *The Federalist* #10. Large republics do more than produce multiple factions, and the Constitution provides for more than a pluralistic politics of compromise and coalition. Large republics are representative rather than direct democracies, and representatives do not simply reflect the opinions of factions that exist in the general public. Instead, Madison wrote, representatives necessarily "refine and enlarge the public views" — sometimes by improving them, and sometimes by making them worse. When legislatures enlarge the public's views for the worse, they threaten to incorporate the dangers of faction within the government. When they improve upon the public's views, they can begin to address the third problem of governments based on consent, by enabling the legislature to resist the people's immediate desires in the name of the people's own long-term good. The aim of the Constitution's provisions on Congress was to create a representative body that would improve upon the public's views, instead of making them worse.

SELF-INTEREST AND AMBITION: SHAPING INSTITUTIONS WITH THE NEW POLITICAL SCIENCE

The Framers, using the "new political science" described in *The Federalist* #9, believed that people in office often would act out of self-interest and ambition. That is one reason why representatives would not simply reflect the public's views. Greedy legislators may use the policy arena to their private advantage; people who love the trappings of office may pander to their constituents; and great-souled people in search of lasting fame may use demagogic talents to undermine the Constitution and usurp power for themselves.

Anti-Federalists agreed with the Federalists up to this point. They believed that people in government have a natural tendency to become corrupted by power. They concluded that the only way the people could make sure a government would serve them would be to maintain a vigilant watch and zealous control over the actions of their representatives. This meant frequent elections. It meant giving the people the legal power to instruct their representatives to vote the way the people wanted on specific legislative issues. It also meant letting the people recall their representatives in mid-term. Most of all, it meant making sure that legislative districts were small enough for people to know and judge their representatives personally.

The Federalists rejected this approach because it relied too much on citizen watchfulness and virtue. Virtue was too uncertain a foundation for protecting liberty—too easily corrupted by demagogic leadership. They sought, therefore, to support virtue with the external controls of institutional incentives. The challenge they saw was to create institutions within which both great and not-so-great people would be motivated to satisfy their personal ambitions by behaving in ways that in fact would serve the public interest. For this, the Federalists looked toward ambition and the love of public honor.

The love of fame, called by Hamilton in *The Federalist* #72 "the ruling passion of the noblest minds," could "prompt a man to plan and undertake extensive and arduous enterprises for the public benefit." Even a lesser person, when elected to serve as a representative, could be led to consider the public's welfare—if not for the public's own good alone, then for his own "pride and vanity," or for his personal concern for the "marks of honor, of favor, of esteem" that he wants the public to continue to bestow upon him through reelection.

A great deal of the discussion about Congress in the Constitutional Convention, and in the state ratifying debates was about how institutions can shape the self-interest of legislators. How large should congressional districts be? How long should a senator's or representative's term of office be? Should constituents have the power to instruct or recall members of Congress? Should there be a limit on the number of consecutive terms a member might serve in office? In each case, institutional decisions were made with an eye toward channeling ambition to achieve the desired political results.

DELIBERATIVE DEMOCRACY IN THE HOUSE OF REPRESENTATIVES

Channeling the ambition of members of the House of Representatives meant, for most of the Constitution's supporters, channeling the members away from the excesses of democracy and toward a deliberative view of their constituents' long-term interests. The principal constitutional means used were large House districts that would keep the size of the House itself under control, and two-year House terms instead of the one-year terms most common for state legislatures.

HOUSE DISTRICT SIZE: THE ISSUE AT THE CONVENTION

The convention did not even begin settling how the House of Representatives would be organized until a majority had first accepted the principle that at least one branch should be elected by the people, with representation based on some kind of proportionality. With this issue apparently resolved in late June, the division over whether there should be a national government was superseded by two others: a large-state/small-state dispute over representation in the Senate, and a north/south or slave-state/free-state cleavage over power in the House.[3] Principled differences over the purpose of representation slid into the background as the convention came close to disbanding in failure. The broader issues were not to be aired fully again until the postconvention ratification debates.

It was not that convention delegates failed to understand the deeper issues raised by large versus small districts or by the relationship between representative and constituent. The convention reached one of its theoretical high points on June 6, during a debate over proportionality in the first branch, when Pennsylvania's James Wilson talked about the advantages of large districts and Madison followed with a preview of *The Federalist* #10. After the early debates, however, the larger issues became swallowed in the details of apportionment.

The original Virginia Plan had left the rules for apportionment open. The plan introduced on May 29 read: "The rights of suffrage in the National Legislature ought to be proportioned according to the Quotas of contribution, or to the number of free inhabitants." Both population and contribution quotas or taxes were involved in the apportionment debates. The idea of basing taxes on population came from a change the Confederation Congress had tried to make in the Articles of Confederation. The Articles required states to contribute to the general treasury "in proportion to the value of all land within each state." However, the Articles did not give Congress the power to compel state legislatures to pay, and the states never conducted the census of land and buildings the Articles required.[4] In April 1783, Congress passed a revenue act that would have taxed states in proportion to the whole number of free inhabitants and three-fifths of all other persons, excluding Indians not taxed—that is, three-fifths of the slaves. But the act was not approved unanimously by the thirteen states, as the Articles required. In fact, New York's 1786 refusal to accept the new tax was one of the events precipitating the Constitutional Convention. Even though the revenue act died, however, its three-fifths clause lived on in the convention's changes to the Virginia Plan.

The first reading of the apportionment clause was on May 30. Madison tried to forestall premature arguments over slavery and stick to the general issue of proportionality, but the whole matter was postponed. During the second reading of the Randolph Plan, the debate over proportionality versus equal representation for the House came on June 9 and 10. After deciding for proportionality, the convention voted 9–2 to adopt a motion made by James Wilson that ignored wealth and based apportionment entirely on population, explicitly following the language of the revenue act's three-fifths clause.

Debate over the three-fifths clause began in earnest during the third reading, after the Paterson Plan had been rejected and the delegates had reaffirmed their commitment to proportionality for the first branch. On July 5, a Committee of Eleven (one from each state present) recommended equal state representation in the Senate and proportionality in the House. The formula for the House was to be one representative for each 40,000 "inhabitants of the description" previously agreed to, specifically incorporating the three-fifths clause. Over the next two weeks, some southern delegates pushed for counting slaves fully, and the North divided between those who thought slaves should not be counted at all and others who thought that, because slaves were treated as property in southern state law, they ought to be counted along with all other forms of property in a national property census. The sectional interests in these positions were clear. If slaves were excluded entirely, or if all property were counted, the North would have many more representatives than the South. If slaves were counted fully, representation would be about equal.[5]

The sectional division was not settled until three further points were resolved. First, the convention spent July 9 and 10 on the allocation of seats in the first meeting of Congress under the new Constitution. The initial House was to have sixty-five members, thirty-five from the North and thirty from the South (including Maryland and Delaware, which had significant slave populations). Then, on July 11, southern delegates led by Randolph insisted that a periodic census be written into the Constitution to prevent the North from freezing its advantage permanently. (Many Southerners believed, erroneously, that their representation would increase over time.[6]) Finally, on July 12, the convention unanimously adopted a motion by Gouverneur Morris that "direct taxation shall be in proportion to Representation." This had the effect of making the South pay a price for the advantage of counting even three-fifths of its slaves for representation. Thus, the final formula required a periodic census, with apportionment to be based on at least 40,000 inhabitants (including three-fifths of all slaves) per representative. That number was reduced to 30,000 on the last day of the convention, upon George Washington's request in his only speech to the assembled delegates.

HOUSE DISTRICT SIZE: DEBATES DURING RATIFICATION

By backing into a district size of at least 30,000 people, the convention firmly rejected the idea that congressional districts had to be small. It set a minimum, but no corresponding maximum, and even a district of 30,000 was very large for the time. Only the country's two largest cities, New York and Philadelphia, had enough people in 1790 (about 30,000 each) to warrant a full representative. Boston's population was about 18,000, Charleston's about 16,000, and Baltimore's about 13,000. No other city reached 10,000, and 90 percent of the population lived outside cities.

One gets a better sense of this decision by comparing the new House districts to state legislative districts of the time. South Carolina's state legislature had a 110-member lower house and a thirty-nine-member upper house, but only five representatives to Congress in 1789. The smallest state legislature was Delaware's, with twenty-one in the lower house and nine in the upper; Delaware had one representative. The largest delegation to the first Congress was Virginia's at ten. Virginia's own lower house had 180 members, and its upper house had twenty-four. Each member of the House of Representatives thus was expected to represent many more people than state legislators in even the smallest of the country's upper chambers. So Anti-Federalists had some real reason to wonder when they heard the House described as the branch of the national government that would be closest to the people.

This became one of the main points in the Anti-Federalists' critique of the Constitution during the ratification debates. Their arguments against large districts were based on three different concerns. First, they argued that members from such large districts could not possibly know enough about local issues to represent constituents adequately. How could one person know, let alone represent, the concerns of the whole city of Philadelphia, or a half dozen rural counties? "Our federal representatives," said Virginia's George Mason in his state's ratifying convention, "must be unacquainted with the situation of their constituents. Sixty-five members cannot possibly know the situation and circumstances of all the inhabitants of this immense continent."

Second, on the other side of the knowledge issue, most constituents in large districts could not know their representatives personally. "The number of the House of Representatives [is] too small," said John Smilie in the Pennsylvania ratifying convention. "They will not have the confidence of the people, because the people will not be known by them as to their characters."

Finally, if constituents could not know their representatives in person, they would be forced to choose people whose names were known to them only by reputation. The result, many Anti-Federalists maintained, would be an aristocratic legislature. No one suggested the United States would develop a hereditary aristocracy. Everyone also admitted that the Constitution extended the franchise as broadly as any of the states, and that the Constitution, unlike many of its state counterparts, excluded all property qualifications for office. The point was that only wealthy or unusually talented people could ever become widely known to strangers, even by reputation. This view was expressed most eloquently by Melancton Smith, who argued that large districts would exclude "middling yeomen" from Congress to favor what he called the "natural aristocracy," among whom he included the learned and able as well as the well-born and rich. Underlying all three of these objections was a view of representation that saw direct democracy as the ideal and saw good representatives as ones who approximated direct democracy by mirroring their constituents.

The Federalists, in contrast, thought that representation inevitably would alter the people's views, and not simply reflect them. The question for the Federalists, therefore, was not how large districts should be to promote citizen control, but how large they should be for Congress to function as the Federalists thought it should. The Federalists wanted a body that would promote deliberation, discussion, and compromise. Protecting liberty meant promoting diversity; it also meant creating a government that was able to act. Action in the face of diversity requires a legislature whose members are able to deliberate together. In the best situation, deliberation would transcend constituents' immediate concerns and be based at least in part on the members' own views about what would be good for the nation. But even if the legislators did not put the national interest first, the legislature should at least be designed to permit members from diverse constituencies, acting in the name of their own and their constituents' self-interest, to engage in a process of informed discussion, compromise, and coalition building.

Madison wrote in *The Federalist* #55 that the House should be large enough to insure "free consultation and discussion" but not so large as to produce the "confusion and intemperance of a multitude." At some point, too large a legislature would produce the form of democratic control without the content. The actual result would be demagogic leadership by a few. "In all very numerous assemblies," Madison continued, "passion never fails to wrest the scepter from reason. Had every Athenian citizen been a Socrates, every Athenian assembly would still have been a mob." An excessively large assembly would enhance the constituents' views, in other words, but would do so by enlarging the flames of immediate passion. That is not what the convention delegates wanted from the Congress. The real effort should be to enlarge toward deliberation rather than demagogy. Keeping the size of Congress within bounds makes deliberation possible.

Making deliberation possible cannot by itself make members of Congress deliberate. The size of the House cannot by itself make self-interested, ambitious legislators, who owe their jobs to their constituents, want to resist their own constituents' momentary passions.

Why should capable, ambitious politicians ever want to look toward the country's long-term needs? Patriotism is one obvious answer, but the authors of the Constitution were looking for self-interested incentives so they would not have to count on the uncertainties of virtue. What could a constitution do to encourage self-interested, democratically elected politicians to feel unsatisfied with pandering to constituents or aggrandizing themselves? To see how the convention tried to address this issue, we must turn to the length of the congressional terms.

LENGTH OF HOUSE TERMS

Ten state legislatures had one-year terms of office for members of the lower house in 1787, two had six-month terms and only one, South Carolina's, had a two-year term. Nevertheless, most of the delegates in Philadelphia knew that one-year terms had been burdensome to members of the Continental Congress. State legislators served fairly close to home, attending short sessions that let them treat politics as a sidelight to their main occupation. Serving in Congress took people far from home, and trying to act as a leader meant staying away for a long time.[7] The convention delegates included many who had been leading figures in the Continental Congress and in their own state houses. Most wanted reelection to come less often.

The first major convention discussion of House terms came on June 12. Roger Sherman and Oliver Ellsworth opened by moving for annual elections, John Rutledge of South Carolina quickly proposed two years and was followed by Maryland's Daniel of St. Thomas Jenifer, who proposed three. "Too great [a] frequency of elections rendered the people indifferent to them, and made the best men unwilling to engage in so precarious a service," Jenifer said. Madison seconded Jenifer because it would take three years for members to learn anything about the interests of states other than their own, and because one-year terms would be consumed traveling to and from the capital. Elbridge Gerry of Massachusetts then voiced the convention's strongest objection to multiyear terms:

> The people of New England will never give up the point of annual election. [T]hey know of the transition made in England from triennial to Septennial elections, and will consider such an innovation here as the prelude to a like usurpation. He considered annual Elections as the only defence of the people agst. tyranny. He was as much agst. a triennial House as agst. a hereditary Executive.

After second speeches by Madison and Gerry, three-year terms were approved by a vote of 7–4.

On June 21, Randolph moved to change three years to two. Randolph said he would have preferred annual elections, but the country's size made that inconvenient. The delegates struck the three-year term by a vote of 7–3, with one state divided, and then adopted a two-year term without further discussion. That was the last time the issue came up at the convention.

No one else at the convention matched Gerry's vehemence against multiyear terms. His ardor may seem somewhat surprising in light of the concern he expressed early in the convention about the "levelling spirit" and excesses of democracy in his home state. But Gerry's passion for one-year terms was more than matched in the state ratifying conventions. The Federalists, however, were able to counter these strong feelings with several different lines of argument. The simplest, although defensive, carried a great deal of persuasive force: two-year terms were still short and still left representatives fully dependent on the people. The ratification debates also brought out a number of affirmative reasons for preferring two years to one. One purpose of large districts was to favor the election of capable people; but short terms would deter capable people from running. They would have to spend all their time "riding post to and from Congress," said Fisher Ames in Massachusetts. But cutting down on travel, and increasing time spent at the seat of government, were desired for reasons more profound than just to serve the convenience of officeholders. The aim was not only to get good people to run but to influence how they looked at policy while in office. The Constitution's supporters placed great emphasis on making sure that members of Congress would serve long enough to learn what they had to do.

The most complete debate on two-year terms took place in Massachusetts, and Fisher Ames was one of the most eloquent Federalist speakers in that state's convention. In his main speech on biennial terms, Ames linked term length to the deepest issues of the representation debate. To act properly as trustees, Ames said, the representatives have to understand what they are doing. What do they need to know? It would not be enough for them only to understand the technical aspects of the great objects of federal legislation: "At least two years in office will be necessary to enable a man to judge of the trade and interests of the state which he never saw." To govern effectively, said Madison in Philadelphia, it will be necessary for representatives to acquire knowledge not only of their own local affairs but "of the affairs of the States in general." What they must acquire, in other words, is the political knowledge of how other people see their own interests as well as the technical knowledge of the subject itself.

If the job is to combine interests, however, people may have to be persuaded about what their real interests are, as opposed to their immediate desires. Without such persuasion, it may be impossible to form durable policy majorities of any kind. But the idea of persuasion implies representatives who do not simply follow their constituents' immediate wishes. The relationship between members and constituents must be two-way: the constituents use elections to make sure their representatives remain dependent, but the representatives use the time between elections to persuade constituents to modify immediate desires in light of their own enlightened self-interest. Once the job of the representative is seen in this light, we can see how General William Heath of Massachusetts was able to portray Congress's ability to adjourn between sessions, go home, and then return to unfinished business, as one of the important advantages of two-year terms. Time, said Ames, will allow "the sober, second thought of the people" to become law, instead of the passionate "volcano" of their "fiery" first impressions.

For the whole process to work, however, members must look toward and deliberate with each other—an impossibility if every moment is spent looking over the shoulder at the home constituency. How two-year terms help achieve this was explained by Theodore Sedgwick of Massachusetts, later the president *pro tempore* of the U.S. Senate (1798) and Speaker of the House (6th Congress, 1799–1801). Speaking at the Massachusetts ratifying convention, Sedgwick said it would take more than a year for a representative to "divest himself of local concerns." With a one-year election cycle, James Madison said in Philadelphia, "none of those who wish to be re-elected would remain at the seat of government." Representatives will need two years to shed local attachments and adopt at least somewhat of a national perspective. They will need time to live among, talk to, and get to know their colleagues—time to learn the interests of the other states as their fellow legislators see them. Only if the representatives adopt this perspective will it be possible for them to combine their interests and pass complex legislation that may in fact serve the national interest.

THE SENATORIAL PERSPECTIVE

Convention delegates thought two-year terms would buy House members some breathing space to consider issues from a national perspective. No one trusted the two-year term, however, to be an adequate check on the "excesses of democracy." Multiplicity of factions was to be the new Constitution's most basic protection for liberty, but supplementary checks were also needed. Creating power and checking it had to go hand in hand.

Pierce Butler of South Carolina told the convention on May 30 that dividing the legislature into two branches was the only thing that would make him willing even to consider augmenting Congress's power. On May 31, the convention decided on two branches without debate. When the issue was discussed at greater length on June 20 and 21, all the delegates who spoke out linked dividing the legislature with adding to Congress's power. This time, the convention approved bicameralism by a vote of 7–3–1, with negative and divided votes coming from the same states that were negative or divided over proceeding with the Virginia instead of the New Jersey Plan two days before.

If the delegates agreed that the second chamber was meant to check the House, they differed over what the character of that check should be. Broadly, we can divide their ideas into three groups: (1) the Senate as the representative of the states in their political capacities; (2) the Senate as a quasi-aristocratic substitute for the British House of Lords; and (3) the Senate as the place for taking a longer-range view from a national, and not simply a state, perspective.

THE SENATE AND THE STATES

After the convention voted a final time on June 29 for proportionality in the House, delegates on the losing side fought doggedly to make the Senate a body that would represent the states as such. Their efforts left a significant, though somewhat ambiguous, mark on the final product.

The first issue to be resolved was the method of election. In the Virginia Plan, the Senate was to have been chosen by the House from nominations made by the state legislatures. On June 7, Dickinson argued for election and not just nomination by state legislatures. His speeches showed a desire to preserve one branch of Congress as a body for representing states. "The sense of the States would be better collected through their Governments," he said in support of his proposal. "The preservation of the States in a certain degree of agency is indispensable." The convention adopted the Dickinson motion, 10–0. The decision was confirmed on June 25, at the height of debates over the nation–state issue, by a vote of 9–2. The context led Max Farrand to conclude:

> Whatever opinions were expressed in debate, and whatever arguments were advanced for or against the election of the members of the upper house by the state legislatures . . . they should be interpreted with reference to the one question at issue, that of proportional representation. It might also be noted that from the moment of the adoption of the great compromise the method of electing the members of the upper house was never questioned in the convention.[8]

Like the method of election, equality of representation was an issue pressed vigorously by delegates who wanted to preserve a role for states within, and not merely alongside or beneath, the national government. The leading advocates of the Great Compromise—Ellsworth, Sherman, and Johnson from Connecticut—all spoke about equal representation and election by the state legislatures as ways to ensure that the Senate would represent the states. Sherman, for example, "urged the equality of votes not so much as a security for the small States; as for the State governments which could not be preserved unless they were represented and had a negative in the general Government." His sentiment was endorsed at one time or another by most of the New Jersey Plan's early supporters. On the other side, Wilson, Madison, and the other leading nationalists continued to think of equal representation for the states as being fundamentally unjust, but were willing to swallow their opposition to let the Constitution go forward.

Equal representation and election by state legislatures meant that senators might see themselves as delegates from their states to the national government. Ironically, however, Sherman's remark was made in the context of a decision that reopened the chance for a Senate that would play a more national role: he was endorsing a motion by Elbridge Gerry to let senators vote per capita. The proposal was put forward primarily to encourage attendance and was endorsed for that reason by Sherman. But letting senators cast their own ballots gives them a chance to act as individuals, instead of as delegates. Gerry acknowledged as much, saying that per capita voting "would give a national aspect and Spirit to the management of business." No vote was taken on per capita voting on July 5, but when the issue was raised again on July 23, Maryland's Luther Martin — perhaps the convention's most forceful defender of states' rights — opposed it "as departing from the idea of the *States* being represented in the second branch." Despite Martin's concern the idea carried, 9–1, with only Maryland voting no.

Per capita voting opened up the possibility of a national Senate, but most delegates did not openly discuss the point in this context. They did talk about it, however, when the question was who should pay senators' salaries. The Committee of Details' report of August 6 had provided that "the members of each House shall receive a compensation for their services to be ascertained and paid by the State, in which they shall be chosen." This issue was debated on August 14. The key participants were "states' rights" participants in support of the committee's position and moderate supporters of the Great Compromise against. Nationalist delegates also opposed the committee on this point, but were willing to let the issue be carried by the moderates. The debate over pay was closed by Maryland's Daniel Carroll, a moderate who argued that "the Senate was to represent and manage the affairs of the whole, and not to be the advocates of State interests. They ought not then to be dependent on nor paid by the States." After Carroll spoke, payment from the national treasury was adopted, 9–2.

During the debate of August 14, in other words, moderate delegates who had spoken a month earlier as if the Senate were meant to represent the states in their political capacities, backed away from this view when the issue was pay. Senators were expected to represent their states, but that is not all they were to do. Too much dependence would make it impossible for the Senate to serve other objectives the delegates thought crucial.

The same ambiguities pervaded the state ratification debates. Anti-Federalists tried to portray the Senate as a body that would become a collection of independent aristocrats. The supporters of the Constitution tried to allay those fears, often by reviving — however qualifiedly — a view of the senators as representatives of the states. Some, including Rufus King of Massachusetts, John Jay of New York, and Wilson Nicholas of Virginia, went so far as to say that the states might instruct their senators how to vote in Congress, a common practice under the Confederation but one never discussed in the Convention. As Roy Swanstrom has observed:

> Defenders of the Constitution . . . in their efforts to dissipate the doubts of those who feared for the sovereignty of their States, seldom missed an opportunity to clothe the future Senators in the full dress of ambassadors sent by the States to defend their sovereignty against the national orientation of President and House of Representatives.[9]

Swanstrom clearly overstated when he used "ambassadors." Madison, for example, did not speak of the Senate as representing state sovereignty in *The Federalist* #62 but as "the portion of sovereignty remaining in the individual states" or "residuary sovereignty." And Hamilton said that the job of the Senate was indeed to represent the states, but not the states' apparent interests as state governments might happen to see them but their "genuine interests," which would consist in the good of the whole union. Such distinctions may well have been lost, however, on people who were inattentive or who preferred later to bolster a state-based perspective for their own political reasons. Swanstrom, therefore, seemed to be on solid ground when he talked about the aftereffects:

> On the whole, constant reiteration of the "council of the States" concept during the ratification campaign — often by those who had opposed it in the Federal convention — extended its circulation to the point where, by the time the Senate was actually formed, it had a sufficient acceptance to be used by Federalists and Republicans alike — when it served their purposes.[10]

The influence of this view of the Senate as the "council of the States" continued to be felt for a long time after 1789. But the "council of states" view cannot be supported in its pure form from the convention debates. Delegates did speak of the Senate as a body that would protect the states, but that was not all they said. The Senate was given more than one function: its very existence protected the states, but in its actual operation the Senate's task was to be profoundly national.

The Senate's national role grew out of the need delegates saw for checking the House of Representatives. This job was not one requiring a statehouse perspective. It is hard to find any supporter of the Constitution whose primary concern about the House was that it would be excessively nationalist. The worry was that the House would be too local, too tied to immediate desires, too inconstant — in short, that it would fall prey to the excesses of democracy. But how could the Senate correct this? What could the delegates do to give Senators a self-interest in adopting a different perspective from that of their House colleagues?

AN ARISTOCRATIC SENATE?

Some delegates thought the best way to make sure the Senate would check the House would be to make the Senate into an aristocratic upper chamber akin to the British House of Lords. John Dickinson, for example, said on June 7, in support of his motion to have state legislatures elect the Senate, that he "wished the Senate to consist of the most distinguished characters, distinguished for their rank in life and their weight of property, and bearing as strong a likeness to the British House of Lords as possible." Dickinson carried the day on the method of election, but none of his colleagues seemed to think this would create anything like a House of Lords. Only one person even came close: Gerry supported Dickinson because he thought state legislatures would favor the "commercial and moneyed interest" over the landed ones (then a majority) that he thought would dominate the House.

Delegates may not have agreed with Dickinson about how to make the Senate aristocratic, but a number did agree with the objective. Interestingly, these delegates seemed to make no distinction between an "aristocratic" body and one that represented wealth. For example, General C. C. Pinckney proposed paying no salary to senators: "As this branch was supposed to represent the wealth of the Country, it ought to be composed of persons of wealth; and if no allowance was to be made the wealthy alone would undertake the service." Pinckney's motion was defeated on June 26 by only 5 – 6. Three days later, on June 29, the idea that the Senate should represent property received another preliminary, tentative boost. Ellsworth had just made his formal motion for equal representation in the Senate after proportionality had been adopted for the House. Abraham Baldwin of Georgia was the first speaker after Ellsworth. Baldwin was reluctant to support Ellsworth until other issues had been settled. "He thought the second branch ought to be the representation of property, and that in forming it therefore some reference ought to be had to the relative wealth of their Constituents."

An even bigger boost came when Gouverneur Morris returned to the convention on July 2 after a long absence. Morris was the leading advocate of using property in the formula for House apportionment. His remarkable speech on the Senate came immediately after the tie vote on equal representation that led to the Committee of Eleven and in turn to the Great Compromise. Morris's notion was that the way to protect the democratic spirit of the House was to give the rich their own, distinct branch of the legislature. Morris was able over the next five weeks to get the delegates to focus attention on the issue of property qualifications — for voting and for House apportionment as well as for Senate qualifications. By the time he was finished, the convention had thoroughly aired, and consistently rejected, the idea that wealth, as such, should be the basis of, or a qualification for, exercising power.

Property qualifications for the Senate was not raised again during July, as the convention finished the third reading of the Randolph Plan before turning its work over the Committee of Detail. The committee's report included a sentence that went well beyond anything the convention had accepted until then:

> The Legislature of the United States shall have authority to establish such uniform qualifications of the members of each House, with regard to property, as to the said Legislature shall seem expedient.

When the sentence came up for discussion on August 10, the initial comments were made by people who supported property qualifications and thought they should be part of the Constitution instead of being left to the legislature's discretion. Charles Pinckney "was opposed to the establishment of an undue aristocratic influence in the Constitution, but he thought it essential that the members of the Legislature, the Executive, and the Judges — should be possessed of competent property to make them independent and respectable." Pinckney's motion "was rejected by so general a no, that the States were not called."

After this vote, discussion returned to the committee's proposal to vest the power to set qualifications in Congress. Madison was against it because:

> A republic may be converted into an aristocracy or oligarchy as well by limiting the number capable of being elected as the number authorised to elect. In all cases where the representatives of the people will have an interest distinct from that of their Constituents, there was the same reason for being jealous of them. . . . It was as improper as to allow them to fix their own wages.

Madison had another reason for opposing property qualifications that he held in check on this day but had expressed more colorfully on June 26, the day C. C. Pinckney had suggested a Senate without pay: "The man who is possessed of wealth, who lolls on his sofa or rolls in his carriage, cannot judge of the wants or the feelings of the day laborer." Madison's principled objections appear not to have been the decisive ones, however. Wilson said he thought the whole sentence should be dropped because "a uniform rule would probably never be fixed." After Wilson spoke, the clause was rejected, 3–7.

So the Constitution ended up with no property qualifications for the Senate, nothing that would legally define it as an aristocratic, oligarchic, or propertied check on the House. Of course, the Senate had always had a significant number of rich or socially prominent people among its members, but this did not come about because of the Constitution. That makes all the difference for understanding how the Senate was expected to check the House. The Constitution's authors wanted the Senate to have a different perspective, but did not think the senatorial perspective had to be based on class.

One reason the convention shied away from thinking of the Senate as an aristocracy was expressed by Charles Pinckney in a long speech on June 25, given while the convention was thinking about who should elect senators and how long they should serve. Pinckney's position was that the United States could not have a branch of government based on birth or wealth because the country did not have a social structure that would make such a branch possible. But in addition to the points stressed by Pinckney, the United States also lacked aristocratic ideas, "the aristocratic spirit." Except for Morris, the people who talked about property qualifications talked not about pride but about interests; the aim was to distribute power, not honor. It takes something more than sociology or economics to make people think in those terms. The ideas that led convention delegates to talk about propertied interests rather than orders or classes rested on a theory whose basic categories (natural rights, equality, and self-interest) were every bit as incompatible with creating an explicitly aristocratic or oligarchic branch of the legislature as were the economic realities.

TERM LENGTH, SIZE, AND THE SENATE'S NATIONAL PERSPECTIVE

What, then, were senators expected to do, and what did the Constitution provide to encourage senators to do it? There was more of a consensus among the delegates about what the Senate should do than on how to achieve it. Madison wanted a Senate that would work with more coolness and wisdom than the House. Randolph wanted one that would be less prone to being swayed by the passionate "turbulence and follies of democracy." Morris was worried about the "precipitation, changeableness and excesses of the first branch." Pinckney in the South Carolina ratifying convention spoke about the Senate providing wisdom, experience, and constancy. Davie in North Carolina said the Senate would be more experienced, more temperate, and more competent than the House. Harrison in New York talked about energy and stability. Wilson in Pennsylvania talked about stability, circumspection, and precision.

Although the delegates agreed on what they wanted the Senate to do, their flirtation with property qualifications showed they were less sure how to obtain it. In the final document, senators were required to be 30 years old, instead of twenty-five for the House, and to be citizens for nine years, instead of the House's seven. Otherwise, the qualifications for office were identical. How would the offices differ? For one thing, senators would be elected by state legislatures instead of directly by the people. Dickinson thought that might help the Senate be more like a House of Lords, and Madison thought "filtration" generally brought better people to office than direct election. But few, as we mentioned, thought that the method of election alone would be enough for the job.

For a clue on this question, it is worth considering *The Federalist* #62 and #63. These were the only two papers on how the Senate would work. In them, Madison brushed quickly over who would elect senators, equal representation, and the qualifications for office to devote the bulk of the essays to two subjects familiar from our consideration of the House: the number of senators and the length of their terms. As with the House, in other words, *The Federalist* describes a Constitution that relies on political and structural incentives for achieving the Senate's institutional objectives.

The length of Senate terms came up for formal debate twice during the convention. On June 12, Senate terms were discussed almost immediately after the convention had temporarily settled on three-year terms for the House. Richard Spaight of North Carolina proposed seven years. Sherman preferred five. That would have been the same as the Maryland Senate, which was the longest in the thirteen states. William Pierce of Georgia was the only delegate who favored the same three-year term as the House. Randolph praised Maryland's Senate but argued that a seven-year term was needed to give senators the will to perform their job. Madison then supported Randolph, and a seven-year term was adopted, 8–1–2.

The biggest objection to long terms was that the Senate might become too insulated from popular control. Nathanial Gorham of Massachusetts suggested four-year terms on June 25 to answer this objection, with one-fourth of the seats up for election every year. This would have followed the practice of five different state constitutions that had staggered multiyear terms for the upper chamber. Randolph suggested seven-year staggered terms. Williamson thought six years would be easier for staggering than seven. By the start of work on July 26, Gorham had accepted a six-year term. Then, Delaware's George Read moved a nine-year term, with one-third to rotate every three years.

Madison supported Read in the convention's clearest statement of the way the Constitution's leading authors saw the relationship between means and ends as they shaped the institutions of government: "In order to judge of the form to be given this institution, it will be proper to take a view of the ends to be served by it. These were first to protect the people against their rules: secondly to protect [the people] against the transient impressions to which they themselves might be led." One precaution to protect the people against their rulers is to "divide the trust between different bodies of men, who might watch and check each other." It is much harder for the people to protect against the temporary errors they themselves were liable to make either through "want of information as to their true interest" or "from fickleness and passion." To guard against these, it was important to have at least one branch of government whose members served long enough to have adequate knowledge of the people's true, long-term interests, and whose terms, methods of selection, and limited number would give them a firmness that "might seasonably interpose against impetuous counsels."

Madison had no doubt that the policies that would need the benefit of time would often have to do with the distribution of wealth. He agreed with Pinckney that the United States would not have the same extremes of wealth and poverty as Europe, but he disagreed that this country could "be regarded even at this time was one homogeneous mass." Class, Madison thought, might well become the basis of future political divisions. He therefore thought it particularly important to find a way to guard against this, without making wealth the basis for forming the institution that would do the guarding. Long terms would help achieve these results not by relying on the senators' individual wealth, and not by relying on them as representatives of their states. Long terms would help senators develop a "sense of national character." Having such a sense would mean being concerned not only for the long-term operation of domestic policy but also for the prestige of the country in the eyes of foreign countries. But prestige required constancy, and constancy required people in government whose term of office gave them a self-interest in what would happen over the long run.

The nine-year term was eventually defeated, 3–8. This happened in part because of a belief, articulated by Gerry, that too long a term would make the Constitution too hard to sell to the people. But Madison's argument, supported by Wilson, led to a 7–4 vote approving the six-year term that the day before had seemed too long to many of the delegates.

RECALL AND ROTATION

Two issues that were very closely related conceptually to the length of Senate terms were recall and mandatory rotation in office. The Articles of Confederation had provided for both. The original draft of the Virginia Plan had included them for the House but not for the Senate. The convention then dropped them on June 12 without debate or dissent. The issues received considerable attention in the ratifying conventions, however.

The Virginia and New York ratifying conventions—especially New York's—brought recall and rotation under more careful scrutiny than any other forum. The New York convention even proposed a constitutional amendment on the subject. The amendment, approved with only minor grammatical changes by the convention, read as follows:

> Resolved, That no person shall be eligible as a senator for more than six years in any term of twelve years, and that it shall be in the power of the legislatures of the several states to recall their senators, or either of them, and to elect others in their stead, to serve for the remainder of the time for which such senator or senators, so recalled, were appointed.

The issue of recall involved both the national purpose of long Senate terms and the role of senators as representatives of their states. Supporters of the amendment said that its purpose was to reinforce the senator's sense of dependence. John Lansing elaborated: "If it was the design of the plan to make the Senate a kind of bulwark to the independence of the states, and a check to the encroachments of the general government, certainly the members of this body ought to be peculiarly under the control, and under the strict subordination to the state who delegated them."

In Virginia, Patrick Henry saw recall and instructions as a state's only protections against "nefarious project[s]":

> At present [under the Confederation] you may appeal to the voice of the people and send men to Congress positively instructed to obey your instructions. You can recall them if their system of policy be ruinous. But can you in this government recall your senators? Or can you instruct them? You cannot recall them. You may instruct them, and offer your opinions; but if they think them improper, they may disregard them.

Nicholas replied to Henry that the state may not recall the senators but they can instruct them. Nicholas begged Henry's question, however, of how states could instruct their senators with security, if they could not recall senators for disobeying. Without the sanction of recalls, instructions became little more than advisory petitions.[11]

The New York opponents of recall refused even this concession about instructions in their rejection of recall. Chancellor Robert R. Livingston disputed the basic premise about the role of the states behind both recall and instructions. Senators, Livingston said, "are not to consult the interests of any one state alone, but that of the union." Hamilton, if anything, was even stronger in his rejection. The purpose of the government, said Hamilton, was to combine protection against tyranny from the government, with strength, stability, and vigor in the execution of government. But achieving strength, stability, and vigor could be achieved only "by the formation of some select body formed particularly on this principle." The Senate was meant to be that body, and to that end was formed "to hold its authority during a considerable period, and . . . have such an independence in the exercise of its powers, as will divest it, as much as possible, of local prejudices." The power of recall would do just the opposite and "render the senator a slave to all the capricious humors among the people." Far from being the servant of the states, Hamilton said that "the Senate should be so formed as in some measure to check the state governments, and preclude the communication of the false impressions which they receive from the people."

Hamilton then talked about the importance of deliberation and compromise. If senators are made to feel a constant dependence on their states, they will intrigue to form their compromises "from local views." But that is contrary to the institution's most important objective. "We are attempting, by this Constitution, to abolish factions, and to unite all parties for the general welfare. . . . He [a senator] is an agent for the Union, and he is bound to perform services necessary for the good of the whole, though his state should condemn him." Hamilton was under no illusion that senators would automatically be concerned about the good of the whole. His point was that the institution was meant to serve this national objective, and the objective would be impossible to achieve if the Constitution included a recall provision.

Rotation raised some of the same issues as recall, and some new ones. From the Federalist perspective, rotation would thwart a healthy ambition. From the Anti-Federalist vantage point, it was the answer to legislators separating themselves from the country and becoming a class unto themselves. Two-year House terms, it will be remembered, were defended by the advantage that they would let members live in the capital city and develop some knowledge of and concern for the opinions of their colleagues. Six-year Senate terms, George Mason was convinced, would let senators "fix themselves in the federal town, and become citizens of that town more than of our state." Mason's answer was mandatory rotation. The opponents of rotation did not dispute that senators would live in the federal town and develop a "national character." Instead, they wondered what would happen if the senators were prevented by law from being reelected. Hamilton asked delegates from the New York convention to imagine a Senate made up of people with large ambitions. How would such people react to forced rotation? "When a man knows he must quit his station, let his merit be what it may, he will turn his attention chiefly to his own emolument: nay, he will feel temptations, which few other situations furnish, to perpetuate his power by unconstitutional usurpations." Mandatory rotation threatened to bring about one of the worst dangers a constitution writer might imagine, by encouraging the most capable officeholders to usurp power and undermine the Constitution. That is why Hamilton immediately followed these sentences with the following: "Men will pursue their interests. It is as easy to divert human nature as to oppose the strong currents of selfish passions. A wise legislator will gently divert the channel, and direct it, if possible, to the public good."

One of the principal sources of public danger or vice comes when a person with the ability to attain power, honor, and rewards finds his ambition frustrated because he cannot pursue those objectives legally within the regime. Conversely, the same, highly capable public leaders—still acting out of the same love of power, hope of honors and rewards, or desire for enduring public applause—can bring important benefits to the government as long as the "principal incentives to public virtue" are made available to them for acting in ways the Constitution's authors thought would serve the public interest.

The Senate had two main purposes. From the states' point of view, the Senate was to protect the continued existence of the states, but not necessarily to be their mouthpiece. In its national role, the Senate was to act as a check on the House by giving its members a stake in being concerned with the effect of legislation on their own states' and the country's real, long-term (or what Alexis de Tocqueville might have called "enlightened") self-interest. To achieve these results, the Constitution relied on two devices: filtration and long terms.

Filtration, given less weight in *The Federalist* than long terms, was achieved by providing for indirect election of senators by state legislatures instead of direct election by the people. Indirect election would help send better people to the Senate. Whatever other policy or personal criteria state legislators might use, they would almost surely limit the field of potential candidates to politicians who had gained a measure of respect from their political colleagues for their previous public performance.

Even more important than how they were to be elected, though, was what future public rewards senators might expect after entering office. To keep senators' eyes focused on the national interest, it was important to give the office sufficient power and stature to be attractive to capable people, and then to give those people a chance to continue in office if they do their job well. Giving senators the power to advise and consent to treaties and executive appointments helped make the office attractive; so did six-year terms. Six-year terms also — when combined with the possibility of reelection and a protection against recall — gave senators a personal reason for considering the effects of their policy decisions over a longer time period than House members. At any given moment, two-thirds of the Senate must look not toward the next election day but to the election or two afterward. The longer time frame gives senators a self-interested motive for making decisions that seem unpopular at the moment, if the senators are convinced the decisions eventually will be seen to have served the country's long-term interest.

CONCLUSION

There was an underlying consistency in the arguments and modes of analysis the Constitution's authors and supporters used for the Senate and House. They wanted to establish a democratic government — one that ultimately was responsible to the will of the people. But they also believed energetic government was essential to preserving liberty, and they therefore wanted a legislature whose members would have the ability and will to act in the people's long-range interest.

The Constitution's Framers believed the United States could become a great nation. But greatness — perhaps just plain survival — called for a government that would attract able people to public service and attach them to the public good. During the Revolutionary War, as Jack Rakove has written, "attendance at Congress was . . . an obligation to be discharged, not an ambition to be fulfilled." [12] Afterward, said Alexander Hamilton in an uncontested remark to the New York ratifying convention, it became "difficult to find men who were willing to suffer the mortification to which so feeble a government, and so dependent a station, exposed them."

People who are satisfied with profit or small honors can be found to fill any public office, no matter how petty. But how can a government attract people of ability to work for the common good? The Framers had learned that even if virtue can call people to office in times of necessity, it cannot be relied on in more ordinary times. Something else, something more personal, was needed. That something was best expressed in the most famous sentences from *The Federalist* #51:

> Ambition must be made to counteract ambition. The interest of the man must be connected with the constitutional rights of the place. It may be a reflection on human nature, that such devices should be necessary to controul the abuses of government. But what is government itself but the greatest of all reflections on human nature? If men were angels, no government would be necessary. If angels were to govern men, neither external nor internal controuls on government would be necessary.

If people are to govern themselves, the task of preserving liberty must be based on human nature. Ambition must be made the cornerstone of self-government. Channeling ambition, therefore, became the Framers' most important objective as they designed the new government's legislative branch.

THE PRESIDENCY AND THE EXECUTIVE POWER

JUDITH A. BEST

One word, *energy,* summarizes the Founders' goals for the presidency as an institution. By energy that meant the capacity for vigorous, forceful, and effective action. Although independence was highly important to their theory of the Presidency, it was not unique to it, for independence was their goal for all three branches of the government. Independence in the executive, furthermore, was the means or instrument necessary to produce the end, the energetic presidency, that they desired. The primary characteristic and special contribution of the presidency to the whole system of government was to be energy. Alexander Hamilton, in *The Federalist* #70, stated this principle most clearly: "Energy in the executive is a leading character in the definition of good government."

In some ways this is a startling conclusion from men who were devoted republicans, for a powerful executive is the hallmark of monarchy. One would expect that these men, who had so recently fought a war to free themselves from a hereditary king, men who constantly claimed that they were not friends of monarchy, would favor powerful, dominant legislatures and weak executives. Yes, they did want a more powerful, more truly national government than the one they had under the Articles of Confederation, but it would seem that this could be accomplished by delegating more power to Congress and by allowing it to legislate directly upon the people rather than only upon the states. Energy in government may be essential, but why is it necessarily and primarily to be placed in the executive branch of a republican government? In order to understand why the Founders drew this conclusion about the proper nature and function of the executive power we must examine not only their experiences in the new world but also the political theory that informed and enlightened that experience.

A republic is a form of government in which all governmental power comes directly or indirectly from the people, that is, from the many as opposed to the one or the few. Over two thousand years ago, Aristotle made the case for the republican form of government when he pointed out that the claims of all the other contenders to rule can also be made by the people in their collective capacity. The claims to rule are based on the contribution of something necessary to the nation: wisdom, wealth, talent, strength. The claim of the one wise man to rule is met by the fact that the people have collective wisdom. Practical wisdom, prudence, which is the form of wisdom most useful in governing, is a product of experience. The people as a collective have more experience than any one man could possibly have, thus the adage that many heads are better than one. The claims of the few talented or the few wealthy or the few strong are likewise met by the fact that the people together have talents, wealth, and strength that match or exceed the claims of the few. Aristotle concluded that the people have a very good case, and that the rule of the people is the best practical regime.

However, since the claim or title of the people is based on their collective contributions, Aristotle pointed out that they should exercise only those governmental powers appropriate to collective action such as deliberation, lawmaking, and judging as jurors. He further pointed out that there are some governmental tasks for which there is no substitute for the talents of *one* man. Those tasks are generally the ones we associate with executive office, with leaders of all kinds. The successful performance of these tasks requires the unity that is inherent in one man as well as the secrecy, dispatch, access to and use of information that collectives almost never possess. It is an axiom of political science that all viable political associations must have leaders. The ship of state cannot do without the pilot who sets the course, who knows where the shoals and reefs lie, and who can direct all hands.

Aristotle may have made a rational argument for the rule of the people, but our Founders discovered a more cogent one in the Lockian concept of the equality of the natural rights of men. Although they did not derive their republicanism from Aristotle's prudential argument, they nonetheless understood and accepted his argument regarding the necessity of energy in the executive, and this, in part, because they could also draw on the subsequent two thousand years of human experience which supports this common sense conclusion.

Their immediate experience in the American context was one of legislative dominance over the executive and of resulting weakness in government. Although there were three kinds of colonies in America — royal, proprietary, and corporate — the general experience in the American colonies was one of continuous struggle between colonial governors and colonial assemblies. Through the years the trend was toward an increase in the power of the assemblies. This was true even in the royal colonies, in part because of the geographical remoteness of the royal governors from the king and from the forces under his command. In the main, however, it was because the power of the local purse was in the hands of the colonial assemblies, and they used it very effectively to encroach upon the executives. They were so effective that "by 1760 the assemblies were dominant in almost every colony in continental America."[1] From their colonial past, the

Founders had learned of the tendency of the legislature to encroach upon the executive.

The period of the Revolutionary War and its aftermath only reinforced this view. It was a period of strong state legislatures and weak executives. To the men of the revolutionary period, republican principles seemingly mandated supreme power in the legislature; power in the executive was monarchical. The concentration of power in the legislature was true also of the Articles of Confederation, for there was no clearly defined, separate executive, and the executive functions of the Confederation were performed by a committee of the Confederal Congress. Of course, the Confederation was weak to begin with, for it had not been granted adequate powers, and the absence of the energy provided by a true executive only compounded its feebleness.

The distaste for monarchy — for any office that even remotely resembled it — and the suspicion of central government resulted in near-anarchy in the national system and something approaching legislative tyranny within the states. The economy was in chaos; there were threats by foreign powers; the law was unstable; factionalism was rampant; and governments were threatened by or actually faced insurrection. To the men who assembled in Philadelphia, the situation was very bad and deteriorating rapidly. Something clearly had to be done, and they knew what to do.

Their solution was the new science of government whose oracle was the celebrated French philosopher Montesquieu. That new science was the separation of powers and the checks and balances that made possible the independent and energetic executive within the republican form. The Founders were overwhelmingly in agreement with Montesquieu's view that when the legislative and executive powers are united, there can be no liberty. The separation of powers was inherent in the Virginia Plan, which was the primary draft for the development of the new Constitution, and even the New Jersey Plan provided for it in rudimentary form.

One of the great advantages of this new science they so wisely endorsed is that it frees the executive from the clutches and control of the legislature. In monarchies the executive dwarfs all; in the old republics the legislature consumed all; but the new science of government promised a balance of power that would supply the advantages of republics and overcome their defects: legislative tyranny, on the one hand, and irresolution and weakness especially in foreign relations, on the other hand. By separating the executive from the legislature, it becomes possible to use the executive power to check the legislature and to provide the whole system with leadership.

It is really rather remarkable that so many of the delegates to the Constitutional Convention, including the ardent and jealous republicans, could overcome their often passionate hatred of monarchy, and by design, by openly stated intent, create an energetic executive office. It is really remarkable when one further considers the temper of the people they represented, a temper that found nearly everything resembling monarchy to be odious. In such a context, it took some courage even to discuss the executive office much less to propose a strong one. The first time this delicate subject was raised in the convention the delegates had to be prodded out of their embarrassed silence by the respected Benjamin Franklin's reminder of the importance of the issue. Even those first able to overcome their reticence felt obliged to bow to the social-political taboo, to disassociate themselves from monarchy, and vehemently to deny any intention of proposing an elective king. It is no wonder that the creation of the presidency was their most difficult and divisive task with many of the major features of the office unsettled until the closing moments of the convention.

The power, the authority, and the dignity of the office are in large part the result of their ability to allay passions, to distinguish between an energetic republican executive and a monarch, and to recognize the necessary relationship between energy in the executive and free government. The creation of the presidency is a tribute to the power of critical rational thought in candid discussion, for there are many who believe with Clinton Rossiter that the institution called the American presidency is "one of the few truly successful institutions created by men in their endless quest for the blessings of free government." [2]

Even so, at the time of the state ratification debates, fear of the presidential power almost sank the ship of the Constitution before it was launched. In state after state, voices were raised to object to the "monarchical" office. (To this very day, two centuries later, most vocal critics of a President or the presidency draw on the popular dread of an imperial presidency.) It took a rhetorical tour de force to overcome this obstacle to ratification, and it was supplied by a brilliant, and extremely prescient analysis of the institution by Alexander Hamilton in *The Federalist*. The doubts and misgivings were such that Hamilton felt compelled to devote the whole of one of the papers to a comparison between the presidency and the British monarchy in order to prove their dissimilarity and to establish the innocence of the presidency. His defense of the presidency is a list of the constitutional limitations on the office: the fixed four-year term, impeachment, qualifications on the veto, the congressional powers to declare war and raise armies, the qualifications on the treaty-making power and on appointments. In contrast, he describes the royal prerogatives: hereditary rule, a sacred and inviolable person, an absolute veto, the right to declare war and to raise armies, the sole right to make treaties and appointments, the right to create titles of nobility and to grant charters of incorporation.

But Hamilton was not content to argue the case in the negative, and so in *The Federalist* #70 he argued for the compatibility of a vigorous executive with true republican principles. Those who find a vigorous executive to be "incompatible with the genius of republican government" are simply wrong.

To make his case for energy in the executive, Hamilton drew not only on history and authority but also and especially on common sense. "A feeble executive implies a feeble execution of the government. A feeble execution is but another phrase for a bad execution; and a government ill executed, whatever it may be in theory, must be, in practice, a bad government." His premise established, he went on to analyze the ingredients of this energy and found that they are unity, duration in office, adequate provision for support, and competent powers. Most of the constitutional provisions regarding the presidency were designed to develop and foster these ingredients and thus vigor in the executive.

Unity being the most obvious ingredient, the Founders agreed to one President rather than several. A proposal for a plural executive of at least three members was made in the convention by those who wished to avoid any possible resemblance to or tendency toward monarchy, but it was quickly dismissed. The clinching argument was that a plural executive would be a formula for disaster or defeat in war. A successful army has one head.

The characteristics of a successful military leader were also thought to be applicable to other executive roles in domestic as well as foreign policy. One man can be more resolute and decisive than several, and because he can be decisive he can act quickly and even, when necessary, in secrecy. With three executives the potential for dissension and animosity would produce indecisiveness and delay, and perhaps even divide the country at the worst possible moments — national emergencies. Prolonged discussion, debate, and even obstruction among equals are beneficial in a legislature, but they enervate the executive.

A plural executive not only endangers national security, it destroys republican responsibility. Each executive can hide behind the others; each can claim he was overruled or pressured against his better judgment by the others. That "the buck stops here" (in Harry Truman's favorite maxim) is possible only with a single executive. If you want energy, if you really want a job done and done quickly and well, you hire one man to be in charge. You make the job his responsibility. If it is done well, the praise and honor are his. If it is not, the blame is his. But if you are not sure you want the job done and done quickly, if you are not even sure what should be done, you form a committee. Then, little will be done quickly, and if there is any blame to be given, it is hard to figure out who should be blamed and punished.

Experience teaches that emergencies arise, that there are times when swift action is necessary, that some things can be done only in secrecy, that sometimes decisive action is better than continual debate, and finally that if men are to be accountable for their actions, personal responsibility must be clear. It is simply in the nature of things that the capacity for vigorous, forceful, effective action resides and must reside in a single executive.

Duration in office is directly connected with energy in the executive in large part because it contributes to the independence of the executive. Although the mode of selection of the President is the major factor in his independence, the length of his term has an important impact on his personal attitudes and behavior, and thus on his willingness to exercise his independence. The shorter the term, the less valuable the office is to the man who holds it. We invest our greater efforts in and take the greatest risks for that which is most securely ours. A longer term creates a greater incentive for effort because of a greater personal investment and interest in the position.

An energetic President is a leader, and while a leader by definition must have followers, and must be in touch with the desires and goals of the group, a leader is not simply compliant and submissive. He does not simply take orders, he gives them. He must have the courage and will to keep the followers together and on course. He must on occasion say no to the people. In doing this, he incurs risks to his reputation and to his tenure. He must risk his popularity, at least temporarily, in hopes that the passions of the people will subside, and they will soon see the correctness of his policies. But if his term is too short, he will be more likely to pander to their uninformed or emotional demands either so that he can be reelected or because his interest in the office is so temporary that it is not worth the effort to resist them.

The same point is true with regard to executive–legislative relations. The separation of powers requires an energetic President who will vigorously perform the constitutional role of checking the legislature. But if his term is too short, if the office is a revolving door, if he is to be here today and either up for reelection or gone tomorrow, than why bother to resist? Why not curry favor with the legislature either for its support in a new election or in hopes of finding a comfortable home there once one has left the presidency? Too short a term places the incumbent's personal interest in conflict with his duties.

The convention considered a variety of terms ranging from two or three to fifteen or twenty years. So long as it was considered necessary to make the President ineligible for a second term, a relatively long term of at least seven years was most favored, so that long-term projects could be undertaken and there would be stability of administration. When the obstacles to reeligibility were overcome, four years became the choice. Hamilton himself conceded that there is nothing magical about a four-year term. It does not of itself guarantee firmness and independence but rather, along with reeligibility, contributes to it. The Founders decided that four years was a reasonable balance between two desirable but, in practice, contradictory principles: responsiveness to the will of the people, which requires short terms in office, and independence, which requires long terms in office.

The fact that the President has a fixed four-year term is both an advantage and a disadvantage to him. The advantage is that he cannot be turned out of office during that four-year term merely for unpopularity with either the people or the legislature; thus he is independent. The disadvantage is that he has no flexibility in seeking reelection. He cannot, as a prime minister in a parliamentary system may, call for a new election at a time when he is riding high in public opinion polls.

The third ingredient in energy in the executive is adequate provision for support, for to be energetic the President must be independent, and if he is to be independent the legislature must not be able to control his salary. This point seemed so clear that almost without debate the convention agreed that the President should be compensated, but that his salary could neither be increased nor decreased, nor was he permitted to receive any other salary or fee from the national or state governments during the term for which he was elected.

Only Franklin suggested that the President should not be paid at all on the grounds that to pay him united the passions of the love of power and the love of money. That proposal was not taken seriously very probably because its practical effect would be to limit the office to men of great wealth, and perhaps even exclude the very man for whom the office was being designed, George Washington (Washington had to borrow a hundred pounds to pay his way to his inauguration). Washington was the president of the convention by unanimous choice and a man so respected and admired that many historians are convinced that without his constant presence before them, the delegates would not have created a powerful executive office. When the proponents of the energetic executive spoke, they spoke not in the abstract, for the delegates saw before them the very man for the job. Their trust in him no doubt reduced their fears of monarchy. Franklin to the contrary notwithstanding, the President was to be paid and paid in such a way that the legislature could neither starve him nor bribe him into submission.

However, adequate provision for support, though necessary, would not of itself suffice to make the President independent. The key to presidential independence lay in the method of selecting the President. This was the most difficult facet of this most delicate subject, and no vote seemed to settle it. Time and again the issue was reintroduced, and the problem was not finally resolved until the very last days of the convention. Among the proposals considered were: election by the people, by Congress, by the state governors, by the state legislatures, and by special electors chosen for that sole purpose.

The initial choice, influenced no doubt by the practice in most states, was election by Congress. On at least five separate occasions, the delegates endorsed this plan. Since even most of those who favored this method did want a President free from congressional leading strings, it was agreed that he should have a long — seven-year — term and not be eligible for reelection. Fear of cabal, of corrupt bargains between the legislature and the executive, necessitated a single long term if Congress were to choose the President.

Some of the most eloquent and, as it turned out, persuasive speakers, Wilson, Gerry, Morris, and Madison, argued that it was imperative for the President to be truly independent if the separation of powers was to work. Again and again they rose to point out the tendency of republican legislatures to absorb the powers of the executive. Again and again they warned that legislative tyranny would be the consequence of an executive chosen by the national legislature. Again and again they reminded the delegates that one of the great purposes of the executive is to check the legislature. They were adamant that a President chosen by Congress would be its creature.

They were so persuasive on the point of independence that the convention rejected election by Congress, by the state legislatures, and by the state governors. The convention finally decided to have the President chosen by special electors and expressly forbade anyone holding national office from serving as an elector. These electors could be chosen in a variety of ways, according to the decisions of the individual state legislatures, and each state would have as many electors as it had representatives in both houses of Congress.

This choice had a number of advantages. First and foremost it made the President truly independent, for he owed his office to no single existing and continuous governmental authority. He would not be indebted to or controlled by Congress, the state governors, the state legislatures, or any factional group among the people as a whole. The agency that chose him, the Electoral College, would exist for but one day, the day on which they cast their ballots. It would not meet as a united body, but rather each set of state electors would meet in its own state capital for that single day and then would be dissolved. This method of selection was designed to create a truly independent President, one who was not produced by intrigue, secret plotting, or corrupt bargains.

This choice had the further advantage of making it possible for the President to be indefinitely eligible for reelection, thus of allowing the people their full and free choice and the use of talented and experienced men. Finally, it made it possible to reduce the term of office from seven to four years, thus making the presidency more responsive to the will of the people. If Congress chooses the President, it is essential that he be limited to one long term lest he curry favor with them and acquiesce in all their proposals and demands in hopes of being reelected by them. If, however, his reelection does not depend upon their favor but rather upon some outside agency, he can serve as a check upon their excesses without abandoning hope of returning to finish the projects he has begun.

The last ingredient of an energetic executive is competent powers, and here more than anywhere else, with the possible exception of the mode of presidential selection, the Founders' purposes are laid bare. They gave the President the power of a qualified veto for two reasons: first, as constitutional armor to protect the executive against legislative encroachment; second, as a safeguard against bad laws. The first is the instrument or means, the second is the end. The President was to use the veto to produce the reconsideration necessary to protect the people against legislative errors and even oppression. But in order to use the veto to protect the people, he must first be able and willing to use it — he must be independent. Therefore, he must use it to protect the office of the presidency itself.

That the office was in need of protection was the theme of some of the most impassioned speeches in the convention and of some of the most compelling rhetoric in *The Federalist Papers.* It is clear that the Founders feared legislative tyranny in republican government and, therefore, were determined to buttress the executive to make it a match for the legislature. "The real source of danger," said Madison in the convention, was "the powerful tendency in the legislature to absorb all power into its vortex." Indeed, for a time some of those who saw the necessity of an internal control on the legislature wanted to have the judiciary serve as a council to share the veto with the President because they thought an unaided executive would be no match for the legislature. In the end, there was a general consensus that the President alone would exercise the veto power since he must be independent of even the judiciary in order to obtain the unity that produces clear responsibility. (Could the Founders return today and see how Congress has used its constitutional power to define a bill in order to evade a veto by presenting the President with omnibus bills filled with venial pork barrel legislation and legislative riders, I believe they would be convinced they were right to fear legislative encroachment.)

They qualified the veto, allowing a legislative override with a two-thirds vote of each chamber rather than giving the President an absolute veto, because, as Hamilton said in *The Federalist* #73, the absolute veto is "a power odious in appearance, useless in practice." The absolute veto is a royal prerogative and rests on a principle antithetical to republicanism — the superiority of one man. The modern republican principle of the equality of men does not assume the equal superiority of men but rather their common fallibility as well as their capacity for collective rightful judgment. The Founders believed in man's sober second thoughts, not in his hasty and passionate first ones. Thus the policy that was to be produced by the separation of powers, the policy of the entire governmental solar system, was to be, as Madison defined it in *The Federalist* #51, the "policy of supplying by opposite and rival interests, the defect of better motives." The policy was designed to insure that free government will be good government because it will be reasonable government.

While it is true enough to say that the qualifications on the veto serve as a check against abuse by the executive, that explanation is not sufficient. The veto was also qualified so that it would be used often and on ordinary occasions to prevent legislative errors. The veto was qualified so that reconsideration would be institutionalized in the lawmaking process, so that legislators would think twice, enlarge their views, and control their passions, either because a bill was actually vetoed or because a veto could always be anticipated. The qualified veto is an internal control on government because it gives the legislature a rival, because it forces legislators to reassess their proposals in light of objections actual or anticipated. Reexamination and reflection produce more mature judgment and better laws.

An absolute veto in a republic is too powerful a weapon to be used except in the extreme case of legislative treachery — an open attack on the rights of the people. The major effectiveness of the veto is not its actual invocation but its anticipation, and a republican legislature would almost never anticipate an absolute veto. The President would not dare to use it. Thus, to give the President an absolute veto would be to give him a power he cannot use, and to possess power you cannot use is to be weak and incompetent. The qualified veto is designed for energy in the executive.

Of all the powers of the presidency the veto power was the most widely debated in the convention, but the debate was not over the advisability of such a power. All were agreed that it was a necessary check on the legislature. Rather, the debate was over the advisability of a shared veto. They resolved the issue in favor of energy, competence, and responsibility.

The other powers of the presidency are those generally associated with the executive office from the most ancient of times, which have survived either because experience proved them most appropriate to the executive, or because of long usage, or both. And, there was relatively little disagreement or debate about most of them in the convention. The four major remaining powers are: the power of commander-in-chief, the power to pardon, the power to make treaties, and the power to make appointments. In each case the decision to place these powers in the executive contributed, though more in some cases than in others, to the creation of energy in the executive.

The power of commander-in-chief is the power to direct and employ the military forces created by Congress. There was no disagreement that this power of necessity belongs to the executive; in fact, it was probably the recognition that unity of command is the essence of military victory that led the convention to reject a plural executive. Apparently, the only real concern was that Congress, which originally had been given the power "to make war," would not be able to swiftly respond to attack. This problem was quickly resolved by changing the language to give Congress the power "to declare war." This, of course, greatly enlarged the presidential power, for it made it possible for the President, by deploying troops at his discretion, to create a state of war without a declaration of war, a state of war that Congress might find it difficult to reverse. In light of dangers from foreign powers, they preferred to take this risk. On balance their choice was rational, for not only is the President subject to reelection and impeachment but also Congress controls the purse, and can reduce or disband an army.

The pardoning power had been associated with the executive office through long custom as a delicate action best suited to the judgment of one man. It was granted to the President except in cases of impeachment as a matter of course and almost without discussion. Some members of the convention wished to exclude treason as well as impeachment, fearing, as Randolph put it, that "the President himself may be guilty." These men would have given the power to pardon treason to the legislature. Since not only the President but all officers of the United States can be impeached for treason, and since no pardon for impeachment was to be permitted, the anomaly of the President judging in his own case was thought to be sufficiently avoided. Further, involving the legislature in any part of the pardoning power struck most of the delegates as unwise and improper. Hamilton's argument in *The Federalist Papers* against excluding treason from the pardoning power was pure prudence. There are times when an offer of pardon may either arrest a treason or at least undermine it. Such moments are fleeting, and the executive can act more quickly than the legislature.

The history of the convention's actions on the treaty-making power is further evidence of the development of the Founders' thoughts regarding the executive, a development always toward the utility of a more vigorous executive. The original proposal was to give the treaty-making power to the Senate. After debate, the convention concluded that, although treaties might have the force of law, the negotiation of them was more appropriate to the executive, and so they gave the treaty-making power to the President subject to ratification by two-thirds of the Senate. Hamilton's argument for this in *The Federalist* #75 is based on the attributes unique to the executive, "decision, secrecy and dispatch," qualities essential in negotiation. It was not that they first decided to give the treaty-making power to the President and then included the Senate as a safety precaution. Rather, they first favored the Senate as the instrument, and later modified the Senate's power by adding the executive as initiator and negotiator because of the vigor he could bring to the process.

A similar situation can be discovered with regard to the appointment of ambassadors and judges. The first proposal in the convention was for appointment by the Senate, but eventually they decided that the power of nomination should be given to the executive because of his special attribute of clear personal responsibility. A close reading of *The Journal of the Federal Convention* indicates that there was a gradual but clear movement toward utilizing the special characteristics inherent in a single executive in order to introduce energy into the whole governmental solar system. Their first proposals, if adhered to, would have produced legislative dominance. The modifications introduced during the sixteen weeks of their deliberations were almost invariably ones that fortified the executive either by conjoining the executive with the legislature in the performance of governmental tasks or by providing the executive with weapons to defend the office against legislative trespass.

Of all the powers of the Presidency none had, and has, more potential for development in the hands of a dynamic leader than that found in the amorphous executive power. The Constitution states that "The executive Power shall be vested in a President of the United States." But what is the executive power? The Constitution does not define it. Perhaps this is wise, for men do not have perfect foresight. The ambiguity of this phase, "the executive Power," not only provides the system with flexibility and responsiveness to emergencies but also makes the office a kind of blank canvas on which each incumbent can paint his own colors, and some have chosen to paint it with bright, bold ones.

We do, of course, have some general thoughts about what constitutes the executive power: law enforcement and appointments, but these are specifically mentioned in the Constitution. The real issue is what does the phrase mean to the incumbent? What does he think it authorizes? Some Presidents have read it to mean a general grant of power that in effect enlarges the specific constitutional grants, an interpretation actually anticipated by some members of the convention, by men like Morris who saw the President as "the general guardian of the national interests."

For a President like Abraham Lincoln, this constitutional phrase gave the specific tasks of commander-in-chief and faithful executor of the laws a bolder aspect. The Lincoln who issued the Emancipation Proclamation and who, on his own authority and in opposition to the Supreme Court, suspended the politically sacred writ of habeas corpus, is a man who broadly interpreted his duties and powers. Lincoln was not the only President so to read the executive power. Both Roosevelts, Woodrow Wilson, Truman, Andrew Jackson, and even Thomas Jefferson are prominent among the Presidents who, to one degree or another, conceived of the executive power on a grand scale.

All governments possess the inherent power, the power to do whatever is necessary in an emergency to preserve the state, but it was this ambiguous statement in the Constitution vesting the executive power of the United States in the President that led men like Lincoln to claim that the inherent power belonged to the President. In an emergency, Lincoln asserted, the President could do anything that was not forbidden to Congress. More than this, if the Constitution must be preserved, it is the executive who must act to preserve it, even if this means he must break a law. With regard to the suspension of the writ of habeas corpus, Lincoln asked, "Are all the laws, *but one,* to go unexecuted, and the government itself go to pieces, lest that one be violated?"[3] The very nature of the executive power, the power to enforce the laws and the Constitution, makes the inherent power a presidential power. The President alone possesses the executive power of the United States; if he cannot exercise the inherent power, no one can. It is no wonder that some historians have described this constitutional phrase as the "joker" or "wild card" the Founders placed in the deck of the Constitution.

The Founders wanted to create an energetic presidency. Were they successful? Yes! Critics and friends of the presidency alike agree that the presidency is one of the most vigorous, effective, and powerful offices in the world. Of course, this is in part a product of the current power and wealth of the country as a whole. Nonetheless, one is entitled to ask the cause and effect question here. Would the country have grown so much in power and wealth, would it even be one country rather than several if the Founders had not established the energetic presidency? Think of Jefferson's farsighted purchase of the Louisiana territory or of Lincoln's resoluteness in holding the Union together, or of Franklin Roosevelt's inspirational confidence in the nation during the dark days of the Great Depression. These striking events do not begin to exhaust the list that gives us pause, and lead us to honor our Founders for their wisdom in creating the energetic Presidency.

THE COURTS AND THE JUDICIAL POWER

RALPH A. ROSSUM

The significance the Framers attached to the courts and the judicial power can be surmised by noting the placement, brevity, and generality of the judicial article of the Constitution. To begin with, Article III follows Article I, establishing the legislative branch, and Article II, establishing the executive branch. By so arranging the articles, the Framers addressed each branch, in James Wilson's words, "as its greatness deserves to be considered."[1] Further, Article III is only one-sixth as long as the legislative article, and about a third as long as the executive article. Finally, whereas Article I specifies in great detail the qualifications of representatives and senators, the size of the two houses of Congress, the procedures they must follow, and the powers they are authorized or prohibited to exercise, and whereas Article II likewise is quite detailed in its discussion of the President's qualifications, mode of appointment, powers, and responsibilities, Article III merely vests "the judicial power of the United States" in one Supreme Court—its size is unspecified—and in "such inferior Courts as the Congress may from time to time ordain and establish." It imposes no qualifications on the judges—not even the requirement of citizenship—and outlines no procedures they are obliged to follow.

The Framers left the judicial article as brief and incomplete as they did because they believed what Alexander Hamilton would later declare in *The Federalist* #78: "The judiciary is beyond comparison the weakest of the three departments of power." With him, they understood the judiciary to be "the least dangerous to the political rights of the constitution; because it will be least in a capacity to annoy or injury them." They recognized that in any republican government the greatest threat of tyranny would come from the legislative branch, which, as James Madison declared in the Constitutional Convention, "had evinced a powerful tendency . . . to absorb all power into its vortex." Consequently, they devoted much of their time and energies during the Constitutional Convention to designing institutional arrangements and drafting specific delegations of power that would obviate the threat of legislative tyranny. Most of their discussions and decisions on the judiciary—its powers and functions—were influenced by that objective. The judicial branch was one more means by which they sought to check legislative oppression. They did not perceive that the judiciary would itself be a potential source of oppression; to the extent that it might pose any danger, they believed it could be adequately checked by the very same Congress that the judiciary helped to curb.

The Farmers' deliberations on the judiciary began with two resolutions in the Virginia Plan. Resolution 8 proposed the establishment of a "council of revision," composed of "the Executive and a convenient number of the National Judiciary," which would have "authority to examine every act of the National Legislature before it shall operate, and every act of a particular Legislature before a Negative thereon shall be final. . . ." It further proposed that "the dissent of the said Council shall amount to a rejection, unless the Act of the National Legislature be again passed, or that of a particular Legislature be again negatived by _____ of the members of each branch." Since language in Resolution 6 would have allowed the national legislature "to negative all laws passed by the several States, contravening in the opinion of the National Legislature the articles of Union," Resolution 8 authorized the Council of Revision to review legislation not only of the general government but of the states as well.

Resolution 9 then provided for the actual establishment of the judiciary. It proposed that "a National Judiciary be established to consist of one or more supreme tribunals, and of inferior tribunals to be chosen by the National Legislature, to hold their offices during good behavior; and to receive punctually at stated times fixed compensation for their services, in which no increase or diminution shall be made so as to affect the persons actually in office at the time of such increase or diminution." It further proposed that "the jurisdiction of the inferior tribunals shall be to hear and determine in the first instance, and of the supreme tribunal to hear and determine in the dernier resort, all piracies and felonies on the high seas, captures from an enemy; cases in which foreigners or citizens of other States applying to such jurisdictions may be interested, or which respect the collection of the National revenue; impeachments of any National officers, and questions which may involve the national peace and harmony."

As the convention proceeded with its work, these resolutions were repeatedly taken up and continually refined until they ultimately emerged as the completed Article III. The delegates gave these resolutions their full and careful attention. They did so, however, not because they viewed the judiciary as a serious threat to the political liberty of the people but because, as they confronted the questions of how to structure and empower the judiciary, they wee obligated to think through the principal features of separation of powers and federalism, key elements of what *The Federalist* #9 would call the Framers' improved "science of politics."

The delegates turned their attention to these resolutions for the first time on June 4, at which time they agreed to postpone consideration of the council of revision and adopted unanimously language to establish "one supreme tribunal" and "one or more inferior tribunals." Their deliberations continued on June 5, and focused first of all on the method of appointment. Wilson opposed the Virginia Plan's proposal that judges be appointed by the national legislature. "Experience shewed the impropriety of such appointments by numerous bodies. Intrigue, partiality, and concealment were the necessary consequences." He argued that the national judiciary should be appointed by a single, responsible executive. John Rutledge "was by no means disposed to grant so great a power to any single person. The people," he feared, "will think we are leaning too much towards Monarchy." He also objected to "establishing any national tribunal except a single supreme one. The State Tribunals are most proper to decide in all cases in the first instance." At this juncture, as at several other critical junctures during the convention, Benjamin Franklin sought to restore "a sense of proportion and of the obligations of statesmanship which the Convention seemed in danger of losing."[2] He observed that only two modes of appointment had been mentioned: by the legislature and by the executive. He urged his fellow delegates to suggest such other modes as might occur to them, "it being a point of great moment." He then related "in a brief and entertaining manner" a mode he understood was practiced in Scotland, "in which the nomination proceeded from the Lawyers, who always selected the ablest of the profession in order to get rid of him and share his practice among themselves." He urged the delegates to find some method of making it in the interest of the electors to select the best possible individuals for the judiciary.

Madison thereupon suggested a third method: appointment by "the Senatorial branch." The Senate would be "numerous enough to be confided in," and yet not so numerous as to be governed by the intrigue and partiality of the full legislature. Moreover, it would be "sufficiently stable and independent" to follow its own deliberate judgments. He only "hinted" at this, however, and his motion, seconded by Wilson, was merely that the convention give up for the present selection of the judiciary by the national legislature and leave the choice to some better method to be settled "on maturer reflection." His motion passed, nine states to two, and on June 13, the convention unanimously agreed to appointment by he Senate.

After the delegates quickly agreed that the members of the national judiciary should hold their offices "for good behavior" and receive "a fixed compensation" for their services, Rutledge moved, and Roger Sherman seconded the motion, to expunge the provision in the Resolution 9 establishing inferior tribunals under the national authority. Rutledge stressed that the creation of lower federal courts unnecessarily encroached on the jurisdiction of the states and unnecessarily created obstacles to the adoption of any new constitution. He argued "that the State Tribunals might and ought to be left in all cases to decide in the first instance, the right of appeal to the supreme national tribunal being sufficient to secure the national rights and uniformity of Judgments." Sherman "dwelt chiefly on the supposed expensiveness of having a new set of Courts, when the existing State Courts would answer the same purpose." Their arguments were met by the defenders of a lower federal judiciary. Madison observed that unless inferior tribunals were dispersed throughout the new republic, with final jurisdiction in many cases, "appeals would be multiplied to a most oppressive degree." Besides, without lower federal courts, an appeal would typically provide no remedy. "What was to be done," Madison queried, "after improper Verdicts in State tribunals obtained under the biassed directions of a dependent Judge, or the local prejudicies of an undirected Jury? To remand the cause for a new trial would answer no purpose," for it would presumably end in no better verdict. Madison insisted that "an effective Judiciary establishment commensurate to the legislative authority was essential. A Government without a proper Executive and Judiciary would be a mere trunk of a body without arms or legs to act or move." Wilson argued that the admiralty jurisdiction ought to be given wholly to the national government as it related to cases outside the jurisdiction of particular states, and Rufus King challenged Sherman's argument, contending that "the establishment of inferior tribunals would cost infinitely less than the appeals that would be prevented by them."

Despite these objections, Rutledge's motion to strike out the establishment of inferior tribunals passed on a vote of five states for the motion, four opposed, and two divided. The most that Wilson and Madison could secure on their following motion was the delegates' consent to giving the national legislature the discretion "to institute inferior tribunals" if it chose to do so. Despite Pierce Butler's prediction that "the people will not bear such innovations" and that "the States will revolt at such encroachments," the motion passed, eight states voting yes, two voting no, and one divided.

On June 6, Wilson and Madison moved to reconsider the vote excluding the judiciary from a share in the revision of the laws. Wilson focused on the "expediency of reinforcing the Executive" with the influence of selected judges, while Madison went further and stressed that the Council of Revision "would also enable the Judiciary Department the better to defend itself against Legislative encroachments." He replied to those who contended that the Council of Revision constituted a violation of the principle of separation of powers, in that "the Judiciary Department ought to be separate and distinct from the other great Departments," by observing that it represented no more a violation of the principle than giving the negative to the executive alone: "The maxim on which the objection was founded required a separation of the Executive as well as of the Judiciary from the Legislature and from each other." He then shifted to a policy argument and concluded by noting that "whether the object of the revisionary power was to restrain the Legislature from encroaching on the other co-ordinate Departments, or on the rights of the people at large, or from passing laws unwise in their principle, or incorrect in their form, the utility of annexing the wisdom and weight of the Judiciary to the Executive seemed incontestable."

Madison's arguments, however, failed to convince his colleagues. Elbridge Gerry's response was typical: he believed that "the Executive, whilst standing alone would be more impartial than when he could be covered by the sanctions and seduced by the sophistry of the judges." As a consequence, Wilson's motion to join the judges in the Council of Revision was defeated by a vote of eight states to three.

With the exception of the delegates' action on June 13, when they unanimously resolved that the judges should be appointed by the second branch of the national legislature and that the jurisdiction of the national judiciary should extend to "cases which respect the collection of the national revenue, impeachments of any national officers, and questions which involve the national peace and harmony," the convention did not address the judicial branch again until July 18. Nevertheless, the convention's early and brief deliberations on the judiciary were of decisive importance; not only did they give form to the final shape of Article III but they also prompted the Framers to think profoundly and profitably about the fundamental principles of the new Constitution they were drafting. Thus, the debate over judicial appointment and the proposal to associate the judiciary with the executive in the Council of Revision squarely confronted the Framers with the need to think through their understanding of separation of powers, just as the proposals to establish lower federal courts and to authorize the national legislature to negative state laws — which negative was, in turn, subject to the veto of the Council of Revision — compelled them to work out the principle of federalism.

The Farmers' debate over the Council of Revision was particularly helpful in the development of their new understanding of separation of powers. At the time of the Constitutional Convention, two traditional understandings of separation of powers were extant: the understanding present in the British regime and the understanding present in many of the early state constitutions. In Great Britain power was separated among the three departments of government according to the principle of rule that each department embodied. Thus, the Crown had the powers it did because they were powers associated with the principle of rule by the one, monarchy; the House of Lords had the powers it did because they were associated with the principle of rule by the few, aristocracy; and the House of Commons had the powers it did because they were associated with the principle of rule by the many, democracy. The result of this British understanding was not a functional separation of powers but rather a balance of powers described by Sir William Blackstone in his *Commentaries on the Laws of England* as "the true excellence of the English government." Blackstone explained the advantages of this checking and balancing as follows: "Like three distinct powers in mechanics, they jointly impel the machine of government in a direction different from what either, acting by itself, would have done; but at the same time in the direction partaking of each, and formed out of all; a direction which constitutes the true line of the liberty and happiness of the community." [3]

The understanding of separation of powers present in many of the early state constitutions was entirely different. These constitutions were drafted in the hope of keeping the legislative, executive, and judicial departments separate and distinct from each other. Each department was understood to have a separate and distinct function and was to exercise only the powers associated with that function. As the Massachusetts Constitution put it: "The legislative department shall never exercise the executive and judicial powers, or either of them: The executive shall never exercise the legislative and judicial powers, or either of them: The judicial shall never exercise the legislative and executive powers, or either of them." Since tyranny was understood to consist in the accumulation of all power in one branch of the government, this rigid, functional separation of powers — secured through absolute constitutional prohibitions — was seen by many who helped to draft these early state constitutions as an essential means for the preservation of liberty.

The Framers rejected both of these traditional understandings. They rejected the British understanding of separation of powers, despite its ability to check and balance powers, because it was impossible to duplicate in America. The United States lacked the social raw materials necessary to bring it into existence, namely, a millennium's experience with aristocracy and monarchy. They also rejected the understanding of a rigid, functional separation of powers present in the state constitutions as unable to check the will of tyrannical majorities as expressed through a compliant or demogogic legislature. With Madison, they appreciated that "[w]herever the real power in a Government lies, there is the danger of oppression. In our Governments the real power lies in the majority of the community, and the invasion of private rights is chiefly to be apprehended, not from acts of Government contrary to the sense of its constituents, but from acts in which the government is the mere instrument of the major number of the Constituents." [4] They knew that in any republican government the greatest threat of tyranny came from the legislative branch, which, in the words of *The Federalist* #48, was "everywhere extending the sphere of its activity and drawing all power into its impetuous vortex." "Parchment barriers" could not be trusted to contain this "encroaching spirit of power." The only effective solution to this threat of legislative tyranny was, they recognized, a new kind of separation of powers that provided the executive and the judiciary with the necessary constitutional means to resist these legislative encroachments — one that provided for the checks and balances of the British constitution but by wholly popular means. The Council of Revision, and the Framers' deliberations over it, served as the catalyst for the development of this new separation of powers.

The catalytic effect that the Council of Revision had in developing and clarifying the Framers' new understanding of separation of powers is apparent by examining the debate over associating the judiciary with the executive in the revisionary power that occurred on June 6 and by contrasting it with the next debate on this subject, which occurred on July 21. On June 6, Wilson simply stressed that the council would reinforce the executive, and Madison responded to the charge that the council would result in an "improper mixture" of executive and judicial powers by asserting that it would not violate the principle of separation of powers any more than would the presidential veto itself. He only hinted (and that may be too strong a word) that what is important is not so much a separation of powers as a balance of powers among the three departments of government.

On July 21, when the council was next debated, the quality of the arguments on its behalf were considerably improved. Wilson and Madison both had been forced in the interim to assess the objections based on separation of powers that had been raised to the Council of Revision and, in so doing, to think through exactly what separation of powers meant, or ought to mean. Thus, Madison was now able to defend the council as not inconsistent with separation of powers but as vital to its preservation. He "could not discover in the proposed association of the Judges with the Executive in the Revisionary check on the Legislature any violation of the maxim which requires the great departments of power to be kept separate and distinct. On the contrary he thought it an auxiliary precaution in favor of the maxim." Critical of the rigid, functional separation of powers present in the state constitutions of his day, he observed that "if a Constitutional discrimination of the departments on paper were a sufficient security to each against encroachments of the others, all further provisions would indeed be superfluous. But," he continued, "experience had taught us a distrust of that security; and that it is necessary to introduce such a balance of powers and interests, as will guarantee the provisions on paper. Instead therefore of contenting ourselves with laying down the Theory in the Constitution that each department ought to be separate and distinct," he urged his fellow delegates "to add a defensive power to each which should maintain the Theory in practice." In so doing, they would not be blending the departments together; they would be erecting "effectual barriers for keeping them separate."

Wilson likewise had come to appreciate that separation of powers did not require a separation of the functions of government. In fact, for separation of powers to prevent legislative encroachments, the functions of government had to be blended and balanced among the three departments of government. "The separation of the departments does not require that they should have separate objects but that they should act separately though on the same objects." In this respect, separation of powers would operate in the same manner as bicameralism, where "it is necessary that the two branches of the Legislature should be separate and distinct, yet they are both to act precisely on the same object."

On the theoretical groundwork laid by Madison and Wilson, Gouverneur Morris built a powerful, practical example:

> Suppose that the three powers, were to be vested in three persons, by compact among themselves; that one was to have the power of making — another of executing, and a third of judging, the laws. Would it not be very natural for the two latter after having settled the partition on paper, to observe, and would not candor oblige the former to admit, that as a security against legislative acts of the former which might easily be so framed as to undermine the powers of the two others, the two others ought to be armed with a veto for their own defense, or at least to have an opportunity of stating their objections against acts of encroachment? And would any one pretend that such a right tended to blend and confound powers that ought to be separately exercised? As well might it be said that if three neighbours had three distinct farms, a right in each to defend his farm against his neighbours, tended to blend the farms together.

While the Framers rejected once again Wilson's and Madison's call for a Council of Revision (this time, with three states voting yes, four voting no, and two divided), they ultimately embraced the new understanding of separation of powers that would have supported the Council. They came to appreciate that the only way to solve the problem of "the encroaching spirit of power" was, in the words of *The Federalist* #51, "by so contriving the interior structure of the government . . . that its several constituent parts . . . [are] by their mutual relations, the means of keeping each other in their proper places." They came to realize that separation of powers requires coordinate and equal branches, with each performing a blend of functions, thereby balancing as opposed to strictly separating powers. The Framers thereafter employed this understanding of separation of powers to resolve debates over the relationships among, and the powers appropriately assigned to, the three branches. One of these debates centered on judicial appointment and was ultimately resolved by their recognition that both the executive and the legislative branch could separately participate in the same appointment process; this led to the unanimous agreement on September 7 that the presidential appointment of all judges should be "by and with the advice and Consent of the Senate."

Just as the debate over the Council of Revision was the catalyst for the development of the Framers' new understanding of separation of powers, so, too, the proposals to establish lower federal courts and to authorize the national legislature to negative state laws (subject, in turn, to the Council of

Revision's veto) were of decisive importance in determining the principles and shape of the new federal structure the Framers were creating. The Virginia Plan's resolutions requiring the establishment of lower federal courts and authorizing the national legislature to "negative all laws passed by the several states, contravening in the opinion of the national legislature, the Articles of Union" were clearly national in character and were defended on that ground. Madison, for instance, contended that the lower federal courts were the arms and legs that would complete the national body. He also seconded Charles Pinckney's motion to broaden the authority of the national legislature to negative state laws to include "all laws which they should judge to be improper," arguing that "he could not but regard an indefinite power to negative legislative acts of the States as absolutely necessary to a perfect system." Wilson likewise supported the motion, insisting that "we are now one nation of brethren."

Those delegates opposing these resolutions objected on federal grounds. John Rutledge opposed the establishment of lower federal courts, as they would constitute "an unnecessary encroachment on the jurisdiction of the States," and Hugh Williamson objected to giving the national legislature power to negative state laws because it "might restrain the States from regulating their internal police."

As the debate over these resolutions continued, however, it became increasingly clear to the delegates that the political structure they were creating — in part in response to this debate — could be "neither wholly federal nor wholly national." The new political structure could not be wholly federal, for the new government would operate, in the words of William R. Davie, "in some respects . . . on the states [but] in others on the people." Therefore, the new government could not depend completely on state courts, for, as Edmund Randolph observed, they could not "be trusted with the administration of the national laws. The objects of jurisdiction are such as will often place the general and local policy at variance." On the other hand, the new political structure also could not be wholly national. The states existed as political societies, and few of the delegates seriously urged their abolition. William Johnson's question to the convention was, therefore, apposite: "Does it not seem to follow, that if the states as such are to exist they must be armed with some power of self-defense"? Empowering the national legislature to veto state laws was seen to jeopardize that self-defense, at least for small states. Under the Virginia Plan, the states were not represented equally, and as Gunning Bedford of Delaware animadverted, the large states, which would dominate the national legislature, could use this veto power to crush the small states, "whenever they stood in the way of their ambitious and interested views."

Eventually, after extended and often acrimonious debate, a majority of the delegates came to realize with William Johnson that the states were both distinct "political societies" and "districts of people composing one political society," and agreed to the Great Compromise, with the Senate representing each state equally and with the House representing the people based on the population of each state. Eventually, they acknowledged that the new Constitution would have to be "in strictness neither a national nor a federal constitution; but a composition of both." With that acknowledgment, the delegates were quickly able to dispatch with the resolutions concerning the lower federal courts and the national legislative negative of state laws.

On July 17, the very day after the Great Compromise was accepted, they decisively rejected by a vote of seven states to three the resolution giving Congress the power to reject state laws and agreed instead to a motion by Luther Martin of Maryland that made "the Legislative acts of the U.S. made by virtue and in pursuance of the articles of Union, and all treaties made and ratified under the authority of the U.S. . . . the supreme law of the respective States, as far as those acts or treaties shall relate to the said States, or their Citizens and inhabitants." The same motion declared that "the Judiciaries of the several States shall be bound thereby in their decisions, any thing in the respective laws of the individual States to the contrary notwithstanding." This language had come almost literally from the New Jersey Plan (or the Small State Plan, as it was also called), and had been drafted by delegates who embraced the federal principle and who, while they recognized the need to strengthen the general government, sought only to improve, not replace, the Articles of Confederation. Martin and his allies proposed to add it now to a Constitution that was not wholly federal, because it was also not wholly national; the presence of federal elements in the proposed general government,[5] in this case, the equal representation of all states in the Senate, convinced them that the laws that the new Congress would pass, even though supreme, would not jeopardize the self-defense of the states. The delegates who had unsuccessfully sought approval of the national legislative veto saw this as a way to achieve national supremacy without arousing the suspicions of those who continued to embrace the federal principle; as a consequence, the vote on behalf of Martin's motion was unanimous.

Likewise, on July 18, the convention unanimously agreed to empower Congress to establish lower federal courts at its discretion. Since the Constitution was not wholly national, there was no need for its judiciary to be either whole — that it, complete — or national. Its courts, described by Madison as the government's arms and legs, could be provided by the states. If, however, the courts of the states provided to be biased and untrustworthy, Congress was given the power to establish the general government's own courts, for the new government was also not wholly federal. Once again, the equal representation of the states in the Senate ensured that Congress would exercise this power only when necessary to protect national interests and not to encroach on the states' jurisdiction.

With the resolution of these issues, the judicial article was largely complete. The convention had modified the ninth resolution of the original Virginia Plan so that there was to be only one Supreme Court and such inferior courts as "Congress may from time to time ordain and establish." It determined that federal judges were to be appointed by the President and confirmed by the Senate, were to serve during good behavior, and were to receive compensation that "shall not be diminished during their Continuance in Office"—the delegates having accepted Gouverneur Morris's argument that "the value of money may not only alter, but the state of society may alter." The convention also accepted the language of the Committee of Detail specifying the federal judiciary's jurisdiction as a substitute for the ill-defined provisions of the Virginia Plan, and, with the exception of the delegates' decision on September 4 to transfer the impeachment power from the courts to Congress, this language found its way—without further substantive revision—into Article III, section 2.

The issues of federalism and separation of powers were crucial to the delegates as they drafted the judicial article, and they have been no less so for anyone who has sought an answer to what has been the most enduring judicial question since the founding: Did the Framers intend the Supreme Court to exercise a general power of judicial review, that is, the power to expound the Constitution, and, in so doing, to invalidate those actions of Congress, the executive, and the states that are, in its estimation, contrary to the Constitution? Since the Constitution itself does not explicitly authorize the Court to exercise judicial review over either the acts of the states or those of Congress and the President, those who claim that the Court has this power are obliged to argue inferentially.

Beginning with the federalism issue, that is, the power of the Court to review state acts, Luther Martin's resolution, unanimously accepted by the convention, that national legislation and treaties are the supreme law of the states and that state courts are bound thereby, would seem to imply judicial review of state laws. However, neither Martin's resolution nor the final version of the supremacy clause in Article VI, section 2—which went further still and declared the Constitution itself to be the supreme law of the land—even provides for appeals from state to federal courts, to say nothing of authorizing this kind of judicial review. There is reason to believe that many delegates assumed that the federal courts, and especially the Supreme Court, had power to hear appeals from state courts. For example, since they refused to establish lower federal courts and provided instead only for Congress to establish them if it so chose, the delegates must have recognized that state courts would be, in many if not all instances, courts of first instance for federal cases, and they must have appreciated that uniformity of decisions under such circumstances could be secured only by appeals from state courts to the Supreme Court. However, while the delegates may well have contemplated the possibility of appeals to the Supreme Court, it does not follow that they therefore regarded the implied right of appeal as in turn implying the existence of a general power in the federal judiciary to interpret in a comprehensive way the extent of state authority under the Constitution.

Judicial review of the acts of Congress and the President is also based on inference. The way in which the Constitution provides for a separation of powers that so "connects" and "blends" the three departments of government "as to give to each a constitutional control over the others" would seem to imply this kind of judicial review: this power would give the Court a means of checking and restraining the popular branches and thereby of protecting itself from their encroachments, much as the popular branches —through such constitutional controls as impeachment; Congress's power to make exceptions to the Supreme Court's appellate jurisdiction under Article III, section 2; presidential appointment and senatorial confirmation of judges; congressional determination of the size, shape, and composition of the federal courts; and congressional appropriation of money for the judicial branch—have means at their disposal of restraining the courts.[6] This inference would therefore appear defensible; it is further supported by (1) statements made by several delegates during the convention explicitly favoring judicial review; (2) the contention that judicial review was so well known and normal a function of the courts that the Framers took it for granted and saw no need to make explicit provision for it in the Constitution; and (3) the specific acknowledgment of judicial review made by Alexander Hamilton in *The Federalist* #78. These three specific arguments will be briefly considered before addressing the more general claim that the separation of powers present in the Constitution implies judicial review.

Several delegates to the convention clearly believed that the Court should have some power of judicial review. Gouverneur Morris, for one, observed that the judiciary should not "be bound to say that a direct violation of the Constitution was law." Luther Martin, for another, argued against the Council of Revision, contending that "the constitutionality of laws . . . will come before the judges in their official character. In this character, they have a negative on the laws." Similar statements can be found by Elbridge Gerry, Caleb Strong, Rufus King, and John Rutledge. The problem with these statements, however, is that they imply neither a general power to expound the Constitution nor an obligation on the part of the other branches to regard a judicial decision on the constitutionality of their actions as binding. Moreover, other convention delegates made statements unequivocally rejecting judicial review. Thus, for example, John Mercer "disapproved of the doctrine that the judges as expositors of the Constitution should have authority to declare a law void"; so, too, did John Dickinson, who thought that "as to the power of the Judges to set aside the law, . . . no such power ought to exist."

The contention that judicial review was so normal a judicial function at the time of the convention that no provision had to be made for it in the Constitution likewise collapses upon close scrutiny. Leonard W. Levy has shown that during the period 1776–1787, there were in fact only two legitimate instances where state courts actually invalidated state laws: the "Ten Pound Case" in New Hampshire and *Bayard v. Singleton* in North Carolina. In the former case, the court's action resulted in an abortive attempt to impeach the offending judges, and in the latter, the legislature angrily summoned the judges before it to explain their disregard for its authority. As Levy observes, these cases show that judicial review "was nowhere established, indeed that it seemed novel, controversial, and an encroachment on legislative authority. Its exercise . . . was disputed and liable to provoke the legislature to retaliation." [7] If the Framers had intended judicial review, it is highly unlikely that they would have allowed it to rest on so precarious a foundation or have failed to make specific provision for it.

Hamilton's arguments in *The Federalist* #78 also fail to provide much support for the inference that the Framers intended judicial review. It must be recalled that his argument there were primarily in response to a series of Anti-Federalist essays written by "Brutus." Brutus sought to discredit the Constitution by, among other things, magnifying the powers of the federal judiciary and presenting it as an instrument for consolidating national powers at the expense of the states. In his response in *The Federalist* #78, Hamilton was not so much advocating judicial review as turning Brutus's arguments against himself when he suggested that the Court's power was intended to hold Congress in check and thereby safeguard the states against national aggrandizement by a Congress seeking consolidation. If Congress were to act "contrary to the manifest tenor of the Constitution" and were to attempt to scuttle the federal structure that the Framers had established, the Court could be trusted to invalidate those congressional efforts. As Leonard Levy has observed on this matter as well, Hamilton's remarks "are evidence of shrewd political tactics, not of the Framers' intention to vest judicial review in the Supreme Court over acts of Congress." [8]

Hamilton's personal views toward the Court and its exercise of judicial review were quite different and are apparent elsewhere. Thus, for example, at the Constitutional Convention on June 8, when Hamilton introduced his own plan for a new Constitution as a substitute for the Virginia and New Jersey Plans, he made no provision for any kind of judicial review. Likewise, in *The Federalist* #33, when Hamilton discussed the necessary and proper clause, regarded by many Anti-Federalists as the source of unlimited power for Congress, he did not so much as allude to the Supreme Court when he answered his own question of "who is to judge the necessity and propriety of the laws to be passed for executing the powers of the Union?" For him, the Congress was to judge "in the first instance the proper exercise of its powers; and its constituents in the last." He then continued by observing that "if the federal government should overpass the just bounds of its authority, and make a tyrannical use of its powers; the people whose crea-ture it is must appeal to the standard they have formed, and take such measures to redress the injury done to the constitution, as the exigency may suggest and prudence justify." Again, he made no reference to Supreme Court intervention or its exercise of judicial review. Finally, in *The Federalist* #84, Hamilton made no mention of the judiciary as a means of securing the guarantees of a bill of rights but again insisted that, despite "whatever declarations may be inserted in any constitutions" respecting these rights, they "must altogether depend on public opinion, and on the general spirit of the people and the government."

As these three specific arguments on behalf of judicial review cannot by themselves establish that the Framers intended the Court to have this power, it is necessary to return to the more general claim that the separation of powers present in the Constitution implies that the Court has the final authority to pass on the constitutionality of the acts of its coequal branches. As with the more specific arguments, this more general claim is also impos-sible to sustain. It is possible to argue that the separation of powers present in the Constitution implies the existence of judicial review as a means by which the Court can check and balance the popular branches, just as Con-gress and the President have means by which they can check and balance the judiciary, but this line of reasoning is fatally flawed. The Constitution simply does not make explicit provision for judicial review. The Constitu-tion does, however, explicitly provide for impeachment; congressional con-trol of the Court's appellate jurisdiction; congressional determination of the size, shape, and composition of the entire federal judiciary; presidential appointment of judges subject to Senate confirmation; congressional appro-priations for the courts; etcetera. It is not so much that judicial review can be inferred from separation of powers, as that separation of powers can be inferred from the specific powers that the Constitutional assigns to the branches, thereby enabling each one to be "a constitutional check on the others."

The general claim that the separation of powers present in the Consti-tution implies judicial review is also contradicted by the fact that James Madison, whose contributions to the delegates' emerging understanding of separation of powers were second to none—whose contributions to the framing of the Constitution were so great that he is commonly called "the Father of the Constitution"—flatly denied that the Supreme Court had a general power to interpret the Constitution. During a debate on August 27 over extending the jurisdiction of the Supreme Court to "all cases arising under this Constitution" and the laws passed by Congress, James Madison argued that it was going "too far to extend the jurisdiction of the Court generally to cases arising under the Constitution" and that the Court's jurisdiction ought "to be limited to cases of a Judiciary Nature." He pleaded that "the Right of expounding the Constitution in cases not of this nature ought not to be given to that Department . . . it being generally supposed that the jurisdiction given was constructively limited to cases of a Judiciary nature." [9] Madison reiterated his belief that the judiciary did not possess the general power of expounding the Constitution in October 1788, when he declared that such a power would make "the Judiciary Department paramount in fact to the Legislature, which was never intended and can never be proper." [10] He held to this same belief once he was in the House of Representatives, as his statement during the June 16, 1789, debate on the President's removal power shows: after acknowledging the duty of the judiciary to expound the laws and Constitution, he demanded to know "upon what principle it can be contended that any one department draws from the Constitution greater powers than another, in marking out the limits of the powers of the several departments." He insisted that no provision was made in the Constitution "for a particular authority to determine the limits of the constitutional division of power between the branches of government."

Madison never asserted that the Court possessed a general power to expound the Constitution or that a judicial decision regarding the constitutionality of the actions of Congress or the executive was binding on the political branches. He did not contend that the Court's interpretations were superior to or entitled to precedence over those of Congress or the President. He claimed only that the Court should have final authority to pass on constitutional questions that affected its own duties and responsibilities, that is, that were of "a judiciary nature." Chief Justice John Marshall's opinion in *Marbury v. Madison* (in which the Court for the first time exercised the power of judicial review to invalidate an act of Congress — but, and this is important, it was an act that dealt specifically with the judiciary) is wholly consistent with Madison's understanding of the limited nature of judicial review. In it, he did not contend that the Court had a special function vested in it to enforce the Constitution or to police the other branches of government; rather, he argued that the Court must decide a litigated issue within its jurisdiction and, in so doing, must give effect to the supreme law of the land.

Madison's and Marshall's understanding of the limited nature of judicial review still gives the Court some advantage over the popular branches, and necessarily so since most legislation potentially involves questions of individual legal rights that can be construed as appropriate for judicial determination. Nonetheless, the Framers did not fear that this limited judicial review would jeopardize separation of powers, as they had explicitly provided the other branches with ample power to control the courts. To begin with, Congress could determine — and subsequently alter as circumstances dictated — the size, shape, and composition of the federal court system. It could thereby protect itself from judicial encroachments, if necessary, by limiting the entire federal judiciary to one Supreme Court consisting of a single justice. In addition, most decisions of the courts are not self-enforcing, and thus, as *The Federalist* #78 observed, the judiciary is necessarily obliged to "depend upon the aid of the executive even for the efficacy of its judgments." Further, the delegates agreed to language in Article III, section 2, that granted to Congress plenary power to make exceptions to the appellate jurisdiction of the Supreme Court. Commenting on the exceptions clause in *The Federalist* #80, Hamilton observed that "if some partial inconveniences" should appear to be connected with the incorporation of any of the particular powers the Framers gave to the Supreme Court, "it ought to be recollected that the national legislature will have ample authority to make such exceptions and prescribe such regulations as will be calculated to obviate or remove these inconveniences." [11] Finally, the Framers provided Congress with the power to impeach members of the judiciary, a power which Hamilton in *The Federalist* #81 described as "a complete security" against "the supposed danger of judiciary encroachments on the legislative authority."

While the federal judiciary generated little controversy during the drafting of the Constitution, that all changed during the ratification debates. The Anti-Federalists perceived the judicial article as a threat to democracy, to separation of powers, and to the continued existence of the states. It was perceived as a threat to democracy, because it vested enormous power over the vital daily concerns of men in a small group of nonelected judges serving during good behavior. As Brutus declared, "I question whether the world ever saw, in any period of it, a court of justice invested with such immense powers, and yet placed in a situation so little responsible." The Anti-Federalists recognized that "there is no feature in a free government more difficult to be well formed" than the judiciary. This was so because of the nature of the judicial function. As the "Federal Farmer" observed:

> It is true, the laws are made by the legislature: but the judges and juries, in their interpretations, and in directing the execution of them, have a very extensive influence for preserving or destroying liberty, and for changing the nature of the government. It is an observation of an approved writer, that when we have ascertained and fixed its limits with all the caution and precision we can, it will yet be formidable, somewhat arbitrary and despotic—that is, after all of our cares, we must leave a vast deal to the discretion and interpretation—to the wisdom, integrity, and politics of the judges.

While the Anti-Federalists recognized that judicial discretion was inevitable under any constitution, they faulted the Framers for failing to fix any limits on it. Article III, after all, was both brief and incomplete and, while it did provide Congress with powers to check judicial encroachments, the Anti-Federalists expected that Congress would be loath to restrain the judiciary, for the courts would be the principal means of consolidating all power into the general government and thereby enhancing the powers of Congress.

Moreover, Article III extended federal court jurisdiction to "all cases in law and equity." Equity—the power to dispense with the harsh rigor of the written law and to formulate decrees of relief in certain cases as a court deems necessary—was seen by the Anti-Federalists to pose a particular threat to liberty in that, in the words of the "Federal Framer," it enhanced "an arbitrary power of discretion in the judges, to decide as their conscience, their opinions, their caprice, or their politics" might dictate. England had established a system for drawing the line between law and equity that was rooted in tradition and bound by precedent, but the United States had no such system. Further, with political separation from England had also come legal separation from the binding precedents of the English common law. As the "Federal Farmer" animadverted: "We have no precedents in this country, as yet, to regulate the divisions of equity as in Great Britain; equity, therefore, in the Supreme Court for many years will be mere discretion." In any government dedicated to the rule of law, such discretion is inherently dangerous, and the Anti-Federalists charged that the Constitution's lack of precision in defining the limits of equity was a serious defect. "It is a very dangerous thing," the "Federal Farmer" warned, "to vest in the same judge power to decide on the law, and also general powers in equity; for if the law restrain him, he is only to step into his shoes of equity, and give what judgment his reason or opinion may dictate." [12]

The Anti-Federalists particularly feared this vast judicial discretion because, unlike legislative or executive abuse, judicial abuse would be difficult for the people fully to discern—judicial proceedings are, the "Federal Farmer" sagaciously noted, "far more intricate, complex, and out of the . . . [people's] immediate view." Thus, "bad law immediately excites a general alarm" but "a bad judicial determination, though no less pernicious in its consequences," does not, for it is "immediately felt, probably, by a single individual only, and noticed only by his neighbors, and a few spectators in the Court." Thus, the Anti-Federalists concluded—in direct contradiction to Hamilton's claim in *The Federalist* #78—that "we are more in danger of sowing the seeds of arbitrary government in this department than in any other."

The Anti-Federalists also perceived the judicial article as a threat to democracy because of the way in which it weakened that most democratic of institutions: jury trial. While Article III, section 2, guaranteed the right to trial by jury in criminal cases, it did not in civil cases. Moreover, even in criminal cases, it conferred upon the Supreme Court appellate jurisdiction "both as to law and fact," thereby prompting many Anti-Federalists to fear that the Supreme Court could overturn verdicts of acquittal returned by juries. As Luther Martin complained in his "Genuine Information":

> The appellate jurisdiction extends, as I have observed, to cases criminal as well as to civil, and on the appeal the Court is to decide not only on the law

but on the fact, if therefore, even in criminal cases the general government is not satisfied with the verdict of the jury, its officer may remove the prosecution to the supreme court, and there the verdict of the jury is to be of no effect, but the judges of this court are to decide upon the fact as well as the law, the same as in civil cases.

Martin's objections were part of a more general Anti-Federalist objection to the Court's appellate jurisdiction. They saw in it the tracks of aristocracy. As "A Friend to the Rights of the People" observed, the Court's appellate jurisdiction "extends to all cases and disputes which may happen between man and man; and so may prove, in the issue, a source of mischief and ruin to thousands—The rich and wilful citizen may," he warned darkly, "after passing through the lower forms of law, appeal up to this federal court, at four, or five hundred miles distance; there the other party must repair, at an amazing expence, or else lose his case however just and righteoce [sic]—Hereby the course of public justice may be much obstructed, the poor, oppressed, and many undone—Every door therefore against such a pernicious effect, ought to be shut in the Constitution." "Brutus" was in full agreement. Expecting that the Supreme Court would hold its session "at the seat of the general government," thereby obligating the parties to "travel many hundred miles, with their witnesses and lawyers to prosecute or defend a suit," he anticipated that "no man of midling fortune" could sustain the expense of such a lawsuit and "therefore the poorer and midling class of citizen will be under the necessity of submitting to the demands of the rich and the lordly, in cases that will come under the cognizance of this court."

The Anti-Federalists also perceived the judicial article as a threat to separation of powers. "Brutus" was one of a few who predicted that the Court would come to exercise judicial review and that this in turn would result in the supremacy of a politically irresponsible judiciary, and he saw this as problematical under any understanding of separation of powers. He put the matter bluntly: "If . . . the legislature pass any laws, inconsistent with the sense the judges put upon the constitution, they will declare it void; and therefore in this respect their power is superior to that of the legislature." Hamilton's attempt in *The Federalist* #78 to suggest that judicial review would be used to check the consolidationist tendencies of the Congress was not convincing.

Finally, the Anti-Federalists perceived the judicial article as a threat to the continued existence of the states. They feared with "Brutus" that the Court would "operate to effect, in the most certain, but yet silent and imperceptible manner, what is evidently the tendency of the constitution: —I mean, an entire subversion of the legislative, executive, and judicial powers of the individual states." The judges would "lean strongly in favor of the general government" and would rule in such a way as "will favor an extension of its jurisdiction" not only because the Constitution's provisions permit it — they are "conceived in general and indefinite terms, which are either equivocal, ambiguous, or which require long definitions to unfold the extent of their meaning" — but also because it will "enlarge the sphere of their own authority." "Brutus" was quick to point out that "every extension of the power of the general legislature, as well as of the judicial powers, will increase the powers of the courts; and the dignity and importance of the judges, will be in proportion to the extent and magnitude of the powers they exercise."

Despite the Anti-Federalists' serious misgivings concerning the judicial article — and despite their other and extensive objections to the Constitution more generally — the Constitution was ratified, and the new government it established came into being. However, the framing of the federal judiciary did not end with ratification; the judicial article was not complete until Congress passed the Judiciary Act of 1789. This act provided for a Supreme Court consisting of a chief justice and five associate justices and created a system of inferior federal courts. It established thirteen federal district courts of one judge each — one district for each of the eleven states that had, by that time, ratified the Constitution and two additional districts, in Virginia and Massachusetts for Kentucky and Maine, and it provided for three circuit courts, each composed of two justices of the Supreme Court sitting in conjunction with one district court judge. It stated the jurisdiction of the various courts in great detail and their organization and procedure to a lesser degree.

The Federalist #39 had described the Constitution as neither wholly national nor wholly federal but a composition of both. The members of the First Congress acted in conformity with this statement as they drafted the Judiciary Act. Parts of it were unquestionably national in character. Thus, in addition to establishing lower federal tribunals rather than simply relying on state courts, the Congress also included section 25, which brought the state courts directly under federal appellate jurisdiction by providing for appeals from state courts to the federal judiciary. Under this section, appeals could be taken to the U.S. Supreme Court whenever the highest state court having jurisdiction of the case ruled against the constitutionality of a federal law or treaty; ruled in favor of the validity of a state act that had been challenged as contrary to the Constitution or federal law; or ruled against a right or privilege claimed under the Constitution or federal law. In brief, appeals could be taken whenever the state judiciary assertedly failed to give full recognition to the supremacy of the Constitution or to federal laws and treaties. The Constitution, of course did not specifically provide for appeals from state or federal courts, but the Congress assumed the right to be implied and thought it vital to the uniform upholding of federal laws throughout the Union.[13]

Although the creation of lower federal courts and section 25 were national in character, other provisions of the Judiciary Act of 1789 were federal. Thus, it granted state courts concurrent original jurisdiction in all civil suits at common law and equity — it conferred upon the federal courts exclusive jurisdiction only in admiralty and maritime cases and in cases involving crimes and offenses cognizable under the authority of the United States. Since state courts were more numerous, Congress clearly expected them to be the principal courts of first instance in the federal judicial system. Another provision that was definitely federal in character was Section 34, which required that "the laws of the several States, except where the Constitution, treaties, or statutes of the United States shall otherwise require or provide, shall be regarded as rules of decision in trials at common law in the courts of the United States in cases where they apply."

With the passage of the Judiciary Act of 1789, the First Congress completed the work of establishing the federal judiciary. The Framers were willing to let Congress complete their work because they were confident that separation of powers and federalism — the key elements in their improved "science of politics," which arose in large part out of their deliberations over the judicial article — would oblige Congress to establish a federal court system that was consistent with those key elements. The Judiciary Act both vindicated their confidence and affirmed Hamilton's concluding remarks on the judiciary in *The Federalist* #83: 'The truth is that the general genius of a government is all that can be substantially relied upon for permanent effects. Particular provisions, though not altogether useless, have far less virtue and efficacy than are commonly ascribed to them; and the want of them will never be with men of sound discernment a decisive objection to any plan which exhibits the leading characters of a good government."

WAR POWERS, TREATIES, AND THE CONSTITUTION

CHARLES A. LOFGREN

"Experience is a severe preceptor, but it teaches useful truths," wrote John Jay in 1788 as he reviewed events full of sobering lessons for America's security within the international arena.[1] Jay was correct. When the Second Continental Congress resolved in favor of American independence on July 2, 1776, its action did not assure the result. Transforming the colonies into free and independent states required satisfactory progress in the war, which had begun over a year earlier, in the spring of 1775. Not until 1783 did the American government, now operating under the Articles of Confederation, conclude a final treaty of peace with Great Britain. This outcome required a trained Continental Army, able to face British professionals in open battle, and it turned as well on a formal treaty of alliance with France, Britain's archrival in Europe. With peace came other problems. Large chunks of territory remained under foreign control; military weakness enfeebled diplomacy; and treaty obligations went unheeded at the state level.

Against this background, it is not surprising that the Framers of the American Constitution, meeting a scant four years after Britain formally acknowledged American independence, recognized the requirements of security within a world of sovereign nations. To understand both the grants and, as best as one can, the question marks of the Constitution in the twin areas of national defense and foreign affairs, we need first to turn to the Articles of Confederation and their record of operation.

Although the fact is often overlooked, the Articles granted Congress a near-monopoly of overtly war-related and foreign relations powers. Article IX, which included the Confederation's major substantive powers, began by vesting Congress with "the sole and exclusive right and power of determining on peace and war." Congress alone could send and receive ambassadors, enter into treaties and alliances, and grant letters of marque and reprisal in peacetime. Earlier, Article VI provided that, unless Congress consented, no state could enter into diplomatic activities with foreign governments or keep an army or navy in time of peace, nor could a state engage

242

in war without congressional consent "unless such State be actually invaded by enemies, or shall have received certain advice of a resolution being formed by some nation of Indians to invade such State, and the danger is so imminent as not to admit of a delay, till the United States in Congress assembled can be consulted. . . ." States could issue letters of marque and reprisal in wartime, but only under congressional direction.

To provide military forces, Congress could "build and equip" a navy and set the size of land forces, "mak[ing] requisitions from each State for its quota, in proportion to the number of white inhabitants in such State. . . ." For "[a]ll charges of war, and all other expenses that shall be incurred for the common defense or general welfare," Article VIII authorized Congress to assess sums on the individual states (in proportion to the value of all land within each state), the legislatures of which were then obligated to collect the necessary taxes. Decisions to raise military forces and levy taxes, to make war or peace, to issue letters of marque and reprisal in time of peace, and to enter into treaties or alliances, all required the votes of nine states.

Despite the broad grants, complex and interrelated military and diplomatic problems emerged under the Confederation government. Although the source of the difficulties was not simply constitutional, they pointed up serious deficiencies in the Articles of Confederation. The problems involved two major foreign nations, Indian tribes in the West, individual states, and the Mediterranean trade.

Great Britain was one culprit. Following the Treaty of Peace in 1783, it had refused to withdraw its forces from a line of posts south of the Canadian border in northern New York and the Great Lakes region. These forts had both strategic and economic value. Without them, the Americans were forced to rely on less tenable positions further south and lost out in the fur trade of the region. Not least, Americans suspected that the British, operating out of the posts, continued to instigate Indian warfare. Another grievance was Britain's refusal to admit shipping from the now independent United States to full trading privileges with the empire, particularly the British Isles and the lucrative British West Indies.

Spain's derelictions paralleled England's. The Treaty of Peace between America and Great Britain (to which Spain was not a party) had set the line of 31 degrees north latitude as the northern boundary of West Florida and hence the southeastern boundary of the United States. But Spain, again in control of Florida as the result of the general peace settlement in 1783, noted that when Florida had been under English rule, the boundary had run further to the north. The Spaniards accordingly refused to recognize the new nation's southern border. Ensconced in Louisiana since the end of the Seven Years War, they also sat athwart and blocked the lower Mississippi River, which constituted the major commercial outlet of the growing trans-Appalachian West. From both Florida and Louisiana, they, too, allegedly encouraged Indian raids. Finally, the Americans eyed trade with continental

Spain, but the Spanish government balked at a treaty conceding most-favored-nation treatment.

Throughout the West, Indians remained a barrier to easy white settlement. The problem was partly that Britain and Spain did encourage resistance to American incursions. (The peace settlement, they told the natives, had not really established permanent American control of the area.) More fundamentally, strong tribes both in the Ohio Valley and in the Southwest saw initial American survey efforts as only the first stage in white domination, a conclusion helped along by the inability of the Confederation government to impose any order on settlement. Casualties ran high, with some 1,500 whites killed in Kentucky alone between 1783 and 1790 (when policies of the new government under the Constitution began to be felt). Giving the situation a still more ominous cast, whites west of the mountains had little reason not to flirt with separatist schemes until such time as the central government could guarantee safety in the region.

Within the existing states, other difficulties arose. The peace settlement forbade the United States from placing lawful impediments in the way of Britishers who sought collection of prewar debts; it also outlawed further confiscation of British property. Several states ignored the provisions, probably contrary to the mandate of the Articles of Confederation, which (in Article XIII) bound the states to observe the lawful determinations of Congress. In New York, in *Rutgers v. Waddington* (1784), Alexander Hamilton gained court reversal of a portion of one confiscation action, but the broader problem remained unresolved, thereby giving the British an excuse for not abiding by their commitment to withdraw from the northern forts. Elsewhere, states continued to treat directly with the Indian tribes; quasi-independent Vermont toyed with a Canadian connection; a dispute over the Canadian-American boundary threatened peace in the northern counties of Massachusetts (the present state of Maine); and rumors circulated about British influence in Shays' Rebellion.

Along the North African coast, Tripoli, Algiers, and Morocco added still another irritant. For revenue, the rulers of the Barbary states exacted tribute from the nations whose commercial ships plied Mediterranean trade routes. Pirates swooped on those not paying the protection; and crews were held for ransom, kept in brutal slavery until it was paid. While under colonial rule, the Americans had benefited from British arrangements with the North Africans. Once independent, they became fair game. From his post as American minister to France, an angry Thomas Jefferson suggested that John Paul Jones could discipline the offenders with a few ships — but there were no ships. Nor could Congress afford the cheaper option — tribute.

In fairness, none of these difficulties met quick solution once the new government under the Constitution began operation. They nonetheless pointed up the weaknesses of the Confederation. In truth, until the central American government secured a source of funds, the British had little to fear. The same was true of the Spanish to the south and the Barbary states across the ocean. An instructive episode began in 1784, when Congress recommended a 700-man, one-year army, primarily to operate against Indians north of the Ohio River, and the next year replaced it with a three-year force. The units only slowly materialized and proved largely ineffective against the pro-British tribes, not least because the men generally went unpaid owing to the failure of individual states to respond to Confederation assessments.

Nor, quite apart from lack of military muscle, could the American government shape an effective diplomatic campaign on either the northern posts issue or the trade front. John Jay, as the Confederation's secretary of foreign affairs, forcefully argued that the Treaty of Peace bound the individual states, but so long as state courts had jurisdiction over disputes involving British debts and Tory confiscations, treaty guarantees remained hollow, which the British recognized. Other factors further reduced English incentives to treat with the Americans. Although West Indian interests in Parliament protested the restrictions on importation of American goods, they were outmatched by representatives of British shipping and commercial groups, who distinctly benefited from exclusion of the Americans and saw no chance of American retaliation. In particular, the American government had no authority to enact the navigation acts and impost measures that could keep out British goods. While discussing trade policy before Parliament in 1787, Lord Grenville declared, "We do not know whether they [the United States] are under one head, directed by many, or whether they have any head at all."[2] Only individual states could strike back at the British regulations, and although several did, no uniform policy of retaliation emerged. John Adams, the first American minister to the Court of St. James, could do nothing.

The new nation's straits became distressingly apparent when Secretary Jay attempted to gain a treaty with Spain. (The same series of events sensitized the southern states to the dangers of allowing treaty approval by simple majority.) In 1785, Jay secured authorization from Congress to negotiate an agreement covering trade with peninsular Spain, the Florida boundary, and navigation of the Mississippi River. Attuned to the security of Louisiana and Spain's possessions farther south and west, the Spanish envoy, Don Diego de Gardoqui, flatly refused to concede the last point, but indicated that if the United States renounced free navigation of the Mississippi, a trade and boundary agreement might follow. With nothing else available for bargaining, Jay asked Congress to modify his instructions, to allow him to offer American forebearance of Mississippi navigation for twenty-five years. Southern representatives in Congress, whose states had claims and commercial ties in the Southwest, vehemently objected; but on a 7–5 vote, along strict sectional lines, Jay received his new instruction. (The Articles, however, required nine votes for the approval of treaties, which made further negotiation pointless.)

Solutions to the Confederation's military and diplomatic difficulties were thus readily apparent. Most of all, the government required a source of income that it could tap without reliance on the states. With money, military forces would follow, although, to be sure, it would further help if Congress could recruit directly rather than have to rely on the states as recruiting agents. As for convincing other nations that American treaties would be enforced, a mechanism was needed to produce state compliance. In addition, although perhaps not so crucial, clarification of the constitutional status of treaties as binding law would be useful. To allow diplomatic leverage short of military force, Congress required authority to regulate foreign commerce.

The Constitution drafted in Philadephia neatly remedied the deficiencies disclosed by the Confederation's record in military affairs and foreign policy. Indeed, we often forget—and need reminding—how many of the new document's grants involved national security. Most obviously, Congress received powers

> to define and punish Piracies and Felonies committed on the high Seas, and Offences against the Law of Nations;
>
> to declare War, grant Letters of Marque and Reprisal, and make Rules concerning Captures on Land and Water;
>
> to raise and support Armies, but no Appropriation of Money to that Use shall be for a longer Term than two Years;
>
> to provide and maintain a Navy;
>
> to make Rules for the Government and Regulation of the land and naval Forces;
>
> to provide for calling forth the Militia to execute the Laws of the Union, suppress Insurrections and repel Invasions; [and]
>
> to provide for organizing, arming, and disciplining, the Militia, and for governing such Part of them as may be employed in the Service of the United States, reserving to the States respectively, the Appointment of the Officers, and the Authority of training the Militia according to the discipline prescribed by Congress.

These provisions amplified and clarified powers contained in the Articles. In particular, the authority to raise armies without reliance on state requisitions and to call forth the state militias represented major accretions. Yet the overtly war-related powers of Congress were less crucial than two others— the powers "to lay and collect Taxes, Duties, Imposts and excises, to pay the Debts and provide for the common Defence and general Welfare," and "[t]o regulate Commerce with foreign Nations. . . ."

The President, too, received significant responsibilities, although, as we shall discover, contemporaries almost certainly construed his duties narrowly. He became "Commander in Chief of the Army and Navy of the United States, and of the Militia of the several States, when called into the actual Service of the United States," and was ordered to "take Care that the Laws be faithfully executed." He shared another key grant—the "Power, by and with the Advice and Consent of the Senate, to make Treaties, provided two thirds of the Senators present concur." He was given sole authority to nominate ambassadors and other diplomatic officials, but his choices were made subject to Senate confirmation, and he alone could receive diplomatic representatives from other nations.

Less commonly noticed in discussions of the Constitution and national security, the Philadelphia Convention assigned a key task to the judiciary. The jurisdiction of federal courts would extend to cases involving treaties of the United States, diplomatic representatives, and citizens of foreign nations. As an added safeguard, it clarified the status of treaties as supreme law, "any Thing in the Constitution or Laws of any State to the Contrary notwithstanding."

More stringently than the Articles, the proposed Constitution limited state participation in war-making and foreign relations. States were flatly forbidden to conclude treaties or alliances or issue letters of marque and reprisal. Without the consent of Congress, they could not maintain troops or navies in peacetime, nor "engage in War, unless actually invaded, or in such imminent Danger as will not admit of delay."

These extensive provisions entered the Constitution at various times during the Constitutional Convention's nearly four months of deliberations, but from the start the delegates realized their need. In introducing the Virginia Plan, on May 29, Governor Edmund Randolph began by underscoring the urgency of the military and foreign situation. His remarks (in their fullest recorded version) deserve extended quotation:

> It [the Confederation] *does not provide against foreign invasion.* If a State acts against a foreign power contrary to the laws of nations or violates a treaty, it cannot punish that State, or compel its obedience to the treaty. It can only leave the offending States to the operations of the offended power. It therefore cannot prevent a war. If the rights of an ambassador be invaded by any citizen it is only in a few States that any laws exist to punish the offender. A State may encroach on foreign possessions in its neighbourhood and Congress cannot prevent it. . . . None of the judges in the several States [are] under the obligation of an oath to support the confederation. . . .
>
> Imbecility of the Confederation [is] equally conspicuous when called upon to support a war. The journals of Congress [provide] a history of expedients. The States [are constantly] in arrears to the federal treasury. . . .
>
> What reason [is there] to expect that the treasury will be better filled in the future, or that money can be obtained under the present powers of Congress to support a war [?] *Volunteers* [are] not to be depended on for

such purpose. *Militia* [are] difficult to be collected and almost impossible to be kept in the field. *Draughts* stretch the strings of government too violently to be adopted. Nothing short of a regular military force will answer the end of war, and this [is] only to be created and supported by money.

Rather than delineate the specific military and foreign relations powers that a new constitution should contain, the Virginia Plan offered the principle of assigning the legislative powers of the Confederation Congress to a national legislature, and the executive powers of the old Congress to a national executive. The plan implied a power to raise revenue and proposed that the legislature have authority to veto state legislation and militarily coerce recalcitrant states.

Despite Randolph's initial observations, the convention's proceedings disclose a striking characteristic: the delegates *said* relatively little about military and foreign affairs. But their silence hardly constituted a lack of concern. Instead, the provisions just reviewed emerged almost as a matter of course from the Committee of Detail (in early August), the Committee on Postponed Parts (at the beginning of September), and the Committee of Style (just before final adjournment). Extended debate was unnecessary. A clear consensus existed that effective government demanded authority regarding national security.

In several respects, however, the Constitution's war-related and foreign affairs provisions did attract a degree of attention. We turn next to three areas that drew comments in the convention and produced controversy either in the ratification debates or in subsequent years: the armies and militia clauses; the war-making authority of Congress and the President's role as commander-in-chief; and the treaty-making powers of the President and the Senate (with a brief look at the legal status of treaties).

Within the convention, the armies and militia clauses together drew more commentary than the others. This is not surprising, for they represented the clearest *addition* to the military powers of the Confederation — save, of course, for the power of taxation itself. Furthermore, for over a century Americans had followed the attacks by English radicals on standing armies. Pictured as a force officered by aristocrats and composed of rank-and-file soldiers who were drawn from the dregs of society, brutalized by harsh discipline, and turned into near-automatons, a standing army emerged in this view as a tool of tyranny. Direct experience with the British army during a series of colonial wars that culminated in the Seven Years War, as well as during the decade preceding the outbreak of the War for Independence, only confirmed the description. Yet it is another measure of the convention's consensus on military matters that despite the prevalent anti-army ideology, the only limitation on armies included in the Constitution was the two-year restriction on appropriations. No state voted for Elbridge Gerry's motion to place a numerical limit on peacetime armies.

By contrast, the militia represented a bulwark of liberty. Comprising, for example, all free men between the ages of sixteen and sixty, it both protected the community from external attack and prevented domestic tyranny. That the actual militia system had deteriorated — and unquestionably had proved inadequate in the Revolutionary War — mattered less than the continued emotional commitment that it stirred. Indeed, the armies clause gave increased importance to the militia as a counterweight, a consideration reflected in the convention's careful refinement of the central government's authority to regulate and call up the state militias. The remarkable feature of the militia clause is nonetheless not the existence of limitations but the grant itself — and not least because the delegates surely expected that, like the armies clause, it would become a prominent target in the ratification debates.

The two clauses in fact came under sustained attack once the Constitution went before the states. The dissent of the Anti-Federalist minority in Pennsylvania's convention conveys the flavor and contains a subtle contrast to which we shall soon return. The dissenters charged:

> A standing army in the hands of a government placed so independent of the people may be made a fatal instrument to overturn the public liberties; it may be employed to enforce the collection of the most oppressive taxes, and to carry into execution the most arbitrary measures. An ambitious man who may have the army at his devotion may step up into the throne, and seize upon absolute power.
>
> The absolute command that Congress have over the militia may be made instrumental to the destruction of all liberty, both public and private; whether of a personal, civil, or religious nature.
>
> First, the personal liberty of every man probably from sixteen to sixty years of age may be destroyed by the power Congress have in organizing and governing of the militia. . . .
>
> Secondly, the rights of conscience may be violated, as there is no exemption of those persons who are conscientiously scrupulous of bearing arms. . . .
>
> Thirdly, the absolute command of Congress over the militia may be destructive of public liberty; for under the guidance of an arbitrary government, they may be made the unwilling instruments of tyranny.[3]

The Federalists met such attacks by conceding that the Constitution granted the powers in question, but they stressed that the contingencies the nation would face were indefinite. As Alexander Hamilton put it in *The Federalist* #23,

> These powers ought to exist without limitation, *because it is impossible to foresee or define the extent and variety of national exigencies, or the correspondent extent and variety of the means which may be necessary to satisfy them.* The circumstances that endanger the safety of nations are infinite; and for this reason no constitutional shackles can wisely be imposed on the power to which care of it is committed [emphasis in original].

Whatever the disagreement over the wisdom of giving the central government authority to raise and support armies, and call up the militia, the result of New Constitution was a clear understanding that the powers existed.

During the Civil War, and again in both World War I and the Vietnam War, an intriguing constitutional issue arose: does the central government's authority to raise armies encompass the power to draft troops? Nowhere did the Framers and ratifiers explicitly address the problem, but their remarks implicitly provide an answer. At first glance, of course, the proper response appears to be an obvious "yes," particularly in light of the indefinite contingency arguments that the Federalists advanced in 1787–1788. (The comment from Hamilton quoted in the preceding paragraph is an example.) "[A]s the mind cannot conceive an army without the men to compose it," commented the United States Supreme Court in 1918, "on the face of the Constitution the objection that it does not give the power to provide for such men would seem to be too frivolous for further notice." [4]

Yet it seems probable that Americans in the 1780s would have taken the opposite view. For them, *as a matter of definition,* armies comprised men who served for pay, not out of compulsion. A decade later, a Federalist congressman delineated the distinction in the course of a debate over authorizing an army during the Quasi-War with France; "if there be any characteristic marks by which to distinguish a militia from regulars," he explained, "it is that the former are compelled to serve, and the latter enter voluntarily into service." [5] (It needs noting that his Republican opponents in the immediate debate had agreed regarding the distinction.) By this analysis, the militia is the sole body in which service can be required, and the Constitution places strict limitations on its use. One bit of the circumstantial and implicit but wide-ranging evidence comes from the already-quoted statement of the Pennsylvania minority. Because the Anti-Federalists seized every opportunity to attack the Constitution, it is significant that while the Pennsylvanians saw central control of the militia as a threat to personal, religious, and public liberty, they portrayed a federal army as a threat only to public liberty. Armies, they thus implied, could not threaten personal and religious liberty, because the men comprising them served voluntarily. Nor, when read carefully, do the indefinite-contingency arguments of the Federalists deny the conclusion, for their authors were intent on defending the Constitution's omission of strict limitations on funding. But should a military draft ever be reinstituted, young men and women would be well-advised to head the Supreme Court's version of history.

The power of Congress to declare war produced less discussion in the Philadelphia Convention, but proved ambiguous enough in later years to draw considerable attention during periods of undeclared war. As early as the day after Edmund Randolph introduced the Virginia Plan, Charles Pinckney anticipated these subsequent disputes when he questioned the operation of the principle that the national legislature should exercise the legislative powers of the Confederation Congress, while the national executive received its executive powers. He "was for a vigorous Executive," as James Madison recorded Pinckney's remarks, "but was afraid the Executive powers of the existing Congress might extend to war & peace &c[,] which would render the Executive a Monarchy, of the worst kind, towit [sic] an elective one." James Wilson responded that the prerogatives of the British monarch were not an accurate guide to what qualified as executive powers. "Some of these prerogatives were of a Legislative nature. Among others that of war & peace &c." Madison agreed with Wilson. By the time the Committee of Detail began its work, on July 26, the convention had not formally clarified the locus of the power, but the committee nevertheless assigned the power "to make war" to Congress.

The committee apparently reached this decision without difficulty, which strongly hints that the convention members generally assumed that the Confederation Congress's "power of determining on peace and war" was properly assigned as a legislative power. What did cause minor controversy was the committee's choice of wording. When the convention took up the clause on August 17, Charles Pinckney urged that the power "to make war" should be assigned solely to the Senate, which could act more expeditiously than both Houses together. Pierce Butler, also of South Carolina, went further and urged that the President alone should hold the power. The records of the deliberations indicate no support for either proposal, but Madison and Elbridge Gerry "moved to insert 'declare'; striking out 'make' war; leaving the Executive the Power to repel sudden attacks." Rufus King of Massachusetts soon added "that 'make' war might be understood to 'conduct' it[,] which was an Executive function."

The convention accepted the Madison-Gerry amendment, which the delegates *probably* understood as a means to clarify that the executive could act against surprise attacks and would direct war once Congress had authorized it. But the recorded comments surrounding the change are too brief and ambiguous to allow full certainty. Other evidence, both direct and inferential, indicates that in any event the convention continued to regard *Congress* as holding the dominant position in *deciding on* war. Undeclared wars — known then as "imperfect" wars (in the sense of being incomplete) — had frequently occurred within recent history, but no one indicated that the change in wording would allow the executive to commit the nation to them. Quite the contrary, the convention later explicitly gave Congress the authority to grant letters of marque and reprisal. In international practice, issuance of such letters to private vessels, along with the closely related authorization of reprisals by public naval vessels, typically signaled the inauguration of imperfect war.

Once the states began debating the Constitution, the war-*supporting* powers of the proposed government were widely discussed, but the contestants seldom mentioned the war-*making* powers. In view of then current suspicions of executive authority, this in itself lends support to the conclusion that contemporaries regarded Congress as the principal, if not the sole, repository of the power to commit the nation to war.

The few recorded comments that bear directly on the issue support the conclusion. In the Pennsylvania convention, James Wilson declared:

> This [new] system will not hurry us into war; it is calculated to guard against it. It will not be in the power of a single man, or a single body of men, to involve us in such distress; for the important power of declaring war is vested in the legislature at large; this declaration must be made with the concurrence of the House of Representatives; from this circumstance we may draw a certain conclusion that nothing by our national interest can draw us into a war.

Although Wilson spoke of "declaring war," the thrust of his comment indicates that he ruled out war-making by the President. He evidently regarded congressional authority, whether derived solely from the power "to declare war" or from this power plus the authority to issue letters of marque and reprisal, as covering both fully declared wars and imperfect wars. In response to Anti-Federalist attacks, Robert R. Livingston in New York conveyed the same point: "But, say the gentlemen, our present [Confederation] Congress have not the same powers [as the proposed Congress]. I answer, They have the very same . . . [including] the power of making war. . . ." [6]

In New York, while discussing the position of commander-in-chief, Alexander Hamilton corroborated the restricted role of the President. The executive's authority, he argued in *The Federalist* #69,

> would be nominally the same with that of the King of Great Britain, but in substance much inferior to it. It would amount to nothing more than the supreme command and directly of the military and naval forces, as first general and admiral of the confederacy; what that of the British king extends to the *declaring* of war, and to the *raising* and *regulating* of fleets and armies; all which by the constitution under consideration would appertain to the Legislature [emphasis in original].

This arrangement would guarantee unity of command in the *conduct* of war, consistent with the lessons of the War for Independence. It would also put command itself into hands different from those charged with the power of the purse, and would thus help guard against legislative tyranny. And contemporaries may have concluded that the President as commander-in-chief would have a significant role in repelling sudden attacks, a conclusion probably helped along by the common assumption that George Washington would fill the presidential office. Overall, however, the narrow characterization of the position of commander-in-chief accords both with the lack of controversy surrounding the office in the ratification process and with the indications that participants in the state debates equated the power of the new Congress "to declare war" with the Confederation Congress's power "of determining on" war.

But here, too, the indefinite contingency arguments of the Federalists would seem to indicate the opposite conclusion. "There ought to be a capacity to provide for future contingencies, as they may happen," Hamilton explained; "and as these are illimitable in their nature, so it is impossible safely to limit that capacity." Again, though, the context and object of this and similar arguments shows that their object was not to defend enhanced executive authority. Instead, their authors sought to justify the powers of the proposed central government irrespective of branch, and in particular the all-important power of taxation, against exceptions in favor of the states. A similar qualification applies to Hamilton's comment in *The Federalist* #34: "Energy in the executive is a leading character in the definition of good government. It is essential to the protection of the community against foreign attacks. . . ." This alluded to a role for the President as commander-in-chief in meeting sudden attacks—which is consonant with expectations of broad congressional authority in other regards—but Hamilton's actual target was the Anti-Federalist idea of a plural executive. He was not addressing the issue of executive-versus-legislative authority.

In 1787–1788, there could be little doubt about the relation between the treaty power and American security within the international arena. The Treaty of Alliance with France had been vital to success in the War for Independence; and the Treaty of Peace with Great Britain not only ended the conflict but had secured more favorable terms than the battlefield victories of the Americans may have warranted. It is not surprising, then, that the treaty power, like the war-making power, went almost without comment in Philadephia. A method to insure the supremacy of treaties over state law was less easily agreed on.

The Virginia Plan, as we have already seen, allocated the legislative and executive powers of the Confederation Congress to the proposed "national Legislature" and "national Executive," respectively, without further specification. When Charles Pinckney initially questioned this scheme on the grounds that "the Executive powers of the existing Congress might extend to peace & war &c," he doubtlessly had in mind the treaty power along with the war-making powers. Similarly, James Wilson probably intended to include it when he reassured the South Carolinian that "[s]ome of these prerogatives [of the British Monarch] were of a Legislative nature. Among others[,] that of war & peace &c." In any event, the question of whether treaty-making was properly a legislative or an executive function had drawn no further attention by the time the Committee of Detail commenced its work on July 26.

The draft reported by the Committee gave the Senate both treaty-making authority and the power to appoint ambassadors. The sole diplomatic duty given the President was the power to receive ambassadors. In the final Constitution, however, the treaty power fell within the executive article, which provided that the President "shall have Power, by and with the Advice and Consent of the Senate, to make Treaties, provided two thirds of the Senators present concur. . . ." The President similarly received the power to appoint ambassadors, subject to senatorial confirmation. These shifts in wording and placement hint that the members of the convention came to view treaty-making and perhaps the general control of foreign relations as executive functions. If so, then the Framers reached conclusions rather at odds with their view of the proper locus of the war-making power. But it seems unlikely that the final wording reflects an understanding that the President would have extensive authority. As Arthur Bestor, a most careful student of the subject, has remarked, "One searches in vain the records of the Convention and the discussions of the period for the slightest bit of evidence that the framers intended any such result or that contemporaries expected the proposed constitution to operate in this way." [7]

Instead, the convention sought to establish that the President would act as a check on the Senate in the making of treaties. This became important once the so-called Connecticut Compromise gave the states equal representation in the upper house, for senatorial treaty-making dominated by small states could adversely affect the interests of the more populous states. One solution was to join the House of Representatives in the treaty process, but the greater size of the lower house would complicate the secrecy and dispatch sometimes needed in the deliberations on treaty-making. A presidential check became the acceptable alternative once the convention had worked out a method of electing the President that stripped the Senate of any role in presidential selection and thus established executive independence from the body. Even then, the requirement of a two-thirds majority for approval of treaties remained as an additional check to allay fears engendered by the recent Jay-Gardoqui negotiations over the Mississippi River and New England's parallel concern over possible loss of fishery rights. (Defending the two-thirds requirement, Gouverneur Morris went so far as to label fisheries and the Mississippi "the two great objects of the Union.")

The evidence that the delegates in fact understood the President's role as the narrow one of checking the Senate is both indirect and direct. When the Committee on Postponed Parts reported the treaty provision substantially as it appeared in the final Constitution, no objections arose to an enhanced presidential role, not even from delegates who on other occasions voiced suspicions of executive authority. Moreover, in its final form, delegates still spoke of the President as a "check" on the Senate and of treaties as requiring the "concurrence" of the President.

In the ratification stage, most of the contestants were not privy to the history of the treaty provision in Philadelphia. One might accordingly expect that they would interpret the wording and placement of the treaty clause as assigning the President the dominant role in the treaty process. If an assumption of this sort had gained any currency, it would surely have triggered Anti-Federalist attacks on the clause. There were attacks—but none suggesting an independent presidential role. Critics charged instead that the Senate would dominate the process, or else that the Senate and President, working together in secrecy, would compromise the national interests. The House of Representatives, some said, should have been included in treaty-making, along with the more aristocratic Senate.

Federalist responses indicate that both sides agreed about what the Constitution mandated in treaty-making. The few Federalist comments hinting at the possibility of a broad and independent presidential role were only that—hints. James Wilson remarked in Pennsylvania, for example, that "[w]ith regard to their power in forming treaties, they [the Senate] can make none[;] they are only auxiliaries to the President." His larger point, however, was that the Senate was checked in its various powers; and he later restated the conclusion with a rather different emphasis: "They [the Senate] can make no treaty without his [the President's concurrence." Two of *The Federalist Papers*—#64 by John Jay and #75, by Alexander Hamilton—are more representative in this instance. Each defended the propriety of joining the Senate and the President, although, as Hamilton remarked, treaty-making, while not neatly classified, had more the character of legislative activity. Including the President in the treaty process, Jay explained, was desirable because he could act with "that perfect *secrecy* and immediate *dispatch* [which] are sometimes requisite" to negotiation (emphasis in original).

But this defense did not propose an independent presidential role. Jay revealed a fundamental assumption when he wrote, "The convention have done well therefore in so disposing of the power of making treaties, that although *the president must in forming them act by the advice and consent of the senate*, yet he will be able to manage the business of intelligence in such manner as prudence may suggest" (emphasis added). The President's efforts, that is, would take place within the context of senatorial guidance. A bit later he further clarified how "[t]hose matters which in negotiations usually require the most secrecy and the most dispatch, are those *preparatory and auxiliary* measures which are no[t] otherwise important in a national view, then as they tend to facilitate the attainment of the objects of negotiation" (emphasis added). As if to underscore this aspect, Jay remarked that if, during negotiation, "should any circumstance occur which requires the advice and consent of the senate, he [the President] may at any time convene them." From this happy conjunction of characteristics, Jay could conclude in *The Federalist* #64: "Thus we see that the constitution provides that our negociations for treaties shall have every advantage which can be derived from talents, information, integrity, and deliberate investigations on the one hand, and from secrecy and dispatch on the other."

If anything, Hamilton went further in minimizing the President's role, holding that the presidential qualities that were "indispensable in the *management* of foreign negotiations, point out the executive as the most fit *agent* in those transactions; while the vast importance of the trust, and the operation of treaties as laws, plead strongly for the participation of the whole or a part of the legislative body in the office of making them" (emphasis added). Jack N. Rakove correctly observes that "the most striking feature of Hamilton's essay is that he seems almost to strain to justify *any* presidential involvement."[8]

What gave the subject special urgency was the status of treaties as supreme law. In retrospect, the supremacy clause of Article VI — combined, of course, with an adequate federal judiciary — seems a simple and obvious remedy for the problem of state noncompliance with treaties that the Confederation confronted. Yet the solution emerged only haltingly during the deliberations in Philadelphia. The nationalistic Virginia Plan approached the problem in a quite different fashion, through provisions for a federal legislative veto on state legislation and federal military coercion of "any member of the Union failing to fulfill its duty under the articles [of Union]." A supremacy provision appeared first in the New Jersey Plan, which proposed that "all Treaties made & ratified under the authority of the U. States shall be the supreme law of the respective States, . . . any thing in the respective laws of the Individual States to the contrary notwithstanding." The convention rejected the New Jersey Plan itself, but it also abandoned the Virginia Plan's provisions for a legislative veto and military coercion, in effect substituting the approach of the New Jersey Plan. (Even then, however, the nationalists in the convention seem not to have realized the full extent of their victory, for a month later they tried unsuccessfully to reinstate a legislative veto.)

As finally approved, the wording of the supremacy clause contains a superficially curious contrast in its treatment of laws and treaties. Only laws of the United States "which shall be made in pursuance of" the Constitution become "the supreme law of the law," but the same status attaches to "all Treaties made, or which shall be made, under the Authority of the United States," with no mention of a requirement that the treaties be made in pursuance of the Constitution. On its face, then, the clause leaves "open to question whether the authority of the United States means more than the formal acts prescribed to make the convention," as Justice Oliver Wendell Homes, Jr., observed when he gave the issue its classic formulation in *Missouri v. Holland* (1920).[9]

The direct evidence from Philadelphia is slight. The conventional explanation stresses that the delegates chose the phrase "authority of the United States" in order to insure that preexisting treaties (like the 1783 treaty with Britain) would remain valid under the new government. But the record displays no such clarity. It was on August 23 that the convention approved the wording "all Treaties made under the authority of the U.S. shall be supreme law." Yet this formulation did not solve the problem, and the topic was reopened two days later. As Madison recorded, the clause "was reconsidered and after the words 'all treaties made,' were inserted . . . the words 'or shall be made[.]' This insertion was meant to obviate all doubt concerning the force of treaties preexisting, by making the words 'all treaties made' refer to them, as the words inserted would refer to future treaties." The new insertion, not the use of "authority of the United States," was thus the crucial one in insuring the validity of earlier treaties. Once more, it is perhaps the silence of delegates that provides the best evidence. None charged that the clause elevated treaties over the Constitution.

In the ratification debates, by contrast, Anti-Federalists observed that "[i]t is not said that these treaties shall be made in pursuance of the constitution—nor are there any constitutional bounds set to those who shall make them," as the "Federal Farmer" elaborated. Almost without exception, however, their explicit or implicit concern was the supremacy of treaties over *state* constitutions. Those Federalists mentioning the issue agreed with George Nicholas, who explained in Virginia that the wording of the clause meant "no treaty . . . shall be repugnant to the spirit of the [federal] Constitution, or inconsistent with the delegated powers." [10] It is also significant that only a year later, in section 25 of the Judiciary Act of 1789, Congress recognized the possibility of court review of treaties on federal constitutional grounds.

The Constitution, as the Framers and ratifiers perceived it, rectified the failings and incorporated the strengths of the Articles of Confederation in the realm of national security. Most of all, it gave new government the source of funds necessary to raise armies and the power to raise them directly. The old Congress had not lacked authority to determine on war; the new Congress would continue to hold the power, although the President gained the power of command and would conduct wars once they were begun. Similarly, the old Congress held the treaty power, which now devolved on the Senate, subject to the concurrence of the President, who (analogous to his conduct of war) would superintend negotiations within the broad guidelines laid down by the upper house. Not least, the Constitution placed beyond dispute the supremacy of treaties over state law, but left them subservient to the Constitution itself.

How confidently can we accept these conclusions and where do they lead us? To some extent they all rest on the silent-dog approach to historical interpretation. Anti-Federalists, that is, did not bark when they should have if they had glimpsed contrary meanings in the Constitution. Federalists, or at least some of them, would also have barked. Interpreting silence is risky, of course, but fortunately it is not all we have to go on. Some direct evidence exists, and it points to the same conclusions. What may be hard for us to grasp is that provisions that have subsequently been the focus of sometimes sharp controversy could pose few or no difficulties to the Framers and ratifiers. We fail as historians, however, if we allow our puzzlement to become their puzzlement by importing ambiguities into their Constitution. Do we fail as constitutionalists if we try to use their Constitution to resolve our puzzlement?

THE CONSTITUTION: AN ECONOMIC DOCUMENT?

JAMES H. HUTSON

To prepare for the Bicentennial of the United States Constitution, the history department of a major university invited a group of scholars in October 1985 to consider the topic "Beyond Beard." To the organizers of the conference, who wanted an assessment of the continuing impact of Charles Beard's *An Economic Interpretation of the Constitution of the United States*, the Beard thesis was not "dead," as Gordon Wood declared in 1968. Nor was Richard Hofstadter's 1969 obituary acceptable. Far from standing "like an imposing ruin on the landscape of American historiography," as Hofstadter asserted, *An Economic Interpretation*, a defiant admirer claimed in 1981, was an "enduring monument" to Beard's scholarly prowess.[1] *An Economic Interpretation* still lives, then, despite its apparent disintegration under the onslaught of scholars in the 1950s. That the book will ever regain the dominance of the interpretation of the Constitution which it exercised in the 1930s and 1940s is scarcely conceivable, but it continues to be a presence in the scholarship on the Constitution, and so, of course, does its thesis that the Constitution was an economic document.

Charles Beard published *An Economic Interpretation of the Constitution of the United States* in 1913, when at the age of thirty-nine he was professor of American politics and government at Columbia University. The son of a wealthy Indiana businessman, Beard was a crusading liberal at DePauw College, 1895–1898. His passion for political reform caused him to gravitate toward socialist and Labourite intellectual circles during postgraduate work at Oxford; he was "almost-a-socialist" during this period, he later told a friend.[2] Beard apparently became familiar with the writings of Karl Marx during his English sojourn. The extent to which *An Economic Interpretation of the Constitution* was inspired by Marxist theory has been a matter of disagreement among historians. From the moment *An Economic Interpretation* was published, Beard was obliged to defend himself against charges that it was "Marxian." He replied that the theoretical underpinnings of the work, the idea that economic factors dictated political ones, was suggested to him by James Madison's *Federalist* #10, which Beard quoted extensively and, as later critics charged, selectively, in his monograph. Whether Madisonian or Marxian, Beard's attempt to "explain" historical events by the rigorous application of theory intrigued scholars and has gained *An Economic Interpretation* a continuing audience among historians interested in methodology—even methodology gone wrong—and in the use of models to control bodies of data.

Settling in at Columbia, Beard devoted his reformist energies, as many of his colleagues did, to the political movement known as Progressivism, an effort, cutting across political parties, that sought in the years between 1900 and World War I to tame corporate power in the interests of a more humane society. Beard wrote position papers for Progressive causes, organized supporters, made speeches, and put his considerable energies at the disposal of the movement in numerous ways. Indeed, some scholars contend that *An Economic Interpretation* was less a work of dispassionate scholarship— Beard tried hard to give it that appearance—than a Progressive tract, a muckraking exposé whose intention was to discredit the Constitution for partisan purposes. What about *An Economic Interpretation* makes these charges credible?

The thesis of *An Economic Interpretation* is that the creation of the Constitution was the archetype of conflict of interest in American history, a seminal event in which a group of politicians, ostensibly acting in the public interest, enriched themselves and their friends by actions they knew would produce these results. Beard divided American society at the time of the Constitution into two groups: realty and personalty. By realty he meant small farmers who were a "large debtor class." Personalty he defined as "money, public securities, manufactures, trade and shipping."[3] According to Beard, personalty was under duress during the Confederation period. Agrarian debtors in control of state legislatures defrauded creditors by issuing paper money; public securities plummeted in value because Congress could not lay taxes to fund them; trade and manufacturing languished because Congress lacked the power to assist them. As a result, personalty interests across America mobilized to bolster their economic interests; they did so, Beard asserted, by planning and writing the Constitution of the United States and contriving its ratification.

The Constitution served personalty in two ways, Beard claimed, "one positive, the other negative."[4] Positively, the Constitution catered to personalty by granting the government power to tax and thus redeem public securities and power to regulate commerce and thus stimulate trade and manufacturing. Negatively, it protected creditors by thwarting parliamentary majorities (presumably soft on debtors and depreciating currency) with institutional contrivances such as checks and balances and "control" by an uneffected judiciary, a favorite topic of Progressive declamation. The Constitution was a document written to gratify the economic interests of its drafters, who were, in Beard's oft-quoted words, "immediately, directly, and personally interested in, and derived economic advantages from, the establishment of the new system."[5] The leaders in the ratifying conventions, Beard added, "represented the same economic groups as the members of the Philadelphia Convention; and in a large number of instances they were also directly and personally interested in the outcome of their efforts." The Constitution, in short, was an economic document, the work of a "consolidated interest group whose interests knew no state boundaries and were truly national in their scope"[6] and whose motives were, in all cases, personal gain, not the public welfare or justice or any of what Beard scornfully called the "abstract principles" of political science.[7]

What was new about Beard's thesis? Certainly not the assertion that there were economic dimensions to the creation of the Constitution. Numerous pre-Civil War writers had emphasized that the attitudes of various groups in American society toward the Constitution were dictated by economic self-interest. John Marshall's *Life of Washington*, written between 1804 and 1807, described creditors and debtors taking positions on the Constitution according to its impact on their economic welfare. Richard Hildreth, in his *History of the United States* (1849), found on one side of the Constitution merchants "who hoped much from the regulation of commerce" and on the other side debtors, fearing the demise of paper money.[8] To the holders of public securities Beard assigned special importance—"as personalty was the dynamic element in the movement for the Constitution, so securities were the dynamic element in personalty"[9]—but as early as 1817 David Ramsay, in his *History of the United States*, reported that "the mass of public creditors expected payment of their debts, from the establishment of an efficient government, and were therefore decidedly for its adoption."[10]

After the Civil War writers continued to call attention to the economic aspects of the contest over the Constitution. Professional scholars like Woodrow Wilson wrote of the document being employed by the "wealthy classes" to check "popular majorities"; popularizers like Henry J. Ford described the establishment of a "government of the masses by the classes."[11] Similar statements appeared on the eve of the publication of Beard's book. In 1912, for example, Algie Simon claimed that the Constitution was written so that "the interests of a small body of wealthy rulers might be served."[12] Progressive scholars, while leaning toward a sociopolitical analysis of the Constitution, portraying its creation as a struggle between "democracy" and "aristocracy," did not ignore economic factors. The Constitution, wrote J. Allen Smith in his celebrated *The Spirit of American Government* (1907), "was in form a political document but its significance was mainly economic," since aristocrats intended it to thwart popular efforts to abolish "all private monopoly" and to regulate other ill-gotten gains.[13]

In what way, then, did Beard's approach differ from that of his predecessors? Alert though they were to the economic dimensions of the Constitution, they produced little hard evidence to prove their claims, and many of them implied that economic factors operated principally during the ratifying contests, at a considerable remove from the drafters of the Constitution. Beard's innovation was to bring economic self-interest onto the floor of the Philadelphia Convention, to thrust it foremost into the calculations of the Framers of the Constitution, and to offer dramatic new evidence to support his case. Beard's new evidence was "unworked" Treasury Department records of the 1790 funding operation. Beard described his discovery of these records in Washington with the controlled excitement of an archeologist finding a treasure; he could use the records, he revealed, "only after a vacuum cleaner had been brought in to excavate the ruins." [14]

These records revealed to Beard the power of economic self-interest in its most compelling form. He asserted that the adoption of the Constitution produced an economic bonanza for public security holders, transforming at a stroke roughly $60,000,000 of nearly worthless paper into assets yielding a profit of $40,000,000.[15] The "Records of the Treasury Department" revealed that forty of the fifty-five men who attended the convention owned public securities. These men, Beard argued, knew that the Constitution would create a bull market in securities; they knew "the precise results which the new government that they were setting up was designed to attain." [16] Therefore, Beard concluded, their motive in writing the Constitution was to profit from a rise in the value of public securities as well as from other forms of personalty in which they were "immediately, directly, and personally interested." The key word is immediately, for although Beard denied that he was accusing the "members of the Convention of working merely for their own pockets," [17] the irresistible impression produced by his emphasis on immediate, direct gratification of economic self-interest was that the drafters wrote the Constitution to make a financial killing, to make big money fast.

Progressives admired Beard's methods and conclusions. By diligent digging for the facts, he removed the halo from the Constitution and exposed its "true" nature. Just as muckraking journalists were uncovering the "hidden cesspools" beneath the respectable institutions of the age, Beard argued that the Constitution had its own secrets, that it was the instrument of self-seeking, special interests. The Constitution, then, did not deserve what Beard's colleague Frank J. Goodnow called the "superstitious reverence" which many Americans afforded it and which standpatters manipulated to prevent political reform. By desanctifying it, Beard hoped to promote the Progressive political and social agenda.

Opponents of Progressivism and "patriotic" votaries of the Constitution were scandalized by Beard's book. Ex-President William Howard Taft denounced it and the conservative press fulminated against it, none more passionately than the Marion *Ohio Star*, which printed the famous headline "Scavengers, Hyena-Like, Desecrate the Graves of Dead Patriots We Revere" and urged its readers to condemn Beard and "the purveyors of his filthy lies and rotten aspersions."

Reviews in the scholarly journals of the day anticipated the searching critiques of the 1950s. While many reviewers approved of attention to the economic aspects of the Constitution—"the economic factor in history is significant and influential," conceded Owen R. Libby in the *Mississippi Valley Historical Review* (June 1914)—Beard's efforts to construct an economic interpretation of the document were considered to have been compromised by his sloppy scholarship. If the Framers of the Constitution were motivated by economic self-interest, how explain, asked John Latané in the *American Political Science Review*, the fact that leading *opponents* in the Philadelphia Convention owned securities worth $87,000, four times more than the value, $21,000, of securities held by a like number of leading proponents? How could Beard's theory be true, asked E. S. Corwin in *The History Teacher's Magazine*, when his evidence showed that only seven members owned securities before the meeting and two-thirds of the value of these securities were owned by an opponent of the Constitution?

An Economic Interpretation of the Constitution survived these early challenges as well as the massive, though indirect, refutation contained in Charles Warren's *The Making of the Constitution* (1929), an account that reiterated the venerable conviction that the Framers of the Constitution were inspired by selfless, patriotic motives. The 1930s, with their focus on the economic fortunes of the nation, provided a congenial atmosphere for the Beard thesis. By 1935, thirty-seven of forty-two new college textbooks incorporated it. In 1938 *An Economic Interpretation of the Constitution* was one of the two volumes most frequently mentioned by American intellectuals in a survey of "Books That Changed Our Minds." After a quarter-century Beard's thesis had established itself so firmly that "what at first seemed audacious to the point of lèse majesté came ultimately to be taken as commonplace."[18]

The Beard thesis emerged unscathed from the 1940s, but seemed to disintegrate under a series of scholarly assaults in the 1950s. The first thrust was an article by Robert Thomas in 1953 showing that supporters and opponents of the Constitution in Virginia, far from being divided in personalty–realty camps, were coalitions of similar economic interests. Far heavier blows were delivered by Robert Brown in 1956 and Forrest McDonald in 1958. Brown's work, *Charles Beard and the Constitution*, was a 200-page scourging of Beard for sins committed in the name of scholarship. According to Brown, there were so many innocent as well as deliberate mistakes in *An Economic Interpretation of the Constitution* that no statement in the book was reliable. In dissecting Beard's famous chapter on "The Economic Interests of the Members of the Convention," Brown demonstrated, for example, that Beard ignored the totality of the property holdings of the members, that the realty of a delegate like Washington exceeded his personalty by a margin of 95.44 to 4.56 percent, and that similar ratios prevailed for other delegates. In fact, Brown's research indicated that "only six delegates had personal property in excess of realty," that "eighteen delegates definitely had realty which outweighed personalty," and that the other thirty delegates "prove nothing in particular on the basis of Beard's evidence." [19] So much, then, for the power of personalty at the Constitutional Convention.

In *We the People* (1958) Forrest McDonald carried the investigation of Beard's scholarship even further than Brown, extending his scrutiny not only to members of the Philadelphia Convention but to all the members of all the state ratifying conventions. About the men at Philadelphia McDonald reached a conclusion similar to Brown's: the preponderant property interest, 25 to 14, represented among the signers of the Constitution was realty. Furthermore, thirty-three of forty-one convention delegates whose "attitudes are ascertainable" opposed the clauses that Beard claimed were especially inserted to protect personalty. McDonald's research suggested that in the convention Beard's categories should be reversed: the contending sides were "men of considerable personalty interests, who opposed the Constitution, and men having realty-agrarian interests, a band of debtors, and a few men having modest personalty interests," who favored it.[20]

In examining the ratifying conventions McDonald discovered that the Beardian world was equally topsy-turvy, that substantial realty interests supported the Constitution and substantial personalty interests opposed it. He showed that small farmers overwhelmingly supported the Constitution is every ratifying convention except those in North Carolina and New Hampshire, where they were evenly divided, in Massachusetts, where they were opposed, 55 percent to 45 percent, and in South Carolina. It was in demonstrating the existence of substantial personalty interests among the Anti-Federalists that McDonald made his most significant contribution, for their extensive presence among opponents of the Constitution had not been previously suspected by scholars. Not only did McDonald find that large numbers of merchants and manufacturers were Anti-Federalists but he also demonstrated that those identified by Beard as the movers and shakers among the Federalists — the holders of public securities — were conspicuous in the Anti-Federal camp and were as little inhibited by conflicts of interest as Beard intimated their Federalist counterparts to be. In Pennsylvania, New York, and Rhode Island, McDonald showed Anti-Federalists lining their pockets by using inside knowledge to buy cheap public securities which they then funded by issuing paper money. The result was that in states like Pennsylvania a larger proportion of Anti-Federalist than Federalist delegates owned securities (73.9 percent to 50 percent); Anti-Federalists owned a larger amount of securities than their adversaries ($70,852 to $67,666), and a larger amount per person ($4,167 to $2,942). The desire of

Anti-Federalist leader Charles Pettit to transform Pennsylvania "into a speculator's paradise" seemed to have been realized.

McDonald's work showed that supporters and opponents of the Constitution were not compartmentalized into holders of realty and personalty, as Beard contended, but that the two groups were amalgams of both kinds of property holders, often in roughly similar proportions state by state. His conclusions for Pennsylvania and South Carolina, that "the distribution of occupations and the holdings of most forms of property were about the same on both sides," applied to most of the thirteen states. Economically, therefore, Anti-Federalists and Federalists appeared to have been coalitions of the same kinds of interests. McDonald concluded that the Anti-Federalists matched the Federalists in "intelligence, education, experience, and political savoir faire, and they comprehended a similar assortment of rich men, poor men, virtuous men, and thieves." [21]

The thoroughness and vigor of Brown and McDonald's assault convinced some historians that they had dealt Beard a mortal blow. Beard's friends rallied, however, and they soon began giving his critics stiff doses of their own medicine. In 1960 Jackson Turner Main published an article impugning McDonald's research methods, and Lee Benson used his *Turner and Beard: American Historical Writing Reconsidered* to score McDonald for employing a "logically fallacious design of proof" which caused him to "direct his critique against a nonexistent thesis" and to assail Brown for "theoretical confusion" and "a fundamental misreading of Beard." Though sympathetic to Beard, Benson did not spare him either, criticizing his work as "inconsistent, ambiguous, and incomplete," even as he tried to salvage some of Beard's insights by recasting them.[22] These exchanges, as Professor Main admitted, produced "anarchy and confusion." [23] For if Beard was wholly or partly wrong and if his critics were wholly or partly wrong, who could say what was the right way to understand the creation of the Constitution? Historians seemed to be thrown upon their own resources; to form a judgment on the dispute between Beard and his critics appeared to require nothing short of an independent—and possibly an interminable—research project. Many scholars, puzzled by events, retreated behind disclaimers that they intended neither to support Beard nor to rebut him.

Compounding the confusion were sequels that Brown and McDonald published to their broadsides against Beard. Both authors—Brown in his *Reinterpretation of the Formation of the American Constitution* (1963) and McDonald in *E Pluribus Unum* (1965)—employed an economic interpretation of the Constitution; by embracing Beard's methodology, they seemed to repudiate their earlier strictures against him. The authors' intentions, however, were to show that a correct application of the theory, as opposed to Beard's mismanagement of it, offered the best hope of comprehending the creation of the Constitution.

Instead of ascribing the Constitution to the machinations of personalty,

Brown and McDonald offered other groups or combinations of groups as the "dynamic" element in the constitutional drama. Brown argued that because the drafters of the Constitution were men of large (primarily real) property and the average American in 1787 was a prosperous middle class farmer, a broad segment of the population was interested in the protection of property and it supported the Constitution because it promised to provide that protection. McDonald drew a more complicated picture. To replace Beard's theory, he offered, in *We the People*, four alternative hypotheses about the role of economic forces in the creation of the Constitution. Before proposing these hypotheses, McDonald argued that there were at least seventy-five discrete economic interest groups in the United States in 1787 and that the construction of a valid economic interpretation would require the evaluation of the impact of the Constitution of each of these groups, a formidable assignment because their condition differed from state to state and some groups were affected by the Constitution in contradictory ways. "The interplay of conditioning and determining factors was extremely complex," McDonald conceded.[24] In *E Pluribus Unum* McDonald attempted to explain how this aggregation of interest groups interacted to create the Constitution. He found the task so daunting that, to the amusement of his critics, who deplored his "crude economic determinism," he was obliged to resort, at last, to a Bancroftian explanation that a miracle had occurred at Philadelphia in 1787.

No less than Beard and McDonald, Lee Benson emphasized the economic dimensions of the historical process. His quarrel with Beard was over the "intellectual confusion" created by his (Beard's) equation of economic determinism and economic interpretation. "When adequately tested, the economic deterministic parts of Beard's main hypothesis will not work," Benson asserted, "but, restated, some of his claims can be incorporated into a social interpretation of the Constitution that may work."[25] A social interpretation, in Benson's view, required that economic factors be associated with a number of other variables — religion, education, geography, communications — to describe the social milieu that shaped political decisions. In his *Political Parties before the Constitution* (1973) Jackson Turner Main presented a social interpretation of the divisions over the Constitution along the lines suggested by Benson. On one side, favoring the Constitution, was a group which Main called Cosmopolitans; their opponents he designated Localists. Economic circumstances were important in forming positions on the Constitution, but so, Main argued, were a myriad of other factors that produced the Cosmopolitan and Localist mentalities.

The scholarly strife of the 1950s and 1960s discredited substantial parts of Beard's thesis — although some scholars were reluctant to make this concession — but it did not deter historians from proposing alternative economic interpretations of the Constitution. These tended to conceive of economic forces as displaying themselves among a profusion of interest groups and in competition with a profusion of noneconomic factors. In so complicated a universe measuring the economic influences on the creation of the Constitution was not easy. That the Constitution was an economic document, in the sense that economic forces helped to produce it, seemed to be taken for granted. But the exact nature, power, and configuration of those forces was difficult to discern.

Not all of Beard's critics in the 1950s were wedded to an economic interpretation of the Constitution. Douglass Adair, for example, in influential articles written in 1951 and 1957 attacked the validity of the economic interpretation as well as the long tradition in American historiography, predating Beard and the Progressives, that considered the Framers as "practical" men with no concern for ideas or theories. Adair contended that, on the contrary, the Revolutionary generation believed that ideas—which he variously called "theories," "philosophy," the "science of politics," and the lessons of history—could and should guide statesmen in their tasks and that they had, in fact, done so at Philadelphia.

There were two corollaries to Adair's emphasis on ideas. One concerned the motives of the Framers. If they were guided by theories about establishing a viable political regime, if their objectives were the implementation of principles of "liberty, justice, and stability," as Adair said they were,[26] they could be considered, not as narrowly self-interested politicians, but as public-spirited citizens, even as patriots. Again, if the Framers were moved by ideas, not by selfish desires to protect their property against popular majorities, the Constitution need not be pressed into the Progressive mold of an antidemocratic conspiracy. Adair, in fact, viewed it as "quasi-mixed," as having a "strong and inevitable tendency . . . towards the national democracy that would develop in the nineteenth century."[27] Adair's importance in the historiography of the Constitution was that by insisting on the significance of ideas in the framing of the document he made it possible to reconceptualize the Founders, to view them as patriots and, if not as outright democrats, at least as men leaning in that direction. The result was the flourishing of what might be called, for want of better words, a democratic interpretation of the creation of the Constitution, which for a time seemed capable of establishing a new dominance over the subject.

The political scientist Martin Diamond was a major force in propagating the democratic interpretation of the Constitution. Developing an argument made first by Adair, Diamond contended that Madison's theory in *The Federalist* #10 was the intellectual plan which guided the Philadelphia Convention in constructing a government that retained the essentials of democracy while eliminating its unpalatable aspects. Although Diamond stressed that the Framers deplored and intended to check the excesses of popular government, he emphasized the ardor of their democratic commitment, since his intention was to restore from Progressive expropriation "their bona fides as partisans of democracy." The Framers, he wrote, wanted "to make démocratie safe for the world." The Constitution was an "effort to constitute democracy."[28]

In an influential article published in 1961, John Roche continued the emphasis on democracy by saluting the members of the convention as "superb democratic politicians" and the Constitution as a "vivid demonstration of effective democratic political action."[29] The momentum of the democratic interpretation continued in 1966 and 1967 with the appearance of an expanded version of Cecilia Kenyon's 1955 article on the Anti-Federalists, which shattered the Beardian view of these adversaries of the Constitution, and of Clinton Rossiter's *1787: The Grand Convention* and Richard B. Morris's *The American Revolution Reconsidered*. Rossiter and Morris described the Constitution in almost identical terms — "a notable exercise in the art of democratic . . . politics."[30] And they considered the writers of the Constitution patriots, not economic opportunists. Rossiter, in fact, was emboldened "in deliberate defiance of the ban placed upon the word by serious minded historians" to hail them as heroes and to compete with the English encomiasts William Gladstone and Alfred North Whitehead by quoting John Adams to the effect that the Constitutional Convention was "if not the greatest exercise of human understanding, the greatest single effort of national deliberation that the world has ever seen."[31]

The democratic interpretation of the creation of the Constitution never achieved an ascendancy, however. In 1968 Paul Eidelberg produced a monograph, *The Philosophy of the American Constitution*, intended as a rebuttal of Diamond, in which he disputed the notion that the ideas of the Framers indicated that they wanted to establish a democratic government. In Eidelberg's view, the Framers feared the "leveling spirit" of the people and were apprehensive "that the national legislature might repeat the experience of those state legislatures which . . . had succumbed to 'democracy'" during the Confederation period. Consequently, their major objective was, as Eidelberg presented it, to introduce the "aristocratic principle" into the new government to check and restrain rampant democracy.[32]

In *The Creation of the American Republic* (1969) Gordon Wood reached the same conclusion. Unlike Eidelberg, however, Wood adopted a modified version of the Progressive approach, rejecting Beardian economic determinism but emphasizing social conflict. The Framers, he asserted, intended "to confront and retard the thrust of the Revolution with the rhetoric of the Revolution." There were, he explained, "partisan and aristocratic purposes that belied the Federalists' democratic language." What he meant was this: the makers of the Constitution were alarmed by the strength of the democratic forces — to which he ascribed an irrepressible social mobility — that were released by the Revolution and manifested themselves in the vicious conduct of many state legislatures during the Confederation period. To control the ebullient democracy became their goal; to do this, they relied on the strategy, later explained in *The Federalist* #10, of monopolizing national offices for the "natural aristocracy" by enlarging the electoral districts in which they ran. By bringing the "natural aristocracy of the country back into dominance in politics" the problems of the nation would be solved. The Constitution, Wood concluded, "was intrinsically an aristocratic document designed to check the democratic tendencies of the period."[33]

By integrating an analysis of ideas with Progressivism Wood challenged the conclusions of the democratic interpretation of the Constitution and, with the assistance of Eidelberg and others, brought its progress to a halt. But Wood's work was immediately attacked by two of the most conspicuous heirs of the Progressive tradition, Merrill Jensen and Jackson Turner Main, who complained that his treatment of republicanism had infused a "conservative bias" into the historiography of the 1770s and 1780s.[34] Then, in 1973, Wood appeared to repudiate the thesis of the *Creation of the American Republic* by asserting that the "talk prevalent in 1787 of aristocracy versus democracy cannot perhaps be taken literally," that "American society in 1787–88 does not appear to have been sharply or deeply divided into two coherent classes," and that the contest over the Constitution was a manifestation of "antagonism between elites."[35] Neither the Progressive nor the democratic interpretation worked, Wood evidently concluded. The result was a situation similar to that in the aftermath of Brown and McDonald's assaults on Beard: if Diamond, Rossiter, and proponents of the democratic interpretation of the Constitution's creation were untenable and if Wood was also untenable, whose account could be accepted?

Confusion compounding confusion—such was the condition the historiography of the Constitution seemed to have reached by the 1970s. Uncertainties about the validity of the democratic and Progressive interpretations combined with the problems of the economic interpretations proposed as alternatives to Beard seemed to place the creation of the Constitution almost beyond the reach of ordinary understanding. Scattered articles written by Beardian apologists in the 1980s offered no help, because their authors reinterpreted Beard into a scholar he himself would scarcely have recognized. One writer claimed, for example, that what really concerned Beard was not the play of economic forces but the question of "power and authority" in American history.[36] Another, saluting Beard as "a patriotic celebrant of the Founding Fathers' handiwork," described him as examining a "premodern political world" from the context of a "Ruskinian skepticism about modern thought."[37] Such analyses promise little balm to perplexed understandings.

The muddle in which the historiography of the creation of the Constitution now finds itself is not surprising. The demise of any theory as dominant as Beard's was, in any discipline, will produce an interval of uncertainty, a period of groping and trial and error. What is, perhaps, surprising is the optimism expressed in the early 1960s that the situation would soon clarify itself. In 1962 Elkins and McKitrick observed that because of the impact of recent scholarship "the entire subject of the Constitution and its creation has become a little murky . . . one is not altogether certain what to think." But they hoped that "new work . . . excellent and system- atic . . . still in progress" would cut through the mist.[38] Writing the next year, Robert E. Brown was equally optimistic: "Doubtless the great healer time—plus additional research—will do much to resolve the controversy over the Constitution."[39] Two decades have passed with no results.

No new scholarly consensus seems to be forming about the creation of the Constitution. Nor does there seem to be any new synthesis in prospect, nothing resembling what physicists call a grand unified theory that will knit all the theads of the subject into an explanation at once compelling and coherent. When a grand new explanation emerges, it seems certain that it will not assert that the Constitution was an economic document in the sense Beard alleged that it was, a document written purely for the personal profit of its authors and their associates. It seems equally certain that any credible explanation of the creation of the Constitution will have to reckon with the impact of economic forces, a fact appreciated by the earliest writers on the Constitution. Just how this impact will be assessed is unclear at the moment. Perhaps the scholarship stimulated by the Bicentennial of the Constitution will bring the economic dimensions of the document into better focus.

THE CASE AGAINST RATIFICATION: ANTI-FEDERALIST CONSTITUTIONAL THOUGHT

MURRAY DRY

To be for or against the constitution, as it stands is not much evidence of a federal disposition; if any names are applicable to the parties, on account of their general politics, they are those of republicans and anti-republicans. The advocates are generally men not very friendly to those rights, and properly anti-republicans.

Federal Farmer VI, 2.8.72.

I take it for granted, as an axiom in politic, that the people should never authorize their rulers to do anything, which if done, would operate to their injury.

Brutus X, 2.9.98.

What place should the views of the Anti-Federalists have in the bicentennial celebration of the Constitution? After 200 years under the same Constitution, none of whose amendments has changed its essential character, are we not all Federalist constitutionalists? If the opponents of the Constitution were truly "men of little faith" in the possibilities of a new form of republican government, as Cecelia Kenyon has argued, then studying their thought today can serve only as a foil for the victorious Federalists, whose arguments and accomplishment can be more fully understood and appreciated in the comparison.[1] Likewise, if Gordon Wood is correct in describing the ratification controversy in terms of a social conflict pitting the aristocratic few against the democratic many, then the entire founding debate is of merely historical interest. That is because, as Wood presents it,

NOTE: I would like to acknowledge with gratitude the assistance I received from Dan Kahan, who graduated from Middlebury College in 1986. He was my research assistant for this and other projects during the summer of 1985 and he made many valuable comments on an earlier draft of this chapter.

271

the Anti-Federalists' argument for a substantial representation conflicted with and undermined the Revolutionary attachment to an organic theory of society, and the Federalist appeal to election as the sufficient cause of representation eliminated the possibility of a genuine aristocratic politics.[2]

There is some truth to each of these interpretations, but they fail, in my opinion, to take sufficient account of the constitutional issues the country faced in 1787–1788. A sounder and more instructive approach is taken by Herbert Storing, whose authoritative edition of the Anti-Federalist writings facilitates a full study of the founding dialog over the Constitution. While he concluded that the Anti-Federalists had the weaker argument, Storing saw the Anti-Federalists as expressing sound moral reservations about the possibility that republican government could prosper by relying so fundamentally on "enlightened self-interest" and ambition checking ambition.[3]

After introductory remarks about who the Anti-Federalists were, why they objected to that name, and how they approached the Constitution, this chapter focuses on the relationship between the Anti-Federal conception of republican government and their proposals for constitutional change. The Anti-Federalists present a distinctive view of republicanism which, when combined with a theory of representation, supports a more genuine federalism than the Constitution guarantees. Nonetheless, even though the Constitution was ratified, the Anti-Federal conception of federalism has remained alive in our constitutional history. Other aspects of Anti-Federal republicanism can also be identified in contemporary constitutional debate. The conclusion to this chapter will briefly illustrate this contention that Anti-Federal constitutionalism has been assimilated into American constitutional law.

WHO WERE THE ANTI-FEDERALISTS?

The following members of the Constitutional Convention did not sign the Constitution and opposed unconditional ratification: Elbridge Gerry of Massachusetts, Robert Yates and John Lansing of New York, Luther Martin of Maryland, and George Mason and Edmund Randolph of Virginia. Martin, Yates, and Lansing opposed any radical change in the Articles of Confederation. In the convention they favored the New Jersey Plan, which retained most of the features of the Articles but proposed to add a plural executive, a limited tax power on imports, a power to regulate commerce, and a coercive power over those states delinquent in raising their tax requisitions. When the convention voted to work from the nationalist Virginia Plan, these delegates returned home to prepare their opposition. Their arguments, both in the convention and later, were both conservative and legal: the convention went beyond its authority in proposing a national government, rather than merely revising the Articles; and the people would not consent to it.

The other three nonsigners stayed through to the end of the convention and expressed their opposition only in the final week. Mason emphasized the lack of a bill of rights and the inadequacy of representation, and he opposed both the unitary executive and his reeligibility. But his opposition seems to have been due to his failure to secure tariff protection for the South; he urged the requirement of a two-thirds vote in both Houses for navigation acts. Likewise Randolph, who also opposed the unitary and reeligible executive, began to think the convention was getting ahead of the people only after the compromise on slave importation and navigation. Randolph, who presented the Virginia Plan, wrote a public letter explaining why he favored a second convention, and then reconsidered and supported ratification in the Virginia Convention in 1788. And Gerry presented a list of numerous items, none of which fully explained his opposition.

Among the state ratification conventions, leaving aside Rhode Island, which did not ratify the Constitution until 1790, and North Carolina, which rejected the Constitution in 1788, there was significant Anti-Federal opposition in only Pennsylvania, Massachusetts, New York, and Virginia. William Findley, John Smilie, and Robert Whitehill, along with George Bryan, were the major opponents in Pennsylvania, but most of what is recorded of the debate in that state is the Federalist position, especially the speeches of James Wilson. *The Reasons of Dissent* of the Pennsylvania Convention Minority presents the Anti-Federal opposition. Massachusetts had the first close state convention, where Gerry was present to answer questions but did not sit. Opposition was substantial, but when John Hancock and Samuel Adams came out in favor of unconditional ratification, accompanied by recommendatory amendments, the Federalists won, 187–168. Substantial Anti-Federal arguments were made by Melanchton Smith, John Lansing, and G. Livingstone in New York, and by Patrick Henry and George Mason in Virginia. Each major convention considered the Constitution clause by clause, and the discussion focused on the grant of legislative powers and the provisions regarding elections and apportionment.

When we turn to the major writings of the opponents, we encounter numerous pseudonyms. The eighteenth-century practice was to emphasize the argument rather than the authority of the individual, but the Federalists had the advantage: everyone knew that Washington and Franklin supported the Constitution, and the authors of the famous *Federalist Papers* were known soon after publication. The case is different with the Anti-Federalists. "Centinel," the major Pennsylvania Anti-Federal writer, was probably George Bryan, but his son, Samuel, also claimed authorship. "Agrippa," the major Massachusetts Anti-Federalist, appears to have been James Winthrop, but it is unclear whether New York's "Cato" was Governor George Clinton or not. "Maryland Farmer" may have been John Francis Mercer, but the evidence is circumstantial. And authorship of the two best and most important series of essays, the *Essays of Brutus* and the *Letters from the Federal Farmer,* cannot be identified with certainty. The common identifications, Robert Yates as Brutus and Richard Henry Lee as Federal Farmer, have been called into question.

As for the controversy over the names, each side had a claim on the term "federalist," and the confusion stems from the Constitution, which was based on the Virginia Plan rather than on the more limited New Jersey Plan. In the convention, which was held in secret to facilitate candor, the plans were clearly identified with the national principle and the federal principle, respectively. The national principle did not mean that states would be eliminated, but it did mean that the structure and powers of the new government would reflect the priority of union. The federal principle assumed an arrangement of states into a league or treaty—the terms were then indistinguishable—in which the states composing the new whole remained primary. The Constitution, in a departure from the national principle, recognized the existence and importance of the states in the construction of the Senate: each state legislature was to elect two senators. The apportionment compromise, which also affected the election of the President, won over all but the staunchest supporters of old-style federalism—Martin, Yates, and Lansing.

This compromise and the critical sectional compromise over slavery and navigation acts had the effect of neutralizing the sectional divisions as well as the large-state–small-state divisions. It also permitted the supporters of the Constitution to claim the name Federalists. They could point to efforts during the Confederation period to strengthen the federal authority, that is, Congress, by passing an amendment providing for a limited tax power. Usage during that period identified federal men and measures with strengthening Congress; those who opposed such measures were Anti-Federal. During that debate, of course, state primacy, reinforced by state control over their delegates, equality in voting, and reliance on requisitions for troops and taxes, was the rule; the proposed change would have given Congress a limited tax on imports. With the work of the Constitutional Convention, the debate on federalism took place within an entirely different framework. Requisitions, understood to be the essence of the federal principle, were replaced by a complete legislative power to raise armies and taxes. That is why the Anti-Federalists claimed to be the true federalists; they stood for the primacy, or at least the coordinate status, of the states. Furthermore, they argued that the proposed Constitution would lead to a consolidated national government, where the states would function as mere administrative units.

Because they were firmly attached to union, and because they too agreed that the period was critical and something had to be done to strengthen the federal authority, the Anti-Federalists had a difficult time explaining their opposition to the Constitution, especially in light of the compromises described above. It is not surprising that their most effective argument in debate concerned the absence of a bill of rights. But, this position does not necessarily get to the core of Anti-Federal constitutionalism. A bill of rights may describe express limitations on governmental powers or it may expressly secure individual rights. We shall see that the Anti-Federal interest in rights goes together with an interest in mild, and hence decentralized, government.

ANTI-FEDERAL CONSTITUTIONALISM

All major Anti-Federal discussions of federalism aim at a balance between the two levels of government. To appreciate the importance of this approach to federalism, we must begin with the Anti-Federalist understanding of republican government.

REPUBLICAN GOVERNMENT

Brutus begins his discussion of republican government with this passage from the eighth book of Montesquieu's *Spirit of the Laws:*

> It is natural to a republic to have only a small territory, otherwise it cannot long subsist. In a large republic, there are men of large fortunes, and consequently of less moderation; there are trusts too great to be placed in any single subject; he has interest of his own; he soon begins to think that he may be happy, great and glorious, by oppressing his fellow citizens; and that he may raise himself to grandeur on the ruins of his country. In a large republic, the public good is sacrificed to a thousand views; it is subordinate to exceptions, and depends on accidents. In a small one, the interest of the public is easier perceived, better understood, and more within the reach of every citizen; abuses are of less extent, and of course are less protected.

Montesquieu's argument is made in terms of the primacy of the public good in republican government, as opposed especially to monarchy, the other form of free government. A small territory and population facilitate equality of wealth and make the idea of "public good" intelligible.

The Anti-Federalist conception of the small republic could not, and did not, simply follow Montesquieu's account. First, Montesquieu's discussion on republics makes no reference to representation; the people retain the general lawmaking power and choose magistrates for specific affairs exceeding their own abilities. The Anti-Federalists, on the other hand, with one notable exception,[4] presented their small-republic argument in con junction with an argument for substantial representation. The representation argument was necessary to make the Anti-Federal position practical in the United States.

Second, Montesquieu described the principle of republics, in contrast to monarchy and despotism, as virtue, that is, love of country, love of equality, and love of frugality. He approved of sumptuary laws for republics, to encourage commerce and industry and discourage luxury. The Anti-Federalists, in agreement with the Federalists and against Montesquieu, viewed republican government as deriving from the principles of liberty enunciated in the Declaration of Independence. These principles include political independence as well as individual rights, but the former is in the service, ultimately, of the latter. For example, Brutus begins his second letter with a discussion of natural liberty and the origin of civil society, individual insecurity. "The common good, therefore, is the end of civil government, and common consent, the foundation on which it is established. To effect this end, it was necessary that a certain portion of natural liberty should be surrendered, in order, that what remained should be preserved. . . ."[5] As Federal Farmer put it, "liberty, in its genuine sense, is security to enjoy the effects of our honest industry and labours, in a free and mild government, and personal security from illegal restraints."[6]

While the Anti-Federalists agree that liberty is the core principle for American government, their conception is more public and less individualist than that of the Federalists. For them, republican government requires greater attention to virtue, that is, to public spiritedness, than is manifested in the proposed Constitution. Consequently, Anti-Federal republicanism requires more than the elective principle plus institutional checks and balances. In this respect, they stand closer to Montesquieu's account of traditional republicanism, while the Federalists stand closer to his account of England, "a republic disguised under the form of monarchy."

In his treatment of Anti-Federal republicanism, Herbert Storing identifies "three fundamental considerations bearing on the kind of government needed for a free society":

> Only a small republic can enjoy a voluntary attachment of the people to the government and a voluntary obedience to the laws. Only a small republic can secure a genuine responsibility of the government to the people. Only a small republic can form the kind of citizens who will maintain republican government.[7]

A popular and mild government, in which the governors are aware of the sentiments and interests of the people, will produce voluntary attachments and responsibility. The citizenship requirement suggests the need for actual participation in government by all citizens and some agency of moral education and training. The main devices recommended by the Anti-Federalists to accomplish these three ends are representation and jury trial, in civil as well as criminal cases, and over matters of law as well as fact. Federal Farmer puts it this way:

> The essential parts of a free and good government are a full and equal representation of the people in the legislature, and the jury trial of the vicinage in the administration of justice — a full and equal representation, is that which possesses the same interests, feelings, opinions, and views the people would were they all assembled — a fair representation therefore, should be so regulated, that every order of men in the community, according to the common course of elections, can have a share in it — in order to allow professional men, merchants, traders, farmers, mechanics, etc. to bring a just proportion of their best informed men respectively into the legislature, the representation must be considerably numerous.[8]

A substantial representation, combined with short terms and rotation in office, produces a confidence in government, a strict accountability, and therefore a government resting on persuasion rather than coercion. It also gives a greater number of individuals direct experience in government. Jury trial, in civil as well as criminal cases, including general verdicts (covering questions of law as well as fact), succeeds in giving the people a check in the administration of justice analogous to their check in the legislature via representation. Federal Farmer says that both devices "are the means by which the people are let into the knowledge of public affairs — are enabled to stand as the guardians of each others rights, and to restrain, by regular and legal measures, those who otherwise might infringe upon them."[9] But Federal Farmer could have gone further in his defense of jury trial, since, unlike even a substantial representation, it permits every citizen, over time, to have direct experience in the administration of government. And, for the same reason that Federal Farmer urges the adoption of a bill of rights — to "establish in the minds of the people truths and principles which they might never otherwise have thought of, or soon forgot"[10] — a juror's responsibility to deliberate and decide in a particular case reinforces the habits and spirit of republican government even more so than having confidence in someone else's honesty and judgment.

These arguments should be contrasted with those of The Federalist, where energetic and effective administration is identified with the most refined selections, and where representation in America, which is identified with election, is celebrated precisely because, in contrast to Greece and Rome, it excludes the people, in their collective capacity, from government.

In addition to representation and jury trial, the Anti-Federalists, following Montesquieu, thought that "the manners, sentiments, and interests of the people should be similar."[11] Otherwise, opinions will clash, representatives will be in continual strife, and the public good will not be promoted. Where Madison, in The Federalist #10, took diversity and majority rule for granted and focused on the problem of preventing majority tyranny, that is, of securing the rights of individuals in minorities, the Anti-Federalists assumed the importance of a basic homogeneity to prevent faction and support a voluntary attachment to the government. Cato likened the effects of size and diversity on the attachments of citizenship to "a pebble cast on the calm surface of a river, the circles begin in the center and are small, active, and forcible, but as they depart from that point, they lose their force, and vanish into calmness." [12] The Anti-Federalists regarded both religion and written statements of rights as means of maintaining the manners and morals of the people.

REPUBLICANISM AND FEDERALISM

The Anti-Federalists assumed that the people within each state were sufficiently homogeneous to support republican government. They also assumed that relations among the states could be administered with a far less energetic government than the one embodied in the Constitution. To demonstrate that their proposals for constitutional change satisfied their conception of republican government, however, the Anti-Federalists had to show that the representation in the states was substantial. They did this with a discussion of classes, notably aristocracy and democracy.

The argument is essentially the obverse of *The Federalist* #10, where Madison reversed traditional republican theory and argued that the increased competition from a large constituency would be "most favorable to the election of proper guardians of the public weal." To Federal Farmer, and Melanchton Smith, who made the same argument in the New York Convention, those "proper guardians" are the natural aristocracy; a substantial representation must include the democracy as well:

> In my idea of our natural aristocracy in the United States, I include about four or five thousand men; and among these I reckon those who have been placed in the offices of governors, of members of Congress, and state senators generally, in the principal officers of Congress, of the army and militia, the superior judges, the most eminent professional men, & men of large property—the other persons and orders in the community form the natural democracy; this includes in general the yeomanry, the subordinate officers, civil and military, the fishermen, mechanics and traders, many of the merchants and professional men.[13]

The men of the first class "associate more extensively, have a high sense of honor, possess abilities, ambition, and general knowledge"; the men in the second class "are not so much used to combining great objects . . . possess less ambition, and a larger share of honesty: their dependence is principally on middling and small estates, industrious pursuits, and hard labour, while that of the former is principally on the emoluments of large estates, and of the chief offices of government." [14]

Federal Farmer wanted "the two great parties" to be "balanced," and the only way to do that was to balance the powers of the state and federal governments. That is because the effect of the greater competition for places in the House of Representatives would be to give the advantage to the natural aristocrats. Smith argued in the New York Convention that the middling class was the best overall representative class for republican government. From circumstance and ability, their passions and ambitions are limited, and on the matter of taxes, "from their frugal habits, and feeling themselves the public burdens, [they] will be careful how they increase them." [15]

In reply to Smith, Alexander Hamilton, who was even more candid in convention speeches than in the *The Federalist,* after denying the existence of an aristocracy in the United States, did express the following important conviction:

> It is a harsh doctrine that men grow wicked in proportion as they improve and enlighten their minds. Experience has by no means justified us in the supposition that there is more virtue in one class of men than in another. Look through the rich and the poor of the community, the learned and the ignorant. Where does virtue predominate? The difference indeed consists, not in the quantity, but kind, of vices which are incident to various classes; and here the advantage of character belongs to the wealthy. Their vices are probably more favorable to the prosperity of the state than those of the indigent, and partake less of moral depravity. [16]

If we add to that the contention, in *The Federalist* #72, that love of fame is "the ruling passion of the noblest minds," where Hamilton is supporting executive reeligibility, we see that the republicanism of the Federalists, in contrast to that of the Anti-Federalists, seeks to make substantial use of the love of distinction, political and economic. Such a position appeals to public recognition and is fully consistent with the individualist basis of natural liberty, the principle from which both sides begin their reflections on government. But it acknowledges and makes use of the love of inequality to a greater extent than the Anti-Federalists consider appropriate for republican government. While the Anti-Federalists urge the necessity of restraining individual interest and ambition more than the Federalists do, I do not think this means that they reject liberalism for an older form of republicanism. The Anti-Federalists did not oppose the elective principle, in favor of selection by lot, and, with the one exception of Maryland Farmer, they did not recommend sumptuary laws as a means of restraining luxury.

REPUBLICAN GOVERNMENT AND THE SEPARATION OF POWERS

The Anti-Federalist definition of republican government also informed their understanding of the separation of powers. While their criticism of the Constitution on this score is secondary to their federalism argument, the Anti-Federalists thought the proposed Constitution placed too much power in the less popular branches of the federal government, particularly the Senate.

The Anti-Federalists attacked the separation of powers from two different perspectives. On the one hand, some, such as Centinel, alleged that there was too much mixing and not enough separation; on the other hand, it was alleged, by Patrick Henry and the Maryland Farmer in particular, that there were no genuine checks, only paper checks. The explanation for these apparently contradictory approaches goes back to Montesquieu and the difference between republics and constitutional monarchies. To the Anti-Federalists, the English example of the separation of powers depends on the existence of a constitutional monarch and social classes, or orders, in society, specifically a hereditary nobility as the aristocratic class. With those materials, an institutional separation of powers, based on social class checking social class in a bicameral legislature, mediated by a monarchical executive, can work. Henry takes the Federalist celebration of the extension of the elective principle to form a wholly new form of checks and balances and compares it unfavorably to the English system. Election by the people, directly or indirectly, is a "paper check"; the self-love of the hereditary nobility stands as a genuine check against both the king and the commons. To combine Henry's point here with the earlier discussion of election and the natural aristocracy, the elected officials will all partake of the same class, the natural or elected aristocracy, and the only check, "the negative power of not reelecting them," "is but a feeble barrier, when their personal interest, their ambition and avarice, come to be put in contrast with the happiness of the people." [17]

The republican alternative to such a complex system of checks and balances inclines toward a simpler structure, with more of the powers remaining in the legislature. In the extreme case, this points to Pennsylvania's unicameral legislature. It surely rules out combining executive powers in the small Senate. For that reason, the Anti-Federalists proposed a special elected council to assist the executive in appointments, and they favored full legislative approval for all commercial treaties.

THE ANTI-FEDERAL PROPOSALS FOR CONSTITUTIONAL CHANGE

We turn now to the Anti-Federalists' recommendations for constitutional change. While there was no strict uniformity among the opponents, the effect of the major compromises in the Constitutional Convention, as noted above, was to mute the north–south and the large-state–small-state divisions. This survey focuses on the major issues and draws on the state convention debates and the major newspaper essays and pamphlets.

THE PREAMBLE AND ARTICLE VII (ON RATIFICATION)

The Preamble's reference to "We the people," in place of the listing of the separate states, as in the Articles, signaled the change in governmental structure, and, hence, a significant revision of federalism. Patrick Henry dramatically objected to this phrase in the Virginia Convention: "My political curiousity, exclusive of my anxious solicitude for the public welfare, leads me to ask who authorized them to speak the language of *We the People,* instead of *We the States?* States are the characteristic, and the soul of a confederation." [18] This referred back to the Congress's limited instructions to the Constitutional Convention: that the convention was to meet "for the sole and express purpose of revising the Articles of Confederation." The standard answer to this objection, which was first raised in the convention, was that the Constitution was but a proposal until ratified by the people, through specially chosen conventions. But this reply was not sufficient to legitimate the ratification provision, which violated the amendment provision of the Articles of Confederation in two ways: the ratification of nine states, rather than all thirteen, was sufficient to bring the Constitution into being, and the state legislatures were bypassed for the conventions. Luther Martin was virtually alone in pressing this objection, both in the convention and in his *Genuine Information.* He claimed that the dissolution of the federal government did not produce a state of nature as long as the state governments existed, and therefore the people did not have the right to agree to changes in the federal Constitution that affected the state constitutions. [19] The fullest reply to this, made in the convention and in *The Federalist* #40, was that the mode of ratification was an exercise of the people's right of revolution. The moderate Anti-Federalists did not press the legal argument, since they acknowledged that changes were necessary, and they did not want to give Rhode Island, the only state not to send delegates to Philadelphia, an easy veto.

ARTICLE I: THE LEGISLATURE AND LEGISLATIVE POWER

The major discussions under Article I took place in connection with: (1) elections, apportionment, and the terms of and qualifications for office (sections 2, 3, 4, and 6); (2) the enumeration of powers (section 8); and the provision regarding the slave trade (section 9).

ELECTIONS, APPORTIONMENT, AND QUALIFICATIONS FOR OFFICE. The Framers of the Constitution deserve high marks for their work on suffrage, apportionment, and qualifications for office. They compromised, to the satisfaction of the small states and of moderate nationalists from the large states, on the mode of election and apportionment for the Senate. Moreover, notwithstanding diverse practices in the states, they wrote specific suffrage and apportionment provisions for the House and office qualifications for both houses of Congress. Nonetheless, the Anti-Federalists objected to almost every provision.

To begin with the terms of office, Anti-Federalists in Massachusetts and New York argued for annual elections in the lower house, and for a four-year Senate term. Furthermore, in the New York Convention, G. Livingstone moved amendments to require rotation and recall in the Senate, and many Anti-Federalists, including Federal Farmer, agreed with those proposals.[20] No one objected to the suffrage provision for the House (which is understandable, since each state's suffrage requirement for its most popular branch became that state's federal requirement), but there was some objection, from Impartial Examiner in Virginia, for example, to state legislative election for the Senate; he favored popular election.[21] In this case, deference to the state governments, in the name of federalism, conflicted with the republican principle of consent, direct consent, of the people. Most Anti-Federalists favored the "federal" nature of the senate, as was reflected in the equal representation as well as the mode of election. However, Centinel, for one, objected to the equality of representation.[22] On the other side, Martin, consistently adhering to the traditional federal principle, objected to the individual form of voting, instead of voting by state delegation.[23] The important apportionment formula for the House, which included "three-fifths others" in order to produce a sectional balance of power, drew criticism from Massachusetts and New York Anti-Federalists for including slaves. In addition, Smith, who had argued that the number of representatives was too small, wanted to increase the ratio from one representative for every 30,000 to one for every 20,000. As an example of their distrust, Smith and other Anti-Federalists wondered why the Framers used the construction "shall not exceed" rather than one guaranteeing maximum representation.[24] The language proposed by the Anti-Federalists would have necessitated a constitutional amendment at some time in the future, to keep the size of the House manageable.

The Anti-Federalists frequently objected to the vagueness of Congress's power over the states regarding the time, place, and manner of holding elections. That Congress must have ultimate control over its own elections seemed reasonable, but the Anti-Federalists argued that all fundamental provisions should be set by the Constitution and not left to legislative discretion. Federal Farmer speculated on the effect that statewide elections for representatives, with a plurality sufficient for victory, would have on the representation.[25]

The liberal qualifications for office, which included age, citizenship for a prescribed number of years, and state residency, were criticized by some, including Federal Farmer, as follows: "It can be no objection to the elected, that they are Christians, Pagans, Mahometans, or Jews; that they are of any colour, rich or poor, convict or not. Hence, many men may be elected who cannot be electors.[26] This reflected the importance of homogeneity for a mild government. David Caldwell made the same point in the North Carolina Convention, when the prohibition on any religious test as a qualification for office was discussed. There, Samuel Spencer, another Anti-Federalist, took issue with Caldwell, arguing in favor of full religious liberty. These concerns about who might get elected to office appear to contradict the Anti-Federalist critique of an aristocratic representation in Congress. But their concern was for a sufficiently middle class representation, not with the widest possible diversity, especially as applied to religion. The Anti-Federalists were the democrats in the sense that they favored a popular participation in and influence on government; but in their preference for homogeneity, in order that mild republican government might work, they were less liberal than the Federalists. This does not make them nonliberals, however, since the universality of natural rights does not necessitate extending civil rights without regard to racial, religious, or ethnic differences.

THE ENUMERATION OF POWERS.   The Anti-Federalist critique of the Constitution focused on representation and taxation; there would be too little of the former and too much of the latter in the proposed government. Moreover, while the Anti-Federalists proposed increases in the representation, since the representation would always be more substantial in the states, their major argument was for a reduction in the powers of Congress, specifically the power over the purse and the sword.

Of all Anti-Federalists Brutus provided the fullest discussion of the enumeration of powers. His account of the possible scope of the powers, and the assistance that Congress was likely to receive from a judicial interpretation of the Constitution, reads like a preview of Justice John Marshall's opinion in *McCulloch v. Maryland*. For example, in his first letter, after quoting from the necessary and proper and the supremacy clauses, Brutus writes:

> The government then, so far as it extends, is a complete one, and not a confederation. . . . It is true this government is limited to certain objects, or to speak more properly, some small degree of power is still left to the states, but a little attention to the powers vested in the general government, will convince every candid man, that if it is capable of being executed, all that is reserved for the individual states must very soon be annihilated, except so far as they are barely necessary to the organization of the general government.

Brutus notes that the tax power, "the most important of any power that can be granted," is given completely, and "the idea of confederation is totally lost, and that of one entire republic is embraced." And the power "to raise and support armies at pleasure, as well in peace as in war, and their controul over the militia, tend, not only to a consolidation of the government, but the destruction of liberty."[27]

The Anti-Federalists attempted to draw a line between federal and state powers, conceding to the federal government only those powers that were necessary for security and defense. Brutus took on *The Federalist's* strongest argument, which was that the means must be proportional to the ends, and since the end, securing the objects of union, depends on the actions of other nations, it requires unlimited means.[28] Brutus replied that the end is not limited to preserving the common defense and general welfare of the union. Since the government is "complex in its nature, the end it has in view is so also. . . ."

> Neither the general government, nor the state governments, ought to be vested with all the powers proper to be exercised for promoting the ends of government. The powers are divided between them—certain ends are to be attained by the one, and other certain ends by the other; and these, taken together, include all the ends of good government. This being the case, the conclusion follows, that each should be furnished with the means, to attain the ends, to which they are designed.[29]

The most important applications of this argument involved the powers to tax, to raise and support armies, to regulate the militia, and to borrow money. The most common tax proposal was to limit the federal government to a tax on foreign imports, leaving internal taxes, both those on individuals and those on commodities to the states. This would guarantee the states a source of revenue, since the Anti-Federalists feared that any concurrent tax power would lead to federal preemption of the states' sources of funds. It would also eliminate the need for numerous federal assessors and collectors and federal ordinances that would interfere with state laws.[30] The Anti-Federalists in the Massachusetts Convention and Federal Farmer recommended that if Congress found the import tax insufficient, it could turn to the states for requisitions.[31] To clarify this proposal, the Constitution's mode of raising direct taxes, which had to be proportional to each state's representation, may or may not have involved the state governments, but the coercive authority was the federal government's and that government would determine the mode of taxation. The requisitions approach left the mode of taxation and its execution to the state governments.

Turning to the war power, there was substantial support for the proposition that there shall be no standing armies in time of peace. Brutus proposed a limited power to raise armies to defend frontier posts and guard arsenals to respond to threats of attack or invasion. Otherwise, standing armies could be raised only on the vote of two-thirds of both houses. Federal Farmer first proposed that a special majority, two-thirds or three-quarters, be required in Congress, until the representation was increased; he later proposed employing the principle of requisitions for raising armies, with the states retaining a right to refuse. In addition, he recommended that land forces could not be maintained for more than a year without congressional approval.[32] The Anti-Federalists also objected to the provisions relating to the militia. Luther Martin wanted a percentage limit on the militia that could be sent out of the state, and Federal Farmer regarded a "select militia" as inconsistent with republican government. Only a strong general militia, composed of all men capable of bearing arms, especially "the substantial men, having families and property," with officers appointed by the states, combined energy and safety.[33]

Anticipating the debate over the assumption of state debts, Brutus objected to the unlimited power to borrow money. "[B]y this means [Congress] may create a national debt, so large, as to exceed the ability of the country ever to sink." He proposed that the power be restricted to "the most urgent occasions, and then we should not borrow of foreigners if we could possibily help it."[34]

Finally, Federal Farmer first supported and then opposed federal bankruptcy laws, on the grounds that the state laws differed, making a uniform federal practice unworkable, and that this power would involve the federal judiciary in internal matters best left to the state courts.[35]

RESTRICTIONS ON CONGRESS: THE SLAVE TRADE. The Constitutional Convention handled the critical sectional division in the country—which refers to the fact that over 90 percent of the nation's nearly 700,000 slaves were concentrated in the five southern states, constituting over one-third of the population there—so successfully that it played a very small role in the ratification debate. Still, the twenty-year embargo on federal legislation prohibiting slave importation drew criticism for its tolerance in Massachusetts, and for its limited protection in North Carolina.

ARTICLE II: THE EXECUTIVE POWER

We shall begin with the office of the presidency—its unity, mode of election, and tenure—and then consider executive powers, which includes the general grant of executive power, the qualified veto power, the commander-in-chief power, the appointment power (with the advice and consent of the Senate), the treaty-making power (with two-thirds of the Senate necessary for ratification), the pardoning power, and the power to convene and adjourn Congress.

To begin with the decision for a single executive, while there was a brief but full debate in the convention, in which Randolph and Mason charged that unity in the executive was the "foetus of monarchy," during the ratification debate no Anti-Federalist objected to the single executive. The only qualification came in the form of a frequently made argument for a council of appointment.

As for the mode of election, Publius, citing Federal Farmer, noted how this part of the Constitution "escaped without severe censure." Federal Farmer judged the election "to be properly secured," and later said it represented "a judicious combination of principles and precautions."[36] Cato urged a direct election, since "it is a maxim in republics, that the representatives of the people should be of their immediate choice."[37] This was a minority view among the opponents, probably because a direct popular election was unlikely to produce a majority choice.

The Anti-Federalists generally opposed reeligibility, however. Federal Farmer, who favored unity for decisiveness and responsibility, turned *The Federalist*'s argument that reeligibility provided a constructive use for ambition around by charging that once elected, a man will spend all his time and exercise all his influence ("he will spare no artifice") attempting to stay in office. James Monroe, however, agreed with *The Federalist* on this point and supported reeligibility.[39]

Turning to the powers, first, no one questioned the suitability of the general assignment of "the executive power" to the President. Perhaps it was unclear how that could be construed to grant the President additional, nonenumerated powers, such as the removal power. The Anti-Federalists were divided on the executive's veto; Federal Farmer and Monroe supported it, while Impartial Examiner opposed it, as an inappropriate borrowing from the British Constitution.[39] The Anti-Federalists' most common criticism, after reeligibility, pertained to the Senate's participation in the treaty-making and appointment powers. In general, the Anti-Federalists favored a council of appointment, although Federal Farmer thought that Congress should appoint some of the major offices and the Senate could retain its participation in appointing foreign affairs officers.[40] While Federal Farmer feared that the Senate would become the source of aristocracy, he could not suggest an alternative arrangement for treaty-making. But several Anti-Federalists objected to treaties having the force of law; they wanted treaties to be approved by both houses of Congress, and Federal Farmer proposed that Congress approve all commercial treaties.[41]

Patrick Henry, who said that the Constitution "squints toward monarchy," and some other Anti-Federalists expressed a fear that as commander-in-chief the President would acquire absolute power, and George Mason and Centinel feared that the President might exercise the pardoning power to screen criminals from punishment, but these objections were less prominent than the others noted above. And Cato feared that the President would use his power to call "either House" into session to work with the Senate to further aristocratic designs.[42]

The experience of government without an independent executive, the common expectation that George Washington would be the first President, and uncertainty about the strength of the office compared to the Senate, explain the Anti-Federalists' moderate support for the office.

ARTICLE III: THE JUDICIAL POWER

Brutus's account of the judicial power anticipated the full development of judicial review as well as the importance of the judicial branch as a vehicle for the development of the federal government's powers. By extending the judicial power "to all cases, in law and equity, arising under this Constitution," Article III permits the courts "to give the constitution a legal construction." Moreover, Brutus continued, the equity jurisdiction, which referred to separate courts in England, gave the courts power "to explain the constitution according to the reasoning spirit of it, without being confined to the words or letter." This is why Brutus concludes that "the real effect of this system of government will therefore be brought home to the feelings of the people through the medium of the judicial power." [43] The judicial power will be able to attribute certain powers to the legislature "which they have not exercised," and they will also use the Preamble to expand the legislative powers.[44] Brutus does not object to the life tenure for judges, but he opposes extending the judicial power to the Constitution. Without that power, the courts would be limited to interpreting congressional statutes; they would not be able to exercise judicial review over federal legislation.

Brutus and Federal Farmer objected to the extensive appellate jurisdiction of the Supreme Court, especially as it affected the right to trial by jury. Article III, section 2, may have guaranteed a jury trial in criminal cases, but an appellate reconsideration of the facts would negate that right, and the Anti-Federalists wanted that right extended to civil cases and protected against appellate reconsideration there also.[45]

Finally, the Constitutional Convention, in a compromise between those who favored a full federal court system and those who opposed lower federal courts, provided that Congress could "ordain and establish" lower courts. Brutus agreed with those who thought that, aside from the Supreme Court's original jurisdiction, much of the judicial power could have been left to originate in the state courts.[46]

AMENDMENTS PROPOSED BY THE ANTI-FEDERALISTS IN THE STATE RATIFICATION CONVENTIONS

The Anti-Federalists are best known for the Bill of Rights, since the Constitution would not have been ratified without the promise, first made in the Massachusetts Convention and subsequently accepted, that recommendatory amendments accompanying a vote for unconditional ratification would be considered in Congress. But the Bill of Rights was as much a Federalist as an Anti-Federalist victory. This can be shown by considering the argument for a bill of rights and then by examining the Anti-Federalist proposals.

The Anti-Federalists wanted a bill of rights to curb governmental power. When the Federalists denied the necessity of a federal bill of rights,

TABLE 1. List of Proposed Amendments

1. jury trial in civil cases: Pennsylvania, Massachusetts, New Hampshire, Virginia, New York, North Carolina, Rhode Island
2. no interference in state election laws unless the state fails to provide for elections: Pennsylvania, Massachusetts, South Carolina, New Hampshire, Virginia, New York, North Carolina, Rhode Island
3. state control of its own militia: Pennsylvania, Virginia, New York, North Carolina, Rhode Island
4. strict separation of powers: Pennsylvania, Virginia, North Carolina, Rhode Island
5. nonsupremacy of treaties: Pennsylvania, North Carolina
6. restriction on federal judicial jurisdiction: Pennsylvania, Massachusetts, New Hampshire, Virginia, New York, North Carolina, Rhode Island
7. limitation of powers to those "expressly" or "clearly" delegated: Massachusetts, South Carolina, New Hampshire, New York
8. no direct taxation unless the import tax is insufficient and/or requisitions fail: Massachusetts, South Carolina, New Hampshire, Virginia, New York, North Carolina, Rhode Island
9. no Congressionally authorized commercial treaties: Massachusetts, New Hampshire, New York, North Carolina, Rhode Island
10. restrictions on standing army: New Hampshire, Virginia, New York, North Carolina, Rhode Island
11. limitation on Presidential reeligibility: Virginia, New York, North Carolina
12. limitation on Senate reeligibility: New York
13. state recall of Senators: New York, Rhode Island
14. oath not to violate state constitutions: New York

on the ground that whatever power was not enumerated could not be claimed, the Anti-Federalists pointed to the Constitution's supremacy and to the extensiveness of the powers enumerated. If what became the bill of rights, the first ten amendments, is compared with the proposed amendments in Table 1, it becomes clear how the content of the amendments was completely Federalist: neither the Anti-Federal proposals to restrict federal powers, especially the tax and war powers, nor their proposals to change the governmental structure were accepted.

From the proposals in Table 1, Madison, who proposed the amendments that became the Bill of Rights, included only the jury trial provision, which was ratified, the separation of powers statement, which was not, and the statement that powers not delegated are reserved to the states, or to the people, without the adverb "expressly." The Anti-Federalists attempted to get "expressly" put into the amendment, which became the tenth, but failed. Madison made a point of saying, in his speech introducing the amendments, that he was not proposing that any changes he made in the government's structure or powers, but only that certain rights, which he considered beyond the government's power, be made more secure by being written into the Constitution.

In one sense, however, the Anti-Federalist demands for a bill of rights derives from their understanding of republican government. That goes back to the importance of mild government and the educational value of proclaiming the rights and keeping the people aware of them. As Federal Farmer wrote, "If a nation means its systems, religious or political, shall have duration, it ought to recognize the leading principles of them in the front page of every family book." [47] The affirmation of rights against the government does reflect Anti-Federal constitutionalism. Unlike several state bills of rights, however, the rights enumerated are largely individual rather than collective. Consequently, the civic education that the Bill of Rights has provided has been primarily to support individual rather than community claims. That such a bill of rights has served to strengthen the federal courts reflects Federalist constitutionalism.

CONCLUSION

With the ratification of the Constitution, one would expect the victory of the Federalist view of federalism and republican government. And yet, the strict construction of congressional powers, and even more so, the states' rights view of the union, reflect a retention of the Anti-Federalist view of federalism. The only difference is that the debate is now over the meaning of the Constitution, not over whether it should be ratified.

The Federalist #39, which takes every reference to the states in the frame of government as proof of federalism, easily lends itself to a view of nation–state relations similar to the Anti-Federal position. Consider the important "necessary and proper" clause. The Anti-Federalists claimed that it provided for unlimited power for Congress, and the Federalists denied it, without, however, indicating what could not be implied. Unlike the debates on the tax power and the power to raise armies, this discussion was inexact. That is, did "necessary" mean "convenient and useful" or "without which, the enumerated power is nugatory"? This was the original debate over "loose," or liberal construction versus strict construction. It took place in 1791, first in the House, where Madison urged strict construction and lost, and then in the executive branch, where Jefferson urged strict construction and lost to Hamilton, who argued, to President Washington's satisfaction, for a liberal construction. Chief Justice Marshall later established liberal construction in our constitutional law in *McCulloch v. Maryland* (1819). I think *The Federalist's* position clearly supports liberal construction. If so, that means that the Anti-Federal view of federalism survived the Constitution in the form of strict construction and states' rights. The leading advocates of these constitutional theories were Madison and Jefferson.

In addition to the "necessary and proper" clause, we should take note of the commerce clause. This was barely discussed during ratification. That is because everyone agreed on its clearly intended applications, to permit Congress to make commercial treaties and to pass tariffs. (The exception to the latter was sectional and minor, as we noted.) And for nearly a century, Congress did not enact legislation under the commerce clause that raised serious questions about how far this power might invade a state's internal affairs. Only then did the question arise whether commerce is merely buying and selling across state lines or whether it comprehends any and all economic activities with a national impact. Put another way, which branch of government should decide the question, Congress or the Supreme Court?

The view that Congress should is called "cooperative federalism," while the view that the Supreme Court should is called "dual federalism." Edward Corwin, who coined these terms, thought that the latter was constitutionally prescribed and that it was repudiated during the New Deal. On the first point, I think he was wrong. The line-drawing approach to the powers of Congress resembles the Anti-Federalist attempt to use the internal – external distinction to make the states at least coordinate partners with the national government. The Federalists defended extensive taxing and war-making powers by arguing that national needs are in principle unlimited. That argument focused on defense and the later debate turns on commerce and general welfare, but it is hard to imagine the major arguments of *The Federalist* #10, which refers to regulating "various and interfering interests," supporting anything but a strong government and a broad commerce power.

On the second point, Corwin was right for twenty-five years, but since 1976 we have seen a revival of interest in the Tenth Amendment as a source of constitutional, and hence, judicial, protection of states' rights. The current Court majority holds to cooperative federalism, but it clings to a narrow 5 – 4 majority, and the minority is not inclined to respect precedent on this issue.

In addition, the Supreme Court has interpreted the Eleventh Amendment as a source for the states' claim to immunity, under the sovereign immunity doctrine, from lawsuits in federal courts by individuals raising federal questions. This position has little support from the Framers' intent, since the amendment was intended to prevent individuals from one state from suing another state to recover a debt, but it is another example of judicial support for a view of federalism that is closer to the Anti-Federalist than the Federalist position.

It is not so easy to find contemporary examples of Anti-Federalist republicanism today, although it surely was present in the constitutionalism of Jefferson and his followers, including Madison after 1791. Still, suspicion of "big government," and a preference for Congress, against presidential power or the bureaucracy, resembles Anti-Federal republicanism. Specifically, the War Powers Act of 1973 strikes me as a modern equivalent of the Anti-Federal hostility to standing armies in peacetime.

On another point, the Anti-Federal interest in homogeneity and civic responsibility, as reflected in their concern about qualifications for office, jury trial, and the militia, bears some relation to the contemporary interest in referenda and in the "communitarian" critique of our traditional emphasis on individual rights. This critique is present in controversies over the regulation of obscenity and prayer in public schools.[48]

The point is that our constitutional founding settled some important issues, but it did not settle all of them, at least not once and for all. That these issues reoccur in American political and constitutional history is testimony to the thoughtfulness of the founding debate as well as the incompleteness of any political founding that relies on the rule of law. Thanks to the Anti-Federalists, we have a fuller understanding of the tension between individualism and citizenship in a modern liberal republic.

THE CASE FOR RATIFICATION: FEDERALIST CONSTITUTIONAL THOUGHT

DAVID F. EPSTEIN

The speeches and writings that made the case for ratification of the United States Constitution reveal most of what we can know about the intentions of those who made the Constitution legally authoritative, the American people of 1787–1788. It is true that these speeches and writings offer the opinions only of the most articulate supporters of the Constitution, but their intended audience was the people and their elected representatives at the ratifying conventions; and so they also indicate what considerations those articulate supporters thought would or should lead others to support the Constitution.

Federalist ratification statements differed from the private deliberations of the Constitutional Convention by having this public, argumentative character; and also because many of the detailed questions addressed by the convention were now of secondary importance. The proponents of ratification did not have to believe or prove that each decision by the Framers had been perfect in order to support a judgment that, on balance, adopting this Constitution was a better course than rejecting it. The assertion that the proposal was "such a constitution as, upon the whole, is the best that can possibly be obtained" [1] was consistent with the position that it "must be examined with many allowances, and must be compared not with the theory, which each individual may frame in his own mind, but with the system which it is meant to take the place of, and with any other which there may be probability of obtaining. . . ." [2]

The broad claims made on the Constitution's behalf, rather than the reasoning that explained each of its provisions, are the subject of this chapter. These claims may conveniently be divided into promises and reassurances: promises that the new government could supply blessings not available under the Articles of Confederation (peace, prosperity, and justice), and reassurances that it would not extinguish blessings Americans thought they already enjoyed (limited and popular government). In surveying these claims, I will emphasize but not confine myself to the most famous Federalist writings, the essays of Alexander Hamilton, James Madison, and John Jay published as *The Federalist* under the pen name "Publius." That work was "the boast of the advocates of this new constitution"[3] and influenced speeches and writings of others; and its authors were also prominent participants in their states' ratifying conventions. But some Federalist themes were given more emphasis elsewhere (for example, the economic advantages of the Constitution, the continuing powers of the states, the case against a bill of rights); and *The Federalist's* length and depth were not universally appreciated. Federalist Rufus King thought some more modest essays of "'the Landholder' will do more service our way, than the elaborate works of Publius."[4]

PROMISE: DEFENSE, PROSPERITY, JUSTICE

[I]t may in general be demanded, what indication is there of national disorder, poverty, and insignificance that could befall a community so peculiarly blessed with natural advantages as we are, which does not form a part of the dark catalogue of our public misfortunes?[5]

Federalists charged that the "imbecility" of the Articles of Confederation had caused economic "ruin and decay everywhere,"[6] and would sooner or later cause worse: disunion, civil war, anarchy, usurpation by a despot, or conquest by a foreign power. The economic problem was already clear: "The husbandman finds no encouragement to encrease his stock and produce, for he finds no vent for them — the mechanick stands idle half his time, or gets nothing for his work but truck — half our sailors are out of business — the labourer can find no employ . . . wealth . . . lies dormant for want of encouragement to loan it, under the security of just and equal laws."[7] However, a dispassionate historian might evaluate American economic circumstances of 1787–1788, the Federalists thought this issue cut sharply with the people: "these things are too severely felt to be omitted; the people feel them; they pervade all classes of citizens and every situation from New Hampshire to Georgia; the argument of necessity is the patriot's defense, as well as the tyrant's plea."[8]

The necessities imposed by war were not yet severely felt but had to be anticipated:

. . . if a hostile attack were made at this moment on the United States, it would flash conviction on the minds of the citizens of the United States of the necessity of vesting the government with this power [to impose direct taxes], which alone can enable it to protect the community. I do not wish to frighten the members into a concession of this power, but to bring to their minds those considerations which demonstrate its necessity.[9]

It would be "deceiving ourselves" to think that "we shall always have peace, and need make no provision against wars. . . . Did there ever exist a nation which, at some period or other, was not exposed to war?"[10] Indeed,

American weakness was likely to invite attack by a European power; "nations in general will make war whenever they have a prospect of getting anything by it."[11] If American military power depended on the separate action of each state government, "state will fall after state. . . . United we are strong, divided we fall."[12]

America's economic problems were caused in part by military weakness. For some Americans, navigation of the Mississippi River appeared indispensable to prosperity and an "unalienable right," but that right could "only be secured by one of two ways—by force or by treaty"; and even obtaining a treaty depended upon being "more powerful and respectable" and thus "more feared."[13] More generally, foreign nations found it unnecessary to confer reciprocal commercial benefits on America. The individual states were in a poor bargaining position, but a national government "able to counteract the oppressive acts of other nations respecting our trade" would "set all the springs of action in motion."[14]

Notwithstanding the people's reluctance to allow a national government extensive powers of taxation, or the authority to maintain a standing army in peacetime, Americans had to imitate the "customary and ordinary modes practiced in other governments."[15] The existence of other countries made it a matter of necessity that a national government be able to command revenues and raise troops from the entire United States. In principle, Congress already had the necessary powers under the Articles of Confederation, but it had to address its commands to the state governments. What would distinguish the new government was that it could enforce its laws against individual citizens, who could be punished and were therefore subject to coercion by "the arm of the ordinary magistrate."[16] State governments, by contrast, could be subdued (if at all) only by force of arms, and therefore decided for themselves whether to accept the national decisions. As a result, the Confederation's "requisitions" of money were simply "pompous petitions for public charity."[17]

National safety depended not only on giving the national government certain powers but also on that government's qualities or characteristics. For example, the assignment of the executive power to a single officer (attacked by some Anti-Federalists as monarchical) is conducive to "energy in the executive," which is "essential to the protection of the community against foreign attacks. . . . Decision, activity, secrecy, and dispatch will generally characterize the proceedings of one man in a much more eminent degree than the proceedings of any greater number. . . . In the conduct of war, in which the energy of the executive is the bulwark of the national security, everything would be to be apprehended from its plurality." The objection that "a vigorous executive is inconsistent with the genius of republican government" must give way to the fact that an energetic executive is essential to "good government."[18]

Besides this matter of speed and decisiveness, the wisdom and consistency of the government's decisions could be of crucial importance in foreign policy. "Every nation . . . whose affairs betray a want of wisdom and stability, may calculate on every loss which can be sustained from the more systematic policy of its wiser neighbors." [19] Speaking to the New York ratifying convention, Alexander Hamilton went so far as to announce a "trut[h] . . . not often held up in public assemblies": that "a community will ever be incompetent to . . . that branch of administration, especially, which involves our political relation with foreign states." [20] Accordingly, elections should not simply transmit public opinion into the councils of government, but should be used to "obtain for rulers men who possess most wisdom to discern, and most virtue to pursue, the common good of the society." This "aim" of obtaining excellent rulers is one that popular governments have or ought to have in common with "every political constitution." [21]

On the basis of this concern with "good government," that is, with the results of government, Federalists defended the relatively small number and long terms of officers that Anti-Federalists thought departed from the spirit of popular government. The new government could "collect and avail itself of the talents and experience of the ablest men, in whatever part of the Union they may be found," in contrast to state governments composed from a smaller supply of candidates. The terms of office established by the Constitution departed from the "simple and familiar standard" of annual elections so as to permit rulers to learn from their experience in office. The number and term of officers affect not only their likely abilities and opportunities but also their incentives. The ambition of rulers means that "a change of men" in office leads to "a change of measures"; and frequent elections lead to a "continual change even of good measures," which "is inconsistent with every rule of prudence and every prospect of success." The Senate's small size makes "a sensible degree of the praise and blame of public measures . . . the portion of each individual." The President, with an unlimited opportunity to seek reelection, might in the best case be moved by "the love of fame" to "plan and undertake extensive and arduous enterprises for the public benefit. . . ." In general, the Constitution's arrangement of offices was seen as putting rulers in situations where their own personal motives would direct them toward the "positive merit of doing good." [22]

Energy, wisdom, and stability appeared indispensable with respect to foreign countries, but were also advantageous at home. For example, stability in the laws is favorable to economic enterprise, and thus to national wealth. But the Federalists' general case for "good government" becomes more complicated when one turns from foreign to domestic affairs. While government's powers and qualities enable it to serve Americans by restraining foreigners, its promotion of domestic tranquillity and the general welfare requires it to restrain some Americans. This harsh fact may be unexceptionable if those restrained are common criminals or "those irregular and high-handed coalitions which sometimes interrupt the ordinary course of justice." [23] Shay's Rebellion suggested the value of a national government that could rescue states from insurrection and anarchy. But the Federalists' own description of confederated America pointed to a more fundamental difficulty. America's problems were not the work of only a few trouble-makers, but the result of a failure of the states spontaneously to cooperate for their common good. A government that could make the states cooperate would thwart the impulses that resisted cooperation in the first place. So strong were those impulses that Federalists bluntly predicted war among disunited American states. Commercial rivalries, disputed borders, and other particular issues of contention — as well as the general fact that neighboring countries are "natural enemies" — meant that disunited American states would be "the victim of mutual rage, rancour, and revenge." [24]

For example, under the Articles of Confederation importing states could raise revenue for themselves by excise taxes on imported goods that citizens of neighboring states would pay as well. Federalists appealed both to justice and to the domestic tranquillity that injustice would sooner or later interrupt:

> [T]he principles of reason and justice require, that states and individuals should so exercise their rights as not to injure and depress their neighbours. If this [argument] should not induce them to adopt a proper mode of conduct, we have no doubt but argument derived from our natural strength, operating on their natural weakness will produce the desired conviction — the opinion of any statesman is not much to be regarded who supposes that a powerful and enlightened people, uncontrouled by any tie of government, will consent to become perpetual tributaries to a weaker neighbour. [25]

Similarly, some states were endangering the others by provoking the hostility of the Indians or foreign countries. In general, the Federalists could not claim that the new government would simply preserve all the advantages enjoyed by all the states; they had to argue that the "local interests of a state ought, in every case, to give way to the interests of the Union" because the "small good ought never to oppose the great one." [26] To this end, the new Constitution would deny the states the power to tax imports and make war, and would assign disputes between states to a national court.

But while Federalists hoped Americans would see the "necessity of sacrificing private opinions and partial interests," they did not want to see a sacrifice of anyone's *rights*. "Justice is the end of government. It is the end of civil society." The problem was not only to protect the people of some states from injustice by other states but to protect the minority of the people within each state from injustice by the majority. The same facts of human diversity and partiality that explain one state's unjust policies toward another operate in any society. The principle of popular government permits a majority of the people, moved by passionate opinion or economic interest, to violate the rights of the minority. A widely deplored example of this problem was state legislation that defrauded creditors by making paper money legal tender for debts. The "factious spirit" which had "tainted our public administration" caused a general "alarm for private rights." [27]

Thus Federalist constitutional thought was not satisfied with the promise of a government that would promote the good of the public in general. The Federalists' more exacting standard was that government must "establish Justice," that is, protect the private rights of each individual citizen. Madison and James Wilson both explained the rights of human beings in terms of their "faculties." Government must protect "the faculties of men" by protecting their right to possess the property that they acquire by exercising their faculties. Government's task is not to satify human desires or needs, but only to protect men's right to exercise their human capacities so as to satisfy their own desires or needs. Thus, for example, for government to arrange "an equal division of property," whether for the moral improvement of the rich or the material satisfaction of the poor, is an "improper or wicked project." [28] The view that government's fundamental purpose is to secure the private rights of individuals is founded on the argument made by John Locke and accepted by American founders that government is voluntarily instituted by naturally free individuals so as to secure the enjoyment of their freedom. The community as a whole ultimately exists for no other purpose, although its existence is an indispensable condition for the security of private rights and thus its common defense and even general welfare are of great importance.

Injustice not only contradicts the fundamental purpose of government, it tends to injure the general welfare and disrupt domestic tranquillity — making possible a prudential argument for justice to those whose self-love attaches them to their own rights but makes them heedless of the rights of others. For example, paper money schemes that defrauded existing creditors had the additional consequence of drying up further credit. America's economic problems could be attributed in part to these policies; "if there be no confidence, property will sink in value, and there will be no inducement or emulation to industry." [29] Moreover, the majority's oppression of the minority may cause the kind of "turbulence and contention" that made the ancient democracies "in general . . . as short in their lives as they have been violent in their deaths." [30]

The Constitution would prohibit state governments from issuing paper money or adopting ex post facto laws or bills of attainder, and thus promised relief from those forms of injustice. James Madison offered a general argument that the new national government would be more just than the state governments. Because the new government operated over an extensive sphere of territory and population, groups of men with a particular factious motive would be less likely to constitute a majority of the entire population and less likely to find it easy to unite their efforts and carry out their plans.

Federalists did not differ from Anti-Federalists in seeing protection of private rights as the fundamental purpose of government; but they doubted that Anti-Federalists understood what most threatened those rights and what was necessary to protect them. Rejecting the view that strong government is the overriding danger to men's rights, Federalists insisted that rights were threatened by anarchy, by conquest, and even by the lawful majority of a heterogeneous society. Accordingly, the problem of limiting government so as to protect rights was more complicated than the Federalists' opponents assumed.

REASSURANCE: LIMITED AND POPULAR GOVERNMENT

> Yet, however weak our country may be, I hope we shall never sacrifice our liberties.[31]

To Anti-Federalists, the extensive powers conferred on the new government suggested the danger that those powers would be abused and the state governments extinguished; and the qualities of energy, stability, and wisdom emphasized by Federalists justified the suspicion that the government would be somewhat removed from the people in spirit as well as location. Much Federalist argument was devoted to refuting specific charges that seemed far-fetched — such as that the national provision for impeachment would apply to state officials, or that Congress's power over the time of elections would allow it to extend its term of office to twenty years. But these lame objections reflected the more fundamental fear that the Constitution would sooner or later replace America's local, limited, popular governments with a distant, oppressive, and aristocratic government.

The Federalists' first line of defense was that the new Constitution left the existing state governments intact and would merely secure the people's enjoyment of the benefits of those trusted, popular, local governments. The state legislatures "exclusively retain such powers as will give the states the advantages of small republics, without the danger commonly attendant on the weakness of such governments."[32] The national government was necessary to defend the states and to serve certain national purposes, but "the Constitution does not suffer the federal powers to controul in the least, or so much as to interfere in the internal policy, jurisdiction, or municipal rights of any particular State: except where great and manifest national purposes and interests make that controul necessary."[33] Within each state the existing form of government would rule on almost all matters; state governments could

> . . . cut canals; regulate descents and marriages; license taverns; alter the ciminal law; . . . establish poor houses, hospitals, and houses of employ-

ment; regulate the police; and many other things of the utmost importance to the happiness of their respective citizens. In short, besides the particulars enumerated, every thing of a domestic nature must or can be done by them.[34]

The fact that some constitutional provisions relied on state governments (for example, state legislative election of senators) was a further proof that the states would be preserved.

But it could not be denied that, in the name of "great and manifest national purposes and interests," the authority previously enjoyed by popular, local governments would be in some measure curtailed; and policies those governments had chosen would be changed by a newly authoritative national government. Accordingly, much Federalist argument offered reassurances about the national government's own character. In answer to a variety of charges concerning the national government's threat to liberty, the Federalists insisted that its powers were properly limited and its character "wholly popular."

In answer to the objection that the new Constitution contained no bill of rights, James Wilson offered an argument widely praised on one side and widely ridiculed on the other. The new government needed no bill of rights because all of its powers were "enumerated." In contrast to the state governments, which could exercise *any* powers except those specifically denied by a bill of rights, the national government could exercise *only* those powers specifically granted. A bill of rights that specified exceptions to national power would imply that those were the only exceptions, and thus expand rather than limit the national government's power.[35] The problem with this argument was that the Constitution's enumeration appeared to assign broad objects or purposes to the national government, and without a bill of rights the government might choose to serve those purposes by means that would violate rights.

Eventually, Federalists temporized on this question and insisted only that universally popular amendments such as a bill of rights could easily be adopted subsequent to ratification and so ought not be made a condition for (and endanger the prospect of) ratification.[36] But the fact that Federalists thought a bill of rights unimportant is worth noting, given the prominent place of the Bill of Rights in more recent constitutional thought. A bill of rights is "but a paper check," meaningless unless someone can be relied on to enforce it. States with bills of rights had been guilty of grossly violating them.[37] A bill of rights is also not likely to be unequivocal in meaning; one proposed restriction on punishments would use the "expressions 'unusual and severe' or 'cruel and unusual,'" which "surely would have been too vague to have been of any consequence, since they admit of no clear and precise signification."[38]

Moreover, some very dangerous powers of government could not prudently be limited at all. Some Anti-Federalists wanted to forbid a standing army in time of peace, and permit the national government to impose excise taxes but not direct taxes. Federalists defended granting the important powers of purse and sword "without limitation," on the grounds that *"it is impossible to foresee or to define the extent and variety of national exigencies, and the correspondent extent and variety of the means which may be necessary to satisfy them."* [39] For example, although the national government could usually rely on excise taxes for its revenue, the additional power to impose direct taxes would be essential in time of war. And not the immediately foreseeable circumstances but the "probable exigencies of ages" should guide the assignment of the government's powers. [40] A primary response to fears that such unlimited powers made the government dangerous was expressed by the following question: "Would any man choose a lame horse [lest] a sound one should run away with him; or will any man prefer a small tent to live in, before a large house, which may fall down and crush him in its ruins." [41]

Federalists insisted that the form of the government — that is, its arrangement of offices, not the words that would define or limit its powers — was the people's fundamental guarantee against oppression. Thus the important question was not the extent and wording of the legislative powers, but "how are Congress formed? how far have you a control over them? Decide this, and then all the questions about their power may be dismissed for the amusement of those politicians whose business it is to catch flies. . . ." [42] Anti-Federalists should not offer "unmeaning cavils about the extent of the powers"; they should consider whether the proposed government is "modeled in such a manner as to admit of its being safely vested with the requisite powers." [43] The most important aspect of how that government was modeled was its representative character:

> Independent of all other reasonings on the subject, it is a full answer to those who require a more peremptory provision against military establishments in time of peace to say that the whole power of the proposed government is to be in the hands of the representatives of the people. This is the essential, and, after all, the only efficacious security for the rights and privileges of the people which is attainable in civil society. [44]

Anti-Federalists who also saw representation as the essential security for the people's rights charged that the new government would have only a "shadow" of representation because so few officials would be elected to represent such a large and diverse population. In this view, the state governments could better be trusted with dangerous powers because they were more likely to satisfy the Anti-Federalist Brutus's standard "that those who are placed instead of the people, . . . should bear the strongest resemblance of those in whose room they are substituted." [45] But Federalists did not accept that standard. The people's security is that representatives must answer to them, not that representatives resemble them. Federalists described representation not as an imperfect simulation of an assembled people but as a positive improvement over it. The proposed Constitution compared favorably to ancient democracies by its *"total exclusion of the people in their collective capacity,* from any share" in the government.[46] The people participate only in their individual capacities as voters, so as to elect fit characters to serve the public good and judge their demonstrated fitness and fidelity in subsequent elections. Representatives should fully *understand* the interests and opinions of the people they represent, but should not simply convey a sample of those interests and opinions. And sufficient knowledge to support the limited tasks of the national government could be conveyed by a less minute representation than was needed by the state governments. "I apprehend it is of more consequence to be able to know the true interest of the people, than their faces, and of more consequence still, to have virtue enough to pursue the means of carrying that knowledge usefully into effect."[47]

To the Federalists, then, representation is not a matter of reproducing or resembling the people but of being responsible to them. Rulers have room to exercise judgment, although the people's ultimate power of judgment means that "the general sense of the people will regulate the conduct of their representatives."[48] The people are spared the task of devising policies themselves, but must judge the policies of the rulers they elect; and they can judge with the advantage of hindsight, according to their experience of the effect of those policies. Whereas Anti-Federalists doubted that the people would or should trust representatives so few, durable, and remote, Federalists thought elected officials could earn the people's trust by their deeds. The people's confidence depends not on a numerous representation but on "a good administration" and "a train of prosperous events."[49] Moreover, it would be just as well if the people were not excessively confident of their representatives' trustworthiness. Paradoxically, it was safer to confer more dangerous powers on the less trusted federal government; such powers "had better be in those hands of which the people are most likely to be jealous than in those of which they are least likely to be jealous."[50]

The "interior structure" of the proposed government provided additional safeguards. "A dependence on the people is, no doubt, the primary control on the government; but experience has taught mankind the necessity of auxiliary precautions."[51] Without such auxiliary precautions, rulers might misuse their powers between elections, deceive an inattentive electorate, or even cancel future elections altogether.

One such precaution was the separation of legislative, executive, and judicial powers. The effect of this separation is that the legislators cannot dictate to whom the laws will be applied, which gives them an incentive to pass such laws as they would not mind having the executive enforce against themselves and their friends. Moreover, the people will be directly coerced or punished only by an "executive" who carries out rules made by others rather than rules according to his own whim. The executive's veto both permits him to defend his independence of the legislature and thereby preserve the advantages just mentioned, and, like the division of the legislature into two branches, serves as an additional security against oppressive laws. The judiciary's term of good behavior secures its independence of the executive and the legislature; it can judge both whether the executive's attempted executions are consistent with the law and whether the legislature's legislation is consistent with the Constitution. And the state governments will jealously watch the national government and sound an alarm among the people against any encroachments.

Without describing these checks in detail, I will summarize their nature and purpose. While elections are designed to obtain wise and virtuous rulers, they cannot be expected to yield rulers of perfect wisdom and perfect virtue. While Federalists accused Anti-Federalists of excessive distrust of elected officials, they denied expecting "nothing but the most exalted integrity and sublime virtue." [52] Rather than simply try to calm popular suspicions concerning the private motives of potential rulers, the Federalists argued that these motives could be put to useful effect—both (as noted earlier) in provoking public service and in urging resistance to the overbearing ambitions of their fellow rulers. "Ambition must be made to counteract ambition"; "opposite and rival interests" are used to supply "the defect of better motives." [53]

> In a compound government, such as that now recommended by the Convention, the talents, ambition, and even avarice of great men, are so balanced, restrained and opposed, that they can only be employed in promoting the good of the community. Like a mill-race, it will convey off waters which would otherwise produce freshes and destruction, in such a manner as only to produce fruitfulness, beauty and plenty in the adjacent county. [54]

In some cases, an official's motive in checking other rulers is a desire to preserve his own office's powers against encroachment. In other cases, he may expect to win immediate popularity by resisting another branch's assault on the people's political liberty. In this respect, "checks" serve to secure "the rights of representation" (and representation, in turn, secures "the rights of the people"). [55] Checks may also more directly defend the people as a whole from unwise or oppressive measures instigated by hasty or ambitious representatives. Finally, and with least certainty, checks may be employed to defend a minority's rights against an overbearing majority. A majority's unjust plans can be delayed by a senate or president acting in expectation of eventual reward by a repentant people or simply from a love of justice.

But Federalists strongly insisted that none of these checks departed from the "strictly republican," "wholly popular" character of the proposed government. In contrast to the English constitution's King and Lords, in

America "the whole is elective; all are dependent upon the people. The President, the Senate, the Representatives, are all creatures of the people."[56] No "hereditary or self-appointed authority" with a "will independent of the majority — that is, of the society itself."[57] is relied on to defend the rights of minorities — or, for that matter, to contribute the energy, wisdom, or stability traditionally attributed to monarchical or aristocratic institutions. Despite the apparent advantages of the British "mixed" constitution in these respects, the American Constitution's "strictly republican" character was given great weight:

> It is evident that no other form would be reconcilable with the genius of the people of America; with the fundamental principles of the Revolution; or with that honorable determination which animates every votary of freedom to rest all our political experiments on the capacity of mankind for self-government.[58]

I have earlier noted difficulties concerning foreign policy and minority rights which suggested that popular government is a mixed blessing when considered as a means; but in this argument popular government appears as an end in itself, both to the American people and to the votaries of freedom who address them. The Constitution is defended not simply as conducive to the people's interest, but as consistent with the people's honor.

An "honorable determination" about human "capacity" requires that government protect not only the acquisitive faculties by which men gain property but also the political faculties manifested (in different degrees) by opinionated partisans and ambitious politicians. No restrictions on suffrage are introduced by the Constitution (although existing state restrictions are deferred to); and no political offices are reserved for any hereditary or self-appointed authorities. "This new offered government is equal, every individual is a fair candidate for the highest seat in the empire, which is a matter unknown to every other nation in the world. . . ."[59] The political opportunities a republican government preserves for its citizens as a matter of principle are desirable in themselves.

On the question of popular government Federalist reassurances should perhaps be described also as a promise. The republican governments of the states, which Anti-Federalists feared the new Constitution would destroy, were in the Federalist view unlikely to survive without the new Constitution. The danger of war between them would drive each state to "resort for repose and security to institutions which have a tendency to destroy their civil and political rights"; or factious rule within the states would bring about the same "instability, injustice, and confusion" that have "been the mortal diseases under which popular governments have everywhere perished." Only "a more perfect structure" would permit "the excellencies of republican government" to be "retained and its imperfections lessened or avoided."[60] This would both serve the interests of America and promote the cause of popular government in general: "Republics, we trust in Heaven, can be energetic, wise and upright. Yet we must candidly acknowledge, that *it yet remains* for America to establish, by her example, the truth of this position." [61]

The Federalists' intention to provide "energetic, wise and upright government" for America is the most conspicuous theme in their case for the Constitution. But that intention is accompanied by an "honorable determination" to vindicate republican government in general. Only if a "wholly popular" form can be designed to protect men's rights not only from overbearing government but also from foreign conquest, domestic violence, or majority faction, can "this form of government . . . be rescued from the opprobrium under which it has so long labored and be recommended to the esteem and adoption of mankind." [62]

FRAMING AND RATIFYING THE FIRST TEN AMENDMENTS

ROBERT A. RUTLAND

When George Mason suggested, during the closing days of the Constitutional Convention, that a bill of rights ought to preface the proposed Constitution he opened a political Pandora's box. Unimpressed with Mason's argument that "a Bill of Rights . . . would give great quiet to the people," not a single state delegation voted in favor of Mason's motion. Perhaps the delegates, eager to move ahead with the business of erecting a government "of *energy & stability*" (to use James Madison's phrase), believed a bill of rights was unnecessary. And they may have doubted Mason's statement that "with the aid of the State declarations, [such] a bill might be prepared in a few hours." [1] Hard at work since May, most of the forty-two delegates still working on the Constitution in September were skeptical because they had written and rewritten sections of the frame of government until their impatience outweighed their judgment.

What turned a small spat into a bitter public controversy over the bill-of-rights issue was Mason's reluctance to drop the matter. Since the convention debates had been secret, the public was not aware of any disagreement related to a bill of rights until the delegates adjourned. Unhappy with the final draft of the Constitution, Mason took the printed committee report and used the blank side to set down his "Objections to this Constitution of Government." "There is no Declaration of Rights," Mason began, "and the laws of the general government being paramount to the laws and constitution of the several States, the Declarations of Rights in the separate States are no security." Because the week was out, Mason served notice he would not sign the Constitution as it stood, and he carried out the threat on September 17, when he was joined by two other delegates with similar misgivings.

Possibly within a few hours after the ceremonial signing of the Constitution, Mason showed his list of objections to other public men who were displeased with the final draft. Anxious to share his objections, Mason made several copies for his friends before he departed from Philadelphia. One copy found its way into a print shop and became the first salvo in the paper war over ratification of the Constitution. At first Mason was perturbed that his objections had been hurried into print "without my Approbation, or Privity," but on second thought Mason was pleased with his handiwork. In friendly fashion he sent the pamphlet to neighbor George Washington. Washington reacted with chagrin and sent it on to Madison with the notation: "To alarm the people, seems to be the ground work of his plan." [2]

In fact, Mason's opening argument struck the most damaging blow dealt to the Constitution as it went to the states for ratification. By calling attention to the absence of a bill of rights, which most states had enacted during the Revolution, Mason developed a propaganda weapon for the shaping opposition forces (soon to be known as "Anti-Federalists"). For the next ten months the overriding political question in America was: Will the states ratify or reject the Constitution? The major roadblock to ratification was the lack of a bill of rights, and not until its supporters conceded that they would offer amendments in the First Congress was a fair trial for the Constitution assured.

Storm warnings over the omitted bill of rights filled Anti-Federalist newspapers, where Mason's alarm-bell phrase was picked up and repeated. Some Anti-Federalists who wanted to talk about "necessary amendments" demanded a second convention, but the idea never took hold. Dissenting Protestant groups, particularly the Baptists, were galvanized into action by the implied threat in Mason's outcry. James Madison, who had returned to the Continental Congress to await developments and coordinate the Federalist ratification campaign, soon perceived the inroads made by the "no bill of rights" arguments. Then his friend Thomas Jefferson read the Constitution in Paris and wrote to say he liked the document in general. But, Jefferson added, he was disappointed by "the omission of a bill of rights providing clearly & without the aid of sophisms" for the civil rights Americans had come to believe were their birthright.[3]

From his message center in New York Madison took heed of the changing public sentiment. Starting with the Massachusetts ratifying convention in February 1788, the Anti-Federalists found that their opponents were defensive whenever the subject arose. To beat down efforts to make acceptance of a bill of rights a condition to ratifying, the Federalists conceded "recommendatory amendments," a list of proposed amendments dealing with freedom of the press, free speech, trial by jury, and other civil rights. Looking ahead to the crucial Virginia and New York conventions, the Federalist managers conceded their tactical error. What they wanted to prevent was a snowballing of any Anti-Federalist scheme that would make ratification conditioned to a premature amending process for a bill of rights.

"The plan of Massts. is unquestionably the Ultimatum of the foederalists," Madison observed. "Conditional amendments or a second general Convention, will be fatal." As Virginians elected their delegates for a ratifying convention, Madison told Governor Edmund Randolph (one of the three nonsigners of the Constitution): "Recommendatory alterations are the only ground that occurs to me." [4] As a co-author of the *Federalist Papers*, Madison never mentioned the bill of rights in his essays, but Alexander Hamilton finally faced the issue in late May 1788 when only the New York convention mattered. Hamilton assured New Yorkers that trial by jury was not all that important, and reminded voters that in a technical sense, their state had no separate bill of rights. "I go further, and affirm that bills of rights . . . are not only unnecessary in the proposed constitution, but would even be dangerous." [5] The Constitution was one of delegated powers, hence "why declare that things shall not be done which there is no power to do?"

Madison did not take the declamation over a bill of rights seriously, for he was preoccupied with what he thought was the central issue involved: preservation of the Union. Approaching the June 1788 ratifying convention in Richmond, he saw the Anti-Federalist leadership as disorganized, "taking very different grounds of opposition." But once the Virginia convention was under way, Madison found the opposition was united on at least the main issue of a bill of rights, and when Anti-Federalists proposed a second convention to add "a declaration of rights asserting and securing from encroachment the great principles of civil and religious liberty," some conciliatory remarks were in order. Looking directly at Patrick Henry and George Mason, Madison asked the convention to ratify the Constitution without any strings attached. Trust us, Madison said, once the Constitution is operating. "Then we shall freely, fairly and dispassionately consider and investigate your propositions, and endeavour to gratify your wishes." [6]

By a vote of 89 to 79, the Federalists had it their way, with only a list of recommended amendments sent along with the Virginia ratification. Madison had promised to work for a bill of rights, however, and ultimately that campaign promise proved to be the Anti-Federalists' trump card. Meanwhile, New York ratified in July with another list of recommended amendments. The strategy of seeking a second convention fell flat. The old Continental Congress was dismantled. With a mixture of apathy and misgivings, Rhode Island and North Carolina decided to stay out of the Union for a while (in part because of apprehensions over adding a bill of rights).

While various elections took place and arrangements proceeded for establishing the new government in March 1789, one Federalist remembered all the promises concerning a bill of rights. A Richmond printer gathered all the recommended amendments from the seven state conventions making the proposals and printed then in a small pamphlet. Madison obtained several copies and sent one to Jefferson with a comment that he "never thought the omission a material defect." Madison conceded that many opponents wishing a bill of rights spoke "from the most honorable & patriotic motives," and "As far as these may consist of a constitutional declaration of the most essential rights," there would be no harm in adding them to the ratified Constitution. But Madison reminded Jefferson that in their home state the 1776 Declaration of Rights had been violated "in every instance where it has been opposed to a popular current." In a republic, Madison insisted, the real danger to civil liberties was posed by "the majority of the Community . . . not from the acts of Government contrary to the sense of its constituents."[7]

In effect, Madison was arguing with himself as he explained the situation to Jefferson. What protection did a bill of rights afford, if "the tyrannical will" of the majority could not be denied? Madison decided there were only two values in a bill of rights, both of them related to public opinion. "The political truths declared in that solemn manner . . . become incorporated with the national sentiment, [to] counteract the impulses of interest and passion," and if that were not enough, "a bill of rights will be a good ground for an appeal to the sense of the community." In other words, citizens who wanted to exercise their rights might have to get a court order to do it. The line between the federal government having "too much or too little power" was fine, Madison admitted.

Armed with the Richmond printer's pamphlet and newspaper clippings, Madison expected he would have a role in the first Congress scheduled to meet in March 1789. His plans were almost aborted when Patrick Henry vindictively arranged to keep Madison off the Virginia delegation to the U.S. Senate. Instead, the Virginia legislature chose two Anti-Federalists. Then Henry's handpicked committee arranged for a congressional district that would dilute Madison's strength in the piedmont counties. Then as Madison's opponent for a House of Representatives seat the Anti-Federalists chose James Monroe. Madison had thwarted Henry at the Richmond convention, and now he paid the price, for Monroe was an old friend with a comfortable following in tidewater Virginia.

The ensuing campaign forced Madison to return to Virginia. He despised "the appearance of a spirit of electioneering" but realized Monroe was a formidable candidate. "Upon the whole, the Baptist Interest seems to prevail everywhere," a friend warned. Madison met the challenge head-on, by assuring a Baptist minister in his district that he was convinced that the essential liberties of citizens deserved protection in the Constitution, "particularly the rights of Conscience in the fullest latitude." Madison's pledge to work for a bill of rights found its way into a Fredericksburg newspaper, with a cautionary note that the way to procure the required amendments was through the constitutional route, not via a second federal convention "meeting in the present foment of parties."[8] Despite a ten-inch snow on election day, Madison defeated Monroe with a 336-vote majority. His promise to work for a bill of rights seems to have made the difference.

Framing the bill of rights now became a personal matter for Madison. Indeed, no other elected official in President Washington's administration seems to have given the campaign pledges of June–July 1788 much thought, for they now concentrated on the business of making the Constitution a working document. The paper system created at Philadelphia gave the young republic a new lease on life, with its longevity still in doubt. The conventional wisdom was to do nothing about any amendments until the ship of state was under sail again. First let Congress convene, then inaugurate Washington, and then start the business of tax collecting. The national treasury was empty — what deserved a higher priority than to find cash for the impoverished republic? Madison realized an emergency existed, and for a time he deferred to the judgment of his peers who insisted that a bill of rights was not urgently needed. Some even thought Madison ought to forget the whole thing.

Jefferson, watching the American scene from Paris, at first had suggested that a bill of rights ought to be forced on the new government (by nine states ratifying, with the remaining four staying out until "the declaration of rights is annexed to it"). Things were working out almost as he had suggested, but Jefferson disliked the implication that a bill of rights was a party issue. The best argument in favor of a bill of rights, he told Madison, was "the legal check which it puts into the hands of the judiciary." To Madison's charge that it was inadequate to list some rights for fear others would be left out, Jefferson countered: "Half a loaf is better than no bread." [9]

With advice coming from all directions, and the House debating a bill for taxing imports, Madison took advantage of the national attention focused on the congressional debates. In the middle of the debate on import duties, Madison announced his intention to bring up a bill of rights in three weeks. In a sense, Madison forced the hand of his colleagues, and one from Virginia tried to forestall debate on a bill of rights by introducing Patrick Henry's pet bill asking for second federal convention. This Anti-Federalist tactic, and a similar one from New York, died in a legislative pigeonhole once Madison had introduced his proposed amendments.

More than one colleague must have groaned a bit when Madison kept his promise and on June 8 asked the House to go into "a Committee of the Whole on the state of the Union" to discuss the proposed amendments. Some congressmen, such as Aedanus Burke, were sympathetic to the idea, but insisted Madison's timing was way off. A Georgia congressman thought the Constitution as it stood ought to "have a fair trial" and suggested a nine-month postponement of the matter. Madison insisted "that our constituents" would be discouraged if Congress postponed the issue "from time to time, and refuse to let the subject come into view." [10] William Loughton Smith gave Madison credit for a good try and suggested that the Virginian now sit down and keep quiet.

Despite the discouraging reaction in the House, Madison refused to back down. For one thing, both Rhode Island and North Carolina were still outside the Union. Moving forward with amendments embodying a bill of rights, Madison said, would probably mean "that a reunion should take place as soon as possible." He reminded the House that "the great mass of the people" who opposed the Constitution "disliked it because it did not contain effectual provisions against encroachments" upon the paper safeguards to which "they have been long accustomed." Ever mindful of public opinion, Madison added, "nor ought we consider them safe, while a great number of our fellow citizens think these securities necessary."

Then Madison read his proposed amendments, nine in number but with none of the rhetoric trimmed, so that they actually came to twenty-six separate paragraphs. The preliminary wording dealt with a statement from the Virginia Declaration of Rights affirming the people as the source of all power, with a government created by them bound to offer its citizens life, liberty, and the right to acquire property and to pursue "happiness and safety." Then Madison proposed trying a flexible ratio of citizens to representation in Congress after a limit had been reached and a check on Congress in fixing its salaries. Next came the familiar provisions in state bills of rights — guaranteeing citizens freedom of religion, speech, press, peaceable assembly, petition for grievances, and the right to bear arms. All these Madison regarded as "private rights." The quartering of troops in peacetime was disavowed.

Next Madison took up double jeopardy, self-incrimination, the due process of law in matters involving both life and property, excessive bail, searches and seizures, speedy public trials, confrontation by accusers, and aids to accused persons in need of witnesses or counsel. A general statement held that exceptions made in the list of rights "shall not be construed as to diminish the just importance of other rights retained by the people, or . . . enlarge the powers delegated by the constitution." Acknowledging that these amendments applied only to the federal government, Madison's next provision broadened the base of protection. "No State shall violate the equal rights of conscience, or the freedom of the press, or the trial by jury in criminal cases." Another section provided for grand juries, and jury trials when the property in controversy came to a certain amount. In criminal matters the trial was to be in the vicinity of the accusation before an impartial jury. In common law cases, jury trial was "one of the best securities to the rights of the people, [and] ought to remain inviolate."

Madison's catalogue of rights and liberties came to a close with a provision for keeping the legislative, executive, and judicial branches of government separated, and another declaring that all powers not delegated elsewhere or not prohibited to the states should remain reserved to the states.

After he read the proposed amendments, Madison stayed on his feet to deflect arguments that a bill of rights was unnecessary. Everybody knew that in "a few particular states" the provisions in their declaration of rights had been violated. Still, "they may have, to a certain degree, a salutary effect against the abuse of power." More important, Madison added, by placing the guarantees "into the constitution, independent tribunals of justice will consider themselves in a peculiar manner the guardians of those rights." [11]

From his years of legislative service Madison had calculated the effect of introducing the idea of a bill of rights without an accompanying set of proposals. He knew that his colleagues would be more inclined to act only if a well-digested plan was offered, for this stratagem might overcome the inertia that afflicted most legislators. Carefully sifting through the clippings and the Richmond pamphlet, Madison had gleaned his final list from over 200 separate proposals made in the state ratifying conventions. He had distilled the key proposals common to all the state plans, then added his own measure to make it clear that the states would be responsible for the paramount matters of religion, press censorship, or jury trials in criminal trials. At the same time, Madison had skirted the controversial proposals of the states that dealt with regulating elections, taxation, presidential terms, judicial authority, and commercial treaties. These matters did not belong in a set of amendments meant to delineate the inviolable rights of mankind, Madison reasoned. Explaining his selection to Governor Edmund Randolph, Madison said he had tried to limit his amendments "to points which are important in the eyes of many and can be objectionable in those of none." "The structure & stamina of the Govt. are as little touched as possible," he added. [12]

Insofar as the Constitution was concerned, Madison had gone out of his way to prevent an overhaul of the structure by making it possible to incorporate his proposals into the original document. The Constitution signed on September 17, 1787, had seven articles — Madison's additions and rearrangements provided for an enlarged preamble and a total of eight articles. His goal was to cause as few ripples as possible in the amending process, which he realized was an experiment and therefore unpredictable. And Madison exercised his own discretion, too, for he brought forward nothing to appease the seven states that had asked for an amendment barring Congress from interfering with the regulation of elections.

Before the day's business was finished, the House voted to take up Madison's proposals in the Committee of the Whole. But days and weeks went by with all attention focused on ways and means of raising money. In the interim, Madison's amendments were printed in the newspapers from Boston southward to the Carolinas. From Philadelphia Madison learned that "the most ardent & irritable among our friends are well pleased with them," while Anti-Federalists implied approval by their silence. "The proposed amendments," Madison was told, "will greatly tend to promote harmony among the late contending parties and a general confidence in the patriotism of Congress." When Madison's plans were reported in North Carolina, the news "dispersed almost universal pleasure," a Federalist observed, and was held up "as a refutation of the gloomy profecies of the leaders of the opposition." [13]

Madison's House colleagues viewed the list with something less than complete admiration. The New England congressmen thought Madison was trying to sidetrack the House from more important work. Fisher Ames admitted the amendments were "the fruit of much labor and research." "He had hunted up all the grievances and complaints of newspapers, all the articles of conventions, and the small talk in their debates," Ames noted. "Upon the whole, it may do some good towards quieting men, who attend to sounds only, and may get the mover some popularity, which he wishes." [14] Roger Sherman, who had opposed a bill of rights at the Constitutional Convention, thought the House had better uses for its time than debating Madison's plan.

When Madison interrupted "a moment of leisure" in the House to remind members they had work to do on his amendments, it was Ames who complained that a general debate could go on endlessly. He moved for a select committee to take Madison's proposals "and cull out those of the most material kind, without interrupting the principal business of the House." [15] A Georgia congressman confessed that he regarded the whole question "a mere waste of time" and preferred a special committee "as the lesser of two evils." Madison stepped aside to allow the issue a full airing. The result was that a select committee was appointed, with Madison a member but John Vining (of Delaware) named as chairman, on July 21.

The committee went right to work, going along with Madison's proposition to expand the original Constitution rather than add amendments. An upper limit of 175 members for the House was fixed, and pay raises for Congress were to take effect only after an intervening election. Madison's original wording on these proposals was hardly tampered with, but in the bill of rights section some drastic changes occurred in the committee. Madison had followed the Virginia Declaration of Rights in his listing of guarantees to worship, speak, and print freely. He also had said that "no national religion" could be established. In the committee, the article on religion was boiled down to a simple statement: "No religion shall be established by law, nor shall the equal rights of conscience be infringed." Freedom of the press and speech, and the right to assemble peaceably or petition the government were compressed into one sentence. From that point onward, the committee stayed close to Madison's original wording and retained his proposal to make the guarantees apply to states as well as the federal government. The change that would prevent appeals to the Supreme Court in cases involving trifling sums also was retained.

So far, Madison must have thought, so good. On August 13, the Virginia delegation moved together to bring the business forward, only to run into a high wall of indifference. His patience tested, Madison insisted the matter could be postponed no longer. His fellow Virginian, John Page, made the motion to begin the debate and said that if more time passed without action the people "will not think us serious." Thus reminded, the House voted to take up the committee report, but immediately a snag developed when Roger Sherman objected to the notion of incorporating the amendments into the original Constitution. Sherman made a motion to add each article separately, as a kind of appendix to the Constitution as it stood in 1787.

Madison opposed Sherman's motion, saying "it will certainly be more simple, when the amendments are interwoven into those parts" of the Constitution "to which they naturally belong." Two days were spent debating the form of the amendments and the size of the House before attention was focused on the bill of rights itself. The article mentioning religious freedom evoked contempt from Sherman, praise from Catholic Daniel Carroll, and a proposed change from Samuel Livermore. He suggested the article be changed to read: "Congress shall make no laws touching religion, or infringing the rights of conscience." His motion passed, and weary Theodore Sedgwick wanted to know if every right known to man was considered by the committee—"they might have declared a man should have a right to wear his hat"—and he was against filling the Constitution with "these trifles." Another member wanted to add to the clause on peaceable assembly "to instruct their Representatives." Madison was unhappy when the debate took this turn. If they failed to accomplish their mission with a bill of rights, he said, the blame will rest on "the difficulties arising from discussion and proposing abstract propositions." On the other hand, "if we confine ourselves to an enumeration of simple, acknowledged principles, the ratification," he predicted, "will meet with but little difficulty."

Madison's plea for the House to stop the nitpicking went unheeded. On the debates droned. When a South Carolina congressman tried to dump the article preventing states from infringing on the basic rights of speech, press, and religion, Madison was on his feet again. This article was "the most valuable amendment on the whole list," he said. His colleagues beat back the motion to drop the article, and rallied again when Elbridge Gerry almost threw the whole debate into a whirlwind. Let us go back and consider *all* the amendments proposed by the state ratifying conventions, Gerry said, and see if we cannot satisfy everybody. Gerry was probably being facetious at best, or perhaps he hoped to make the impatient delegates vote to drop the whole business. Whatever his point may have been, Gerry failed to carry it.

During the August debates sentiment grew for treating the amendments as additions to the Constitution rather than merely an expansion of the original document. Sherman perceived the change and renewed his motion for "adding the amendments to the constitution by way of supplement." This time the motion passed by a large majority, and Madison made no recorded objection to the change.[16]

Before the House took a vote on the whole package of amendments, Madison realized the debates were dragging on and might lead nowhere. To Edmund Randolph he confessed that "progress has been exceedingly wearisome." To an absentee congressman Madison said in private what he failed to say in debating the question of altogether separate amendments. "It became an unavoidable sacrifice to *a few* who knew their concurrence to be necessary, to the despatch if not the success of the business, to give up the form by which the amendts. when ratified would have fallen in the body of the Constitution, in favor of the project of adding them by way of appendix to it," he wrote to Alexander White. "It is already apparent I think that some ambiguities will be produced by this change, as the question will often arise and sometimes be not easily solved, how far the original text is or is not necessarily superseded, by the supplemental act." Madison predicted that a proposed "middle way," treating all the amendments "as a single act to be adopted or rejected in the gross, and of proposing them as independent amendts. each of which shall take place or not, as it may be individually decided on," offered a solution the majority might accept. The proposed amendments would be regrouped "according to their affinity to each other, which will reduce them to the number of 5 or 6 in the whole." [17]

Madison wrote from inside knowledge, for a committee appointed to combine the proposals reported with a list of seventeen amendments. Representation in the House headed the list, then separate amendments were proposed for fixing congressional salaries, protecting civil liberties and guarding against usurpations of the jury system and due process for accused criminals. The House acted at once to send the proposals to the Senate, where another effort was made to postpone the whole matter until the next session. Senator Richard Henry Lee (who in 1787 tried to append a declaration of rights to the Constitution when the Continental Congress forwarded it to the states) was disgusted by a motion to postpone consideration on the grounds that experience might prove the amendments unnecessary. "As if experience were now necessary to prove the propriety of those great principles of Civil liberty which the wisdom of the Ages has found to be necessary barriers against the encroachments of power in the hand of frail Man!" Lee trumpeted.[18]

After beating that motion back, the senators debated the House list for six days behind closed doors (unlike the House, the Senate allowed no reporters in its chamber). Seeking textual parsimony, the senators merged the House proposals on religious and other personal freedoms into a single amendment. Three other House articles dealing with jury trials and court procedure shrank to two amendments, and Madison's favorite proposition (prohibiting states from infringing on personal liberties) was dropped altogether. Attempts to add a variety of new proposals, including a prohibition on levying direct taxes, were turned back. Finally, the Senate approved the surviving twelve proposed amendments and returned the whole package to the House.

Predictably, the House balked. In a conference committee, the senators would not agree on limits for "the *value* of appeals to the Supreme Court, which they say is unnecessary." The upper house conferees also wanted no mention of holding trials in a certain locality. "The [word] vicinage they contend is either too vague or too strict a term," Madison reported. An amendment rejecting standing armies and ordering an explicit acknowledgment that military forces were controlled by civilian authorities was turned down, along with a stricture affirming the separation-of-powers concept in government. A twelfth amendment, proposing that "The powers not delegated by the Constitution, nor prohibited by it, to the States, are reserved to the States respectively or to the people" sailed ahead with blessings from both houses.

While the conference committee worked for acceptable compromises, George Mason read the propositions sent from the House with a nod of approval. "I hope they will also pass the Senate," Mason wrote. With a few small changes unrelated to personal rights, Mason added, "I cou'd chearfully put my Hand & Heart to the new Government." [19] The citizen who had started all the fuss now seemed content, but Mason's enthusiasm was not universally shared by his fellow Virginians.

Hurrying toward adjournment, the conference committee members resolved outstanding differences with alacrity. On September 24, the House heard that only two amendments kept them apart from the Senate version and they voted to change the third and eighth amendments to read as they would when ratified as the First and Sixth amendments. By a vote of 37 to 14, the House sent its approved version of twelve proposed amendments to the President for transmittal to the states, as provided in Article V. Hours later, the Senate also approved the proposed amendments. Exactly four months had elapsed since Madison first announced his goals.

Congress proved to be a speed demon when compared to the lethargic state legislatures. Nearly two years would pass before the first Ten Amendments—the Bill of Rights—became part of the fundamental Constitution. But at no time was the outcome in doubt. Rhode Island and North Carolina reacted by ending their holdout status and ratifying the Constitution so they could become full partners in the Union. In both states, there was general agreement that with the Bill of Rights in the hopper, there was no good reason to stay aloof from the sister states. Here and there, recalcitrant citizens labeled the twelve proposed amendments as "little more than milk and water." Patrick Henry was said to be disappointed in the extreme because the long list from the Virginia ratifying convention had made only a partial dent. "We might as well have attempted to move Mount Atlas upon our shoulders," Richard Henry Lee reported, as to have the Senate accept the Virginia proposals in toto. Senator William Grayson told Henry that the amendments that survived the conference committee were "good for nothing . . . and will do more harm than benefit." [20]

A strange twist in the ratifying process for the Bill of Rights came from Virginia when Grayson and Lee forwarded to the state legislature a letter disclaiming responsibility for the final version. Perhaps it was a grandstand play on their part, for they hinted that the state governments were being threatened and said they have been unable to insert amendments that would have halted this unfortunate trend. "Such amendments therefore as may secure against the annihilation of the state governments we devoutly wish to see adopted," the senators complained as they hinted a second federal convention was really needed to solve the problem.[21] A delegate who favored prompt action on the Bill of Rights suggested the senators wrote their ill-humored letter to gain popularity with Henry's faction. The Virginia House of Delegates passed the first ten amendments handily, then balked at accepting the last two, and the upshot of the shuffling between the House and state Senate was that nothing was done except a postponement until the fall of 1790.

Forces beyond the control of regional political chieftains were at work, however. Madison viewed this infighting in perspective and told Washington that the "miscarriage of the 3d. art: [First Amendment]" would boomerang.[22] His prediction proved correct, except that petty wrangling continued during another session, and not until the fall of 1791 did the Virginians stop their hair-splitting and ratify ten of the proposed twelve amendments.

What happened in the other state legislatures during the interval is almost lost to history. Few records were kept of state legislative proceedings beyond a simple recording of the vote. Public men seem to have taken the ratification for granted and turned their attention elsewhere. Only the newspapers faithfully reported the course of the twelve amendments through the various state assemblies, and before too long it was clear that the first two (relating to representation in Congress and congressional salaries) would not be ratified by the required number of states. New Jersey began the process, and during the winter of 1790 Maryland, North Carolina, New Hampshire, South Carolina, Delaware, Pennsylvania, and New York had approved ten amendments. Rhode Island approved the amendments in June 1790, and then almost a year went by without further legislative action. Vermont was admitted as a state in March 1791, so that eleven ratifications were now required to make the Bill of Rights operative. On November 3, 1791, Vermont became the tenth ratifying state. Public attention had moved to other arenas when the Virginia legislators ratified the proposed articles on December 15, 1791.

Thus during a fifteen-year period Virginians began the movement toward guaranteed civil liberties and then brought it to a close. The first ten amendments certified by Secretary of State Thomas Jefferson as fully effective confirmed past experience and made no radical imprint on the society that nurtured them into law. The "parchment barriers" Madison spoke of in 1787 were not to become a fortress of American liberty for generations.

ORGANIZING THE NEW NATIONAL GOVERNMENT

JACOB E. COOKE

On September 17, 1787, Philadelphia's Old State House was the scene of one of the most important events in American history. On that day the delegates to the Constitutional Convention signed the frame of government that they had hammered out during the preceding four months in one of the most momentous, and brilliant, debates in our national history. The fate of the new Constitution was now up to the states, or at least to the support of nine of them, the number constitutionally mandated for its adoption. At first the prospects were bright. Delaware, Pennsylvania, and New Jersey joined up almost immediately, followed early in 1788 by Georgia, Connecticut, and Massachusetts, although in the latter there was strenuous opposition. It appeared certain that a favorable decision by the three additional states necessary to launch the new government would be forthcoming, but the probability of its success, once launched, depended on more than numbers. Ratification by Virginia, the most populous state, and New York, strategically located and an important commercial center, were indispensable. Thanks to the brilliant oratory of Federalist leaders such as James Madison of Virginia and Alexander Hamilton of New York, as well as to the pressure of circumstances, both decided to throw in their lot with the Union, which was now established.

The first national elections under the new Constitution were almost immediately held and by the beginning of 1789 it was clear that the First Congress would predictably be controlled by those who had labored for ratification, the nationalists, or, as they were more frequently referred to, Federalists. Nor was there any doubt about the identity of the first President. On February 4, 1789, the Electoral College, entrusted by the Constitution with the responsibility, unanimously elected George Washington, commanding general of the army that had forged American independence and already a legendary national hero. (Although not the Electors' unanimous choice, John Adams of Massachusetts received enough votes to qualify as vice-president.) Upon receiving official word of his election on April 14, 1789, Washington, "with a mind oppressed with more anxious and painful sensations than I have words to express," accepted a post that he neither relished nor had sought.[1] His low spirits must have been somewhat elevated, however, by his eight-day trip to the temporary capitol in New York City, a triumphal process without precedent in the country's history. Once there, he had a week or so to settle in and to recover from his physically arduous journey before his inauguration, scheduled for April 30.

There was no need to hurry. Although scheduled to convene on March 4, 1789, Congress had taken no action of any significance. Congressmen arrived so tardily that it was not until April 6 that a quorum of both the Senate and the House was first present and that transaction of business commenced.

Once underway the initial session of the First Congress compiled an impressive record. Its importance resides not only in the specific measures that it passed but in the manner in which it did so; since it was the *first* Congress virtually all of its proceedings were precedents. During its almost two-century-long history it has, of course, changed in manifold and major ways, but its essential mode of procedure remains that established during its formative years. Because of its unique situation and the problems it confronted, the precedent-setting role of the First Congress is hardly surprising. This was because the Constitution provided only the skeleton of a government and also because the new government itself had few established guidelines to rely on. Major problems, old and new, urgently required solutions. North Carolina and Rhode Island, for example, stubbornly remained outside the new union; citizens of Vermont still schemed with Canada; Great Britain continued to refuse to relinquish its posts in the west; there was only a miniscule army and no navy at all; some system of taxation had to be devised to replace the unworkable requisition system provided for by the Articles of Confederation; the issue of tariff and tonnage laws had to be confronted; and, above all, some provision had to be made for paying the national debt that the Confederation government had miserably failed to handle.

Since in his inaugural address Washington had refrained from making recommendations to Congress and had instead merely expressed his intention to defer to congressional judgment, in its first session Congress initiated most of the measures that it adopted. Among these were provision of salaries for congressmen and other public officials; adoption of titles, forms, and ceremonies consonant with what Senator William Maclay of Pennsylvania called "republican plainess"[2]; recommendation to the states of a federal bill of rights; establishment of a federal judiciary; authorization of executive departments; the passage of tax measures to assure adequate revenues for the Union, including enactment of tariff legislation that was only mildly protectionist; and endorsement of the unencumbered removal power of the President.

Several of these measures deserve emphasis because they were of lasting importance. One notable example was the right of the chief executive to remove from office at his will public officials for whose appointment the Constitution mandated approval of the Senate. The issue was introduced by Madison, perhaps the most influential member of the House, who moved that department heads could be dismissed by the President solely on his own authority. Adoption of Madison's motion represented an important enhancement of presidential power, although the absence of any specific constitutional provision on the subject spawned a century and a half of episodic debate concerning it.

More significant yet in historical perspective was adoption of a bill of rights to be submitted to the states. Such congressional action was in response to urgent requests that had been made by many state ratifying conventions. Once again, leadership was assumed by Madison who compiled from the propositions recommended by these state conventions a number of proposals that emerged from congressional debate as the first ten amendments to the Constitution, the federal Bill of Rights.

The single most important measure of the First Congress was the Judiciary Act of 1789, which remains today the basic charter of the federal court system. It was described (with some pardonable exaggeration) by Chief Justice Charles Evans Hughes a hundred and fifty years later as "a statute which is a monument of wisdom. . . . It may be said to take rank in our annals as next in importance to the Constitution itself." [3] On the organization of the judicial branch the Constitution was purposely vague. Although Article III provided for a Supreme Court, described the cases to which federal judicial power extended, and authorized "such inferior courts as Congress may from time to time ordain and establish," the Constitution neither stipulated the number of judges nor made the creation of inferior courts obligatory. Congress's most difficult assignment was not the composition of the Supreme Court but contriving a satisfactory relationship between state and federal courts, an issue on which there was considerable controversy. (Some committed states' righters, for example, took the position that in the federal judicial system state courts should exercise original jurisdiction with final appeal to the U.S. Supreme Court.) The task of framing a judicial system was assigned to a Senate committee whose most influential member was Oliver Ellsworth of Connecticut, who took the lead in drafting the act that was eventually agreed on.

The Judiciary Act of September 24, 1789, provided for a Supreme Court consisting of a chief justice and five associate justices, thirteen district courts, each presided over by one judge, and three circuit courts composed of two Supreme Court justices sitting with one district court judge. The organization and procedure of these courts were stipulated and their respective jurisdictions defined. Most important of all was section 25 of the act, which made decisions of state tribunals subject to federal appellate jurisdiction by providing for review by the U.S. Supreme Court of judgments and decrees of state courts in certain instances. Specifically, appeals could be taken to the nation's highest tribunal whenever constitutional questions involving the interpretation of the Constitution, federal statutes, and treaties had been answered in favor of the states, or adverse to national power. The overarching importance of this provision, the very core of American federalism, was its solution to the problem of conflicts between state and federal laws.

Also of both contemporary and enduring importance was congressional creation during its initial session of three principal executive departments—state, war, and the treasury—and two executive offices who lacked departments, an attorney general and a postmaster general. Authorized by the Judiciary Act of 1789, the former's principal duties were to prosecute cases for the United States before the Supreme Court and to provide legal counsel to the President and heads of executive departments. To fill the post, Washington selected a close personal friend, Edmund Randolph, who was a former governor of Virginia and an Anti-Federalist apostate. For the more minor post of postmaster general (authorized by temporary acts in 1789, 1790, and 1791, and by a permanent provision in 1793), the President, presumably to achieve sectional balance, designated Samuel Osgood of Massachusetts. Another New Englander was selected as secretary of war: the portly and affable Henry Knox had administered the similar office under the Confederation government and his appointment was widely predicted. Nor was the identity of the first secretary of the treasury a surprise: the President called on Alexander Hamilton of New York, a former and much trusted aide-de-camp who, although a comparatively youthful thirty-four, was one of the country's best known nationalists. More unexpected was Washington's choice to head the state department: Thomas Jefferson, the President's fellow Virginian, had earned public recognition for his service since 1784 as minister to France, a post he had just relinquished.

Washington had no master plan for the use to be made of his cabinet (understandably enough, since the body we know by that name was not expressly provided for by the Constitution) nor the precise duties and authority to be delegated to its members. His relationship with them evolved slowly as practice and policies, once initiated, hardened into a more formal arrangement. At the outset, he consulted with his principal ministers individually, on occasion asking them for written reports on current issues relating to their departments and sometimes requesting them to discuss with him documents previously submitted. Within a couple of years, however, he had begun to meet with them collectively (the attorney general included) on a regular basis, a practice that continued for the remainder of his first term and throughout his second. The precedent thus established was an enduring one. All of Washington's successors have consulted with and relied on their cabinets for advice, although the frequency of such meetings and degree of reliance have varied, depending on changing presidential needs, styles, and circumstances.

Just as the Constitution did not explicitly prescribe the relationship of the President and his cabinet, so it also was silent on the connection between the chief executive and the Supreme Court. On this issue some durable precedents were established during Washington's administration. An initially unresolved but important constitutional question, for example, was whether the President, when confronted by pressing legal questions, might call on the Supreme Court for advice. The initial problem that brought this issue to the fore was the administration's quandary over its response to violations of American neutrality. When Washington requested the opinion of the Supreme Court on some twenty-nine questions involving knotty legal questions, principally concerning interpretations of international law, the justices politely refused, arguing that "the lines of separation drawn by the Constitution between the three departments of government" and "our being judges of a court in the last resort, are considerations which afford strong arguments against the propriety of our extra-judicially deciding the questions alluded to. . . ."

Thus, early on was established a juridical principle that would be steadfastly adhered to. A future justice of the Court expressed the matter this way: the judicial function is confined to the "power of a court to decide and pronounce a judgment and carry it into effect between persons and parties who bring a case before it for decision." Similarly, the Court refused to honor legislative requests that it perform what it construed as nonjudicial duties. This issue arose over a congressional act that directed U.S. circuit courts to act as commissioners in the award of Revolutionary War pensions. The Court declined on the grounds "that neither the *Legislature* nor the *executive* branches, can constitutionally assign to the *judicial* any duties but such as are properly judicial, and to be performed in a judicial manner." [4]

The separation of powers between the executive and judicial branches that the Supreme Court obliged Washington to observe was not applicable to his relationship with the legislative branch. Although disinclined to offer firm congressional leadership, Washington dutifully obeyed the constitutional mandate that the chief executive advise Congress on the state of the Union and "recommend to their consideration such measures as he shall judge necessary and expedient." In fulfilling this responsibility, Washington appeared in person at the opening of each session of Congress to review its record of the previous year and to make recommendations for the forthcoming one. He also submitted special messages on issues that arose during the course of congressional sessions, though these were usually in the form of documentary reports rather than policy proposals. Communications between the two branches of government were characterized by elaborate protocol, with Congress acknowledging the President's formal addresses in stilted replies.

In addition to Washington's annual state of the Union messages his cabinet members also proposed policies and measures to Congress (occasionally at the latter's request). In this respect, Hamilton was far and away the most energetic and aggressive, a characteristic tellingly demonstrated during the second session of the First Congress (January 4 to August 12, 1790). The leadership then exercised by Hamilton was due not only to his personal drive and forcefulness but also to the fact that his program was directly dependent on congressional approval. On the acceptance of that program, as Hamilton and other nationalists saw the matter, hinged the success of the American experiment in nation-building. And they were right, not because the passage of Hamilton's particular policies was an indispensable prerequisite to viable nationhood, but in the sense that the most urgent problem confronting the country was a fiscal crisis that demanded the adoption of some program that would securely establish public credit. The most glaring failure of the Confederation government had been just that, a failure that had been largely responsible for the substitution of a revitalized Constitution for the tottering Articles of Confederation.

Among the most important provisions of the new frame of government was the promise that "all debts contracted and engagements entered into before the adoption of the Constitution shall be as valid against the United States under this Constitution as under the Confederation." Hamilton's program for fulfilling this promise was a series of reports to Congress, which remain among the great state papers in our history. The first, a *Report Relative to a Provision for the Support of Public Credit*, was unveiled in January 1790 and sparked an acrimonious debate that dominated Congress until its adjournment some eight months later. At first glance his proposals appeared unexceptionable enough; on a closer reading it was evident that his report was designed not only to salvage public credit but also to assure a strong central government that would almost certainly diminish state power and perquisites. The treasury secretary's report divided the public debt, accrued interest as well as principal, into three categories: first, the foreign debt ($11.7 million); second, the domestic debt ($40.4 million); and third, the debts of the states (about $25 million). All of these, principal plus interest, were to be paid in full by the central government. Over the discharge of the foreign debt there was virtually no disagreement. The method prescribed for payment of the national domestic debt occasioned a heated but brief debate sparked by James Madison's unsuccessful motion that in funding that debt a distinction be made between original holders and speculators and that an equitable share of the funded value of the stock be paid to the former. The assumption of state debts was fiercely contested, leading to a congressional deadlock that was broken only on the eve of adjournment, some six months later. Objectors disagreed for a number of reasons, but the most obdurate opponents represented states whose Revolutionary War debts had been largely discharged. That assumption was finally approved was owing to timely concessions by which Hamilton won over the requisite number of votes. Another compromise settled the second most controversial issue of this stormy session of Congress: the location of the national capital. In exchange for designating Philadelphia the seat of government for a decade, Pennsylvania congressmen delivered enough votes for passage of a measure making a site on the Potomac River, near Georgetown, the permanent capital.

Adoption of major features of Hamilton's program signaled the onset of a feud between the secretary of the treasury and Thomas Jefferson, secretary of state, which turned out to be one of the most consequential developments in the organization of the first government under the Constitution. For a few months following Jefferson's assumption of his office in March 1790, the relationship between the two men was on the surface harmonious. But an eventual rift between two such dynamic, ambitious men of such markedly different family backgrounds, political experience, social status, and personality traits was doubtless inevitable. Soon after Congress adjourned in August 1790, Jefferson convinced himself that his support of funding and assumption was the greatest "of all the errors of my political life."[5] And he resolved not to err again.

The steadfastness of Jefferson's resolve was demonstrated by his opposition to the next major feature of Hamilton's financial program: a report of December 1790 calling on Congress to charter a national bank, one-fifth of whose $10 million capital would be subscribed to by the United States, on whose resources and credit it would be based and whose financial operations it was designed to facilitate. That another major, though implicit, purpose was the further subordination of the states to the Union and establishment of a broad interpretation of the Constitution were not lost on Jefferson and his growing number of allies — James Monroe and Madison, most conspicuously — who were dismayed by Congress's prompt chartering of the proposed institution in a bill that was presented to the President on February 14, 1791.

Comparatively untutored in economic matters and mindful of the arguments set forth by antibank forces in Congress, Washington had reservations about the measure, particularly its constitutionality. For advice, he turned first to Attorney General Edmund Randolph, who unreservedly though unpersuasively averred that the bank was unconstitutional. The President next turned to his secretary of state. Already appalled by what he viewed as Hamilton's corrupt control of Congress and responsibility for the speculative frenzy that gripped much of the country, Jefferson's opinion should have been predictable, at least to any close associate. Nor did the kind of institution proposed by the treasury secretary "fit snugly into the pattern" of the Virginian's "thought and experience."[6] An exponent of constitutional literalism and agrarian financial orthodoxy, Jefferson propounded a rigidly strict interpretation of the Constitution, which if adopted would have placed the national government in a straitjacket. Among other arguments, Jefferson contended that the incorporation of a bank was not among the powers delegated to Congress, nor could its legality be inferred from the section conferring on the national legislature the power to "make all laws which shall be necessary and proper" for carrying into effect its enumerated powers. As Jefferson's most distinguished twentieth-century biographer has remarked, although the Virginian "was a notably creative personality in many fields, he appears in this particular paper in a predominantly negative and defensive role."[7]

So it may also have appeared to Washington, who sent copies of Randolph's and Jefferson's opinions to the secretary of the treasury, implicitly asking him for a rebuttal. Although aware of Hamilton's extraordinary skill in advocacy, the President could not have predicted the masterful essay in constitutional interpretation that he received a week or so later.

Although he rebutted Jefferson's argument point by point, the gist of Hamilton's position was that Jefferson's constitutional fundamentalism would undermine "the just and indispensable authority of the United States."[8] Every power with which any viable government was invested, Hamilton contended, was "by its nature sovereign, and includes . . . a right to employ all the *means*" not specifically precluded by the Constitution that were "requisite and fairly applicable to the attainment of the *ends* of such power."[9] In thus dismissing Jefferson's confiningly narrow approach to constitutional interpretation, the secretary of the treasury took an expansively broad view, one that affirmed the breadth rather than the bounds of governmental power.

The doctrine of implied powers that Hamilton set forth in his opinion on the constitutionality of the bank has been a fundamental maxim of American legal history from that day to our own. What, he asked, was the test of an act's constitutionality? In words that would be echoed by the nation's "great chief justice," John Marshall, Hamilton replied: The "criterion is the *end*, to which the measure relates as a *mean*. If the *end* be clearly comprehended within any of the specified powers, & if the measure have an obvious relation to that end, and is not forbidden by any particular provision of the Constitution—it may safely be deemed to come within the compass of the national authority."[10] Whether influenced by Hamilton's eloquent persuasiveness or convinced that the will of Congress should prevail, on February 25 Washington signed the bill incorporating the Bank of the United States.

The establishment of the bank and the related question of the scope of national power were not the only issues that divided the rival prima donnas of Washington's cabinet. They also differed on the conduct of U.S. foreign policy, which was Jefferson's official responsibility but which Hamilton strove to influence, both openly and covertly. From Washington's inauguration until 1793, when the French Revolution entered the phase of the Terror, the major diplomatic problems of the Washington administration were the management of Indian affairs and relations with Great Britain and Spain. The most immediate threat to national security was posed by the Indians, or so it must have seemed to those frontier settlers who were subjected to the murderous assaults of marauding Indian tribes whose lands (as the Redmen knew only too well) they also coveted. The Indian menace was met, with varying success, by punitive expeditions of the American army. But the administration's policy toward the Indians — whether warfare or negotiations (which Washington favored) — was inextricably connected with U.S. relations with Spain and Great Britain, both of whom allied themselves with the Redmen in order to secure their own interests in the American West (particularly the fur trade) and to thwart U.S. expansion. None of these problems was solved during the first years of government under the Constitution, though some promising progress was made (including the inauguration of normal diplomatic relations with Britain, signaled by the mutual exchange of ministers in 1791).

For his part, Washington was confident that the new nation had weathered both diplomatic and domestic crises with sufficient success that its administration might now be safely entrusted to a new leader of somewhat less heroic repute than his own. Such confidence, born partly on his intense desire to leave public life, was sapped by concern that without his moderating influence the rivalry between his chief ministers might grow, bringing in its train baneful party strife. It was also undermined by pressure from every quarter — from private citizens as well as public officials, including the importunities of both Hamilton and Jefferson — that he remain in office. His reaction was irresoluteness that was in the circumstances tantamount to reelection, and on February 13, 1793, the Electoral College unanimously chose him for what he viewed as another four-year prison sentence.

Even before the Electoral College had blocked Washington's escape from an unsought and unwanted post, the French Revolution had veered sharply leftward, confronting the United States with far more hazardous foreign problems than it had as yet encountered. Disquieting news concerning changes in Revolutionary France during the summer of 1792 had reached the State Department some months before Washington's second inauguration. That these developments were not merely ephemeral was confirmed by events during the weeks that followed the onset of Washington's second term — the beheading of Louis XVI; the ascendancy of the Girondin party; the French declaration of war on Great Britain and Spain; and the formation of a great European coalition to defeat Revolutionary France. Of more immediate interest to the American State Department was the announcement that the French Republic had appointed a new minister plenipotentiary to the United States.

Many Americans, including Jefferson, hailed these developments as a great triumph of freedom over despotism, just as their own Revolution had been. Others, Hamilton among them, viewed the violence that raged in Paris (the Terror and the concomitant bloodbath) as a mighty social upheaval that threatened traditional rights and freedoms as well as republicanism itself. Such contrasting ideas merit emphasis because they expressed those of the already-burgeoning political parties of which Jefferson and Hamilton were the most prominent spokesmen.

Washington agreed fully with neither of his rival ministers (though his position was closer to Hamilton's) but charted his own course. His overarching concern was not ideological but practical: how to maintain a policy of neutrality that would prevent American involvement in European affairs that might jeopardize the new nation's independence. This was the purpose of his famous Proclamation of Neutrality of April 1793 in which he announced his intention of pursuing "a conduct friendly and impartial toward the belligerent powers" and ordered his countrymen to refrain from aiding either combatant.[11]

Did the President thus have the right to take the initiative in and to direct unilaterally the course of foreign affairs? To this question, his secretary of the treasury emphatically responded "yes." In a series of articles entitled "Pacificus" that appeared in the Gazette of the United States, the administration's mouthpiece, from June 29 to July 27, 1793, Hamilton set forth what was for that time a breathtakingly sweeping claim for executive ascendancy in foreign affairs. In the conduct of diplomacy, Hamilton asserted, the chief magistrate is "the constitutional organ of intercourse" and should possess power commensurate with his constitutionally mandated responsibility.[12] More specifically, the constitutional stipulation that the President "take care that the laws be faithfully executed" conferred on him the authority to impose on Congress and his countrymen his own interpretation both of national treaties and the law of nations. Such executive supremacy was not, of course, explicitly granted by the Constitution, but flowed from Hamilton's concept of the powers derived by implication from Article II. Except for particularized constraints (such as the role of the Senate in the making of treaties and appointments to office) Hamilton contended that the Constitution did not prescribe the limits of executive power. In holding that executive power was limited only by a chief magistrate's own construction of "other parts of the Constitution" and his own interpretation of the "principles of free government," Hamilton was in effect setting forth the audacious claim that the President was to be the judge of the nature and extent of his own powers.[13] The claim was the more audacious when put in the context of Hamilton's familiar insistence that the national interest should be the touchstone of American foreign policy and his implicit contention that only the President had the requisite qualifications for deciding at any given juncture just what the national interest was and what action its defense required. Such a claim for executive authority came close to bestowing on the American President the prerogative that Sir William Blackstone had assigned to the British crown. Had Hamilton's fellow citizens, most of whom deeply distrusted executive power, paid careful attention to the treasury secretary's argument, the resulting clamor might well have obliged Washington to dismiss his outspoken adviser. But to mid-twentieth-century Americans, inured to the exercise of boundless presidential power, Hamilton's prescription describes the realities of a situation that seems unlikely to alter.

In 1793, however, Hamilton's argument astonished even some fellow Federalists who otherwise shared his broad interpretation of the Constitution and appalled his political opponents, particularly the secretary of state. "For God's sake, my dear Sir," Jefferson wrote to Madison, "take up your pen, select the most striking heresies and cut him to pieces in face of the public." [14] Although reluctant to challenge the most skillful polemicist of the day, Madison replied to Hamilton in a series of articles under the pseudonym "Helvidius." [15] Hamilton's "vicious" argument in support of preeminent presidential power, the Virginian asserted, would invest President George Washington with the royal prerogatives of George III. To Madison, Hamilton's most alarming contention was that in upholding the national interest the executive might be obliged to take action creating "an antecedent state of things" that might render war inevitable, without the constitutionally mandated declaration by Congress.[16] The right to declare war was constitutionally conferred on Congress, Madison firmly insisted, and that exclusive and unrestricted right could not in any way be qualified or diminished by presidential diplomacy. Although Madison indisputably described the true intent of the Framers of the Constitution, he evaded — perhaps deliberately so — what was clearly the vital issue: If control of foreign affairs lay exclusively with Congress, how could American diplomacy be efficiently or effectively carried on? Hamilton, aware of Madison's unwillingness to confront the problem, insisted on the imperativeness of presidential supremacy in foreign affairs, despite the risk of war. Hamilton's perception of presidential power, though it won few converts at the time, established a precedent of indeterminable importance.

Futurity aside, no mere proclamation could assure American neutrality in a world at war. And even had the United States succeeded in remaining steadfastly impartial, the turbulence in Revolutionary France would have created other diplomatic problems for the Washington administration. From the vantage point of precedent, the most important of these was United States recognition of the republic that had overthrown the monarchy with whom the United States had negotiated the Franco-American treaties of 1778, still the cornerstone of relations between the two countries. Did the replacement of the monarchy by the Republic annul those treaties? Pushed in both directions by the American partisans of pressure of public opinion and his official advisers, both of whom took different positions on the issue, Washington sagely decided that the United States should accept the fact that "every nation may govern itself according to whatever form it pleases" and consonantly accord it recognition, thus establishing a vitally important precedent in the conduct of American diplomacy.[17] Washington's patient and prudent conduct of foreign relations was also demonstrated by his reception of the new French minister, citizen Edmond Genêt. Despite the latter's arrogant and flagrantly unneutral behavior, the President icily received him and patiently forbore his high-handed behavior. All in all, the maintenance of neutrality in the face of the wars of the French Revolution that constantly threatened to involve the new and militarily unprepared nation was, next to the establishment of sound public credit, the greatest achievement of the first government organized under the new Constitution.

It was not only abroad that the Washington administration confronted difficulties, it also faced the possibility of civil disobedience and violence at home. This was the well-known Whiskey Rebellion (a misnomer for what was in correct legal terminology an insurrection), sparked by the resistance of distillers to the excise on whiskey imposed by a law of 1791. The resistance was centered in the westernmost counties of Pennsylvania. There, disgruntled distillers strenuously objected to what they viewed as an inequitable tax (although it was in fact a moderate one) on one of their most important manufactures. In 1792 passive resistance spilled over into violence, prompting a presidential proclamation in September of that year admonishing all citizens to refrain from further obstructing the enforcement of federal law. For a time most did, but in the summer of 1794, violence was revived and intensified, to the point that the President and his principal advisers concluded that it must be suppressed or else the enforcement of federal laws be suspended at gunpoint, thus jeopardizing the supremacy of constitutional and congressionally mandated measures. Accordingly, Washington decided to call out and assume personal command of some 15,000 militiamen from Pennsylvania and surrounding states. Republican critics alleged that the military expedition was mere show, a farce written and directed by their political opponents—notably the ambitious treasury secretary—for partisan political purposes. The President, along with most other Federalists, emphatically disagreed, arguing that the military mission was an essential means of assuring and demonstrating the supremacy of federal law. And so it was. Despite the fact that the militia met no armed resistance, its dispatch established an important precedent, as the history of school desegregation and other developments in the mid-twentieth century would demonstrate.

Even before the insurrectionists were routed, a more dangerous crisis had arisen. At issue was a dangerous rift in Anglo-American relations, occasioned by England's adoption of policies designed to put a stop to the profitable American trade with French Caribbean ports, opened to the

United States following the onset of war between England and France in the winter of 1793. In the early spring of 1794, members of Congress who previously had differed on the proper conduct of foreign affairs closed ranks and enacted both punitive legislation and a program of national preparedness. Washington and his principal advisers agreed that national honor must thus be upheld but believed that the conference table rather than military confrontation was the appropriate response to Britain's high-handed behavior. To carry out such negotiations, John Jay, Chief Justice of the Supreme Court who had also served as secretary of foreign affairs during the Confederation era, was appointed special envoy to the English Court. In the late spring of 1794 Jay arrived in London where, month after month, he sought concessions, most of which Lord Grenville, the British foreign secretary, stoutly resisted. Even when he yielded he did so as stingily as possible. The treaty to which Jay finally assented faithfully reflected the comparative military and commercial power of the two nations, though its American critics presumably believed that it should have reflected their country's potential rather than its actual power. Although negotiating from a position of superior strength, Grenville had made concessions on some issues, for which Jay had paid a high price—in effect, acquiescence in Britain's interpretation of international law, including the rights of neutrals. Nevertheless, Washington signed the treaty in mid-August, despite some misgivings about the procedural diplomatic problems raised by the Senate's conditional ratification some two months earlier. It was an exercise of commendably characteristic statecraft, based on the President's well-placed conviction that what the new nation needed most was not involvement in affairs abroad, much less war (which it was singularly ill prepared to fight), but an era of peace to allow the development of its immense resources and concomitant economic growth and prosperity, national unity and, above all, a strong viable central government that would enable the United States to stand tall alongside the world's great powers.

The issue did not appear this way to the treaty's critics, who were legion. Jay's handiwork provoked a popular furor and provided a catalyst for the full-fledged development of the new nation's first major political parties, which had been evolving since the division in public opinion prompted both by Hamilton's financial program and differences over the appropriate orientation of American foreign policy. There is virtual unanimity among historians that the drawn-out battle over Jay's Treaty represented the maturation of America's First Party System. As one of them has phrased it, the treaty was "in its political effects, the most important measure . . . between the institution of Hamilton's financial program and the election of 1800." [18]

The partisan nature of the treaty controversy was even more tellingly demonstrated during the congressional debate over authorization of funds for its implementation. Constitutionally, this was the responsibility of the

House of Representatives, whose Republican leaders discovered therein a means of embarrassing a Federalist administration and enhancing the popularity of their own party. Their first maneuver, however, was not financial noncompliance but passage of a measure requesting the President to submit to the House copies of papers relating to the negotiation and conclusion of the treaty. After consultation with his official family (and with Hamilton who had retired as treasury secretary more than a year earlier and was now practicing law in New York City), Washington courteously declined Congress's request, arguing that it was contrary to the Constitution. The Republicans now employed a second stratagem — refusal to appropriate the requisite funds for carrying out certain provisions of the treaty. To many Federalists the outcome of the debate was of crucial importance. Hamilton spoke for them when he commented that "the glory of the President, the safety of the Constitution, the greatest interests depend upon it." [19] Weeks of intense and partisan debate resulted in a tie vote that was broken by the Speaker of the House who forwent party loyalty and supported the administration. To Washington and his supporters the decision represented a triumph for the national interest over myopic maneuvers to secure merely partisan advantage. More important than the immediate effects of the episode, however, were the precedents it established, notably the exercise of executive privilege, the constitutional rights of the House in the treaty-making process, and, above all, presidential ascendancy in foreign affairs.

Perhaps because executive leadership not only in foreign but also in domestic affairs had by then been firmly asserted the latter part of Washington's second term was something of an anticlimax. After an impressively successful record (which added up to the organization and firm establishment of the new nation), this was a period during which earlier gains were consolidated but few innovations attempted. At the same time, the very fact that the new nation was now successfully launched encouraged the unleashing of partisan controversy that, though previously acrimonious, had been attenuated by an underlying consensus on the imperativeness of establishing viable nationhood. Now party politics became vitriolic and often scurrilous. For the first time, as an example, attacks were leveled at the President personally. He was accused, among other things, of being a closet monarchist, an aspirant for political sainthood, or, in the words of one detractor, a man who displayed "the seclusion of a monk and the supercillious [sic] distance of a tyrant." [20] Characteristically refusing to comment publicly on such attacks, Washington expressed his indignation and anger only to the small circle of his most trusted advisers. But his chagrin slowly shoved him toward adoption of a practice that he continued to disavow. During his final years as President, Washington (while continuing to affirm his unswerving belief in "the baneful effects of the spirit of party," which, as he insisted in his Farewell Address, "serves always to distract the public councils and enfeeble the public administration") did not knowingly appoint to office any other than bona fide Federalists.[21] The first President thus inaugurated a practice that would remain a hallmark of the American political system and unwittingly established a precedent for presidential party leadership, a role not conferred by the Constitution whose authors did not foresee the role of political parties.

Partisan animosity also strengthened the President's resolve to retire at the end of his second term. There was no constitutional barrier to a third term nor to repeated reelection, and doubtless nothing would more have pleased most Federalists than lifetime tenure for the new nation's Revolutionary War hero and still most popular citizen. But after forty years of public service Washington had not the slightest intention of obliging them. Weary of affairs of state, dispirited by criticism that stung all the more because to him it was willfully and undeservedly libelous, he was implacably determined to forsake the trials of high office for the always cherished tranquillity of Mount Vernon. By refusing to serve more than two terms he unknowingly established a precedent that would be followed by his successors until Franklin D. Roosevelt, whose election to a third and fourth term prompted adoption of the Twenty-Second Amendment to the Constitution.

As the end of Washington's second term approached, he turned his attention to the manner of his leave-taking. Having long since decided that a "valedictory" address rather than a mere announcement would be appropriate, Washington retrieved from his files a farewell message that James Madison had prepared for him some four years earlier before he had given up hope of leaving office at the end of his first administration. Madison's work, he concluded, had stood the test of time and only needed to be brought up-to-date by discussing the "considerable changes," especially in foreign affairs, that had taken place since then. Having decided to take on that assignment himself, Washington's revision took the form of an addendum to Madison's draft in which the President described the difficulties of his second term: baneful partisanship and other domestic problems; the attacks to which he had personally been subjected; and the overarching importance of foreign affairs. Apropos of the latter subject, Washington indicated the principles and policies that the new nation should follow, among them: prevention of foreign influence in domestic affairs; avoidance of alliances with other nations but adherence to America's treaty commitments; preservation of a policy of steadfast neutrality; and, above all, the preservation of a strong and prosperous union.

Not altogether satisfied with the address as it stood, Washington, as he so often had in the past, solicited Hamilton's assistance. The New Yorker was asked either to edit the original address prepared by Madison as revised by Washington or, should Hamilton think it necessary, "to throw the whole into a new form." [22] The former treasury secretary did both, confident, however, that what he described as his own "Original Major Draft" (about one-half of which was his own work and the rest a paraphrase of the work of Madison and Washington) would, as he recommended, be preferred by the President. It would nevertheless be a mistake to attribute authorship of the Farewell Address to Hamilton. Because of his many years of close official association with Washington during which he had revised or written many documents for him, Hamilton was fully cognizant of the Virginian's views and he included nothing that was not fully consonant with them. It is thus appropriate that this famous state paper has always been described as Washington's Farewell Address. Its enduring importance is indicated each February 22 when the address is read before both the Senate and the House of Representatives.

Contemporaneously, the first President decided that the best way of disseminating his valedictory message was newspaper publication. Accordingly, the address appeared in Philadelphia's *American Daily Advertiser* on September 19, 1796, and was widely reprinted elsewhere. On the same day, President Washington left New York City for the final time, en route to Mount Vernon. The period from his return to Philadelphia on October 31 until the inauguration of his successor on March 4 of the following year was comparatively uneventful. Although obliged to take cognizance of the flagrant abuse of diplomatic protocol by French minister Pierre Adet, who openly sought to promote the chances of a Jeffersonian victory in the mudslinging presidential campaign then underway, Washington largely confined himself to the preparation of his eighth annual message to Congress, his final major official responsibility. That address, delivered on December 7, briefly summarized the accomplishments and still persistent problems of his presidency, among them successful handling of Indian affairs and the prospect of enhanced mutual forbearance, implementation of the provisions of Jay's Treaty and the likelihood of a continued Anglo-American rapprochement, the settlement of U.S.-Spanish controversies, and the regrettable deterioration of relations with our Revolutionary War ally, France.

As to the presidential campaign then raging between his former secretary of state and John Adams, his two-term vice-president, Washington was silent. And he remained so, behavior that for once was not to be emulated by the overwhelming majority of his successors. Carrying restraint to its utmost limits (in view, that is, of his own unacknowledged partisanship), he also refused to comment on the election of Adams as his successor and Jefferson as the next vice-president.

John Adams's inauguration on March 4, 1797, symbolized the successful organization of the new government whose mere skeletal framework and powers had been provided for by the Constitution ratified less than a decade earlier. Problems aplenty remained but the governmental parameters within which they would be settled or left unresolved were permanently established. This explains the overarching importance of the initial implementation of a document that has endured to the present day, though fundamentally altered in ways that George Washington and his colleagues could not have imagined.

CONSTITUTIONALISM AND THE AMERICAN FOUNDING

HERMAN BELZ

Between 1776 and 1789 the American people constituted themselves a nation by creating republican governments in the thirteen former English colonies and then, in the Constitutional Convention, by transforming the Union of confederated states into a genuine law-giving government. The novelty of this achievement was epitomized in the seal of the new nation, "Novus Ordo Seclorum," which announced "a new order of the ages." Yet in founding political societies Americans pursued a goal that had occupied Western man since antiquity: the establishment of government power capable of maintaining the stability and order necessary to realize the purposes of community, yet so defined and structured as to prevent tyranny. This age-old quest for the forms, procedures, and institutional arrangements most suitable for limiting power and implementing a community's conception of political right and justice, we know as constitutionalism. It remains to consider American constitution-making in the perspective of Western and specifically English constitutionalism, and to reflect on its significance in shaping political life in the United States.

Constitutionalism takes as its purpose resolution of the conflict that characterizes political life and makes government necessary, through procedures and institutions that seek to limit government and create spheres of individual and community freedom. Based on the paradoxical idea that the power to make law and to rule can be at once sovereign and effective, yet also defined, reasonable, and responsible, constitutionalism contains an inherent tension that sets it against utopianism and anarchism, which deny the reality of power, and absolutism and totalitarianism, which tolerate no limitations on power. Nevertheless, although constitutionalists can in retrospect be seen as sharing common assumptions, differences among them have sometimes led to irreconcilable conflict. One such division occurred in the eighteenth century when the American people separated from the English nation and adopted a new type of constitutional theory and practice for the conduct of their political life.

Perhaps the most obvious feature of American constitutionalism was its apparent dependence upon legally binding written instruments prescribing the organization of government and fixing primary principles and rules to guide its operation. Texts had of course long been used in law, government, and politics, and the English constitution comprised written elements. Americans' resort to documentary, positive-law techniques of government was more systematic and complete than any previous undertaking, however, so much so as to amount to constitutional innovation. Following the American example, peoples everywhere in the modern world have adopted the practice of forming governments by writing constitutions. But Americans in the founding era did more than invent a new approach to the old problem of limited government. Their constitution-making was informed with a new purpose — the liberal purpose of protecting the natural rights of individuals. American charters of fundamental law were not simply ordinances of government; they were also constitutions of liberty. The meaning of liberty, especially the relation between the individual and the community that was central to any practical definition of it, was a deeply controversial issue that divided Americans in state and national constitution-making. The adoption of the federal Constitution in 1787, however, marked a decisive shift toward protection of individuals in the pursuit of their interests, and away from enforcement of community consensus aimed at making citizens virtuous and moral, as the central purpose of constitutional government in America.

American constitutionalism is thus concerned with organizational and procedural matters, on the one hand, and with substantive questions of political purpose, on the other. Most of the time constitutional politics in the United States deals with the former concern, as groups and individuals assert or deny the existence of proper governmental power or challenge methods used to employ it. Nevertheless, constitutionalism is ultimately normative and purposive. Every state may be said to have a constitution, in the sense of an institutional structure and established procedures for conducting political affairs. But not every state is a constitutional state. In the Western political tradition constitutional government is defined by forms and procedures that limit the exercise of power. American constitutionalism goes farther by pursuing not only the negative goal of preventing tyranny but also the positive end of promoting individual liberty, both in the passive sense of protection against government power and in the active sense of participation in the decisions of the political community. Viewed in this light, American constitutionalism raises basic questions of political value and purpose that connect it with the mainstream of Western political philosophy.

In the history of constitutionalism the great problem has not been to create power but to define and limit it. The Western constitutional tradition has employed two methods toward this end. The first is the theory and practice of arranging the internal structure of government so that power is distributed and balanced. In Greek political thought the purpose of politics was to promote virtue or moral excellence in men, and the founder of a political community was advised to balance the classes of society — kingship, aristocracy, and democracy — in a structure of mixed government which permitted each element to contribute to this end. The pursuit by each class of its special aptitude or interest prevented the others from seeking merely private ends, transforming the polity into despotism, oligarchy, or mob rule depending on which part of society dominated. A second method of constitutionalism has been to subject government to legal limitations, or the rule of law. Roman juristic writing, which regarded natural law as a standard of reason and equity for judging the validity and legitimacy of government enactments, is usually considered the source of the rule-of-law idea. Significant practical steps toward achieving it were taken in medieval England as common law courts created a sphere of law and legal right protecting individual property and liberties against government and constituting a limitation on royal discretionary authority. Further contributing to the rule-of-law tradition was the tendency of courts to regard basic principles of common law adjudication as embodying reason and justice, and hence as a kind of fundamental law limiting the acts of government.

English constitutionalism in the period of American colonization comprised both strands of the constitutional tradition. The common law courts in the early seventeenth century insisted on the superiority of law over the royal prerogative. Sir Edward Coke gave famous expression to the idea of a higher law controlling government in asserting that " 'sovereign power' is no parliamentary word. . . . Magna Charta is such a fellow, that he will have no sovereign." Coke also said that "when an act of Parliament is against common right and reason, or repugnant, or impossible to be performed, the common law will controul it and adjudge such act to be void." [1] Parliament itself, however, subsequently claimed supremacy in lawmaking, and vindication of its authority in the Revolution of 1688 effectively precluded development of the rule of law into a politically relevant form of higher-law constitutionalism. An internally balanced institutional structure, expressed in the revised and revitalized theory of mixed government in the eighteenth century, became the principal model of constitutional government in England.

Essentially descriptive in its connotation, the English constitution was the structure of institutions, laws, conventions, and practices through which political issues were brought to resolution and carried out in acts of government. Yet the constitution was also prescriptive or normative, or at least it was supposed to be. Lord Bolingbroke's well-known definition pointed to this quality: "By constitution we mean . . . that assemblage of laws, institutions and customs, derived from certain fixed principles of reason, directed to certain fixed objects of public good, that compose the general system, according to which the community hath agreed to be governed." [2]

More specifically, as Montesquieu, Blackstone, and other eighteenth-century writers affirmed, the purpose or end of the English constitution was civil and political liberty.[3] From the standpoint of modern constitutionalism the legislative supremacy that contemporaries regarded as the foundation of English liberty was incompatible with effective restraints on government. Nevertheless, Parliament was believed to be under a moral obligation to protect the rights and liberties of Englishmen, and the sanctions of natural law were still seen as effective restraints. Moreover, political accountability to public opinion through elections operated as a limitation on government. Englishmen thus continued to see their constitution as fixed and fundamental, notwithstanding legislative sovereignty.[4]

American constitutionalism began in the seventeenth century when English settlers founded political societies and institutions of government in North America. Two things stand out in this early constitutional experience. First, the formation of government was to a considerable extent based on written instruments. In corporate and proprietary colonies the founding documents were charters granted by the crown conferring enumerated powers on a particular person or group within a designated geographical area for specific purposes. Under these charters the colonists adopted further agreements, organic acts, ordinances, combinations, and frames of government giving more precise form to political institutions. In religiously motivated colonies government was more clearly the result of mutual pledging and association under civil-religious covenants. American colonists thus used constitutionlike instruments to create political community, define fundamental values and interests, specify basic rights, and organize governmental institutions.[5]

The second outstanding fact in early American constitutional history was substantial community control over local affairs. To be sure, the colonies employed the forms and practices of English government and generally emulated the metropolitan political culture. Their institutions at the provincial and local levels were patterned after English models, and the theory of mixed government and the balanced constitution was accepted as valid. Yet discordant tendencies pointed to a distinctive course of constitutional development. The fact that in most colonies the power of the governor depended on royal authority while the power of the assembly rested on a popular base, as well as frequent conflict of interest between them, made separation and division of power a political reality discrepant with the theory of mixed government. Furthermore, popularly elected assemblies responsive to growing constituencies and enjoying de facto local sovereignty under written charters introduced a republican element into American politics.

As English subjects, Americans believed they lived under a free—and fixed—English constitution. Long before the American Revolution they expressed this view in the course of conflicts with imperial officials. Numerous writers asserted that the constitution was a contract between the people and their rulers; that the legislature could not alter the fundamental laws from which government derived its form, powers, and very existence; that government must exercise power within limits prescribed by a civil compact with the people. Moreover, the compact chosen to organize and direct government, as a colonial sermon of 1768 put it, must coincide with "the moral fitness of things, by which alone the natural rights of mankind can be secured." [6] Disputing the descriptive English constitution that included parliamentary sovereignty, Americans were coming to think of a constitution as normative rules limiting the exercise of power for the purpose of protecting the people's liberty, property, and happiness.

In declaring their independence from England, Americans in a sense reenacted the founding experience of the seventeenth century. They took what their history and political circumstances determined to be the logical step of writing constitutions to organize their political communities. Before issuing the Declaration of Independence, Congress recommended that the colonies adopt governments that "in the opinion of representatives of the people, best conduce to the happiness and safety of their constituents in particular, and America in general." [7] Although some argued that the people acting in convention should form the government, political exigencies and Whig political theory conferred legitimacy on legislatures, which in all but two instances were responsible for writing or adopting the first state constitutions.

The most distinctive feature of the state constitutions—their documentary or positive character—followed the decision to form new governments as a matter of course. Given the long tradition of founding documents in America, it seemed obvious that the purposes of political community and limitations on government could be achieved better by writing a constitution than by relying on an unstipulated, imprecise constitution like England's, which did not limit government and was not really a constitution after all. Though consisting in part of written documents, the latter was too subjective, ultimately existing in men's minds and premised on the idea that "thinking makes it so." [8] Americans insisted in contrast that the principles and rules essential to organizing power and preserving liberty be separated from the government and objectively fixed in positive form. Old in the tendency it reflected though new in its comprehensive application, American constitutionalism rested on the idea that "saying makes it so," or at least the hope that putting something in writing so it can be authoritatively consulted makes it easier to achieve specified ends. [9]

Professor Lutz's illuminating research has shown that the state constitutions stand in direct line of descent from colonial founding documents which created political communities and established institutions of government. One type of founding document (compact, covenant, combination, agreement) signified mutual promise and consent by which individuals

formed a political community and identified basic values, rights, and interests. A second type of document (enactment, ordinance, frame, constitution) specified governmental institutions.[10] Half the state constitutions
written between 1776 and 1789 were described as compacts and contained
bills of rights that defined basic community values. In the other constitutions the design of government received principal attention. All the constitutions reflected tendencies of previous political development; none created
institutions on a completely clean slate. This fact appeared more clearly in
documents that were concerned mainly with establishing a framework of
government. In these more modern documents, which anticipated the
course of American constitutional development, community consensus
yielded in importance to protection of individual rights as the main purpose
of constitution-making.

In a formal sense American constitutionalism consisted in the stipulation of principles, institutions, and rules of government by the people or
their representatives in the state legislatures. As constitutions are distinguished and ultimately justified by their political purpose and effect, however, the political character of the revolutionary founding documents requires consideration.

Historical scholarship in the past two decades has firmly established
republicanism as the political philosophy of the American Revolution. Although lacking in precise meaning, the concept is most accurately defined as
government resting on the consent of the people and directed by the public
will expressed through representative institutions. In the perspective of
Western political thought republican philosophy was formulated in the
seventeenth century to defend liberty against absolutism. The state constitutions were republican and liberal insofar as they limited government by
prescribing public decision-making procedures that prevented government
officials from aggrandizing power for private benefit rather than the public
good. The constitutions were liberal in yet another sense in confirming and
extending the right of political participation that according to republican
philosophy constituted true liberty for individuals. In many respects, however, state constitutionalism in the revolutionary era was a doctrine of
community power and control that restricted individual rights in a way that
would now be seen as illiberal.

Under the state constitutions the most important power in modern
government — the power to make law and compel obedience — was lodged
in the legislature. Unimpeded by internal governmental checks under the
extreme version of the separation of powers that prevailed in the first phase
of state-making, and sustained by presumptive identity with popular sovereignty as the source of political authority before the rejection of monarchy,
legislatures acted forcefully to promote public virtue and the common good.
Requirements of public virtue frequently took the form of restrictions on

individual liberty through sumptuary laws and statutes regulating the transfer and use of property. Bills of rights that were part of state constitutions had little effect in curbing legislative power because they were treated as hortatory rather than legally binding. In the name of popular sovereignty and patriotism, state legislatures fashioned a constitutionalism of unity and power in government.

The concentrated power of republican virtue acting through institutions of community control was a useful and perhaps necessary expedient in the wartime emergency. In the doctrines of state sovereignty and the police power, revolutionary republicanism entered into the American constitutional tradition, and has offered a compelling model of constitutional government throughout our history to reformers and radicals on both the left and the right. However, the actions of the state legislatures too plainly contradicted the constitutional meaning of the Revolution to become accepted as the principal or exclusive expression of American constitutionalism. That meaning was nowhere better stated than by the Massachusetts General Court in its Circular Letter of 1768, which declared: ". . . in all free States the Constitution is fixed; & as the supreme Legislative derives its Power & Authority from the Constitution, it cannot overleap the Bounds of it, without destroying its own foundation." [11] Yet this was precisely what was happening in the American republics.

The state constitutions may have been fundamental law in the sense of ordaining a framework of government, but they were not fundamental in the sense of controlling legislative power. In all but two states the constitution was written by the legislature and could be altered or abolished by that body if it so chose. More than language of urging and admonition, contained in many of the constitutions, was needed to transform them into effective restraints on the actual exercise of power. Nor was the technique of internal institutional balance effectively employed to limit the state legislatures. In 1784 South Carolinian Thomas Tucker echoed the complaint increasingly heard in other states when he criticized the people of his state for deriving their ideas of government too much from the British constitution, and giving the legislature powers formerly exercised or claimed under a monarchical government. Tucker argued that the South Carolina constitution, written and adopted by the legislature, was not founded on proper authority. He recommended a popular convention to amend the constitution, "fixing it on the firm and proper foundation of the express consent of the people, unalterable by the legislative, or any other authority but that by which it is to be framed." [12]

Attempts to restrict state legislative power in the 1780s broadened and reformed American constitutionalism. As Tucker suggested, writing and amending constitutions by popularly elected conventions clarified the distinction between legislative law and fundamental or paramount law. Massachusetts in 1780 and New Hampshire in 1784 wrote their constitutions in conventions and required them to be ratified by the people in special elections. In theory this was the most effective way to make the constitution an antecedent higher law secure against legislative alteration. Further restriction of legislative power resulted from changes in the internal structure of government. Executive officers were given greater powers as checks and balances — that is, a partial and limited sharing or mixing of functional powers among the departments — were introduced in some states as modification of the separation of powers. Bicameralism, a carry-over from colonial government, was recognized as a means of making legislative action more deliberate. And courts began to play a more prominent political role by treating constitutions as higher law in relation to legislative enactments.

So strong was the tradition of community self-government under legislative sovereignty, however, that it could not easily be dislodged as the main reliance of constitutionalism. Certainly little could be done to alter it by isolated efforts in the several states. Effective reform, if that was needed, could come only from an interstate collaboration working through the state system created by the colonies when they declared their independence. Heretofore peripheral to republican political development, the union of the states in the Confederation became the focus of constitutional change.

The Continental Congress was formed by the colonies in 1774 as a coordinating and advisory body to protect American interests and eventually to pursue the cause of national independence. Exigencies of war and common concerns among the states gave Congress political power, which it exercised through informal rules and practices that were codified in the Articles of Confederation. Considered from a constitutional perspective as a limiting grant of power, the Articles were inadequate because, while they gave Congress ostensible power to do many things, they did not confer the lawmaking authority that is essential to government. Congress could at best make resolutions and recommendations, which in practice amounted to requests that the states could ignore. The Articles were unconstitutionlike in consequence of having been written by Congress and ratified by the states, rather than based in any direct way on popular authority. They were also unconstitutionlike with respect to institutional structure. Whether considered analogous to a legislative or executive body, Congress was the sole governmentlike organ, and only an evolving departmental system saved it from complete incompetence.

As an alliance or league of friendship (the description used in the document), the Articles were a more successful founding instrument. Yet in the form given it in the Articles, the Confederation was incapable of addressing in a constructive manner the defects in American government revealed in the actions of the states. The confederacy provided a field of political action, however, on which the reform of republican constitutionalism could take place. The practical impossibility of amending the Articles in order to strengthen Congress having been demonstrated, and insecurity of liberty and property in the states apparently increasing, proponents of constitutional reform turned a last-ditch desperation move — the calling of a convention of the states at Philadelphia in May 1787 — into an enduring achievement of statesmanship and constitutional invention.

Perhaps most significant, the Framers gave institutional expression to the idea that a constitution, in order to function as a limiting grant of power, must be higher as well as fundamental law. In addition to originating or organizing power, it must be maintained separate from and paramount to government. In a formal sense the Constitution as a founding document was superficially similar to the state constitutions. A preamble explained the reasons for the document, proclaimed the existence of a people and political community, defined specific purposes, and ordained a framework of government. In reality, however, the Framers departed from the model of the state constitutions. It was unnecessary to return to the fundamentals of the social compact and the purposes of republican government, as state constitution writers to varying degrees were inclined to do. The authors of the Constitution observed that they were not addressing the natural rights of man not yet gathered in society, but natural rights modified by society and interwoven with the rights of the states.[13] They knew that the nation they were creating — or, to be more precise, whose existence they were recognizing — was amorphous, loosely related in its constituent parts, and united by few principles and interests. It was far from being the kind of cohesive, integrated community that the states by contrast seemed to be, and most unlike the nation-state communities of Europe. Hence the Framers briefly addressed in the Preamble those few basic unifying purpose and values — liberty, justice, domestic peace, military defense, the general welfare — and gave virtually the entire document to stipulating the institutions and procedures of government. As fundamental law the Constitution thus was less a social compact for a coherent, like-minded community, and more a contractlike specification of the powers, duties, rights, and responsibilities among the diverse polities and peoples that constituted the American Union.

Far more effectively than writers of earlier founding instruments, the Framers made the Constitution a paramount, controlling law. In a practical sense this boiled down to a question of law enforcement. Creating a real government to operate directly on individuals throughout a vast jurisdiction raised a new and potentially difficult compliance issue, but this received little attention at the convention. It was the old compliance problem of the states that stood in the way of making the Constitution binding and effective. At first the delegates considered a congressional veto on state legislation to deal with this issue. Rejected as impracticable, the veto was replaced by the supremacy clause (Article VI, section 2), stating that the Constitution, laws made in pursuance of it, and treaties made under U.S. authority "shall be the supreme Law of the Land; and the Judges in every State shall be bound thereby, any Thing in the Constitution or Laws of any State to the Contrary notwithstanding." This language expressed the paramountcy of the federal constitution over the states, and by inference over national legislative law as well. Not explicitly stated but implied in the judicial article was the idea that the superior force of the Constitution depended on its application and interpretation by the courts.

The higher-law character of the Constitution was further affirmed and institutionalized in the method of its drafting and in provisions for its ratification and amendment. Although delegates to the Philadelphia Convention were appointed by the state legislatures rather than elected by the people, the Constitution was a more genuine expression of the will of the people than were the Articles of Confederation, which were written by Congress. It has always been difficult for historians convinced of the democratic character of the Articles to admit this fact, but the Framers' acknowledged apprehension about unlimited popular rule does not gainsay their commitment to the republican idea that government derives its just powers from the consent of the governed. Consistent with this commitment, institutions of direct popular consent that were still exceptional at the state level were incorporated into the national constitution. Ratification would be decided by conventions in the states, presumably popularly elected. Amendment of the Constitution could occur through popular approval in state legislatures or special conventions, of proposals recommended by Congress or by a convention to be called by Congress on the application of two-thirds of the state legislatures. The superiority of the Constitution to legislative law was enhanced by this provision for its amendment, since an utterly fixed and inflexible political law would become irrelevant to the task of governing an expanding society. If the Constitution required change, however, the people must amend it. Thus were popular sovereignty and the higher-law tradition incorporated into American constitutionalism.

To make the Constitution paramount law in operational fact, however, it was not enough to assert its supremacy and assume that the people's innate law-abidingness would give it effect. This was to rely on "paper barriers," concerning the efficacy of which there was much skepticism among the Framers. It was necessary also to structure the organs of government so that power would be internally checked and limited.

A persistent theme in constitutional theory since the late nineteenth century has been that power should be concentrated and unified—the more so the better, in order to deal with social problems—provided only that government be kept responsible through institutions of political accountability and the rule of law. Although the Framers' objective was to create coercive authority where none existed, they rejected concentrated sovereign power as a proper constitutional principle. Delegated, divided, reciprocally limiting power formed the motif of their institutional design.

Unlike the state constitutions, which organized the inherent plenary power of the community, the Constitution delegated specific powers to the general government. The contrast was most significant in the plan of the legislative department, to which the state constitutions assigned "the legislative power" and which the federal constitutions defined by the enumeration of congressional powers. Stable and energetic government seeming to require a strong executive and an independent judiciary, the Constitution made grants of power of a more general nature to these branches, which under the separation of powers were a counterweight to the lawmaking department. The separation principle by itself, however, as the state experience showed, was not a sufficient limitation on legislative power. Accordingly, checks and balances, by which each branch was given a partial and limited agency in the others' power, as in executive participation in legislation through the veto or legislative judging in the impeachment process, built further restraints into the Constitution.

The structure of the Union of course presented the most urgent question of institutional arrangements affecting the constitutional reality of a supreme political law. A division of power was already evident in the plan of the Articles of Confederation; what was needed was to transform the Union's political authority into the genuine power to impose lawful requirements on its constituent parts. This was achieved by reconstituting the Confederation as a compound republic, based both on the people and the states. Once this was accomplished, the pertinent fact for the paramountcy of the Constitution was the division of sovereignty. By giving the central government power over objects of general concern and allowing the states to retain almost all of their authority over local matters, the Framers divided sovereignty, thereby effectively eliminating it from the constitutional order. Arguments were certain to arise about the nature and extent of the powers of the several governments in the American state system, but the effect of such controversy would be to focus attention on the Constitution as the authoritative source of answers to questions about the rights of constituent members.

The Constitution was both fundamental and higher law because it expressed the will of the people, the ultimate source of authority in America. But it would truly limit power only if it was superior to the people themselves as a political entity, as well as to the legislative law. At the time some theorists of popular sovereignty argued that the people could alter their government at will, exercising the right of peaceful revolution and disregarding legalities of form and procedure, even as the Framers did in drafting and securing ratification of the Constitution against the express requirements of the Articles of Confederation. However we view their action — as illegal, unconstitutional, revolutionary, or merely statesmanlike — the authors of the Constitution rejected the notion of unlimited popular sovereignty. They provided restraints on the people in the form of a limited number of offices, long terms of office, indirect elections, large electoral districts, and separated and balanced departments of government. Although these provisions have often been viewed as antidemocratic and in conflict with republican theory, they are more accurately seen as modifying the popular form of government adopted during the Revolution. The Framers' intent, as James Madison wrote in *The Federalist* #10, was to supply "a republican remedy for the diseases most incident to republican government." [14] And one should not forget that despite careful distribution and balancing of authority, Congress remained potentially the most powerful branch of the government, most responsive to the people and possessed of the lawmaking power.

Making the Constitution effective as a permanent higher law involved matters of form, procedure, and institutional structure. Yet as procedural issues carry substantive implications, and means sometimes become ends in themselves, it is also necessary to ask what a constitution is for. To prevent tyranny, the constitutionalist goal, is to create a space in which differences among people become manifest, in which politics can appear and questions of purpose arise. If running a constitution always reflects political concerns, making a constitution is all the more a form of political action that derives from or partakes of political philosophy. We thus consider the purposes and ends of the Framers' constitutionalism.

If the end of the English constitution was acknowledged to be political freedom, Americans were all the more emphatic in declaring liberty to be the purpose of their constitutions. Moreover, if the purpose of politics in modern times, as the history of political thought teaches us, is to protect men's natural rights rather than to make them virtuous and good as the ancients thought, then American constitutions were liberal in purpose. Yet the concept of liberty, universally embraced as a political good, can obviously be defined in different ways. And while recognition of natural rights gave modern politics a new purpose, it is equally true that virtue and moral excellence did not disappear from political discourse. In light of these considerations we may discern two conceptions of political freedom in the constitutionalism of the founding period. The first refers to the liberty of self-governing political communities, which were still thought to have an obligation to make men virtuous and on which individuals depended for their happiness and well-being. The second conception of freedom rests on the primacy of natural rights and generally asserts individual liberty over community consensus as the purpose of government.

Although these conceptions of liberty stand in theoretical opposition to each other, they coexisted in the Revolutionary era. After protesting imperial policies in the language of English constitutional rights, Americans justified national independence by appealing to universal natural rights. Wartime exigencies required decisive political action, however, which was based on the right of local communities to control individuals for the sake of the common good. States interfered with the liberty and property of individuals by controlling markets, restricting personal consumption, awarding monopoly privileges, and limiting imports and exports. They also regulated the speech and press freedoms of persons suspected of disloyalty to the patriot cause. In many ways Revolutionary republicanism subordinated the rights of individual citizens to the community, defining true liberty as the pursuit of public happiness through political action.

Reacting against state encroachments on liberty and property, the Constitution makers of 1787 emphasized protection of individual rights rather than promotion of virtue and community consensus as the purpose of government. Rather than an unattainable ideal of public virtue in ordinary citizens, they appealed to enlightened self-interest as the social reality on which the Constitution would rest. The Framers recognized factional conflict as a limiting condition for creating a constitution, yet also as an opportunity for broadening and redefining republican government. Alongside the communitarian ideal, which remained strong in many states, they created a new constitutional model in the complex and powerful government of the extended republic, based partly on the people yet so structured and limited that individual liberty, property, and pursuit of personal interests would be substantially protected against local legislative interference. This is not to say that mere private enrichment at the expense of the community good or general welfare was the end of the Constitution. The concepts of virtue and the public interest remained integral to political thought and discourse. But virtue assumed a new meaning as the prudent and rational pursuit of private commercial activity. Instead of telling people how to live in accordance with a particular conception of political right or religious truth, the Framers promoted ends believed beneficial to all of society—peace, economic growth, intellectual advancement—by accommodating social competition and upholding citizens' natural rights against invasion by the organized power of the community, whether local, state, or national.

The Founding Fathers are often seen as antidemocratic because they created a strong central government, removed from direct popular and local community control, which they expected to be managed by an aristocratic elite. Notwithstanding its foundation in popular sovereignty and protection of individual liberty and rights, the Constitution in this view contradicted the real meaning of the Revolution, defined as rule by local communities guided by republican civic virtue. Yet while the Revolution stood for government by consent, there is no sound reason for regarding Revolutionary state-making as the single true expression of the republican principle. It was an essential part of that principal that government should operate through law to which all were subordinate, both citizens and government officials, and further that legislative law should be controlled by the higher law of the Constitution. This was the meaning of the rule of law in the United States, and its more complete realization in the Constitution of 1787 signified climax and fulfillment of the Revolution.

The Framers' purpose must also be considered in relation to the threat of national disintegration, either from internal discord or foreign encroachment, that has traditionally characterized accounts of the "critical period" in American history. The weakness of Congress in discharging its responsibilities was surely an impediment to protecting American interests, and an embarrassment to patriotic men. Yet the belief that national disintegration was imminent perhaps depends too much on the idea, borne of subsequent crises, that American nationality must be expressed through a strong central government or else it cannot exist. Some degree of formal cooperation among the states was necessary, but America could have existed as a plural nation, as it did in the Confederation period (and to an important extent continued to do under the Constitution). The problem in 1787 was not the threat of total rupture of the Union attended by actual warfare among the states. The problem was the character of American politics and government, or the nature and tendency of republican government. Republicanism was the defining idea of the nation, and without it we may say that America would no longer exist. The country was growing in the 1780s as population expanded, economic development occurred, westward settlement continued. Yet the state system of 1776 was incapable of adequately accommodating and guiding this development. The states were too strong for the good of republican principles, the Union not strong enough. By restructuring the state system, by reconstituting the Union on a republican constitution that crystallized tendencies in congressional–state relations in the 1780s, the Framers sought to reform American government to the end of securing the republican ideals of the Revolution.

We are so accustomed to thinking of constitutions as a reflection of, and hence determined by, social forces that we tend not to consider that the historical significance of the Constitution really was to demonstrate, as Alexander Hamilton wrote in *The Federalist* #1, that men are "capable . . . of establishing good government from reflection and choice." [15] Historical analysis may lead to the conclusion, for example, that the idea of a constitution as a higher, fixed law appealed to colonial Americans as an effective means of protesting imperial policy. Not so readily do we entertain the view that the constitutionalism of 1787 was based on a sound understanding of human nature, that it propounded valid principles of government, that it possessed intrinsic and not merely instrumental value. These are normative reflections more appropriate to political science, and an older political science at that, than to history. In writing about constitutionalism, however, it is hard categorically to deny a normative dimension, because the basic questions — the effectiveness of limitations on government, abuses of power, the nature of liberty — defy objective measurement. [16]

Yet, while historical analysis need not judge whether the Framers formulated a valid science of politics, it can employ as an evaluative criterion the requirement that a constitution must recognize and conform to a people's principal characteristics and nature. Considered from this point of view the achievement of the Founding Fathers is undeniable. They created a complex government of delegated and dispersed, yet articulated and balanced powers based on the principle of consent. Confirmation of that principle was in turn required by the Constitution in the cooperation and concurrence among the branches of government that was necessary for the conduct of public business. Made for an open, acquisitive, individualistic, competitive, and pluralistic society, the Constitution ordered the diverse constituent elements of American politics. More than merely a neutral procedural instrument for registering the play of social forces, it was a statement of ends and means for maintaining the principles that defined Americans as a national people. The Framers made a liberal constitution for a liberal society.

That the nation now marks the bicentennial of the Constitution is perhaps evidence enough of the Framers' success in establishing a new kind of constitutional government. Yer formal continuity may conceal substantive alterations. We need to ask how the higher-law and limited-power constitutionalism expressed in the document of 1787 actually worked in practice.

It is a striking fact, considering the unhappy outcome of most revolutions and the high rate of failure of constitution-makers in the twentieth century, that the Constitution was not only formally ratified but quickly accorded full political legitimacy. The state constitutions, while not merely pretextual or façade documents, were not invoked and applied in the actual conduct of government as the United States Constitution was. And the new federal instrument was more than accepted: it rapidly became an object of veneration. This "cult of the Constitution," as it has unappreciatively been described by many students of American government, requires explanation.

Historians have offered a number of reasons for constitution worship, including popular identification of the document with economic prosperity; the Federalists' propagandizing to create an instant tradition of the Constitution and inculcate public commitment to it; the people's need for a unifying social myth and object of loyalty to replace monarchy as a course of authority. It has further been argued that Anti-Federalist critics of the document in the ratification debate became its most vigorous supporters because of ideological conditioning that led them to treat it as an ancient constitution requiring literalistic defense to prevent political corruption. More broadly we may say that the Constitution took deep and abiding hold on the American political mind because it reflected a sober regard for the propensities of ordinary human nature and the realities of republican society; created powerful institutions capable of attracting men of talent, ambition, and enlarged civic outlook; and introduced changes in the conduct of public affairs that most people saw as improvements and that caused them to form an interest in the government it created.

The Constitution stipulated institutions, rules, and procedures embodying and symbolizing the principles of republican liberty, national unity, and balance and limitation of power. It was a fixed, objective document that could be consulted and applied, not a formless assemblage of principles, statutes, and decisions carried about in men's minds and dependent on social internalization for its effect. Yet the Constitution's principles and provisions were general and ambiguous enough to allow of varying interpretations. Liberty, union, and reciprocally limiting power meant different things to different people, as did the rules and institutional arrangements expressing and embodying them. At a superficial level this circumstance produced conflict, but at a deeper level the effect was unifying. For groups and individuals were encouraged to pursue political goals within the framework of rules and requirements established by the Constitution. Thus the document became permanent and binding. In the language of social science it was an integrative mechanism. Only the most extreme groups in our history — radical abolitionists and slaveholders in the nineteenth century, totalitarian parties in the twentieth — have repudiated the Constitution as a framework for political action.

The Constitution possessed force and effect because it was useful and relevant to political life. Responsive to the social environment, it had instrumental value. At the same time, repeated reference to the document as the source and symbol of legitimate authority confirmed its intrinsic value, apart from the practical results of specific controversies. People believed, in other words, that it was important to follow the Constitution for its own sake or for the common good, rather than for a particular political reason. The intrinsic value of the Constitution lay not only in the wisdom and reasonableness of its principles in relation to the nature of American society but also in the form those principles were given in a written instrument. The effect of the Constitution as binding political law has much to do with its textual character.

The Framers addressed this issue in discussing "parchment barriers." The state constitutions were evidence that written stipulations were no guarantee of performance, especially when it came to limiting legislative power. Madison in particular said it was not enough to erect parchment barriers in the form of constitutional provisions stating that the legislative department must confine itself to lawmaking. It was further necessary to arrange the interior structure of government so that the constituent parts would limit each other. Personal motives of ambition and interest, Madison reasoned, when linked with a constitutional office would lead men to resist encroachments from other departments. These were the "auxiliary precautions" (supplementing accountability to the people) that would oblige government to control itself.[17] Madison was saying that pluralistic differences in opinion and interest are necessary to make the prescriptions of the text function effectively.

Nevertheless, American constitutionalism insists that the text of the fundamental law be given its due. Madison's auxiliary precautions are in fact rules written into the document. We may agree with an early writer who said political legitimacy consisted "not in the words and letters of the Constitution; but in the temper, habits, and the practices of the people." [18] But it is equally true that while the written text may not be sufficient, it is necessary to achieve the purposes of constitutionalism, or so it has seemed most of the time to Americans. In the Constitutional Convention Rufus King said he was aware that an express guarantee of states' rights, which he favored, would be regarded as "a mere paper security." But "if fundamental articles of compact are no sufficient defence against physical power," King declared, "neither will there be any safety against it if there be no compact." [19] The observation of Carl J. Friedrich is in point: "The 'constitution' tends to become a symbol, and its provisions become so many symbols in turn. It is this symbolic function of *words* which makes the constitution a political force." [20]

Reference to the constitutional text has been a fixed feature of American politics. Its significance and effect have been variously estimated. A long tradition of criticism holds that the document has failed to limit government, especially the federal government in relation to the states. Others argue that constant invoking of the Constitution has trivialized politics by translating policy debate into legalistic squabbles that discourage dealing with issues on their merits. Reformers seeking a more programmatic politics have lamented that the Constitution by fragmenting power prevents responsible party government. And still others contend that the Constitution has worked precisely as intended: to eliminate genuine political action and make citizens passive subjects interested in private economic pursuits rather than public happiness and civic virtue.

These criticisms misunderstand the nature of constitutional politics and hence the binding and configurative effect of the Constitution. If politics is concerned with the end or purpose of political community, the proper role of government, the relationship between the individual and society, then it is difficult to see how the Constitution can be said to have brought an end to politics or prevented political action. As an expression of modern liberalism, however, the Constitution did signify a change in the nature of politics. To elevate natural rights into constitutionally protected civil rights, as the Framers did, was to discourage an older politics based on the pursuit of glory, honor, conquest, and political or religious truth, as well as a newer ideological politics borne of modern revolution. The Framers' constitutionalism was a way of organizing political life that paradoxically placed certain principles, rules, and procedures beyond politics, according them the status of fundamental and paramount law. Premised on the idea that citizens could pursue private interests while preserving community, it was intended to limit the scope and intensity of politics, preventing a total absorption of society that would impose tyranny in the name of ruler, party, people, or community.

Starting in the 1790s and continuing with remarkable continuity to the present day, public policy advocates have charted courses of action with reference to the Constitution. Using constitutional language firmly embedded in political rhetoric, such as due process of law, equal protection of the law, separation of powers, etcetera, they invoke its principles and values to justify their goals, argue over the meaning of its requirements, and align themselves with its manifest tenor as explicated in constitutional law and legislation. Political leaders do this not because they are unwaveringly committed to a specific constitutional principle; in different circumstances they may advocate a different principle. The decisive fact is the high public status accorded the Constitution: policymakers and political actors know that the people take the Constitution seriously, regard it as supreme law, believe it is powerful because embodying sound principles of government and society's basic values, and, indeed, venerate it. Aware of this popular prejudice in favor of the Constitution, and seeking the approval of public opinion, political groups and individuals are constrained to act in conformity with its provisions. Thus the Constitution as binding political law shapes the form and content of policies and events.

The constraining effect of the Constitution might nevertheless be questioned, for it will appear obvious that while some requirements are unequivocally clear (for example, the minimal age of the president), many provisions are ambiguous and imprecise in meaning. Facing this fact, many scholars have concluded that there is no single true meaning of the Constitution, rather several possible readings of it none of which possesses exclusive legitimacy. Some contend there is no real Constitution against which arguments about it can be evaluated, only different assertions as to what the Constitution is at any given time, or what we want it to be. Expressed in the oft-cited statement that the Constitution is what the Supreme Court says it is, this view, carried to its logical conclusion, would mean that the American Constitution is a developing, evolving, growing thing that is changed by the actions of judges, lawmakers, and executive officers. In that case the Constitution ceases to be a fixed, prescriptive, paramount law.

Politically and historically realistic as this analysis appears, it has never been accepted as legitimate in constitutional theory or in the conduct of constitutional politics. From the standpoint of the people and their representatives, the Constitution, in both its procedural requirements and essential principles, has a true, fixed, ascertainable meaning. This popular understanding has existed from the beginning of constitutional politics in the debate over ratification, and it will probably continue until the popular belief that the Constitution as a document says what it means and means what it says, is eroded or superseded by a more sophisticated view of the nature of texts and political language. There is still a strong tendency in public opinion to think that written constitutions, in Jefferson's words, "furnish a text to which those who are watchful may again rally and recall the people: they fix too for the people principles for their political creed." [21]

The importance of the constitutional text in American government has been raised anew in recent years in the controversy over original-intent jurisprudence. Many legal scholars have expressed doubt about the wisdom and legitimacy of consulting the original intent of the Constitution or its authors in settling constitutional disputes. The words of the text, it is argued, apart from anything that its authors may have written or said about its meaning, must be considered as expressing the original intent. And the text must be read and understood according to the accepted meaning of words in the interpreter's own time, place, and historical situation. [22] Some dispose of original intent more directly by asserting that constitutional interpretation need not be bound by the constitutional text, but may be based on fundamental social values and conceptions of justice and moral progress that judges are specially qualified to understand and apply. Either way, the Constitution is assured of its status as a "living document" adaptable to changing social conditions.

Although there may be sound reasons for disconnecting constitutional politics from original intent, from a historical standpoint it seems clear that neither the Framers nor the people over 200 years have taken so narrow a view of the meaning and relevance of original intent. The purpose of making a fixed, objective constitution was to decide the most important basic questions about politics and government once and for all—or until the people changed their mind and amended the document. The idea was to bind future generations in fundamental ways. This purpose would be defeated if those who later ran the Constitution were free to substitute their own definitions of its key terms. Yet the fact remains that constitutional principles and rules have been reinterpreted and redefined, in apparent contradiction of the Framers' intent, in decisions and statutes that have been accepted as politically legitimate. The Supreme Court has in a sense acted as a continuing constitutional convention.

Although the Founding Fathers intended the Constitution to be permanent and binding, the language of the document cannot realistically or reasonably, in a categorical sense, be frozen in its eighteenth-century meaning. It is the Constitution's essential purposes, its fundamental principles and procedures that were not intended to change. The question to be asked is whether fundamental principles and values—the values of individual liberty, national union, distributed and balanced power, the consent of the people—can be defined in an authoritative text and thereby realized in public law and policy to the satisfaction of the political community. American political history generally provides an affirmative answer to this question. But it is important to remember that an overriding imperative in American politics, law, and government has been to reconcile public policy with constitutional principles and rules as embodied in the text, and in accordance with the Framers' intentions. Moreover, original intent has not been viewed in the narrowly positivistic manner urged by current critics of original-intent jurisprudence. The text was thought to have a definite and lasting meaning, and speeches, writings, and letters of the authors of the Constitution have always been thought pertinent to the task of elucidating its meaning. Whatever the practical effect of dismissal of the text and repudiation of original intent would be, such a step would alter the historic character of American constitutionalism.

The issue of original intent is pertinent to the larger question of the purpose of the Constitutional Bicentennial. What is it that we seek in study and commemoration of the Constitution? In a sense the purpose is the same that informs all historical investigation, namely, the desire to learn how things came to be as they are. Yet commemoration of the founding has implications different from other historical celebrations and remembrances because the Constitution is peculiarly and directly relevant to public life. Historical knowledge about it therefore acquires special political significance. Of course any number of politically interested purposes may be served by facts about the founding, including defense of the original-intent position in the contemporary debate over constitutional adjudication. Broadly conceived, however, the bicentennial may be viewed as having the fundamental purpose of clarifying and confirming the meaning of American nationality.

Diverse in ethnic, religious, cultural, and social characteristics, Americans were united in 1776 by the political principles set forth in the Declaration of Independence. Inchoate though it was, the new nation was defined by these principles — liberty, equality, government by consent, the pursuit of happiness as an individual right — which in various ways were written into the state constitutions. By establishing a republican government for the nation, the Framers of the Constitution confirmed these principles, completing the Revolution and making it permanent. Since then American politics has derived from and been shaped by the Constitution, and has periodically been renewed by popular movements resulting in electoral realignments that have included a return to the first principles of the founding as an essential element. After more than 200 years the United States may be old enough and sufficiently secure in its national identity to exist apart from the political principles that marked its appearance in the world. On the other hand, it may not be, in which case the nation still depends for its existence on preserving the principles of the founding. And when one reflects that a great deal of writing about the Constitution has been shaped by attitudes hostile to the Framers, such as those of the Beardian school, the possibility of gaining useful insight into the nature of our fundamental law through historical investigation warrants serious consideration.

Bicentennial activities will focus attention on the text of the Constitution, and this as a matter of course. (The American Political Science Association and the American Historical Association, in describing their conjoint Project '87 for commemorating the Constitution, state that its purpose is to promote "public understanding and appraisal of this unique document.") From a social science point of view the documentary character of the Constitution is easily exaggerated; the internalization of principles and values in officials and citizens is seen as the essential thing in achieving constitutionalist purposes. Looked at in this light, the American Constitution is not and never has been simply the text of the Constitution, but consists in addition in concepts not expressly written in the document, such as the rule of law or the presumption of innocence, as well as institutions and practices that derive from political sources, such as the party system. From the standpoint of public opinion, however, legitimacy in American government still appears dependent upon or derived from direct reference to or necessary inference from the text of the Constitution. Perhaps the text-based constitutional order, in a society as open, pluralistic, and dynamic as the United States, has been an obstacle to the kind of internalization of values that characterizes English political life. After 200 years Americans still seem to be constitutional fundamentalists in regarding the text and original intent as conclusive of legitimate authority. Or perhaps we should say that while a narrow, legalistic textualism has not been the dominant characteristic of constitutional government in America, when an issue is made of the constitutional text the people will insist on the indispensable documentary foundation of constitutionalism.

Understanding this attachment to the constitutional text has often been difficult for scholars and intellectuals, who tend to disparage it as Constitution worship. Perhaps reverence for the Constitution expresses not so much a naive literalism, however, as an awareness of the act of foundation as a source of authority. Considered in this perspective the constitutional text stands for the founding, and the principles written into the document symbolically represent values evident in the actions of the Framers. The founding required rational discussion, deliberation, compromise, and choice; consent, concurrence, and mutual pledging. These procedural values are embodied in constitutional provisions which require government under a fixed institutional structure and by deliberative processes that depend on compromise and concurrence, in accordance with substantive principles of natural rights, consent, and limited and balanced power.

We study the making of the Constitution for the same reason Americans have always turned to the founders: to strengthen and preserve our character as a free people, to continue on a course that has brought us prosperity as a nation. In a world in which governments that impose tyranny on their people are described by some as democracies, we study the founding in an effort to achieve the substance of liberty and natural rights that we believe it is the purpose of government to secure. Ultimately, commemoration of the Constitution expresses the belief that the principles, institutions, and procedures of free government cannot be maintained if divorced from the purpose, intention, and spirit of the Framers of our fundamental law.

NOTES

ORIGINS OF THE AMERICAN REVOLUTION: A CONSTITUTIONAL INTERPRETATION (pp. 36–53)

1. Traditionally, historians have referred to the protagonists in the constitutional contests between Britain and the colonies during the 1760s and 1770s as *Britons* who represented the *imperial* position, and as *colonists* or *Americans* those who represented the *colonial* position. This usage is misleading for two reasons. First, Briton was a designation claimed by colonists as well as those who lived in the home islands and ought not therefore to be used to refer to residents of either place. Second, strictly speaking, imperial connotes those things that pertain to an empire. To use imperial in the traditional way is thus to conflate two analytically distinct entities — Britain and the empire.

This point is not merely a pedantic quibble. On the contrary, the linguistic confusion it represents has contributed to an important misperception about the constitutional situation within the British Empire on the eve of the Revolution. Specifically, it has prevented all but a few scholars from understanding that, as many of the parties to the controversy eventually came to perceive and as this chapter maintains, the constitution of the British Empire was not isomorphic with — and therefore should not be conflated with — either the British constitution or the particular constitutions of each of the several colonies. There was not a single constitution that extended to all the entities within the wide extended polity of the British Empire. What was called the British constitution was the constitution of the home islands. Each colony, including Ireland, in turn had its own particular colonial constitution. The British Empire operated under still a third constitution, an imperial constitution composed of the bundle of practices and regulations by which relationships between Britain and the colonies were customarily regulated.

In an attempt to avoid this confusion, I began several years ago to employ "metropolis," "metropolitan," and other related terms to denote Britain and those people in both Britain and the colonies who were representative of the center of the empire, and "imperial" to refer only to those things that appertained to the empire as a whole. This terminology has of course been widely used by historians and other scholars of empires and center–periphery relations.

2. Bernard Bailyn, *The Ideological Origins of the American Revolution* (Cambridge, Mass., 1967), p. 203.

3. Peter S. Onuf, ed., *Maryland and the Empire, 1773: The Antilon–First Citizen Letters* (Baltimore, 1974), p. 29.

4. Onuf, *Maryland and the Empire*, p. 29; Barbara A. Black, "The Constitution of the Empire: The Case for the Colonists," *University of Pennsylvania Law Review,* 124 (1976):1203.

5. John Phillip Reid, "In a Defensive Rage: The Uses of the Mob, the Justification in Law, and the Coming of the American Revolution," *New York University Law Review*, 49 (1974):1063.

6. John Phillip Reid, *In a Defiant Stance: The Conditions of Law in Massachusetts Bay, the Irish Comparison, and the Coming of the American Revolution* (University Park, Pa., 1977), pp. 2, 161; Reid, "In a Defensive Rage," p. 1091; Hendrik B. Hartog, "Losing the World of the Massachusetts Whig," in Hartog, ed., *Law in the American Revolution and the Revolution in the Law* (New York, 1981), pp. 146–47, 152–53, 160.

THE DECLARATION OF INDEPENDENCE AS A CONSTITUTIONAL DOCUMENT (pp. 54–68)

1. George Anastaplo, "The Declaration of Independence," *Saint Louis University Law Journal*, 9 (1965):390–415, at 391–394. The declaration was used in civil pleadings, not in criminal cases. Anastaplo identifies seven component parts: title, venue, commencement, statement, conclusion, declaration (with pledge), and signatures. Anastaplo admits that "even the delineation of the parts, to say nothing of their meaning, is far from unambiguous and invites continuous reappraisal." Ross M. Lence, for example, asserts that the "general format of the Declaration consists of four easily identifiable parts": title and opening paragraph, summary of political principles, enumeration of grievances, and concluding paragraphs. Lence, "The American Declaration of Independence," in George J. and Scarlett G. Graham, eds., *Founding Principles of American Government*, rev. ed. (Chatham, N.J., 1984), pp. 29–59, at p. 31.

2. See Martin Diamond, "Origin of the Republic: The Formative Years," in Martin Diamond, Winston Mills Fisk, and Herbert Garfinkel, *The Democratic Republic: An Introduction to American National Government*, 2nd ed. (Chicago, 1970), pp. 6–7. (But compare the first edition [1966], pages 3–5.)

THE FIRST AMERICAN CONSTITUTIONS (pp. 69–81)

1. For a more detailed discussion of the process, see Donald S. Lutz, "From Covenant to Constitution in American Political Thought," *Publius*, 10 (1980):101–133.

2. Although not admitted as a new state until 1792, Vermont had already written and adopted two constitutions. Therefore, the 1793 document is its first constitution as a state of the Union but its third adopted constitution, and thus simultaneously a reconsideration of its earlier effort.

3. Based upon Willi Paul Adams, *The First American Constitutions* (Chapel Hill, N.C., 1980), esp. pp. 208–217; and Donald S. Lutz, *Popular Consent and Popular Control* (Baton Rouge, La., 1980), esp. chap. 4.

4. See Lee Soltow, "Wealth Inequality in the United States in 1798 and 1860," *The Review of Economics and Statistics*, 66 (1984):444–451; and Chilton Williamson, *American Suffrage: From Property to Democracy, 1760–1860* (Princeton, N.J., 1960).

5. See Jackson Turner Main, "Government by the People: The American Revolu-

tion and the Democratization of the Legislatures," *William and Mary Quarterly*, Third Series, 23 (1966):391–407.

THE ROAD TO PHILADELPHIA, 1781–1787 (pp. 98–111)

1. Madison to Monroe, March 14 and 19, 1786, in William T. Hutchinson, William M. E. Rachal, and Robert A. Rutland, eds., *The Papers of James Madison* (Chicago and Charlottesvile, 1962–   ), vol. VIII, pp. 497–498, 505–506.

2. Grayson to Madison, May 28, 1786, and Madison to Jefferson, August 12, 1786, ibid., vol. IX, pp. 64, 95–97.

3. Edward Carrington to Thomas Jefferson, June 9, 1787, in Julian P. Boyd et al., eds., *The Papers of Thomas Jefferson* (Princeton, 1950–   ), vol. XI, pp. 408–409.

A SYSTEM WITHOUT PRECEDENT: FEDERALISM IN THE AMERICAN CONSTITUTION (pp. 132–150)

1. The most thoughtful treatment of the significance of the names of these two groups is Herbert Storing's *What the Anti-Federalists Were For*, vol. I of *The Complete Anti-Federalist* (Chicago, 1981), pp. 9–14, 79 n.6.

2. The best account of the terminological issue is in Martin Diamond's "What the Framers Meant by 'Federalism,'" in Robert A. Goldwin, ed., *A Nation of States* (Chicago, 1974, 2nd ed.), pp. 26–28. While Diamond corrects the conventional wisdom in some important respects, I believe that wisdom to be nonetheless sounder on the whole than his own alternative interpretation of federalism in the Constitution.

3. Bernard Bailyn, *Ideological Origins of the American Revolution* (Cambridge, Mass., 1967), p. 208.

4. The classic formulation of this doctrine was by Thomas Jefferson in his "A Summary View of the Rights of British America"; John Adams in his "Novanglus" essays; and James Wilson in his *Considerations on the Nature and Extent of the Legislative Authority of the British Parliament*. The former two are reprinted in Merrill Jensen, ed., *Tracts of the American Revolution, 1763–1776* (Indianapolis, 1967). For a discussion of other sources of this theory, see Randolph G. Adams, *The Political Ideas of the American Revolution* (New York, 1939), chap. III.

5. For a more comprehensive analysis of the ends of the new federalism and its relation to unitary systems, see Michael P. Zuckert, "Federalisms and the Founding," *Review of Politics*, 48 (1986):166–210.

6. These points are well brought out by the State of Virginia in *Martin v. Hunter's Lessee*, 1 Wheaton 304 (1816) and *Cohens v. Virginia*, 6 Wheaton 264 (1821).

7. See Michael P. Zuckert, "Federalisms," for a fuller discussion of the extended republic theme. An indispensable discussion is Martin Diamond's statement in "The Federalist" in *History of Political Philosophy*, eds. Leo Strauss and Joseph Cropsey (Chicago, 1964); see also David Epstein, *The Political Theory of the Federalist* (Chicago, 1984).

8. Cf. Michael P. Zuckert, "Congressional Power under the Fourteenth Amendment: The Original Understanding of Section Five," *Constitutional Commentary*, vol. 3, no. 2 (Summer 1986), pp. 123ff.

9. John W. Burgess, *Political Science and Comparative Constitutional Law* (Boston, 1891), chap. III.

THE CONSTITUTION AND THE SEPARATION OF POWERS
(pp. 151–166)

1. *The Records of the Federal Convention of 1787*, Farrand, ed. (New Haven: 1966), II. 56.

2. *American Political Writings During the Founding Era, 1760–1805* Hyneman and Lutz, eds. (Indianapolis: 1983), I. 521.

3. Everyone agrees, of course, that the idea of the separation of powers is at least as old as Aristotle's *Politics*. Aristotle separated government into its deliberative, magistracy, and judicial functions. But there was no indication in Aristotle that this separation of the *elements* of government was to be the source of any limitation on the *power* of government. The idea of a separation of state and society—in which society could make claims and limitations upon government in the name of the rights and liberties of the people—was alien to Aristotle. For Aristotle, the *politeuma* was always identical to the *politeia*. See *Politics*, Bk. IV, ch. 14, 1296b16 ff.

4. M. J. C. Vile, *Constitutionalism and the Separation of Powers* (Oxford: 1967) p. 125 (emphasis in original); see also pp. 122, 134.

5. W. B. Gwyn, *The Meaning of the Separation of Powers* (New Orleans: 1965), p. 27: "the earliest proponents of the separation of powers were republicans. . . ."

6. As late as 1776, a writer in Philadelphia remarked that "Government is generally distinguished into three parts, Executive, Legislative and Judicial; but this is more a distinction of words than things . . . the distinction is perplexing, and however we may refine and define, there is no more than two powers in any government, viz. the power to make laws, and the power to execute them; for the judicial power is only a branch of the executive." *American Political Writings During the Founding Era, 1760–1805*, I, 387.

7. Thomas Pangle, *Montesquieu's Philosophy of Liberalism* (Chicago: 1973), p. 125.

8. Martin Diamond, "The Separation of Powers and the Mixed Regime," *Publius* 8 (Summer, 1978), p. 36.

9. *The Creation of the Presidency*, p. 34; 41, 42–3. "Whatever the theory, there was legislative omnipotence. . . . The legislature was sovereign."

10. *The Political Theory of the Federalist* (Chicago, 1984), p. 192.

11. See Erler, "The Problem of the Public Good in *The Federalist*," 13 *Polity* (Summer, 1981), p. 649.

THE WITCH AT THE CHRISTENING: SLAVERY AND THE CONSTITUTION'S ORIGINS (pp. 167–184)

1. John Hope Franklin, *From Slavery to Freedom: A History of Negro Americans* (New York, 1974), p. 98.

2. William M. Wiecek, "The Blessings of Liberty: Slavery in the American Constitu-

tional Order," in Robert A. Goldwin et al., eds., *The Constitution, Slavery, and Its Aftermath* (forthcoming publication of the American Enterprise Institute.)

3. Don E. Fehrenbacher, *The Dred Scott Case: Its Significance in American Law and Politics* (New York, 1978), p. 27.

4. A. Leon Higginbotham, Jr., *In the Matter of Color: Race and the American Legal Process: The Colonial Period* (New York, 1978), p. 391.

5. William J. Wood, "The Illegal Beginning of American Negro Slavery," *American Bar Association Journal*, 56 (1970):45–49.

6. William B. Allen, "A New Birth of Freedom: Freedom or Derailment," in Goldwin, et al. *Constitution, Slavery, and Its Aftermath*.

7. Bernard Bailyn, *The Ideological Origins of the American Revolution* (Cambridge, Mass., 1967), pp. 239, 245.

8. Benjamin Quarles, "The Revolutionary War as a Black Declaration of Independence," in Ira Berlin et al., eds., *Slavery and Freedom in the Age of the American Revolution* (Charlottesville, 1983), p. 301.

9. Staughton Lynd, "The Abolitionist Critique of the United States Constitution," in Lynd, *Class Conflict, Slavery, and the United States Constitution* (Indianapolis, 1967), p. 167.

10. William W. Freehling, "The Founding Fathers and Slavery," *American Historical Review*, 77 (1972):81–93 at 84.

CONGRESS DURING THE CONVENTION AND RATIFICATION (pp. 185–208)

1. John Locke, *Two Treatises of Government* (New York: New American Library, 1965), *Second Treatise*, Chapter XI, p. 401.

2. Herbert J. Storing, *The Complete Anti-Federalist* (Chicago: University of Chicago Press, 1981), 7 vols. See Volume 1, *What the Anti-Federalists Were For*, pp. 28–37.

3. See Calvin Jillson, "The Representation Question in the Federal Convention of 1787: Madison's Virginia Plan and Its Opponents," *Congressional Studies*, Vol. 8 (1981), pp. 21–41, for an analysis of shifting cleavages at the convention over this issue.

4. Jack N. Rakove, *The Meanings of National Politics: An Interpretive History of the Continental Congress* (Baltimore: Johns Hopkins University Press, 1979), p. 337.

5. C. C. Pinckney of South Carolina brought population estimates to the convention that apparently were used by convention delegates. According to his estimates, the states of Delaware, Maryland, Virginia, North Carolina, South Carolina, and Georgia had populations of 1,323,000 counting all slaves fully, and the states of New Hampshire, Massachusetts, Rhode Island, Connecticut, New York, New Jersey, and Pennsylvania had a combined population of 1,453,000. The 1790 census showed the six leading slave states with a population of 1,851,919 including slaves, the northern states with 1,786,075. Winton U. Solberg, *The Federal Convention and the Formation of the Union of the American States* (Indianapolis: Bobbs-Merrill, 1958), Appendix II, Population Estimates, pp. 407–409.

6. In the legislative debates before South Carolina's ratifying convention, Edward Rutledge—the former governor, not the Constitutional Convention's John

Rutledge—said: "[T]his [census] clause was highly favorable to the southern inter-est. Several of the Northern States were already full of people: it was otherwise with us; the migrations to the south were immense, and we should in the course of a few years, rise high in our representation, while other states would keep their present position." Jonathan Elliot, ed. *The Debates of the Several State Conventions on the Adoption of the Federal Constitution as Recommended by the General Convention at Philadelphia in 1787,* 5 vols., 2nd ed. (New York, 1888), vol. IV, pp. 276–277. General C. C. Pinckney, whose population estimates were used by many delegates in Philadelphia, echoed Rutledge the next day, down to the statement that "the Eastern states are full." Both comments about the land being full were thoroughly agricultural in their assumptions. It is doubtful that "commercial republic" conven-tion delegates from the North would have agreed. If the delegates had different private expectations about future population trends, that would help explain the success of the three-fifths clause as a convention compromise. In any case, the dynamics of the commercial republic did work to undermine southern expectations. States with substantial slave populations started out with 46 percent of all House seats from 1789 until 1810, but dropped to 41 percent after the 1820 census and 34 percent after 1860. That is why the Senate, where the South was better represented, became the focal point for sectional politics by 1820.

7. Rakove, *Beginnings,* pp. 220–224.

8. Max Farrand, *The Framing of the Constitution of the United States* (New Haven: Yale University Press, 1913), p. 112. Two other ideas for electing senators were put forward during the convention. First, on June 18, Alexander Hamilton presented his own plan to the convention. It included election of the Senate for life terms by special electors chosen by the people. Hamilton may have taken some of his idea from the Maryland Constitution of 1776, which used two special electors per county to select senators for five-year terms. Maryland's Senate was praised in *The Federal-ist* #63, and by Randolph and Madison in the Federal Convention. Second, on July 2, Gouverneur Morris suggested executive appointment for life. Delaware's George Read had proposed executive appointment on June 7 and supported life terms on June 25. No one seconded Read on executive appointment; Robert Morris did on life terms.

9. Roy Swanstrom, *The United States Senate, 1787–1801: A Dissertation on the First Fourteen Years of the Upper Legislative Body,* reprinted by the U.S. Senate, 99th Congress, First Session, S. Doc. 99–19, Oct. 23, 1985, p. 20.

10. Swanstrom, *The United States Senate, 1787–1801,* p. 22.

11. William H. Riker, "The Senate and American Federalism," *American Political Science Review,* vol. 49 (1955):452–469. See also George H. Haynes, *The Senate of the United States: Its History and Practice* (New York: Russell & Russell, 1960), 2 vols., vol. II, pp. 1025–1034.

12. Rakove, *Beginnings,* p. 233.

THE PRESIDENCY AND THE EXECUTIVE POWER
(pp. 209–221)

1. Clinton Rossiter, *Seedtime of the Republic* (New York, 1953), p. 23.

2. Clinton Rossiter, *The American Presidency* (New York, 1960), p. 13.

3. Message to Congress, July 4, 1861, in Roy P. Basler, ed., *The Collected Works of Abraham Lincoln* (New Brunswick, N.J., 1953), vol. 4, p. 340.

THE COURTS AND THE JUDICIAL POWER (pp. 222–241)

1. Robert Green McCloskey, ed., *The Works of James Wilson* (Cambridge, Mass., 1967), p. 290.

2. Herbert J. Storing, "The Federal Convention of 1787," in Ralph A. Rossum and Gary L. McDowell, eds., *The American Founding: Politics, Statesmanship and the Constitution* (Port Washington, N.Y., 1981), p. 24.

3. Sir William Blackstone, *Commentaries on the Laws of England*, vol. 1, p. 55.

4. Letter to Thomas Jefferson, October 17, 1788, in *The Writings of James Madison*, 9 vols., ed. Gaillard Hunt (New York, 1904), vol. 5, pp. 271–275.

5. See Martin Diamond, "*The Federalist* on Federalism: 'Neither a National nor a Federal Constitution, But a Composition of Both,'" *Yale Law Journal*, 86 (1977):1273–1285, for an excellent discussion of how federal elements are mixed into the general government.

6. See especially John Agresto, *The Supreme Court and Constitutional Democracy* (Ithaca, N.Y., 1984).

7. Leonard W. Levy, "Judicial Review, History, and Democracy," in *Judicial Review and the Supreme Court*, ed. Leonard W. Levy (New York, 1967), pp. 8–10.

8. Levy, "Judicial Review, History, and Democracy," p. 6.

9. Max Farrand, ed., *The Records of the Federal Convention of 1787*, 4 vols. (New Haven, Conn., 1937), vol. 2, p. 430. While Madison did declare on July 23 that "a law violating a constitution established by the people themselves, would be considered by the Judges as null and void," and while defenders of judicial review cite this passage to support their contention that the Framers intended the Court to exercise the power of judicial review, Madison was referring only to the need, given the supremacy clause, for state judges to declare unconstitutional a state act in violation of the federal Constitution. See Farrand, *Records*, vol. 2, p. 93.

10. "Remarks on Mr. Jefferson's Draft of a Constitution," *The Writings of James Madison*, vol. V, p. 294.

11. *The Federalist* #80, p. 541. See Ralph A. Rossum, "Congress, the Constitution, and the Appellate Jurisdiction of the Supreme Court: The Letter and the Spirit of the Exceptions Clause," *William and Mary Law Review*, 24 (1983):385–428.

12. See, especially, Gary L. McDowell, "Were the Anti-Federalists Right?" *Publius*, 12 (1982):99–108.

13. See Charles Warren, "Legislative and Judicial Attacks on the Supreme Court of the United States: A History of the Twenty-Fifth Section of the Judiciary Act," *American Law Review*, 47 (1913):1–34, 161–189.

WAR POWERS, TREATIES, AND THE CONSTITUTION (pp. 242–258)

1. John Jay, *An Address to the People of the State of New York* (1788), reprinted in *Pamphlets on the Constitution of the United States . . . 1787–1788*, ed. Paul L. Ford (Brooklyn, N.Y., 1888), p. 71.

2. Quoted in Frederick W. Marks, *Independence on Trial: Foreign Affairs and the Making of the Constitution* (Baton Rouge, La., 1973), p. 68.

3. "The Address and Reasons of Dissent . . . ," in *The Documentary History of the Ratification of the Constitution,* vol. II, *Ratification of the Constitution by the States: Pennsylvania,* ed. Merrill Jensen (Madison, Wisc., 1976), pp. 637–638.

4. *Selective Draft Law Cases,* 245 U.S. 366, at 377–378 (1918).

5. Quoted in Charles A. Lofgren, "Compulsory Military Service under the Constitution: The Original Understanding," in Lofgren, *"Government from Reflection and Choice": Constitutional Essays on War, Foreign Relations, and Federalism* (New York, 1986), p. 42.

6. Jensen, ed., *Documentary History . . . Pennsylvania,* p. 583; *Debates in the Several State Conventions on the Adoption of the Federal Constitution,* 2nd ed., ed. Jonathan Elliot (New York, 1888), vol. II, p. 284.

7. Arthur Bestor, "Respective Roles of the Senate and President in the Making and Abrogation of Treaties: The Original Intent of the Framers of the Constitution Historically Examined," *Washington Law Review,* 55 (1979):93.

8. Jack N. Rakove, "Solving a Constitutional Puzzle: The Treaty-Making Clause as a Case Study," *Perspectives in American History,* New Series, I (1984):254.

9. 252 U.S. 416, at 433.

10. "Letters from the Federal Farmer to the Republican," reprinted in Ford, ed., *Pamphlets on the Constitution,* p. 312; Elliot, ed., *Debates,* vol. III, p. 507.

THE CONSTITUTION: AN ECONOMIC DOCUMENT?
(pp. 259–270)

1. Richard Hofstadter, *The Progressive Historians: Turner, Beard, Parrington* (New York, 1968), p. 344; John Diggins, "Power and Authority in American History: The Case of Charles A. Beard and His Critics," *American Historical Review,* 86 (1981):701.

2. Trevor Colbourn, ed., *Fame and the Founding Fathers* (New York, 1974), p. 86.

3. Charles A. Beard, *An Economic Interpretation of the Constitution* (New York, 1935 edition), pp. 28, 324.

4. Ibid., p. 154.

5. Ibid., p. 324.

6. Ibid., p. 325.

7. Ibid., pp. 17–18, 73.

8. Richard Hildreth, *History of the United States,* 6 vols. (New York, 1849–1852), III, p. 535.

9. Beard, *An Economic Interpretation,* p. 257.

10. David Ramsay, *History of the United States* (Philadelphia, 1808), vol. III, (3 vols) pp. 24–25.

11. Woodrow Wilson, *Division and Reunion* (New York, 1893), pp. 12–13; Henry J. Ford, *The Rise and Growth of American Politics* (New York, 1898), p. 59.

12. Quoted in Stanley Elkins and Eric McKitrick, *The Founding Fathers: Young Men of the Revolution* (Washington, D.C., 1962), p. 8.

13. J. Allen Smith, *The Spirit of American Government* (New York, 1907), pp. 198–199.

14. Beard, *An Economic Interpretation*, p. 22.

15. Ibid., p. 35.

16. Ibid., p. 151.

17. Ibid., p. xvi.

18. Elkins and McKitrick, *Founding Fathers*, p. 2.

19. Robert Brown, *Charles Beard and the Constitution* (Princeton, N.J., 1956), p. 89.

20. Forrest McDonald, *We the People: The Economic Origins of the Constitution* (Chicago, 1958), p. 110.

21. Ibid., pp. 231, 252–254, 268, 310, 321, 357.

22. Lee Benson, *Turner and Beard: American Historical Writing Reconsidered* (Glencoe, 111, 1960), pp. 127, 139–144.

23. Jackson Turner Main, "Charles Beard and the Constitution: A Critical Review of Forrest McDonald's *We the People*," *William and Mary Quarterly*, 17 (1960):86–110.

24. McDonald, *We the People*, p. 401.

25. Benson, *Turner and Beard*, p. 215.

26. Douglass Adair, "That Politics May Be Reduced to a Science," in Colbourne, ed., *Fame and the Founding Fathers*, p. 97.

27. Douglass Adair, "Experience Must Be Our Only Guide," ibid., p. 123.

28. Martin Diamond, "Democracy and *The Federalist*: A Reconsideration of the Framers' Intent," *American Political Science Review*, 52 (1959):60, at 67–68; Diamond, *The Founding of the Democratic Republic* (reprint ed., Itasca, Ill., 1981), pp. 7–8, 65.

29. John Roche, "The Founding Fathers: A Reform Caucus in Action," *American Political Science Review*, 55 (1981):799, 816.

30. Clinton Rossiter, *1787: The Grand Convention* (New York, 1966), p. 15; Richard B. Morris, *The American Revolution Reconsidered* (New York: 1967), p. 161.

31. Rossiter, *Grand Convention*, pp. 18, 20, 156.

32. Paul Eidelberg, *The Philosophy of the American Constitution* (New York, 1968), pp. 146–147, 153, 208–209, 259–260.

33. Gordon Wood, *The Creation of the American Republic* (Chapel Hill, N.C., 1969), pp. 462, 510–513, 615.

34. Main, review of *The Creation of the American Republic*, *William and Mary Quarterly*, 26 (1969):604–607.

35. Gordon Wood, ed., *The Confederation and the Constitution: The Critical Issues* (Boston, 1973), p. xiv.

36. Diggins, "Power and Authority."

37. Pope McCorkle, "The Historian as Intellectual: Charles Beard and the Constitution Reconsidered," *American Journal of Legal History*, 28 (1984):318, 354.

38. Elkins and McKitrick, *Founding Fathers*, p. 2.

39. Robert Brown, *Reinterpretation of the Formation of the American Constitution* (Boston, 1963), p. 56.

THE CASE AGAINST RATIFICATION: ANTI-FEDERALIST CONSTITUTIONAL THOUGHT (pp. 271–291)

1. See Cecilia Kenyon's introductory essay on "The Political Thought of the Anti-Federalists," in *The Antifederalists*, ed. Kenyon (Indianapolis, 1966), concluding observations, pp. XCV–CVI. Parts of this chapter were originally published as "Men of Little Faith: The Anti-Federalists on the Nature of Representative Government," in *William and Mary Quarterly*, Third Series, 12 (1955):3–55.

2. See Gordon Wood, *The Creation of the American Republic* (Chapel Hill, N.C., 1969), pp. 471–564, 606–615, on the last point.

3. Herbert J. Storing, *The Complete Anti-Federalist*, 7 vols. (Chicago, 1981). Volume 1 contains Storing's essay on the Anti-Federalists' political thought, and it has been separately published in a paperback, entitled, *What the Anti-Federalists Were For* (Chicago, 1981). Storing's edition of the *Anti-Federalist* is also available in a one-volume abridgment, entitled *The Anti-Federalist*, selected by Murray Dry (Chicago, 1985). All citations to *Anti-Federalists* will be to *The Complete Anti-Federalist*. In addition to the Roman numeral, a three-part number is used to identify the volume, entry in the volume, and paragraph, or group of paragraphs. The same citation is used in the abridgment.

4. Maryland Farmer advocated an imitation of the Swiss cantons, where the citizens themselves vote on the laws (V, 5.1.74–81).

5. II, 2.9.24.

6. VI, 2.8.79.

7. Storing, *What the Anti-Federalists Were For*, p. 16.

8. II, 2.8.15.

9. XVI, 2.8.190.

10. XVI, 2.8.196.

11. Brutus, I, 2.9.16.

12. III, 2.6.19.

13. VII, 2.8.97.

14. *Ibid.*

15. 6.12.17; also in Jonathan Elliot, ed., *The Debates in the Several State Conventions on the Adoption of the Federal Constitution* (Philadelphia, 1891), vol. II, p. 248; hereinafter cited as *Elliot*.

16. *Elliot* II, p. 257.

17. *Elliot* III, pp. 164, 167.

18. 5.16.1.

19. 2.4.114; see also Max Farrand, ed., *The Records of the Federal Convention of 1787*, 4 vols. (New Haven, Conn., 1966), vol. I, pp. 437–438 (June 27). Hereinafter cited as *Farrand*.

20. *Elliot* II, p. 289; see also Federal Farmer, XI, 2.8.147.

21. 5.14.33–34.

22. I, 2.7.23.

23. *Farrand* II, 94 (July 23).

24. *Elliot* II, 259, 243.

25. III, 2.8.25–6; XII, 2.8.151–154; see also Massachusetts Convention, *Elliot* II, 22 (Pierce).

26. XII, 2.8.150; see also Amos Singletary in the Massachusetts Convention, *Elliot* II, 44.

27. I, 2.9.5–6.

28. See *Federalist* 23, quoted by Brutus at VI, 2.9.79.

29. VI, 2.9.80; see also Federal Farmer XVII, 2.8.208.

30. Federal Farmer III, 2.8.36; Brutus V, 2.9.63.

31. *Elliot,* II, 177, XVII, 2.8.209.

32. Brutus VIII, 2.9.125–126; Federal Farmer III, 2.8.39; XVIII, 2.8.220.

33. 2.4.60; XVIII, 2.8.217.

34. VIII, 2.9.94–5.

35. XVIII, 2.8.221

36. *Federalist* 68; III, 2.8.29; XIV, 2.8.177.

37. IV, 2.6.30.

38. XIV, 2.8.178; 5.21.26.

39. XIV, 2.8.182; 5.21.22.

40. XIII, 2.8.170.

41. Mason, 2.2.10; XI, 2.8.147.

42. 5.16.7; 2.2.9; I, 2.7.23; VII, 2.6.45.

43. XI, 2.9.136–137; 2.9.130.

44. XII, 2.9.146, 150.

45. See Brutus, XIV, 2.9.170–172.

46. XIV, 2.9.183.

47. XVI, 2.8.196.

48. See Michael Sandel's introduction to a collection which he edited, *Liberalism and its Critics* (New York, 1984).

THE CASE FOR RATIFICATION: FEDERALIST CONSTITUTIONAL THOUGHT (pp. 292–304)

1. *The Works of James Wilson,* edited by Robert Green McCloskey, Cambridge, Massachusetts, 1967, volume 2, p. 765.

2. James Madison, in *Commentaries on the Constitution: Public and Private,* edited by John P. Kaminski and Gaspare J. Saladino, Madison, Wisconsin, 1981–   , volume 1, p. 512.

3. "Brutus," in *Commentaries,* volume 3, p. 396.

4. *Commentaries,* volume 2, p. 71.

5. *The Federalist* #15.

6. William Davie, in *Debates in the Several State Conventions,* edited by Jonathon

Elliot, second edition, Philadelphia, 1836, volume 4, p. 17; Francis Corbin, in *Debates*, volume 3, p. 105.

7. *Boston Gazette*, 15 October 1787, in *Commentaries*, volume 1, pp. 382–83.

8. Wilson, in *The Documentary History of the Ratification of the Constitution*, edited by Merrill Jensen and Robert Becker, Madison, Wisconsin, 1976–   , volume 2, p. 581.

9. Madison, in *Debates*, volume 3, p. 249.

10. George Nicholas, in *Debates*, volume 3, p. 358.

11. *The Federalist* #2.

12. John Marshall, in *Debates*, volume 3, p. 420.

13. Nicholas, in *Debates*, volume 3, p. 239.

14. *Newburyport Essex Journal*, 10 October 1787, in *Commentaries*, volume 1, p. 361.

15. *The Federalist* #23.

16. Ibid., #16.

17. Robert Livingston, in *Debates*, volume 2, p. 342.

18. *The Federalist* #70.

19. Ibid., #62.

20. *Debates*, volume 2, p. 302.

21. *The Federalist* #57.

22. Ibid., #4, #53, #62, #63, #72.

23. Ibid., #70.

24. Ibid., #6; *Works of Wilson*, volume 2, p. 766.

25. "New England," in *Commentaries*, volume 3, pp. 84–85.

26. Alexander Hamilton, in *Debates*, volume 2, p. 303.

27. *The Federalist* #37, #51, #10.

28. Ibid.

29. Madison, in *Debates*, volume 3, p. 538.

30. *The Federalist* #10.

31. Hamilton, in *Debates*, volume 2, p. 230.

32. Corbin, in *Debates*, volume 3, p. 107.

33. Peletiah Webster, quoted in Herbert Storing, "The Other Federalist Papers," *The Political Science Reviewer*, volume 6, Fall 1976, pp. 218–19.

34. "A Freeman," in *Commentaries*, volume 3, p. 510.

35. *Commentaries*, volume 1, p. 339.

36. Madison, in *Debates*, volume 3, p. 451.

37. Ibid., p. 450.

38. "Marcus," in *Pamphlets on the Constitution of the United States*, edited by Paul L. Ford, Brooklyn, 1888, p. 360.

39. *The Federalist* #23; emphasis in original.

40. Ibid., #34.

41. "A Citizen of Philadelphia," in *Commentaries*, volume 1, p. 301.

42. "A Countryman," quoted in Storing, p. 227.

43. *The Federalist* #23.

44. Ibid., #28.

45. *Commentaries*, volume 2, p. 122.

46. *The Federalist* #63, emphasis in original.

47. Wilson, in *Documentary History*, volume 2, p. 489.

48. Hamilton, in *Debates*, volume 2, p. 252.

49. Ibid., p. 254.

50. *The Federalist* #25.

51. Ibid., #51.

52. Madison, in *Debates*, volume 3, p. 536.

53. *The Federalist* #51.

54. *Pennsylvania Gazette*, 26 September 1787, in *Commentaries*, volume 1, p. 254.

55. Benjamin Rush, in *Commentaries*, No. 680 (typescript, publication forthcoming).

56. Richard Law, in *Commentaries*, volume 3, p. 316.

57. *The Federalist* #51.

58. Ibid., #37.

59. *Northampton Hampshire Gazette*, 31 October 1787, in *Commentaries*, volume 1, p. 517.

60. *The Federalist* #8, #10, #9.

61. *Pennsylvania Gazette*, 2 April 1788, in *Commentaries*, No. 658 (typescript).

62. *The Federalist* #10.

FRAMING AND RATIFYING THE FIRST TEN AMENDMENTS (pp. 305–316)

1. Max Farrand, ed., *Records of the Federal Convention*, 4 vols. (New Haven, Conn., 1966), vol. 2, pp. 587–588; Madison to Philip Mazzei, Oct. 8, 1788, William T. Hutchinson et al., eds. *The Papers of James Madison*, 16 vols. to date (Chicago and Charlottesville, 1962–   ), vol. 11, p. 278.

2. Washington to Madison, Oct. 10, 1787, *Madison Papers*, vol. 10, p. 190.

3. Jefferson to Madison, Dec. 20, 1787, ibid., vol. 10, p. 336.

4. Madison to George Nicholas, April 8, 1788, ibid., vol. 11, p. 12; Madison to Edmund Randolph, April 10, 1788, ibid., vol. 11, p. 19.

5. *The Federalist*, ed. Jacob E. Cooke (Middletown, Conn., 1961), p. 579.

6. Speech of June 25, 1788, *Madison Papers*, vol. 11, p. 177.

7. Madison to Jefferson, Oct. 17, 1788, ibid., vol. 11, pp. 297–298.

8. Burgess Ball to Madison, Dec. 8, 1788, ibid., vol. 11, p. 385; Madison to George Eve, Jan. 2, 1789, ibid., vol. 11, p. 408; "To a Resident of Spottsylvania County" [Jan. 27, 1789], ibid., vol. 11, pp. 428–429.

9. Jefferson to Madison, March 15, 1789, ibid., vol. 12, pp. 13–14.

10. *Annals of Congress,* 1st Cong., 1st Sess., pp. 441–444.

11. *Madison Papers,* vol. 12, pp. 196–209.

12. Madison to Randolph, June 15, 1789, ibid., vol. 12, p. 219.

13. Tench Coxe to Madison, June 18, 1789, ibid., vol. 12, p. 239; William R. Davie to Madison, June 10, 1789, ibid., vol. 12, pp. 210–211.

14. Fisher Ames to Timothy Dwight, June 11, 1789, Seth Ames, ed., *Works of Fisher Ames,* 2 vols. (Boston, 1854), vol. 1, p. 53.

15. *Annals of Congress,* 1st Cong., 1st Sess., p. 686.

16. Ibid., p. 759.

17. Madison to Randolph, Aug. 21, 1789, *Madison Papers,* vol. 12, p. 348; Madison to White, Aug. 24, 1789, ibid., vol. 12, pp. 352–353.

18. Lee to Charles Lee, Aug. 28, 1789, James C. Ballagh, ed., *Letters of Richard Henry Lee,* 2 vols. (New York, 1911–1914), vol. 2, p. 499.

19. Mason to Samuel Griffin, Sept. 8, 1789, Robert A. Rutland, *Papers of George Mason,* 3 vols. (Chapel Hill, 1970), vol. 3, pp. 1172.

20. Lee to Francis Lightfoot Lee, Sept. 13, 1789, *Lee Papers,* vol. 2, p. 500; Grayson to Henry, Sept. 29, 1789, William Wirt Henry, *Life and Correspondence of Patrick Henry,* 3 vols. (New York, 1891), vol. 3, p. 406.

21. *Documentary History of the Constitution,* 5 vols. (Washington, D.C., 1894–1905), vol. 5, pp. 217–221.

22. Madison to Washington, Jan. 4, 1790, *Madison Papers,* vol. 23, p. 467.

ORGANIZING THE NEW NATIONAL GOVERNMENT
(pp. 317–332)

1. Lost diary quoted in Douglas Southall Freeman, *George Washington: A Biography,* 7 vols. (New York, 1948–1957), vol. VI, p. 166.

2. Quoted in Jacob E. Cooke, *Tench Coxe and the Early Republic* (Chapel Hill, N.C., 1978), p. 234.

3. Quoted in David M. Matteson, *The Organization of the Government under the Constitution* (New York, 1970), p. 222.

4. Henry P. Johnson, ed., *The Correspondence and Public Papers of John Jay,* 4 vols. (New York, 1893), vol. III, p. 488.

5. Quoted in Matteson, *Organization of the Government,* p. 290.

6. Jacob E. Cooke, "The Compromise of 1790," *William and Mary Quarterly,* 3rd Series, 27 (1970):545.

7. Dumas Malone, *Jefferson and His Time,* 6 vols. (Boston, 1948–1981), vol. II, p. 339.

8. Dumas Malone, "Hamilton on Balance," reprinted in Jacob E. Cooke, ed., *Alexander Hamilton: A Profile* (New York, 1982), p. 103.

9. Harold C. Syrett et al., *The Papers of Alexander Hamilton,* 26 vols. (New York, 1962–1979), vol. VIII, p. 91.

10. Ibid., p. 98.

11. Ibid., p. 107.

12. John C. Fitzpatrick, ed., *The Writings of George Washington,* 39 vols. (Washington, D.C., 1931–1944), vol. XXXII, p. 430.

13. "Pacificus," No. VII, *Hamilton Papers,* vol. XV, p. 135.

14. "Pacificus," No. I, ibid., vol. XV, p. 39.

15. Thomas Jefferson to James Madison, July 7, 1793. Paul Leicester Ford, ed., *The Works of Thomas Jefferson,* 10 vols. (New York, 1892–1899), vol. VI, pp. 338–339.

16. Madison's essays were published between August 24 and September 18, 1793, and are printed in Gaillard Hunt, ed., *Writings of James Madison,* 10 vols. (New York, 1900–1910), vol. VI, pp. 133–188.

17. See "Pacificus," No. I, *Hamilton Papers,* vol. XV, p. 42.

18. Quoted in James T. Flexner, *Washington the Indispensable Man* (Boston, 1974), p. 276.

19. Joseph Charles, *Origins of the American Party System* (New York, 1961), pp. 101–102.

20. Hamilton to Rufus King, April 15, 1796, *Hamilton Papers,* vol. XX, pp. 112–115.

21. Freeman, *Washington,* vol. VII, p. 319.

22. *Hamilton Papers,* vol. XX, pp. 277, 278.

23. Washington to Hamilton, May 16, 1796, ibid., vol. XX, pp. 174–178.

CONSTITUTIONALISM AND THE AMERICAN FOUNDING
(pp. 333–354)

1. Quoted in Charles H. McIlwain, *Constitutionalism: Ancient and Modern* (Ithaca, 1940; rev. ed., 1947), pp. 126–127, and Edward S. Corwin, *The "Higher Law" Background of American Constitutional Law* (New York, 1955), p. 44.

2. Quoted in McIlwain, *Constitutionalism,* p. 3.

3. Daniel J. Boorstin, *The Mysterious Science of the Law* (Boston, 1958), pp. 155–159.

4. J. W. Gough, *Fundamental Law in English Constitutional History* (Oxford, 1955), pp. 174–191.

5. Donald S. Lutz, "From Covenant to Constitution in American Political Thought," *Publius,* 10 (Fall 1980):101–133.

6. Daniel Shute, *An Election Sermon* (1768), in Charles S. Hyneman and Donald S. Lutz, eds., *American Political Writings during the Founding Era, 1760–1805,* 2 vols. (Indianapolis, 1983), vol. I, p. 117.

7. Quoted in Fletcher M. Green, *Constitutional Development in the South Atlantic States, 1776–1860* (New York, 1966), p. 54.

8. Benjamin Fletcher Wright, *Consensus and Continuity, 1776–1787* (Boston, 1958), p. 10.

9. Walton H. Hamilton, "Constitutionalism," *Encyclopedia of the Social Sciences* (New York, 1937), vol. III, p. 255; Aaron Wildavsky, "Why Amending the Constitution Is Essential to Achieving Self-Control Through Self-Limitation of Expenditure," *The Bureaucrat,* 9 (Spring 1980):53.

10. Lutz, "From Covenant to Constitution"; Lutz, "The Purposes of American State Constitutions," *Publius*, 12 (Winter 1982):27–44.

11. Henry Steele Commager, ed., *Documents of American History* (New York, 1963), p. 66.

12. Thomas Tucker, *Conciliatory Hints, Attempting by a Fair State of Matters, to Remove Party Prejudice*, in Hyneman and Lutz, eds., *American Political Writings*, vol. I, p. 620.

13. Max Farrand, ed., *The Records of the Federal Convention of 1787*, 4 vols. (New Haven, 1911–1937), vol. II, p. 137.

14. *The Federalist*, ed. Edward Mead Earle (New York, 1938), p. 62.

15. Ibid., p. 3.

16. Observing that the purpose of constitutional government is to prevent tyranny, and that the exact definition of where tyranny begins is difficult to establish, M. J. C. Vile writes: "There are inescapable value-judgments here, and we must accept that a discussion of constitutionalism can only begin by pointing to certain specific examples of societies which are asserted to be non-tyrannical, and to attempt to elucidate their major characteristics," *Constitutionalism and the Separation of Powers* (New York, 1967), p. 308.

17. *The Federalist*, p. 337.

18. Samuel Miller, Sermon (1795), quoted in Michael Lienesch, "The Constitutional Tradition: History, Political Action and Progress in American Political Thought," *Journal of Politics*, 42 (1980):7.

19. Farrand, ed., *Records of the Federal Convention*, vol. I, p. 493.

20. Carl J. Friedrich, *Constitutional Government and Democracy*, 4th ed. (Waltham, Mass., 1968), 169; emphasis in original.

21. Quoted in Charles A. Miller, *The Supreme Court and the Uses of History* (Cambridge, Mass., 1969), p. 184.

22. H. Jefferson Powell, "The Original Understanding of Original Intent," *Harvard Law Review*, 98 (1985):855–947.

BIBLIOGRAPHY

PRIMARY SOURCES

Elliot, Jonathan, ed. *Debates in the Several State Conventions, on the Adoption of the Federal Constitution,* 5 vols., 2nd ed. Philadelphia: Lippincott, 1836–1845.

Farrand, Max, ed. *Records of the Federal Convention of 1787,* 4 vols. New Haven, Conn.: Yale University Press, (1937)1966.

Hamilton, Alexander; Madison, James; and Jay, John. *The Federalist.* New York: 1788. (Current editions include: Middletown, Conn.: Wesleyan University Press, 1961 [edited and with introduction by Jacob E. Cooke], and New York: New American Library, 1961 [with introduction by Clinton Rossiter].)

Jensen, Merrill; Kaminski, John; and Saladino, Gaspare, eds. *The Documentary History of the Ratification of the Constitution,* 16 vols. (projected). Madison: State Historical Society of Wisconsin, 1976– .

Storing, Herbert J., ed. *The Complete Anti-Federalist,* 7 vols. Chicago: University of Chicago Press, 1981.

INTRODUCTION

Adams, Willi Paul. *The First American Constitutions.* Chapel Hill: University of North Carolina Press, 1980.

Beard, Charles A. *An Economic Interpretation of the Constitution of the United States.* New York: Macmillan, (1913)1935.

Burnett, Edmund C. *The Continental Congress.* New York: Macmillan, 1941.

Crosskey, William W., and Jeffrey, William, Jr. *Politics and the Constitution in the History of the United States,* 3 vols. Chicago: University of Chicago Press, 1953, 1980.

Jensen, Merrill. *The Articles of Confederation.* Madison: University of Wisconsin Press, 1940.

Kenyon, Cecilia M., ed. *The Antifederalists.* Indianapolis: Bobbs-Merrill, 1966.

McDonald, Forrest. *We the People: The Economic Origins of the Constitution.* Chicago: University of Chicago Press, 1958.

McLaughlin, Andrew C. *The Confederation and the Constitution, 1783–1789.* New York: Harper & Brothers, 1905.

Murphy, William P. *The Triumph of Nationalism: State Sovereignty, the Founding Fathers, and the Triumph of the Constitution.* Chicago: Quadrangle Books, 1967.

Rakove, Jack N. *The Beginnings of National Politics: An Interpretive History of the Continental Congress.* New York: Knopf, 1979.

Warren, Charles. *The Making of the Constitution.* Boston: Little, Brown, 1928.

BRITISH AND COLONIAL BACKGROUND TO AMERICAN CONSTITUTIONALISM

Andrews, Charles McLean. *Colonial Origins of the American Revolution.* New Haven, Conn.: Yale University Press, 1924.

Bailyn, Bernard. *Ideological Origins of the American Revolution.* Cambridge, Mass.: Belknap Press of Harvard University Press, 1967.

Dargo, George. *Roots of the Republic: A New Perspective on Early American Constitutionalism.* New York: Praeger, 1974.

Howard, A. E. Dick. *Road from Runnymede: Magna Carta and Constitutionalism in America.* Charlottesville: University Press of Virginia, 1968.

McLaughlin, Andrew C. *Foundations of American Constitutionalism.* New York: New York University Press, 1932.

Rossiter, Clinton. *Seedtime of the Republic: The Origins of the American Tradition of Political Liberty.* New York: Harcourt, Brace, 1953.

Sutherland, Arthur E. *Constitutionalism in America: Origins and Evolution of Its Fundamental Ideas.* New York: Blaisdell, 1965.

Wormuth, Francis. *The Origins of Modern Constitutionalism.* New York: Harper, 1948.

ORIGINS OF THE AMERICAN REVOLUTION: A CONSTITUTIONAL INTERPRETATION

Bailyn, Bernard. *Ideological Origins of the American Revolution.* Cambridge, Mass.: Belknap Press of Harvard University Press, 1967.

Black, Barbara A. "The Constitution of the Empire: The Case for the Colonists." *University of Pennsylvania Law Review,* 124 (1976):1157–1211.

Greene, Jack P. *Peripheries and Center: Constitutional Development in the Extended Politics of the British Empire and the United States, 1607–1788.* Athens: University of Georgia Press, 1986.

McIlwain, Charles H. *The American Revolution: A Constitutional Interpretation.* New York: Macmillan, 1923.

McLaughlin, Andrew C. *Foundations of American Constitutionalism.* New York: New York University Press, 1932.

Morgan, Edmund S., and Morgan, Helen M. *The Stamp Act Crisis: Prologue to Revolution.* Chapel Hill: University of North Carolina Press, 1953.

Tucker, Robert W., and Hendrickson, David C. *The Fall of the First British Empire: Origins of the War of American Independence.* Baltimore: Johns Hopkins University Press, 1982.

THE DECLARATION OF INDEPENDENCE AS A CONSTITUTIONAL DOCUMENT

Becker, Carl L. *The Declaration of Independence: A Study in the History of Political Ideas.* New York: Vintage, (1922)1958.

Diamond, Martin. "The Declaration of Independence and the Constitution." *Public Interest,* 42 (1976):39–55.

Hawke, David. *A Transaction of Free Men: The Birth and Course of the Declaration of Independence.* New York: Scribner's, 1964.

Hazelton, John H. *The Declaration of Independence: Its History.* New York: Dodd Mead & Co., 1906.

Jaffa, Harry V. *How to Think about the American Revolution: A Bicentennial Celebration.* Durham, N.C.: Carolina Academic Press, 1978.

Lence, Ross M. "Jefferson and the Declaration of Independence: The Power and Natural Rights of a Free People." *Political Science Reviewer,* 6 (1976):1–34.

Strauss, Leo. *Natural Right and History.* Chicago: University of Chicago Press, 1953.

THE FIRST AMERICAN CONSTITUTIONS

Adams, Willi Paul. *The First American Constitutions.* Chapel Hill: University of North Carolina Press, 1980.

Douglass, Elisha. *Rebels and Democrats.* Chicago: Quadrangle Books, 1955.

Peters, Ronald M., Jr. *The Massachusetts Constitution of 1780: A Social Compact.* Amherst: University of Massachusetts Press, 1978.

Selsam, J. Paul. *The Pennsylvania Constitution of 1776: A Study in Revolutionary Democracy.* Philadelphia: University of Pennsylvania Press, 1936.

Wood, Gordon S. *The Creation of the American Republic, 1776–1787.* Chapel Hill: University of North Carolina Press, 1969.

THE FIRST FEDERAL CONSTITUTION: THE ARTICLES OF CONFEDERATION

Greene, Jack P. *Peripheries and Center: Constitutional Relations in the Extended Polities of the British Empire and the United States, 1607–1788.* Athens: University of Georgia Press, 1986.

Jensen, Merrill. *Articles of Confederation.* Madison: University of Wisconsin Press, 1940.

McLaughlin, Andrew C. *The Confederation and the Constitution, 1783–1789.* New York: Harper & Brothers, 1905.

Rakove, Jack N. *The Beginnings of National Politics: An Interpretive History of the Continental Congress.* New York: Knopf, 1979.

———. "Articles of Confederation." Vol. 1, pp. 83–91, in Greene, Jack P., ed., *Encyclopedia of American Political History.* New York: Scribner's, 1984.

Onuf, Peter S. *The Origins of the Federal Republic: Jurisdictional Controversies in the United States.* Philadelphia: University of Pennsylvania Press, 1983.

THE ROAD TO PHILADELPHIA, 1781–1787

Jensen, Merrill. *The New Nation: A History of the United States during the Confederation, 1781–1789.* New York: Knopf, 1950.

Rakove, Jack N. *The Beginnings of National Politics: An Interpretive History of the Continental Congress.* New York: Knopf, 1979.

Ferguson, E. James. *The Power of the Purse: A History of American Public Finance, 1776–1790.* Chapel Hill: University of North Carolina Press, 1961.

Marks, Frederick W., III. *Independence on Trial: Foreign Affairs and the Making of the Constitution.* Baton Rouge: Louisiana State University Press, 1973.

Onuf, Peter S. *The Origins of the Federal Republic: Jurisdictional Controversies in the United States, 1781–1787.* Philadelphia: University of Pennsylvania Press, 1983.

THE CONSTITUTIONAL CONVENTION

Bowen, Catherine Drinker. *Miracle at Philadelphia: The Story of the Constitutional Convention.* Boston: Little, Brown, 1966.

McDonald, Forrest. *Novus Ordo Seclorum: Intellectual Origins of the Constitution.* Lawrence: University of Kansas Press, 1985.

Rossiter, Clinton. *1787: The Grand Convention.* New York: Macmillan, 1966.

Warren, Charles. *The Making of the Constitution.* Boston: Little, Brown, 1928.

Wood, Gordon S. *The Creation of the American Republic, 1776–1787.* Chapel Hill: University of North Carolina Press, 1969.

A SYSTEM WITHOUT PRECEDENT: FEDERALISM IN THE AMERICAN CONSTITUTION

Diamond, Martin. "What the Framers Meant by Federalism." Pages 24–41 in Goldwin, Robert A., ed., *A Nation of States: Essays on the Federal System.* Chicago: Rand McNally, 1963.

Greene, Jack P. "The Imperial Roots of American Federalism." *This Constitution,* 6 (1985):4–11.

McLaughlin, Andrew C. *Foundations of American Constitutionalism.* New York: New York University Press, 1932.

Ranney, John C. "The Bases of American Federalism." *William and Mary Quarterly* Third Series, 3 (1946):1–45.

Vile, M. J. C. *The Structure of American Federalism.* New York: Oxford University Press, 1961.

THE CONSTITUTION AND THE SEPARATION OF POWERS

Diamond, Martin. "The Separation of Powers and the Mixed Regime." *Publius: The Journal of Federalism,* 8 (1978):333–343.

Epstein, David F. *The Political Theory of the Federalist.* Chicago: University of Chicago Press, 1984.

Gwyn, W. B. *The Meaning of the Separation of Powers.* New Orleans: Tulane University Press, 1965.

Storing, Herbert J. *What the Anti-Federalists Were For.* Chicago: University of Chicago Press, 1981.

Thatch, Charles C., Jr. *The Creation of the Presidency, 1775–1789.* Introduction by Herbert Storing. Baltimore: Johns Hopkins University Press, (1923)1969.

Vile, M. J. C. *Constitutionalism and the Separation of Powers.* Oxford: Clarendon Press, 1967.

THE WITCH AT THE CHRISTENING: SLAVERY AND THE CONSTITUTION'S ORIGINS

Freehling, William W. "The Founding Fathers and Slavery." *American Historical Review,* 77 (1972):81–93.

Higginbotham, A. Leon, Jr. *In the Matter of Color: Race and the American Legal Process, the Colonial Period.* New York: Oxford University Press, 1978.

Lynd, Staughton. *Class Conflict, Slavery, and the United States Constitution.* Indianapolis: Bobbs-Merrill, 1967.

Robinson, Donald L. *Slavery in the Structure of American Politics, 1765–1820.* New York: Harcourt, Brace, 1971.

Wiecek, William M. *The Sources of Antislavery Constitutionalism in America, 1760–1848.* Ithaca, N.Y.: Cornell University Press, 1977.

CONGRESS DURING THE CONVENTION AND RATIFICATION

Bell, Rudolph M. *Party and Faction in American Politics: The House of Representatives, 1789–1901.* Westport, Conn.: Greenwood Press, 1973.

Galloway, George B. *History of the House of Representatives.* New York: Thomas Y. Crowell, 1961.

Haynes, George. *The Senate of the United States.* New York: Russell & Russell, 1960.

MacNeil, Neil. *Forge of Democracy: The House of Representatives.* New York: David McKay, 1963.

Morgan, Donald G. *Congress and the Constitution.* Cambridge, Mass.: Belknap Press of Harvard University Press, 1966.

Swanstrom, Roy. *The United States Senate, 1787–1801.* Senate Doc. no. 64, 87th Congress, 1st Session. Washington, D.C.: U.S. Government Printing Office, 1962.

THE PRESIDENCY AND THE EXECUTIVE POWER

Burns, James MacGregor. *Presidential Government: The Crucible of Leadership.* Boston: Houghton Mifflin, 1973.

Corwin, Edward S. *The President: Office and Powers.* New York: New York University Press, 1964.

Cronin, Thomas E. *The State of the Presidency.* Boston: Little, Brown, 1980.

Hart, James. *The American Presidency in Action, 1789.* New York: Macmillan, 1948.

Neustadt, Richard E. *Presidential Power.* New York: Wiley, (1960)1980.

Rossiter, Clinton. *The American Presidency.* New York: New American Library, 1960.

Thatch, Charles C., Jr. *The Creation of the Presidency, 1775–1789: A Study in Constitutional History.* Baltimore: Johns Hopkins University Press, 1923.

THE COURTS AND THE JUDICIAL POWER

Abraham, Henry J. *The Judicial Process,* 5th ed. New York: Oxford University Press, 1986.

Berger, Raoul. *Congress v. the Supreme Court.* Cambridge, Mass.: Harvard University Press, 1969.

Crosskey, William W. *Politics and the Constitution.* Chicago: University of Chicago Press, 1953.

Goebel, Julius, Jr. *Antecedents and Beginnings to 1801.* Volume 1 of Freund, Paul, ed., *History of the Supreme Court of the United States.* New York: Macmillan, 1971.

Haines, Charles Grove. *The American Doctrine of Judicial Supremacy.* New York: Russell & Russell, (1932)1959.

Warren, Charles. "New Light on the Judiciary Act of 1789." *Harvard Law Review,* 37 (1923):49–132.

WAR POWERS, TREATIES, AND THE CONSTITUTION

Bestor, Arthur. "Separation of Powers in the Domain of Foreign Affairs: The Intent of the Constitution Historically Considered." *Seton Hall Law Review,* vol. 5 (1974), pp. 527–665.

———. "Respective Roles of Senate and President in the Making and Abrogation of Treaties: The Original Intent of the Framers Historically Examined." *Washington Law Review,* 55 (1979):1–135.

Kohn, Richard H. *Eagle and Sword: The Beginnings of the Military Establishment in America.* New York: Macmillan, 1975.

Lofgren, Charles A. *"Government from Reflection and Choice": Constitutional Essays on War, Foreign Relations, and Federalism.* New York: Oxford University Press, 1986.

Marks, Frederick W., III. *Independence on Trial: Foreign Affairs and the Making of the Constitution.* Baton Rouge: Louisiana State University Press, 1973.

Rakove, Jack N. "Solving a Constitutional Puzzle: The Treatymaking Clause as a Case Study." *Perspectives in American History,* New Series, 1 (1984):233–281.

Reveley, W. Taylor, III. *War Powers of the President and Congress: Who Holds the Olive Branch?* Charlottesville: University Press of Virginia, 1981.

Sofaer, Abraham D. *War, Foreign Affairs and Constitutional Power: The Origins.* Cambridge, Mass.: Ballinger, 1976.

THE CONSTITUTION: AN ECONOMIC DOCUMENT?

Beard, Charles A. *An Economic Interpretation of the Constitution of the United States.* New York: Macmillan, (1913)1935.

Brown, Robert E. *Charles Beard and the Constitution.* Princeton, N.J.: Princeton University Press, 1956.

————. *Reinterpretation of the Formation of the American Constitution.* Boston: Boston University Press, 1963.

Ferguson, E. James. *The Power of the Purse.* Chapel Hill: University of North Carolina Press, 1961.

Kenyon, Cecelia. "An Economic Interpretation of the Constitution after Fifty Years." *William and Mary Quarterly,* Third Series, 12 (1955):3–43.

Main, Jackson Turner. *The Antifederalists: Critics of the Constitution.* Chapel Hill: University of North Carolina Press, 1961.

McDonald, Forrest. *We the People: The Economic Origins of the Constitution.* Chicago: University of Chicago Press, 1958.

Wright, Benjamin F. *Consensus and Continuity, 1776–1787.* Boston: Boston University Press, 1958.

THE CASE AGAINST RATIFICATION: ANTI-FEDERALIST CONSTITUTIONAL THOUGHT

Kenyon, Cecelia M., ed. *The Antifederalists.* Indianapolis: Bobbs-Merrill, 1966.

Main, Jackson Turner. *The Anti-Federalists: Critics of the Constitution.* Chapel Hill: University of North Carolina Press, 1961.

Rutland, Robert Allen. *The Ordeal of the Constitution: The Anti-Federalists and the Ratification Struggle, 1787–1788.* Norman: University of Oklahoma Press, 1966.

Storing, Herbert J., ed. *The Complete Anti-Federalist,* 7 vols. Chicago: University of Chicago Press, 1981.

Wood, Gordon S. *The Creation of the American Republic: 1776–1787.* Chapel Hill: University of North Carolina Press, 1969.

THE CASE FOR RATIFICATION: FEDERALIST CONSTITUTIONAL THOUGHT

Adair, Douglass. *Fame and the Founding Fathers,* ed. Trevor Colbourn. New York: W. W. Norton, 1974.

Diamond Martin. "The Federalist." Pages 631–651 in Strauss, Leo, and Cropsey, Joseph W., eds., *History of Political Philosophy*, 2nd ed. Chicago: Rand McNally, 1972.

Epstein, David F. *The Political Theory of The Federalist.* Chicago: University of Chicago Press, 1984.

Erler, Edward J. "The Problem of the Public Good in *The Federalist.*" *Polity*, 13 (1981):649–667.

Storing, Herbert J. "The 'Other' Federalist Papers: A Preliminary Sketch." *Political Science Reviewer*, 6 (1976):215–247.

FRAMING AND RATIFYING THE FIRST TEN AMENDMENTS

Brant, Irving. *The Bill of Rights: Its Origins and Meaning.* Indianapolis: Bobbs-Merrill, 1965.

Levy, Leonard W. "Bill of Rights." Vol. 1, pages 104–125, in Greene, Jack P., ed., *Encyclopedia of American Political History*. New York: Scribner's, 1984.

Perry, Richard L., and Cooper, John C., eds. *Sources of Our Liberties: Documentary Origins of Individual Liberties in the United States Constitution and Bill of Rights.* Chicago: American Bar Foundation, 1959.

Rutland, Robert Allen. *The Birth of the Bill of Rights, 1776–1791.* Chapel Hill: University of North Carolina Press, 1955.

Schwartz, Bernard. *The Bill of Rights: A Documentary History*, 2 vols. New York: Chelsea House, 1971.

———. *The Great Rights of Mankind: A History of the American Bill of Rights.* New York: Oxford University Press, 1977.

ORGANIZING THE NEW NATIONAL GOVERNMENT

Bassett, John Spencer. *The Federalist System, 1789–1801.* New York: Harper & Brothers, 1906.

Miller, John C. *The Federalist Era: 1789–1801.* New York: Harper & Row, 1960.

Matteson, David M. *The Organization of the Government under the Constitution.* New York: Da Capo Press, (1943)1970.

McDonald, Forrest. *The Presidency of George Washington.* Lawrence: University of Kansas Press, 1967.

Chambers, William N. *Political Parties in a New Nation: The American Experience, 1776–1809.* New York: Oxford University Press, 1963.

White, Leonard D. *The Federalists: A Study in Administrative History.* New York: Macmillan, 1948.

Goebel, Julius, Jr. *Antecedents and Beginnings to 1801*, volume 1 of the *Oliver Wendell Holmes Devise History of the Supreme Court of the United States*. New York: Macmillan, 1971.

Cooke, Jacob E. "The Federalist Age: A Reappraisal." Pages 85–154 in Billias, George A., and Grob, Gerald N., eds., *American History: Retrospect and Prospect.* New York: Free Press, 1971.

CONSTITUTIONALISM AND THE AMERICAN FOUNDING

Eidelberg, Paul. *The Political Philosophy of the American Constitution: A Reinterpretation of the Intentions of the Founding Fathers.* New York: Free Press, 1968.

McDonald, Forrest. *Novus Ordo Seclorum: The Intellectual Origins of the Constitution.* Lawrence: University of Kansas Press, 1985.

McLaughlin, Andrew C. *Foundations of American Constitutionalism.* New York: New York University Press, 1932.

Wood, Gordon. *The Creation of the American Republic, 1776–1787.* Chapel Hill: University of North Carolina Press, 1969.

INDEX

INDEX